Thomas D'Arcy McGee

A Popular History of Ireland

From the earliest period to the emancipation of the Catholics. Vol. 1

Thomas D'Arcy McGee

A Popular History of Ireland

From the earliest period to the emancipation of the Catholics. Vol. 1

ISBN/EAN: 9783337323134

Printed in Europe, USA, Canada, Australia, Japan

Cover: Foto ©ninafisch / pixelio.de

More available books at **www.hansebooks.com**

A POPULAR

HISTORY OF IRELAND:

FROM THE

EARLIEST PERIOD

TO THE

Emancipation of the Catholics.

BY

THOMAS D'ARCY McGEE, B.C.L.,
CORRESPONDING MEMBER OF THE NEW YORK HISTORICAL SOCIETY.

IN TWO VOLUMES.
VOL. I.

NEW YORK:
D. & J. SADLIER & CO., 31 BARCLAY ST.,
BOSTON:—128 FEDERAL STREET.
MONTREAL:—COR. OF NOTRE DAME AND ST. FRANCIS XAVIER STS.
1861.

Entered according to Act of Congress, in the year 1863,

By D. & J. SADLIER & CO.,

In the Clerk's Office of the District Court of the United States for the Southern District of New York.

DEDICATION.

TO MRS. JAMES SADLIER,

(NEW YORK.)

My Dear Friend:

I proposed to myself long ago, as you are aware, to prepare, for the use and instruction of our countrymen and women in America, a POPULAR HISTORY OF IRELAND. I did not presume to attempt *a* history of our Fatherland, still less *the* history; all that I hoped to accomplish, considering the obstacles to such a work which surround me, was a faithful and tolerably full compendium of that eventful and chequered story.

In making this compilation, the rules which guided me were chiefly to bring out the great events, in their relative degrees of prominence; to subordinate details to general effects; to put the first foremost, and the secondary second; to emphasize the epochs; to throw the strongest light upon the cardinal characters; to assign rational, believable causes, to strange and uncommon results; in short, to bring out the *rationale* of Irish History, under a form not censurable to the rules of art. If I have succeeded even in sketching such an outline as this, I, too, shall have done something for Irish History.

And now, my Dear Friend, that the labors of the Printer are done, and those of the Publisher about to commence, the thought naturally arises, as to which of my friends I should most of all like to derive pleasure from these volumes. Among old allies and colleagues of my own sex I might find it difficult to fix a preference; but among Irish ladies, there is, in America, one whom all true Irishmen delight to honor. You have watched over this little work with a sisterly anxiety, for which I can never be sufficiently grateful; and your own various and admirable sketches of Irish character have been, during its composition, my chief resource and recreation. With the latest chapter, in point of time, of our History, the chapter of the Exodus, your name must be forever associated. No one has known how to paint to the new age, and the new world, the household virtues, the religious graces, the manly and womanly characteristics of this ancient people, like you, my Friend! I feel, therefore, that I but offer another act of homage to the national character, so honorably represented, both heart and intellect, in your person, when I ask you to accept the dedication of this book.   T. D. M.

· QUEBEC, April 13, 1863.

CONTENTS.

BOOK I.

CHAPTER I.
THE FIRST INHABITANTS, ... 1

CHAPTER II.
THE FIRST AGES, ... 4

CHAPTER III.
CHRISTIANITY PREACHED AT TARA—THE RESULT, . . . 10

CHAPTER IV.
THE CONSTITUTION, AND HOW THE KINGS KEPT IT, . . . 17

CHAPTER V.
REIGN OF HUGH II.—THE IRISH COLONY IN SCOTLAND OBTAINS ITS INDEPENDENCE, ... 23

CHAPTER VI.
KINGS OF THE SEVENTH CENTURY, ... 29

CHAPTER VII.
KINGS OF THE EIGHTH CENTURY, ... 35

CHAPTER VIII.

WHAT THE IRISH SCHOOLS AND SAINTS DID IN THE THREE FIRST CHRISTIAN CENTURIES, ... 40

BOOK II.

CHAPTER I.

THE DANISH INVASION, ... 49

CHAPTER II.

KINGS OF THE NINTH CENTURY (CONTINUED)—NIAL III.—MALACHY L.—HUGH VII., ... 58

CHAPTER III.

REIGN OF FLAN "OF THE SHANNON" (A. D. 879 TO 916). . 69

CHAPTER IV.

KINGS OF THE TENTH CENTURY; NIAL IV.; DONOGH II.; CONGAL III.; DONALD IV., ... 76

CHAPTER V.

REIGN OF MALACHY II. AND RIVALRY OF BRIAN, . . . 86

CHAPTER VI.

BRIAN, ARD-RIGH—BATTLE OF CLONTARF, ... 93

CHAPTER VII.

EFFECTS OF THE RIVALRY OF BRIAN AND MALACHY ON THE ANCIENT CONSTITUTION, ... 101

CHAPTER VIII.

LATTER DAYS OF THE NORTHMEN IN IRELAND, . . 107

BOOK III.

CHAPTER I.

THE FORTUNES OF THE FAMILY OF BRIAN, ... 114

CHAPTER II.

THE CONTEST BETWEEN THE NORTH AND SOUTH—RISE OF THE FAMILY OF O'CONOR, ... 120

CHAPTER III.

THORLOGH MORE O'CONOR—MURKERTACH OF AILEACH—ACCESSION OF RODERICK O'CONOR, ... 126

CHAPTER IV.

STATE OF RELIGION AND LEARNING AMONG THE IRISH PREVIOUS TO THE ANGLO-NORMAN INVASION, ... 133

CHAPTER V.

SOCIAL CONDITION OF THE IRISH PREVIOUS TO THE NORMAN INVASION, ... 141

CHAPTER VI.

FOREIGN RELATIONS OF THE IRISH PREVIOUS TO THE ANGLO-NORMAN INVASION, ... 149

BOOK IV.

CHAPTER I.

DERMID M'MURROGH'S NEGOTIATIONS AND SUCCESS—THE FIRST EXPEDITION OF THE NORMANS INTO IRELAND, . . . 156

CHAPTER II.

THE ARMS, ARMOR AND TACTICS OF THE NORMANS AND IRISH, . 163

CHAPTER III.

THE FIRST CAMPAIGN OF EARL RICHARD—SIEGE OF DUBLIN—DEATH OF KING DERMID M'MURROGH, ... 169

CHAPTER IV.

SECOND CAMPAIGN OF EARL RICHARD—HENRY II. IN IRELAND, . 175

CHAPTER V.

FROM THE RETURN OF HENRY II. TO ENGLAND TILL THE DEATH OF EARL RICHARD AND HIS PRINCIPAL COMPANIONS, . . . 181

CHAPTER VI.

THE LAST YEARS OF THE ARD-RIGH, RODERICK O'CONOR, . . 188

CHAPTER VII.

ASSASSINATION OF HUGH DE LACY—JOHN "LACKLAND" IN IRELAND—VARIOUS EXPEDITIONS OF JOHN DE COURCY—DEATH OF CONOR MOINMOY, AND RISE OF CATHAL, "THE RED-HANDED" O'CONOR—CLOSE OF THE CAREER OF DE COURCY AND DE BURGH, ... 195

CHAPTER VIII.

EVENTS OF THE THIRTEENTH CENTURY—THE NORMANS IN CONNAUGHT, ... 201

CHAPTER IX.

EVENTS OF THE THIRTEENTH CENTURY—THE NORMANS IN MUNSTER AND LEINSTER, . . 206

CHAPTER X.

EVENTS OF THE THIRTEENTH CENTURY—THE NORMANS IN MEATH AND ULSTER, ... 213

CHAPTER XI.

RETROSPECT OF THE NORMAN PERIOD IN IRELAND—A GLANCE AT THE MILITARY TACTICS OF THE TIMES—NO CONQUEST OF THE COUNTRY IN THE THIRTEENTH CENTURY, ... 220

CHAPTER XII.

STATE OF SOCIETY AND LEARNING IN IRELAND DURING THE NORMAN PERIOD, ... 227

BOOK V.

CHAPTER I.

THE RISE OF "THE RED EARL"—RELATIONS OF IRELAND AND SCOTLAND, ... 232

CHAPTER II.

THE NORTHERN IRISH ENTER INTO ALLIANCE WITH KING ROBERT BRUCE—ARRIVAL AND FIRST CAMPAIGN OF EDWARD BRUCE, 237

CHAPTER III.

BRUCE'S SECOND CAMPAIGN, AND CORONATION AT DUNDALK—THE RISING IN CONNAUGHT—BATTLE OF ATHENRY—ROBERT BRUCE IN IRELAND, ... 242

CHAPTER IV.

BATTLE OF FAUGHARD AND DEATH OF KING EDWARD BRUCE—CONSEQUENCES OF HIS INVASION—EXTINCTION OF THE EARLDOM OF ULSTER—IRISH OPINION OF EDWARD BRUCE, . 248

BOOK VI.

CHAPTER I.

CIVIL WAR IN ENGLAND—ITS EFFECTS ON THE ANGLO-IRISH—THE KNIGHTS OF SAINT JOHN—GENERAL DESIRE OF THE ANGLO-IRISH TO NATURALIZE THEMSELVES AMONG THE NATIVE POPULATION—A POLICY OF NON-INTERCOURSE BETWEEN THE RACES RESOLVED ON, IN ENGLAND, ... 253

CHAPTER II.

LIONEL, DUKE OF CLARENCE, LORD LIEUTENANT—THE PENAL CODE OF RACE—"THE STATUTE OF KILKENNY," AND SOME OF ITS CONSEQUENCES, ... 261

CHAPTER III.

ART M'MURROGH, LORD OF LEINSTER—FIRST EXPEDITION OF RICHARD II., OF ENGLAND, TO IRELAND, ... 268

CHAPTER IV.

SUBSEQUENT PROCEEDINGS OF RICHARD II.—LIEUTENANCY AND DEATH OF THE EARL OF MARCH—SECOND EXPEDITION OF RICHARD AGAINST ART M'MURROGH—CHANGE OF DYNASTY IN ENGLAND, ... 276

CHAPTER V.

PARTIES WITHIN "THE PALE"—BATTLES OF KILMAINHAM AND KILLUCAN—SIR JOHN TALBOT'S LORD LIEUTENANCY, . . 289

CHAPTER VI.

ACTS OF THE NATIVE PRINCES—SUBDIVISION OF TRIBES AND TERRITORIES—ANGLO-IRISH TOWNS UNDER NATIVE PROTECTION—ATTEMPT OF THADDEUS O'BRIEN, PRINCE OF THOMOND, TO RESTORE THE MONARCHY—RELATIONS OF THE RACES IN THE FIFTEENTH CENTURY, ... 298

CHAPTER VII.

CONTINUED DIVISION AND DECLINE OF "THE ENGLISH INTEREST"—RICHARD, DUKE OF YORK, LORD LIEUTENANT—CIVIL WAR AGAIN IN ENGLAND—EXECUTION OF THE EARL OF DESMOND—ASCENDANCY OF THE KILDARE GERALDINES, . . . 305

CHAPTER VIII.

THE AGE AND RULE OF GERALD, EIGHTH EARL OF KILDARE—THE TIDE BEGINS TO TURN FOR THE ENGLISH INTEREST—THE YORKIST PRETENDERS, SIMNEL AND WARBECK—POYNING'S PARLIAMENT—BATTLES OF KNOCKDOE AND MONABRAHER, . 314

CHAPTER IX.

STATE OF IRISH AND ANGLO-IRISH SOCIETY DURING THE FOURTEENTH AND FIFTEENTH CENTURIES, ... 327

CHAPTER X.

STATE OF RELIGION AND LEARNING DURING THE FOURTEENTH AND FIFTEENTH CENTURIES, ... 333

BOOK VII.

CHAPTER I.

IRISH POLICY OF HENRY THE EIGHTH DURING THE LIFETIME OF CARDINAL WOLSEY, ... 341

CHAPTER II.

THE INSURRECTION OF SILKEN THOMAS—THE GERALDINE LEAGUE —ADMINISTRATION OF LORD LEONARD GRAY, . . . 345

CHAPTER III.

SIR ANTHONY ST. LEGER, LORD DEPUTY—NEGOTIATIONS OF THE IRISH CHIEFS WITH JAMES THE FIFTH OF SCOTLAND—FIRST ATTEMPTS TO INTRODUCE THE PROTESTANT REFORMATION— OPPOSITION OF THE CLERGY—PARLIAMENT OF 1541—THE PROTECTORS OF THE CLERGY EXCLUDED—STATE OF THE COUNTRY—THE CROWNS UNITED—HENRY THE EIGHTH PROCLAIMED AT LONDON AND DUBLIN, ... 350

CHAPTER IV.

ADHESION OF O'NEIL, O'DONNELL AND O'BRIEN—A NEW ANGLO-IRISH PEERAGE—NEW RELATIONS OF LORD AND TENANT— BISHOPS APPOINTED BY THE CROWN—RETROSPECT, . . 361

BOOK VIII.

CHAPTER I.
EVENTS OF THE REIGN OF EDWARD SIXTH, . . . 370

CHAPTER II.
EVENTS OF THE REIGN OF PHILIP AND MARY, ... 376

CHAPTER III.

ACCESSION OF QUEEN ELIZABETH—PARLIAMENT OF 1560—THE ACT OF UNIFORMITY—CAREER AND DEATH OF JOHN O'NEIL "THE PROUD," 380

CHAPTER IV.

SIR HENRY SIDNEY'S DEPUTYSHIP—PARLIAMENT OF 1569—THE SECOND "GERALDINE LEAGUE"—SIR JAMES FITZMAURICE, . 391

CHAPTER V.

THE "UNDERTAKERS" IN ULSTER AND LEINSTER—DEFEAT AND DEATH OF SIR JAMES FITZMAURICE, ... 400

CHAPTER VI.

SEQUEL OF THE SECOND GERALDINE LEAGUE—PLANTATION OF MUNSTER—EARLY CAREER OF HUGH O'NEIL, EARL OF TYRONE—PARLIAMENT OF 1585, ... 407

CHAPTER VII.

BATTLE OF GLENMALURE—SIR JOHN PERROTT'S ADMINISTRATION—THE SPANISH ARMADA—LORD DEPUTY FITZWILLIAM—ESCAPE OF HUGH ROE O'DONNELL FROM DUBLIN CASTLE—THE ULSTER CONFEDERACY FORMED, . . . 413

CHAPTER VIII.

THE ULSTER CONFEDERACY—FEAGH MAC HUGH O'BYRNE—CAMPAIGN OF 1595—NEGOTIATIONS, ENGLISH AND SPANISH—BATTLE OF THE YELLOW FORD—ITS CONSEQUENCES, . . 421

CHAPTER IX.

ESSEX'S CAMPAIGN OF 1599—BATTLE OF THE CURLEW MOUNTAINS—O'NEIL'S NEGOTIATIONS WITH SPAIN—MOUNTJOY LORD DEPUTY, ... 431

CHAPTER X.

MOUNTJOY'S ADMINISTRATION—OPERATIONS IN ULSTER AND MUNSTER—CAREW'S "WIT AND CUNNING"—LANDING OF SPANIARDS IN THE SOUTH—BATTLE OF KINSALE—DEATH OF O'DONNELL IN SPAIN, ... 439

CHAPTER XI.

THE CONQUEST OF MUNSTER — DEATH OF ELIZABETH, AND SUBMISSION OF O'NEIL—"THE ARTICLES OF MELLIFONT," . 451

CHAPTER XII.

STATE OF RELIGION AND LEARNING DURING THE REIGN OF ELIZABETH, ... 457

BOOK IX.

CHAPTER I.

JAMES I.—FLIGHT OF THE EARLS—CONFISCATION OF ULSTER—PENAL LAWS—PARLIAMENTARY OPPOSITION, . . . 465

CHAPTER II.

LAST YEARS OF JAMES—CONFISCATION OF THE MIDLAND COUNTIES—ACCESSION OF CHARLES I.—GRIEVANCES AND "GRACES"—ADMINISTRATION OF LORD STRAFFORD, ... 476

CHAPTER III.

LORD STRAFFORD'S IMPEACHMENT AND EXECUTION—PARLIAMENT OF 1639-'41—THE INSURRECTION OF 1641—THE IRISH ABROAD, ... 486

CHAPTER IV.

THE INSURRECTION OF 1641, ... 494

CHAPTER V.

THE CATHOLIC CONFEDERATION—ITS CIVIL GOVERNMENT AND MILITARY ESTABLISHMENT, ... 504

CHAPTER VI.

THE CONFEDERATE WAR—CAMPAIGN OF 1643—THE CESSATION, 513

CHAPTER VII.

THE CESSATION AND ITS CONSEQUENCES, ... 519

CHAPTER VIII.

GLAMORGAN'S TREATY—THE NEW NUNCIO RINUCCINI—O'NEIL'S POSITION—THE BATTLE OF BENBURB, ... 525

CHAPTER IX.

FROM THE BATTLE OF BENBURB TILL THE LANDING OF CROMWELL AT DUBLIN, ... 532

CHAPTER X.

CROMWELL'S CAMPAIGN—1649-1650, ... 539

CHAPTER XI.

CLOSE OF THE CONFEDERATE WAR, ... 543

CHAPTER XII.

IRELAND UNDER THE PROTECTORATE—ADMINISTRATION OF HENRY CROMWELL—DEATH OF OLIVER, ... 548

BOOK X.

CHAPTER I.

REIGN OF CHARLES II., ... 553

CHAPTER II.

REIGN OF CHARLES II. (CONCLUDED,) 559

CHAPTER III.

THE STATE OF RELIGION AND LEARNING IN IRELAND DURING THE SEVENTEENTH CENTURY, ... 562

CHAPTER IV.

ACCESSION OF JAMES II.—TYRCONNELL'S ADMINISTRATION, . . 568

CHAPTER V.

KING JAMES IN IRELAND—IRISH PARLIAMENT OF 1689, . . 573

CHAPTER VI.

THE REVOLUTIONARY WAR—CAMPAIGN OF 1689—SIEGES OF DERRY AND ENNISKILLEN, ... 578

CHAPTER VII.

THE REVOLUTIONARY WAR—CAMPAIGN OF 1690—BATTLE OF THE BOYNE—ITS CONSEQUENCES—THE SIEGES OF ATHLONE AND LIMERICK, ... 583

CHAPTER VIII.

THE WINTER OF 1690-91, ... 589

CHAPTER IX.

THE REVOLUTIONARY WAR — CAMPAIGN OF 1691 — BATTLE OF AUGHRIM—CAPITULATION OF LIMERICK, ... 592

CHAPTER X.

REIGN OF KING WILLIAM, ... 597

CHAPTER XI.

REIGN OF QUEEN ANNE, ... 605

CHAPTER XII.

THE IRISH SOLDIERS ABROAD, DURING THE REIGNS OF WILLIAM AND ANNE, ... 610

BOOK XI.

CHAPTER I.

ACCESSION OF GEORGE I.—SWIFT'S LEADERSHIP, . . . 613

CHAPTER II.

REIGN OF GEORGE II.—GROWTH OF PUBLIC SPIRIT—THE "PATRIOT" PARTY—LORD CHESTERFIELD'S ADMINISTRATION, . . . 619

CHAPTER III.

THE LAST JACOBITE MOVEMENT—THE IRISH SOLDIERS ABROAD—FRENCH EXPEDITION UNDER THUROT, OR O'FARRELL, . . 624

CHAPTER IV.

REIGN OF GEORGE II. (CONCLUDED)—MALONE'S LEADERSHIP, . 630

CHAPTER V.

ACCESSION OF GEORGE III.—FLOOD'S LEADERSHIP—OCTENNIAL PARLIAMENTS ESTABLISHED, ... 636

CHAPTER VI.

FLOOD'S LEADERSHIP—STATE OF THE COUNTRY BETWEEN 1760 AND 1776, ... 640

CHAPTER VII.

GRATTAN'S LEADERSHIP — "FREE TRADE" AND THE VOLUNTEERS, 644

CHAPTER VIII.

GRATTAN'S LEADERSHIP—LEGISLATIVE AND JUDICIAL INDEPENDENCE
ESTABLISHED, ... 649

CHAPTER IX.

THE ERA OF INDEPENDENCE—FIRST PERIOD, ... 654

CHAPTER X.

THE ERA OF INDEPENDENCE—SECOND PERIOD, ... 663

CHAPTER XI.

THE ERA OF INDEPENDENCE—THIRD PERIOD—CATHOLIC RELIEF
BILL OF 1793, ... 670

CHAPTER XII.

THE ERA OF INDEPENDENCE—EFFECTS OF THE FRENCH REVOLUTION IN IRELAND—SECESSION OF GRATTAN, CURRAN, AND
THEIR FRIENDS, FROM PARLIAMENT, IN 1797, . . . 677

CHAPTER XIII.

THE UNITED IRISHMEN, . . , ... 685

CHAPTER XIV.

NEGOTIATIONS WITH FRANCE AND HOLLAND—THE THREE EXPEDITIONS NEGOTIATED BY TONE AND LEWINES, . . . 690

CHAPTER XV.

THE INSURRECTION OF 1798, ... 696

CHAPTER XVI.

THE INSURRECTION OF 1798—THE WEXFORD INSURRECTION, . 705

CHAPTER XVII.

THE INSURRECTION ELSEWHERE — FATE OF THE LEADING UNITED
IRISHMEN, ... 717

CHAPTER XVIII.

ADMINISTRATION OF LORD CORNWALLIS—BEFORE THE UNION, . 727

CHAPTER XIX.

LAST SESSION OF THE IRISH PARLIAMENT—THE LEGISLATIVE UNION
OF GREAT BRITAIN AND IRELAND, ... 739

BOOK XII.

CHAPTER I.

AFTER THE UNION—DEATH OF LORD CLARE—ROBERT EMMETT'S
EMEUTE, ... 747

CHAPTER II.

ADMINISTRATION OF LORD HARDWICK (1801 TO 1806), AND OF
THE DUKE OF BEDFORD (1806 TO 1808), ... 754

CHAPTER III.

ADMINISTRATION OF THE DUKE OF RICHMOND (1807 TO 1813), 760

CHAPTER IV.

O'CONNELL'S LEADERSHIP (1813 TO 1821), ... 770

CHAPTER V.

RETROSPECT OF THE STATE OF RELIGION AND LEARNING DURING
THE REIGN OF GEORGE III., ... 777

CHAPTER VI.

PAGE

THE IRISH ABROAD, DURING THE REIGN OF GEORGE III., . . 783

CHAPTER VII.

O'CONNELL'S LEADERSHIP—THE CATHOLIC ASSOCIATION (1821 TO
1826), ... 787

CHAPTER VIII.

O'CONNELL'S LEADERSHIP—THE CLARE ELECTION—EMANCIPATION
OF THE CATHOLICS, ... 798

POPULAR
HISTORY OF IRELAND.

CHAPTER I.

THE FIRST INHABITANTS.

IRELAND is situated in the North Atlantic, between the degrees fifty-one and a half and fifty-five and a half North, and five and a quarter and ten and a third West longitude, from Greenwich. It is the last land usually seen by ships leaving the Old World, and the first by those which arrive there from the Northern ports of America. In size it is less than half as large as Britain, and in shape it may be compared to one of those shields which we see in coats-of-arms, the four Provinces—Ulster, Connaught, Leinster, and Munster—representing the four quarters of the shield.

Around the borders of the country, generally near the coast, several ranges of hills and mountains rear their crests, every Province having one or more such groups. The West and South have, however, the largest and highest of these hills, from the sides of all which descend numerous rivers, flowing in various directions to the sea. Other rivers issue out of large lakes formed in the valleys, such as the Galway river which drains Lough Corrib, and the Bann which carries off the surplus waters of Lough Neagh (*Nay*). In a few districts where the fall for water is insufficient, marshes and swamps were long ago formed, of which the principal one occupies nearly 240,000 acres in the very heart of the country. It is called "the Bog of Allen," and, though quite useless for farming purposes, still serves to supply the surrounding district with fuel, nearly as well as coal mines do, in other countries.

In former times, Ireland was as well wooded as watered, though hardly a tree of the primitive forest now remains. One of the earliest names applied to it was "the wooded Island," and the export of timber and staves, as well as of the furs of wild animals, continued, until the beginning of the seventeenth century, to be a thriving branch of trade. But in a succession of civil and religious wars, the axe and the torch have done their work of destruction, so that the age of most of the wood now standing does not date above two or three generations back.

Who were the first inhabitants of this Island, it is impossible to say, but we know it was inhabited at a very early period of the world's lifetime—probably as early as the time when Solomon, the Wise, sat in Jerusalem on the throne of his father David. As we should not altogether reject, though neither are we bound to believe, the wild and uncertain traditions of which we have neither documentary nor monumental evidence, we will glance over rapidly what the old Bards and Story-tellers have handed down to us, concerning Ireland before it became Christian.

The *first* story they tell is, that about three hundred years after the Universal Deluge, Partholan, of the stock of Japhet, sailed down the Mediterranean, "leaving Spain on the right hand," and holding bravely on his course, reached the shores of the wooded western Island. This Partholan, they tell us, was a double parricide, having killed his father and mother before leaving his native country, for which horrible crimes, as the Bards very morally conclude, his posterity were fated never to possess the land. After a long interval, and when they were greatly increased in numbers, they were cut off to the last man, by a dreadful pestilence.

The story of the *second* immigration is almost as vague as that of the first. The leader this time is called Nemedh, and his route is de- .

scribed as leading from the shores of the Black Sea, across what is now Russia in Europe, to the Baltic Sea, and from the Baltic to Ireland. He is said to have built two royal forts, and to have "cleared twelve plains of wood" while in Ireland. He and his posterity were constantly at war, with a terrible race of Formorians, or Sea Kings, descendants of Ham, who had fled from northern Africa to the western islands for refuge from their enemies, the sons of Shem. At length the Formorians prevailed, and the children of the second immigration were either slain or driven into exile, from which some of their posterity returned long afterwards, and again disputed the country, under two different denominations.

The *Firbolgs* or Belgæ are the *third* immigration. They were victorious under their chiefs, the five sons of Dela, and divided the island into five portions. But they lived in days when the earth —the known parts of it at least—was being eagerly scrambled for by the overflowing hosts of Asia, and they were not long left in undisputed possession of so tempting a prize. Another expedition, claiming descent from the common ancestor, Nemedh, arrived to contest their supremacy. These last—the *fourth* immigration—are depicted to us as accomplished soothsayers and necromancers who came out of Greece. They could quell storms; cure diseases; work in metals; foretell future events; forge magical weapons; and raise the dead to life; they are called the *Tuatha de Danans*, and by their supernatural power, as well as by virtue of "the Lia Fail," or fabled "stone of destiny," they subdued their Belgic kinsmen, and exercised sovereignty over them, till they in turn were displaced by the Gaelic, or *fifth* immigration.

This fifth and final colony called themselves alternately, or at different periods of their history, *Gael*, from one of their remote ancestors; *Milesians*, from the immediate projector of their emigration; or *Scoti*, from Scota, the mother of Milesius. They came from Spain under the leadership of the sons of Milesius, whom they had lost during their temporary sojourn in that country. In vain the skilful *Tuatha* surrounded themselves and their coveted island with magic-made tempest and terrors; in vain they reduced it in size so as to be almost invisible from sea;

Amergin, one of the sons of Milesius, was a Druid skilled in all the arts of the east, and led by his wise counsels, his brothers countermined the magicians, and beat them at their own weapons. This Amergin was, according to universal usage in ancient times, at once Poet, Priest, and Prophet; yet when his warlike brethren divided the island between them, they left the Poet out of the reckoning. He was finally drowned in the waters of the river Avoca, which is probably the reason why that river has been so suggestive of melody and song ever since.

Such are the stories told of the *five* successive hordes of adventurers who first attempted to colonize our wooded Island. Whatever moiety of truth may be mixed up with so many fictions, two things are certain, that long before the time when our Lord and Saviour came upon earth, the coasts and harbors of Erin were known to the merchants of the Mediterranean, and that from the first to the fifth Christian century, the warriors of the wooded Isle made inroads on the Roman power in Britain and even in Gaul. Agricola, the Roman governor of Britain in the reign of Domitian—the first century—retained an Irish chieftain about his person, and we are told by his biographer that an invasion of Ireland was talked of at Rome. But it never took place; the Roman eagles, although supreme for four centuries in Britain, never crossed the Irish Sea; and we are thus deprived of those Latin helps to our early history, which are so valuable in the first period of the histories of every western country, with which the Romans had anything to do.

CHAPTER II.

THE FIRST AGES.

SINCE we have no Roman accounts of the form of government or state of society in ancient Erin, we must only depend on the Bards and Story-tellers, so far as their statements are credible and agree with each other. On certain main points they do agree, and these are the points which it seems reasonable for us to take on their authority.

As even brothers born of the same mother, coming suddenly into possession of a prize, will struggle to see who can get the largest share, so we find in those first ages a constant succession of armed struggles for power. The petty Princes who divided the Island between them were called *Righ*, a word which answers to the Latin *Rex* and French *Roi;* and the chief king or monarch was called *Ard-Righ*, or High-King. The eldest nephew, or son of the king, was the usual heir of power, and was called the *Tanist*, or successor; although any of the family of the Prince, his brothers, cousins, or other kinsmen, might be chosen *Tanist*, by election of the people over whom he was to rule. One certain cause of exclusion was personal deformity; for if a Prince was born lame or a hunchback, or if he lost a limb by accident, he was declared unfit to govern. Even after succession, any serious accident entailed deposition, though we find the names of several Princes who managed to evade or escape this singular penalty. It will be observed besides of the *Tanist*, that the habit of appointing him seems to have been less a law than a custom; that it was not universal in all the Provinces; that in some tribes the succession alternated between a double line of Princes; and that sometimes when the reigning Prince obtained the nomination of a *Tanist*, to please himself, the choice was set aside by the public voice of the clansmen. The successor to the Ard-Righ, or Monarch, instead of being simply called *Tanist*, had the more sounding title of *Roydamna*, or King-successor.

The chief offices about the Kings, in the first ages, were all filled by the Druids, or Pagan Priests; the *Brehons*, or Judges, were usually Druids, as were also the *Bards*, the historians of their patrons. Then came the Physicians; the Chiefs who paid tribute or received annual gifts from the Sovereigns, or Princes; the royal stewards; and the military leaders or Champions, who, like the knights of the middle ages, held their lands and their rank at court, by the tenure of the sword. Like the feudal *Dukes* of France, and *Barons* of England, these military nobles often proved too powerful for their nominal patrons, and made them experience all the uncertainty of reciprocal dependence. The

Champions play an important part in all the early legends. Wherever there is trouble you are sure to find them. Their most celebrated divisions were the warriors of the *Red Branch*—that is to say, the Militia of Ulster; the *Fiann*, or Militia of Leinster, sometimes the royal guard of Tara, at others in exile and disgrace; the *Clan-Degaid* of Munster, and the *Fiann* of Connaught. The last force was largely recruited from the Belgic race who had been squeezed into that western province, by their Milesian conquerors, pretty much as Cromwell endeavored to force the Milesian Irish into it, many hundred years afterwards. Each of these bands had its special heroes; its Godfreys and Orlandos celebrated in song; the most famous name in Ulster was Cuchullin: so called from *cu*, a hound, or watch-dog, and *Ullin*, the ancient name of his province. He lived at the dawn of the Christian era. Of equal fame was Finn, the father of Ossian, and the Fingal or modern fiction, who flourished in the latter half of the second century. Gall, son of Morna, the hero of Connaught, (one of the few distinguished men of Belgic origin whom we hear of through the Milesian bards), flourished a generation earlier than Finn, and might fairly compete with him in celebrity, if he had only had an Ossian to sing his praises.

The political boundaries of different tribes expanded or contracted with their good or ill-fortune in battle. Immigration often followed defeat, so that a clan, or its offshoot is found at one period on one part of the map and again on another. As *surnames* were not generally used either in Ireland or anywhere else, till after the 10th century, the great families are distinguishable at first, only by their tribe or clan names. Thus at the north we have the Hy-Nial race; in the south the Eugenian race, so called, from Nial and Eoghan, their mutual ancestors.

We have already compared the shape of Erin to a shield, in which the four Provinces represented the four quarters. Some shields have also *bosses* or centre-pieces, and the federal province of MEATH was the *boss* of the old Irish shield. The ancient Meath included both the present counties of that name, stretching south to the Liffey, and north to Armagh. It was the mensal demesne, or "board of the king's table:" it was exempt from all taxes, except those of the Ard-Righ, and its relations to the other

Provinces may be vaguely compared to those of the District of Columbia to the several States of the North American Union. ULSTER might then be defined by a line drawn from Sligo Harbor to the mouth of the Boyne, the line being notched here and there by the royal demesne of Meath; LEINSTER stretched south from Dublin triangle-wise to Waterford Harbor, but its inland line, towards the west, was never very well defined, and this led to constant border wars with Munster; the remainder of the south to the mouth of the Shannon composed MUNSTER; the present county of Clare and all west of the Shannon north to Sligo and part of Cavan, going with CONNAUGHT. The chief seats of power, in those several divisions, were TARA, for federal purposes; EMANIA, near Armagh, for Ulster; LEIGHLIN, for Leinster; CASHEL, for Munster; and CRUCHAIN, (now Rathcrogan, in Roscommon,) for Connaught.

How the common people lived within these external divisions of power, it is not so easy to describe. All histories tell us a great deal of kings, and battles, and conspiracies, but very little of the daily domestic life of the people. In this respect the history of Erin is much the same as the rest; but some leading facts we do know. Their religion, in Pagan times, was what the moderns call *Druidism*, but what they called it themselves we now know not. It was probably the same religion anciently professed by Tyre and Sidon, by Carthage and her colonies in Spain; the same religion which the Romans have described as existing in great part of Gaul, and by their accounts, we learn the awful fact, that it sanctioned, nay, demanded, human sacrifices. From the few traces of its doctrines which Christian zeal has permitted to survive in the old Irish language, we see that *Belus* or "Crom," the god of fire, typified by the sun, was its chief divinity—that two great festivals were held in his honor on days answering to the first of May and last of October. There were also particular gods of poets, champions, artificers and mariners, just as among the Romans and Greeks. Sacred groves were dedicated to these gods; Priests and Priestesses devoted their lives to their service; the arms of the champion, and the person of the king were charmed by them; neither peace nor war was made without their sanction; their own persons and their pupils were held sacred; the high place at the king's right hand and the best fruits of the earth and the waters were theirs. Old age revered them, women worshipped them, warriors paid court to them, youth trembled before them, princes and chieftains regarded them as elder brethren. So numerous were they in Erin, and so celebrated that the altars of Britain and western Gaul, left desolate by the Roman legions, were often served by hierophants from Erin, which even in those Pagan days was known to all the Druidic countries as the "Sacred Island." Besides the princes, the warriors, and the Druids, (who were also the Physicians, Bards and Brehons of the first ages,) there were innumerable petty chiefs, all laying claim to noble birth and blood. They may be said with the warriors and priests to be the only freemen. The *Bruais*, or farmers, though possessing certain legal rights, were an inferior caste; while of the Artisans, the smiths and armorers only seem to have been of much consideration. The builders of those mysterious round towers, of which a hundred ruins yet remain, may also have been a privileged order. But the mill and the loom were servile occupations, left altogether to slaves taken in battle, or purchased in the market-places of Britain. The task of the herdsman, like that of the farm-laborer, seems to have devolved on the bondsmen, while the *quern* and the shuttle were left exclusively in the hands of the bondswomen.

We need barely mention the names of the first Milesian kings, who were remarkable for something else than cutting each other's throats, in order to hasten on to the solid ground of Christian times. The principal names are: Eber and Eremhon, the crowned sons of Milesians; they at first divided the Island fairly, but Eremhon soon became jealous of his brother, slew him in battle, and established his own supremacy. Irial the Prophet was King, and built seven royal fortresses; Tiern'mass; in his reign the arts of dyeing in colors were introduced; and the distinguishing of classes by the number of colors they were permitted to wear, was decreed. Ollamh ("the Wise") established the Convention of Tara, which assembled habitually every ninth year, but might be called oftener; it met about the October festival in honor of Beleus or *Crom;* Eocaid invented or introduced a new species of wicker boats, called *cassa*, and spent much of his time upon the sea; a solitary queen, named Macha, appears in the succession, from whom Armagh takes its name; except Mab, the mythological Queen of Connaught, she is the sole female ruler of Erin in the first ages; Owen or Eugene Mor ("the Great") is remembered as the founder of the notable families who rejoice in the common name of Eugenians; Leary, of whom the fable of Midas is told with variations; Angus, whom the after Princes of Alba (Scotland) claimed as their ancestor; Eocaid, the tenth of that name, in whose reign are laid the scenes of the chief mythological stories of Erin—such as the story of Queen Mab—the story of the Sons of Usna; the death of Cuchullin (a counterpart of the Persian tale of Roostam and Sohrab); the story of Fergus, son of the king; of Connor of Ulster; of the sons of Dari; and many more. We next meet with the first king who led an expedition abroad against the Romans in Crimthan, surnamed *Neea-Naari*, or Nair's Hero, from the good genius who accompanied him on his foray. A well-planned insurrection of the conquered Belgæ, cut off one of Crimthan's immediate successors, with all his chiefs and nobles, at a banquet given on the Belgian-plain (Moybolgue, in Cavan); and arrested for a century thereafter Irish expeditions abroad. A revolution and a restoration followed, in which Moran the Just Judge played the part of Monk to *his* Charles II., Tuathal surnamed "the Legitimate." It was Tuathal who imposed the special tax on Leinster, of which we shall often hear—under the title of *Borooa*, or Tribute. "The Legitimate" was succeeded by his son, who introduced the Roman *Lex Tulionis* ("an eye for an eye and a tooth for a tooth") into the Brehon code; soon after, the Eugenian families of the south, strong in numbers, and led by a second Owen Mere, again halved the Island with the ruling race, the boundary this time being the *esker*, or ridge of land which can be easily traced from Dublin west to Galway. Olild, a brave and able Prince, succeeded in time to the southern half-kingdom, and planted his own kindred deep and firm in its soil, though the unity of the monarchy was again restored under Cormac Ulla, or *Longbeard*. This Cormac, according to the legend, was in secret a Christian, and was done to death by the enraged and alarmed Druids, after his abdication and retirement from the world (A. D. 266). He had reigned full forty years, rivalling in wisdom, and excelling in justice the best of his ancestors. Some of his maxims remain to us, and challenge comparison for truthfulness and foresight with most uninspired writings.

Cormac's successors during the same century are of little mark, but in the next the expeditions against the Roman outposts were renewed with greater energy and on an increasing scale. Another Crimthan eclipsed the fame of his ancestor and namesake; Nial, called "of the Hostages," was slain on a second or third expedition into Gaul (A.D. 405), while Dathy, nephew and successor to Nial, was struck dead by lightning in the passage of the Alps (A.D. 428). It was in one of Nial's Gallic expeditions that the illustrious captive was brought into Erin, for whom Providence had reserved the glory of its conversion to the Christian faith—an event which gives a unity and a purpose to the history of that Nation, which must always constitute its chief attraction to the Christian reader.

CHAPTER III.

CHRISTIANITY PREACHED AT TARA—THE RESULT.

THE conversion of a Pagan people to Christianity must always be a primary fact in their history. It is not merely for the error it abolishes or the positive truth it establishes that a national change of faith is historically important, but for the complete revolution it works in every public and private relation. The change socially could not be greater if we were to see some irresistible apostle of Paganism arriving from abroad in Christian Ireland, who would abolish the churches, convents, and Christian schools; decry and bring into utter disuse the decalogue, the Scriptures and the Sacraments; efface all trace of the existing belief in One God and Three Persons, whether in private or public worship, in contracts, or in courts of law; and instead of these, re-establish all over the country, in high places and in every place, the gloomy groves of the Druids, making gods of the sun and moon, the natural elements and man's own passions, restoring human sacrifices as a sacred duty, and practically excluding from the community of their fellows, all who presumed to question the divine origin of such a religion. The preaching of Patrick effected a revolution to the full as complete as such a counter-revolution in favor of Paganism could possibly be, and to this thorough revolution we must devote at leats one chapter before going farther.

The best accounts agree that Patrick was a native of Gaul, then subject to Rome; that he was carried captive into Erin on one of King Nial's returning expeditions; that he became a slave, as all captives of the sword did, in those iron times; that he fell to the lot of one Milcho, a chief of Dalriada, whose flocks he tended for seven years, as a shepherd, on the mountain called Slemish, in the present county of Antrim. The date of Nial's death, and the consequent return of his last expedition, is set down in all our annals at the year 405; as Patrick was sixteen years of age when he reached Ireland, he must have been born about the year 390; and as he died in the year 493, he would thus have reached the extraordinary, but not impossible age of 103 years. Whatever the exact number of his years, it is certain that his mission in Ireland commenced in the year 432, and was prolonged till his death, sixty-one years afterwards. Such an unprecedented length of life, not less than the unprecedented power, both popular and political, which he early attained, enabled him to establish the Irish Church, during his own time, on a basis so broad and deep, that neither lapse of ages, nor heathen rage, nor earthly temptations, nor all the arts of Hell, have been able to upheave its firm foundations. But we must not imagine that the powers of darkness abandoned the field without a struggle, or that the victory of the cross was achieved without a singular combination of courage, prudence, and determination—God aiding above all.

If the year of his captivity was 405 or 6, and that of his escape or manumission seven years later (412 or 413), twenty years would intervene between his departure out of the land of his bondage, and his return to it clothed with the character and authority of a Christian Bishop. This interval, longer or shorter, he spent in qualifying himself for Holy Orders or discharging priestly duties at Tours, at Lerins, and finally at Rome. But always by night and day he was haunted by the thought of the Pagan nation in which he had spent his long years of servitude, whose language he had acquired, and the character of whose people he so thoroughly understood. These natural retrospections were hightened and deepened by supernatural revelalations of the will of Providence towards the Irish, and himself as their apostle. At one time, an angel presented him, in his sleep, a scroll bearing the superscription, "the voice of the Irish;" at another, he seemed to hear in a dream all the unborn children of that nation crying to him for help and holy baptism. When, therefore, Pope Celestine commissioned him for this enterprise, "to the ends of the earth," he found him not only ready but anxious to undertake it.

When the new Preacher arrived in the Irish Sea, in 432, he and his companions were driven off the coast of Wicklow by a mob, who assailed them with showers of stones. Running down the coast to Antrim, with which he was personally familiar, he made some stay at Saul, in Down, where he made few converts, and celebrated Mass in a barn; proceeding northward he found himself rejected with scorn by his old master, Milcho, of Slemish. No doubt it appeared an unpardonable audacity in the eyes of the proud Pagan, that his former slave should attempt to teach him how to reform his life and order his affairs. Returning again southward, led on, as we must believe, by the spirit of God, he determined to strike a blow against Paganism at its most vital point. Having learned that the monarch, Leary, (*Laeghaire,*) was to celebrate his birthday with suitable rejoicings at Tara, on a day which happened to fall on the eve of Easter, he resolved to proceed to Tara on that occasion, and to confront the Druids in the midst of all the princes and magnates of the Island. With this view he returned on his former course, and landed from his frail barque at the mouth of the Boyne. Taking leave of the boatmen, he desired them to wait for him a certain number of days, when, if they did not hear from him, they might conclude him dead, and provide for their own safety. So saying he set out, accompanied by the few disciples he had made, or brought from abroad, to traverse on foot the great plain which stretches from the mouth of the Boyne to Tara. If those sailors were Christians, as is most likely, we can conceive with what anxiety they must have awaited tidings of an attempt, so hazardous and so eventful.

The Christian proceeded on his way, and the first night of his journey lodged with a hospitable chief, whose family he converted and baptized, especially marking out a fine child named Beanen, called by him Benignus, from his sweet disposition; who was destined to be one of his most efficient coadjutors, and finally his successor in the Primatial see of Armagh. It was about the second or third day when, travelling probably by the northern road, poetically called "the Slope of the Chariots," the Christian adventurers came in sight of the roofs of Tara. Halting on a neighboring eminence they surveyed the citadel of Ancient Error, like soldiers about to assault an enemy's stronghold. The aspect of the royal hill must have been highly imposing. The building towards the north was the Banquet Hall, then thronged with the celebrants of the King's birthday, measuring from north to south 360 feet in length by 40 wide. South of this hall was the King's Rath, or residence, enclosing an area of 280 yards in diameter, and including several detached buildings, such as the house of Cormac, and the house of the hostages. Southward still stood the new rath of the reigning king, and yet farther south, the rath of Queen Mab, probably uninhabited even then. The intervals between the buildings were at some points planted, for we know that magnificent trees shaded the well of Finn, and the well of Newnaw, from which all the raths were supplied with water. Imposing at any time, Tara must have looked its best at the moment Patrick first beheld it, being in the pleasant season of spring, and decorated in honor of the anniversary of the reigning sovereign.

One of the religious ceremonies employed by the Druids to heighten the solemnity of the occasion, was to order all the fires of Tara and Meath to be quenched, in order to rekindle them instantaneously from a sacred fire dedicated to the honor of their God. But Patrick, either designedly or innocently, anticipated this striking ceremony, and lit his own fire, where he had encamped, in view of the royal residence. A flight of fiery arrows, shot into the Banqueting Hall, would not have excited more horror and tumult among the company there assembled than did the sight of that unlicensed blaze in the distance. Orders were issued to drag the offender against the laws and the gods of the Island before them, and the punishment in store for him was already decreed in every heart. The Preacher, followed by his trembling disciples, ascended "the Slope of the Chariots," surrounded by menacing minions of the Pagan law, and regarded with indignation by astonished spectators. As he came he recited Latin Prayers to the Blessed Trinity, beseeching their protection and direction in this trying hour. Contrary to courteous custom no one at first rose to offer him a seat. At last, a chieftain, touched with mysterious admiration for the stranger, did him that kindness. Then it was demanded of him, why he had dared to violate the laws of the country, and to defy its ancient gods; on this text the Christian Missionary spoke. The place of audience was in the open air, on that eminence the home of so many kings, which commands one of the most agreeable prospects in any landscape. The eye of the inspired orator, pleading the cause of all the souls that hereafter, till the end of time, might inhabit the land, could discern within the spring-day horizon, the course of the Blackwater and the Boyne before they blend into one; the hills of Cavan to the far north; with the royal hill of Tailtean in the foreground; the wooded heights of Slane and Skreen, and the four ancient roads, which led away towards the four subject Provinces, like the reins of empire laid loosely on their necks. Since the first Apostle of the Gentiles had confronted the subtle Paganism of Athens, on the hill of Mars, none of those who walked in his steps ever stood out in more glorious relief than Patrick, surrounded by Pagan princes and a Pagan Priesthood, on the hill of Tara.

The defence of the fire he had kindled, unlicensed, soon extended into wider issues. Who were the gods against whom he had offended? Were they true gods or false? They had their priests: could they maintain the divinity of such gods, by argument, or by miracle? For his God, he, though unworthy, was ready to answer, yea, right ready to die. His God had become man, and had died for man. His name alone was sufficient to heal all diseases; to raise the very dead to life. Such, we learn from the old biographers, was the line of Patrick's argument. This sermon ushered in a controversy. The king's guests, who had come to feast and rejoice, remained to listen and to meditate. With the impetuosity of the national character—with all its passion for debate—they rushed into this new conflict, some on one side, some on the other. The daughters of the king and many others—the Arch-Druid himself—became convinced and were baptized. The missionaries obtained powerful protectors, and the king assigned to Patrick the pleasant fort of Trim, as a present residence. From that convenient distance, he could readily return at any moment, to converse with the king's guests and the members of his household.

The Druidical superstition never recovered the blow it received that day at Tara. The conversion of the Arch-Druid and the Princesses, was, of itself, their knell of doom. Yet they held their ground during the remainder of this reign—twenty-five years longer (A. D. 458). The king himself never became a Christian, though he tolerated the missionaries, and deferred more and more every year to the Christian party. He sanctioned an expurgated code of the laws, prepared under the direction of Patrick, from which every positive element of Paganism was rigidly excluded. He saw, unopposed, the chief idol of his race, overthrown on "the Plain of Prostration," at Sletty. Yet withal he never consented to be baptized; and only two years before his decease, we find him swearing to a treaty, in the old Pagan form —" by the Sun, and the Wind, and all the Elements." The party of the Druids at first sought to stay the progress of Christianity by violence, and even attempted, more than once, to assassinate Patrick. Finding these means ineffectual they tried ridicule and satire. In this they were for some time seconded by the Bards, men warmly attached to their goddess of song and their lives of self-indulgence. All in vain. The day of the idols was fast verging into everlasting night in Erin. Patrick and his disciples were advancing from conquest to conquest. Armagh and Cashel came in the wake of Tara, and Cruachan was soon to follow. Driven from the high places, the obdurate Priests of Bel took refuge in the depths of the forest and in the islands of the sea, wherein the Christian anchorites of the next age were to replace them. The social revolution proceeded, but all that was tolerable in the old state of things, Patrick carefully engrafted with the new. He allowed much for the habits and traditions of the people, and so made the transition as easy, from darkness into the light, as Nature makes the transition from night to morning. He seven times visited in person every mission in the kingdom, performing the six first "circuits" on foot, but the seventh, on account of his extreme age, he was borne in a chariot. The pious munificence of the successors of Leary, had surrounded him with a household of princely proportions. Twenty-four persons, mostly ecclesiastics, were chosen for this purpose: A bell-ringer, a psalmist, a cook, a brewer, a chamberlain, three smiths, three artificers and three embroiderers, are reckoned of the number. These last must be considered as employed in furnishing the interior of the new churches. A scribe, a shepherd to guard his flocks, and a charioteer, are also mentioned, and their proper names given. How different this following from the little boat's crew, he had left waiting tidings from Tara, in such painful apprehension, at the mouth of the Boyne, in 433. Apostolic zeal, and unrelaxed discipline had wrought these wonders, during a lifetime prolonged far beyond the ordinary age of man.

The fifth century was drawing to a close, and the days of Patrick were numbered. Pharamond and the Franks had sway on the Netherlands; Hengist and the Saxons on South Britain; Clovis had led his countrymen across the Rhine into Gaul; the Vandals had established themselves in Spain and North Africa; the Ostrogoths were supreme in Italy. The empire of barbarism had succeeded to the empire of Polytheism; dense darkness covered the semi-Christian countries of the old Roman empire, but happily daylight still lingered in the West. Patrick, in good season, had done his work. And as sometimes, God seems to bring round His ends, contrary to the natural order of things, so the spiritual sun of Europe was now destined to arise in the West, and return on its light-bearing errand towards the East, dispelling in its path, Saxon, Frankish, and German darkness, until at length it reflected back on Rome herself, the light derived from Rome.

On the 17th of March, in the year of our Lord 493, Patrick breathed his last in the monastery of Saul, erected on the site of that barn where he had first said Mass. He was buried with national honors, in the Church of Armagh, to which he had given the Primacy over all the churches of Ireland; and such was the concourse of mourners, and the number of Masses offered for his eternal repose, that from the day of his death till the close of the year, the sun is poetically said never to have set—so brilliant and so continual was the glare of tapers and torches.

CHAPTER IV.

THE CONSTITUTION, AND HOW THE KINGS KEPT IT.

WE have fortunately still existing the main provisions of that constitution which was prepared under the auspices of Saint Patrick, and which, though not immediately, nor simultaneously, was in the end accepted by all Erin as its supreme law. It is contained in a volume called "the Book of Rights," and in its printed form (the Dublin bilingual edition of 1847), fills some 250 octavo pages. This book may be said to contain the original institutes of Erin under her Celtic Kings: "the Brehon laws," (which are also shortly to be published,) bear the same relation to "the Book of Rights," as the Statutes at large of England, or the United States, bear to the English Constitution in the one case, or to the collective Federal and State Constitutions in the other. Let us endeavor to comprehend what this ancient Irish Constitution was like, and how the Kings received it, at first.

There were, as we saw in the first chapter, beside the existing, four Provinces, whose names are familiar to every one, a fifth principality of Meath. Each of the Provinces was subdivided into chieftainries, of which there were at least double or treble as many as there are now counties. The connection between the chief and his Prince, or the Prince and his monarch, was not of the nature of feudal obedience; for the fee-simple of the soil was never supposed to be vested in the sovereign, nor was the King considered to be the fountain of all honor. The Irish system blended the aristocratic and democratic elements more largely than the monarchical. Everything proceeded by election, but all the candidates should be of noble blood. The Chiefs, Princes, and Monarchs, so selected, were bound together by certain customs and tributes, originally invented by the genius of the Druids, and afterwards adopted and enforced by the authority of the Bishops. The tributes were paid in kind, and consisted of cattle, horses, foreign-born slaves, hounds, oxen, scarlet mantles, coats of mail, chess-boards and chess-men, drinking cups and other portable articles of value. The quantity in every case due from a King to his subordinate, or from a subordinate to his King—for the gifts and grants were often reciprocal—is precisely stated in every instance. Beside these rights, this constitution defines the "prerogatives" of the five Kings on their journeys through each other's territory, their accession to power, or when present in the General Assemblies of the Kingdom. It contains, besides, a very numerous array of "prohibitions"—acts which neither the Ard-Righ nor any other Potentate may lawfully do. Most of these have reference to old local Pagan ceremonies in which the Kings once bore a leading part, but which were now strictly prohibited; others are of inter-Provincial significance, and others, again, are rules of personal conduct. Among the prohibitions of the monarch the first is, that the sun must never rise on him in his bed at Tara; among his prerogatives he was entitled to banquet on the first of August, on the fish of the Boyne, fruit from the Isle of Mann, cresses from the Brosna river, venison from Naas, and to drink the water of the well of Talla: in other words, he was entitled to eat on that day, of the produce, whether of earth or water, of the remotest bounds, as well as of the very heart of his mensal domain. The King of Leinster was "prohibited" from upholding the Pagan ceremonies within his province, or to encamp for more than a week in certain districts; but he was "privileged" to feast on the fruits of Almain, to drink the ale of Cullen, and to preside over the games of Carman, (Wexford.) His colleague of Munster was "prohibited" from encamping a whole week at Killarney or on the Suir, and from mustering a martial host on the

Leinster border at Gowran; he was "privileged" to pass the six weeks of Lent at Cashel (in free quarters), to use fire and force in compelling tribute from north Leinster; and to obtain a supply of cattle from Connaught, at the time " of the singing of the cuckoo." The Connaught King had five other singular "prohibitions" imposed on him—evidently with reference to some old Pagan rites—and his "prerogatives" were hostages from Galway, the monopoly of the chase in Mayo, free quarters in Murrisk, in the same neighborhood, and to marshal his border-host at Athlone to confer with the tribes of Meath. The ruler of Ulster was also forbidden to indulge in such superstitious practices as observing omens of birds, or drinking of a certain fountain " between two darknesses ;" his prerogatives were presiding at the games of Cooley, " with the assembly of the fleet ;" the right of mustering his border army in the plains of Louth; free quarters in Armagh for three nights for his troops before setting out on an expedition; and to confine his hostages in Dunseverick, a strong fortress near the Giant's Causeway. Such were the principal checks imposed upon the individual caprice of Monarchs and Princes; the plain inference from all which is, that under the Constitution of Patrick, a Prince who clung to any remnant of ancient Paganism, might lawfully be refused those rents and dues which alone supported his dignity. In other words, disguised as it may be to us under ancient forms, " the Book of Rights" establishes Christianity as the law of the land. All national usages and customs, not conflicting with this supreme law, were recognized and sanctioned by it. The internal revenues in each particular Province were modelled upon the same general principle, with one memorable exception—the special tribute which Leinster paid to Munster – and which was the cause of more bloodshed than all other sources of domestic quarrel combined. The origin of this tax is surrounded with fable, but it appears to have arisen out of the reaction which took place, when Tuathal, " the Legitimate," was restored to the throne of his ancestors, after the successful revolt of the Belgic bondsmen. Leinster seems to have clung longest to the Bilgce revolution, and to have submitted only after repeated defeats. Tuathal, therefore, imposed on that Province this heavy and degrading tax, compelling its Princes not only to render him and his successors immense herds of cattle, but also 150 male and female slaves, to do the menial offices about the palace of Tara. With a refinement of policy, as far-seeing as it was cruel, the proceeds of the tax were to be divided one-third to Ulster, one-third to Connaught, and the remainder between the Queen of the Monarch and the ruler of Munster. In this way all the other Provinces became interested in enforcing this invidious and oppressive enactment upon Leinster, which, of course, was withheld whenever it could be refused with the smallest probability of success. Its resistance, and enforcement, especially by the kings of Munster, will be found a constant cause of civil war, even in Christian times.

The sceptre of Ireland, from her conversion to the time of Brian, was almost solely in the hands of the northern Hy-Nial, the same family as the O'Neills. All the kings of the VIth and VIIth centuries were of that line. In the VIIIth century (from 709 to 742), the southern annalists style Cathal, King of Munster, Ard-Righ; in the IXth century (840 to 847), they give the same high title to Felim, King of Munster; and in the XIth century, Brian possessed that dignity for the twelve last years of his life, (1002 to 1014). With these exceptions, the northern Hy-Nial, and their co-relatives of Meath, called the southern Hy-Nial, seem to have retained the sceptre exclusively in their own hands, during the five first Christian centuries. Yet on every occasion, the ancient forms of election, (or procuring the adhesion of the Princes,) had to be gone through. Perfect unanimity, however, was not required; a majority equal to two-thirds seems to have sufficed. If the candidate had the North in his favor, and one Province of the South, he was considered entitled to take possession of Tara; if he were a Southern, he should be seconded either by Connaught or Ulster, before he could lawfully possess himself of the supreme power. The benediction of the Archbishop of Armagh seems to have been necessary to confirm the choice of the Provincials. The monarchs, like the petty kings, were crowned or "made" on the summit of some lofty mound prepared for that purpose; an hereditary officer, appointed to that duty, presented him with a white wand perfectly straight, as an emblem of the purity and uprightness which should guide all his decisions, and, clothed with his royal robes, the new ruler descended among his people, and solemnly swore to protect their rights and to administer equal justice to all. This was the civil ceremony; the solemn blessing took place in a church, and is supposed to be the oldest form of coronation service observed anywhere in Christendom.

A ceremonial, not without dignity, regulated the gradations of honor, in the General Assemblies of Erin. The time of meeting was the great Pagan Feast of Samhain, the 1st of November. A feast of three days opened and closed the Assembly, and during its sittings crimes of violence committed on those in attendance were punished with instant death. The monarch himself had no power to pardon any violator of this established law. The *Chiefs* of territories sat, each in an appointed seat, under his own shield; the seats being arranged by order of the Ollamh, or Recorder, whose duty it was to preserve the muster-roll, containing the names of all the living nobles. The *Champions*, or leaders of military bards, occupied a secondary position, each sitting under his own shield. Females and spectators of an inferior rank were excluded; the Christian clergy naturally stepped into the empty places of the Druids, and were placed immediately next the monarch.

We shall now briefly notice the principal acts of the first Christian kings, during the century immediately succeeding St. Patrick's death. Of OLLIOL, who succeeded Leary, we cannot say with certainty that he was a Christian. His successor, LEWY, son of Leary, we are expressly told, was killed by lightning (A. D. 496), for "having violated the law of Patrick"—that is, probably, for having practised some of those Pagan rites forbidden to the monarchs by the revised constitution. His successor, MURKERTACH, son of Erc, was a professed Christian, though a bad one, since he died by the vengeance of a concubine named Sheen, (that is, *storm*,) whom he had once put away at the instance of his spiritual adviser, but whom he had not the courage - though brave as a lion in battle—to keep away (A. D. 527). TUATHAL "the Rough" succeeded and reigned for seven years, when he was assassinated by the tutor of DERMID, son of Kerbel, a rival whom he had driven into exile. DERMID immediatly seized on the throne (A. D. 534), and for twenty eventful years bore sway over all Erin. He appears to have had quite as much of the old leaven of Paganism in his composition—at least in his youth and prime—as either Lewy or Leary. He kept Druids about his person, despised "the right of sanctuary" claimed by the Christian clergy, and observed, with all the ancient superstitious ceremonial, the national games at Tailteen. In his reign the most remarkable event was the public curse pronounced on Tara, by a Saint whose sanctuary the reckless monarch had violated, in dragging a prisoner from the very horns of the altar, and putting him to death. For this offence—the crowning act of a series of aggressions on the immunities claimed by the clergy—the Saint, whose name was Ruadan, and the site of whose sanctuary is still known as Temple-Ruadan, in Tipperary, proceeded to Tara, accompanied by his clergy, and, walking round the royal rath, solemnly excommunicated the monarch, and anathematized the place. The far-reaching consequences of this awful exercise of spiritual power are traceable for a thousand years through Irish history. No king after Dermid resided permanently upon the hill of Tara. Other royal houses there were in Meath—at Tailteen, at the hill of Usna, and on the margin of the beautiful Lough Ennell, near the present Castlepollard, and at one or other of these after monarchs held occasional court; but those of the northern race made their habitual home in their own patrimony near Armagh, or on the celebrated hill of Aileach. The date of the malediction which left Tara desolate is the year of our Lord 554. The end of this self-willed semi-Pagan (Dermid) was in unison with his life; he was slain in battle by Black Hugh, Prince of Ulster, two years after the desolation of Tara.

Four kings, all fierce competitors for the succession, reigned and fell, within ten years of the death of Dermid, and then we come to the really interesting and important reign of Hugh the Second, which lasted twenty-seven years (A. D. 566 to 593), and was marked by the establishment of the Independence of the Scoto-Irish Colony, in North Britain, and by other noteworthy events. But these twenty-seven years deserve a chapter to themselves.

CHAPTER V.

REIGN OF HUGH II.—THE IRISH COLONY IN SCOTLAND OBTAINS ITS INDEPENDENCE.

TWENTY-SEVEN years is a long reign, and the years of King Hugh II. were marked with striking events. One religious and one political occurrence, however, threw all others into the shade, —the conversion of the Highlands and Islands of Scotland (then called Alba or Albyn by the Gael, and Caledonia by the Latins), and the formal recognition, after an exciting controversy, of the independence of the Milesian colony in Scotland. These events follow each other in the order of time, and stand partly in the relation of cause and effect:

The first authentic Irish immigration into Scotland seems to have taken place about the year of our Lord 258. The pioneers crossed over from Antrim to Argyle, where the strait is less than twenty-five miles wide. Other adventurers followed at intervals, but it is a fact to be deplored, that no passages in our own, and in all other histories, have been so carelessly kept as the records of emigration. The movements of rude masses of men, the first founders of states and cities, are generally lost in obscurity, or misrepresented by patriotic zeal. Several successive settlements of the Irish in Caledonia can be faintly traced from the middle of the III. till the beginning of the VI. century. About the year 503, they had succeeded in establishing a flourishing principality among the cliffs and glens of Argyle. The limits of their first territory cannot be exactly laid down; but it soon spread north into Rosshire, and east into the present county of Perth. It was a land of stormy friths and fissured headlands, of deep defiles and snowy summits. "'Tis a far cry to Lough Awe," is still a lowland proverb, and Lough Awe was in the very heart of that old Irish settlement.

The earliest emigrants to Argyle were Pagans, while the latter were Christians, and were accompanied by priests, and a bishop, Kieran, the son of the carpenter, whom, from his youthful piety and holy life, as well as from the occupation followed by his father, is sometimes fancifully compared to our Lord and Saviour himself. Parishes in Cantyre, in Islay and in Carrick, still bear the name of St. Kieran as patron. But no systematic attempt—none at least of historic memory—was made to convert the remoter Gael and the other races then inhabiting Alba—the Picts, Britons, and Scandinavians, until in the year of our era, 565, Columba or COLUMBKILL, a Bishop of the royal race of Nial, undertook that task, on a scale commensurate with its magnitude. This celebrated man has always ranked with Saint Patrick and Saint Bridget as the most glorious triad of the Irish Calendar. He was, at the time he left Ireland, in the prime of life—his 44th year. Twelve companions, the apostolic number, accompanied him on his voyage. For thirty-four years he was the legislator and captain of Christianity in those northern regions. The King of the Picts received baptism at his hands; the Kings of the Scottish colony, his kinsmen, received the crown from him on their accession. The islet of I., or Iona, was presented to him by one of these princes. Here he and his companions built with their own hands their parent-house, and from this Hebridean rock in after times was shaped the destinies, spiritual and temporal, of many tribes and kingdoms.

The growth of Iona was as the growth of the grain of mustard seed mentioned in the Gospel, even during the life of its founder. Formed by his teaching and example, there went out from it apostles to Iceland, to the Orkneys, to Northumbria, to Man, and to South Britain. A hundred monasteries in Ireland looked to that exiled saint as their patriarch. His rule of monastic life, adopted either from the far East, from the recluses of the Thebaid, or from his great contemporary, Saint Benedict, was sought for by Chiefs, Bards, and converted Druids. Clients, seeking direction from his wisdom, or protection through his power, were constantly arriving and departing from his sacred isle. His days were divided between manual labor and the study and transcribing of the Sacred Scriptures. He and his disciples, says the Venerable Bede, in whose age Iona still flourished, "neither thought of nor loved anything in *this* world." Some writers have represented Columbkill's *Culdees*, (which in English means simply "Servants of God,") as a married clergy; so far is this from the truth, that we now know, no woman was allowed to land on the island, nor even a cow to be kept there, for, said the holy Bishop, "wherever there is a cow there will be a woman, and wherever there is a woman there will be mischief."

In the reign of King Hugh, three domestic questions arose of great importance; one was the refusal of the Prince of Ossory to pay tribute to the Monarch; the other, the proposed extinction of the Bardic Order, and the third, the attempt to tax the Argyle Colony. The question between Ossory and Tara, we may pass over as of obsolete interest, but the other two deserve fuller mention:

The Bards—who were the Editors, Professors, Registrars and Record-keepers—the makers and masters of public opinion in those days, had reached in this reign a number exceeding 1,200 in Meath and Ulster alone. They claimed all the old privileges of free quarters on their travels and freeholdings at home, which were freely granted to their order when it was in its infancy. Those chieftains who refused them anything, however extravagant, they lampooned and libelled, exciting their own people and other princes against them. Such was their audacity, that some of them are said to have demanded from King Hugh the royal brooch, one of the most highly prized heir-looms of the reigning family. Twice in the early part of this reign they had been driven from the royal residence, and obliged to take refuge in the little principality of Ulidia (or Down); the third time the monarch had sworn to expel them utterly from the kingdom. In Columbkill, however, they were destined to find a most powerful mediator, both from his general sympathy with the Order, being himself no mean poet, and from the fact that the then Arch-Poet, or chief of the order, Dallan Forgaill, was one of his own pupils.

To settle this vexed question of the Bards, as well as to obtain the sanction of the estates to the taxation of Argyle, King Hugh called a General Assembly in the year 590. The place of meeting was no longer the interdicted Tara, but for the monarch's convenience a site farther north was chosen—the hill of Drom-Keth, in the present county of Derry. Here came in rival state and splendor the Princes of the four Provinces, and other principal chieftains. The dignitaries of the Church also attended, and an occasional Druid was perhaps to be seen in the train of some unconverted Prince. The pretensions of the mother-country to impose a tax upon her Colony, were sustained by the profound learning and venerable name of St. Colman, Bishop of Dromore, one of the first men of his Order.

When Columbkill "heard of the calling together of that General Assembly," and of the questions to be there decided, he resolved to attend, notwithstanding the stern vow of his earlier life, never to look on Irish soil again. Under a scruple of this kind, he is said to have remained blindfold, from his arrival in his fatherland, till his return to Iona. He was accompanied by an imposing train of attendants; by Aidan, Prince of Argyle, so deeply interested in the issue, and a suite of over one hundred persons, twenty of them Abbots or Bishops. Columbkill spoke for his companions; for already, as in Bede's time, the Abbots of Iona exercised over all the clergy north of the Humber, but still more directly north of the Tweed, a species of supremacy similar to that which the successors of St. Benedict and St. Bernard exercised, in turn, over Prelates and Princes on the European Continent.

When the Assembly was opened the holy Bishop of Dromore stated the arguments in favor of Colonial taxation with learning and effect. Hugh himself impeached the Bards for their licencious and lawless lives. Columbkill defended both interests, and, by combining both, probably strengthened the friends of each. It is certain that he carried the Assembly with him, both against the monarch and those of the resident clergy, who had selected Colman as their spokesman. The Bardic Order was spared. The doctors, or master-singers among them, were prohibited from wandering from place to place; they were assigned residence with the chiefs and princes; their losel attendants were turned over to honest pursuits, and thus a great danger was averted, and one of the most essential of the Celtic institutions being reformed and regulated, was preserved. Scotland and

Ireland have good reason to be grateful to the founder of Iona, for the interposition that preserved to us the music, which is now admitted to be one of the most precious inheritances of both countries.

The proposed taxation Columbkill strenuously and successfully resisted. Up to this time, the colonists had been bound only to furnish a contingent force, by land and sea, when the Kings of Ireland went to war, and to make them an annual present called "chief-rent."

From the Book of Rights we learn that (at least at the time the existing transcript was made), the Scottish Princes paid out of Alba, seven shields, seven steeds, seven bondswomen, seven bondsmen, and seven hounds all of the same breed. But the "chief-rent," or "eric for kindly blood," did not suffice in the year 590 to satisfy King Hugh. The colony had grown great, and, like some modern monarchs, he proposed to make it pay for its success. Columbkill, though a native of Ireland, and a prince of its reigning house, was by choice a resident of Caledonia, and he stood true to his adopted country. The Irish King refused to continue the connection on the old conditions, and declared his intention to visit Alba himself to enforce the tribute due; Columbkill, rising in the Assembly, declared the Albanians "forever free from the yoke," and this, adds an old historian, "turned out to be the fact." From the whole controversy we may conclude that Scotland never paid political tribute to Ireland; that their relation was that rather of allies than of sovereign and vassal; that it resembled more the homage Carthage paid to Tyre, and Syracuse to Corinth, than any modern form of colonial dependence; that a federal connection existed by which, in time of war, the Scots of Argyle, and those of Hibernia, were mutually bound to aid, assist and defend each other. And this natural and only connection, founded in the blood of both nations, sanctioned by their early saints, confirmed by frequent intermarriage, by a common language and literature, and by hostility to common enemies, the Saxons, Danes, and Normans, grew into a political bond of unusual strength, and was cherished with affection by both nations, long ages after the magnates assembled at Drom-Keth had disappeared in the tombs of their fathers.

The only unsettled question which remained after the Assembly at Drom-Keth related to the Prince of Ossory. Five years afterwards (A. D. 595) King Hugh fell in an attempt to collect the special tribute from all Leinster, of which we have already heard something, and shall, by and by, hear more. He was an able and energetic ruler, and we may be sure "did not let the sun rise on him in his bed at Tara," or anywhere else. In his time great internal changes were taking place in the state of society. The ecclesiastical order had become more powerful than any other, in the state. The Bardic Order, thrice proscribed, were finally subjected to the laws, over which they had at one time insolently domineered. Ireland's only colony—unless we except the immature settlement in the Isle of Man, under Cormac Longbeard—was declared independent of the parent country, through the moral influence of its illustrious Apostle, whose name many of its kings and nobles were of old proud to bear—*Mal-Colm*, meaning "servant of Columb," or Columbkill. But the memory of the sainted statesman who decreed the separation of the two populations, so far as claims to taxation could be preferred, preserved, for ages, the better and far more profitable alliance, of an ancient friendship, unbroken by a single national quarrel during a thousand years.

A few words more on the death and character of this celebrated man, whom we are now to part with at the close of the sixth, as we parted from Patrick at the close of the fifth century. His day of departure came in 596. Death found him at the ripe age of almost four score, *stylus* in hand, toiling cheerfully over the vellum page. It was the last night of the week when the presentiment of his end came strongly upon him. "This day," he said, to his disciple and successor, Dermid, "is called the day of rest, and such it will be for me, for it will finish my labors." Laying down the manuscript, he added, "let Baithen finish the rest." Just after Matins, on the Sunday morning, he peacefully passed away from the midst of his brethren.

Of his tenderness, as well as energy of character, tradition and his biographers have recorded many instances. Among others, his habit of ascending an eminence every evening at sunset, to look over towards the coast of his native land. The spot is called by the islanders to this day, "the place of the back turned upon Ireland." The fishermen of the Hebrides long believed they could see their saint flitting over the waves after every new storm, counting the islands to see if any of them had foundered It must have been a loveable character of which such tales could be told and cherished from generation to generation.

Both Education and Nature had well fitted Columbkill to the great task of adding another realm to the empire of Christendom. His princely birth gave him power over his own proud kindred; his golden eloquence and glowing verse—the fragments of which still move and delight the Gaelic scholar—gave him fame and weight in the Christian schools which had suddenly sprung up in every glen and island. As prince, he stood on equal terms with princes; as poet, he was affiliated to that all-powerful Bardic Order, before whose awful anger kings trembled, and warriors succumbed in superstitious dread. A spotless soul, a disciplined body, an indomitable energy, an industry that never wearied, a courage that never blanched, a sweetness and courtesy that won all hearts, a tenderness for others that contrasted strongly with his rigor towards himself—these were the secrets of the success of this eminent missionary—these were the miracles by which he accomplished the conversion of so many barbarous tribes and Pagan Princes.

CHAPTER VI.

KINGS OF THE SEVENTH CENTURY.

The five years of the sixth century, which remained after the death of Hugh II., were filled by Hugh III., son of Dermid, the semi-Pagan. Hugh IV. succeeded (A. D. 599) and reigned for several years; two other kings, of small account, reigned seven years; Donald II. (A. D. 624) reigned sixteen years; Connall and Kellach, brothers, (A. D. 640) reigned jointly sixteen years; they were succeeded (A. D. 656) by Dermid and Blathmac, brothers, who reigned jointly seven years; Shanasagh, son of the former, reigned six years; KENFALA, four; FINNACTA, "the hospitable," twenty years, and LOINGSECH (A. D. 693) eight years.

Throughout this century the power of the Church was constantly on the increase, and is visible in many important changes. The last armed struggle of Druidism, and the only invasion of Ireland by the Anglo-Saxons, are also events of the civil history of the seventh century.

The reign of Donald II. is notable for the passing away of most of those saintly men, the second generation of Irish abbots and bishops; for the foundation of the celebrated school of Lismore on the Munster Blackwater; and the battle of Moira, in the present county of Down. Of the school and the saints we shall speak hereafter; the battle deserves more immediate mention.

The cause of the battle was the pretension of the petty Prince of Ulidia, which comprised little more than the present county of Down, to be recognized as Prince of all Ulster. Now the Hy-Nial family, not only had long given monarchs to all Ireland, but had also the lion's share of their own Province, and King Donald as their head could not permit their ascendancy to be disputed. The ancestors of the present pretender, Congal, surnamed "the squint-eyed," had twice received and cherished the licentious Bards when under the ban of Tara, and his popularity with that still powerful order was one prop of his ambition. It is pretty clear also that the last rally of Druidism against Christianity took place behind his banner, on the plain of Moira. It was the year 637, and preparations had long gone on on both sides for a final trial of strength. Congal had recruited numerous bands of Saxons, Britons, Picts and Argyle Scots, who poured into the harbors of Down for months, and were marshalled on the banks of the Lagan, to sustain his cause. The Poets of succeeding ages have dwelt much in detail on the occurrences of this memorable day. It was what might strictly be called a pitched battle, time and place being fixed by mutual agreement. King Donald was accompanied by his Bard, who described to him, as they came in sight, the several standards of Congal's host, and who served under them. Conspicuous above all, the ancient banner of the Red Branch Knights—"a yellow lion wrought on green satin"—floated over Congal's host. On the other side the monarch commanded in person, accompanied by his kinsmen, the sons of Hugh III. The red hand of Tirowen, the cross of Tirconnell, the eagle and lion of Innishowen, the axes of Fanad, were in his ranks, ranged closely round his own standard. The cause of the Constitution and the Church prevailed, and Druidism mourned its last hope extinguished on the plains of Moira, in the death of Congal, and the defeat of his vast army. King Donald returned in triumph to celebrate his victory at Emania and to receive the benediction of the Church at Armagh.

The sons of Hugh III., Dermid and Blathmac, zealous and pious Christian princes, survived the field of Moira and other days of danger, and finally attained the supreme power—A. D. 656. Like the two kings of Sparta they reigned jointly, dividing between them the labors and cares of State. In their reign, that terrible scourge, called in Irish "the yellow plague," after ravaging great part of Britain, broke out with undiminished virulence in Erin (A. D. 664). To heighten the awful sense of inevitable doom, an eclipse of the sun occurred concurrently with the appearance of the pestilence on the first Sunday in May. It was the season when the ancient sun-god had been accustomed to receive his annual oblations, and we can well believe that those whose hearts still trembled at the name of Bel, must have connected the eclipse and the plague with the revolution in the national worship, and the overthrow of the ancient gods on that "plain of prostration," where they had so long received the homage of an entire people. Among the victims of this fearful visitation—which, like the modern cholera, swept through all ranks and classes of society, and returned in the same track for several successive seasons—were very many of those venerated men, the third and fourth generation of the Abbots and Bishops. The Munster King, and many of the chieftain class shared the common lot. Lastly, the royal brothers fell themselves victims to the epidemic, which so sadly signalizes their reign.

The only conflicts that occurred on Irish soil with a Pictish or an Anglo-Saxon force—if we except those who formed a contingent of Congal's army at Moira—occurred in the time of the hospitable Finnacta. The Pictish force, with their leaders, were totally defeated at Rathmore, in Antrim (A. D. 680), but the Anglo-Saxon expedition (A. D. 684) seems not to have been either expected or guarded against. As leading to the mention of other interesting events, we must set this inroad clearly before the reader.

The Saxons had now been for four centuries in Britain, the older inhabitants of which—Celts like the Gauls and Irish—they had cruelly harassed, just as the Milesian-Irish oppressed their Belgic predecessors, and as the Normans, in turn, will be found oppressing both Celt and Saxon in England and Ireland. Britain had been divided by the Saxon leaders into *eight* separate kingdoms, the people and princes of several of which were converted to Christianity in the fifth, sixth, and seventh century, though some of them did not receive the Gospel before the beginning of the eighth. The Saxons of Kent and the Southern Kingdoms generally were converted by missionaries from France or Rome, or native preachers of the first or second Christian generation; those of Northumbria recognize as their Apostles St. Aidan and St. Cuthbert, two Fathers from Iona. This Kingdom of Northumbria, as the name implies, embraced nearly all the country from the Humber to the Pictish border. York was its capital, and the seat of its ecclesiastical primacy, where, at the time we speak of, the illustrious Wilfrid was maintaining, with a wilful and unscrupulous king, a struggle not unlike that which Becket maintained with Henry II. This Prince, Egfrid by name, was constantly engaged in wars with his Saxon cotemporaries, or the Picts and Scots. In the summer of 683 he sent an expedition under the command of Beort, one of his earls, to ravage the coast of Leinster. Beort landed probably in the Boyne, and swept over the rich plain of Meath with fire and sword, burning churches, driving off herds and flocks, and slaughtering the clergy and the husbandmen. The piety of an after age saw in the retribution which overtook Egfrid the following year, when he was slain by the Picts and Scots, the judgment of Heaven, avenging the unprovoked wrongs of the Irish. His Scottish conquerors, returning good for evil, carried his body to Iona, where it was interred with all due honor.

Iona was now in the zenith of its glory. The barren rock,

about three miles in length, was covered with monastic buildings, and its cemetery was already adorned with the tombs of saints and kings. Five successors of Columbkill slept in peace around their holy Founder, and a sixth, equal in learning and sanctity to any who preceded him, received the remains of King Egfrid from the hands of his conquerors. This was Abbot Adamnan, to whom Ireland and Scotland are equally indebted for his admirable writings, and who might almost dispute with Bede himself, the title of Father of British History. Adamnan regarded the fate of Egfrid, we may be sure, in the light of a judgment on him for his misdeeds, as Bede and the British Christians very generally did. He learned, too, that there were in Northumbria several Christian captives, carried off in Beort's expedition and probably sold into slavery. Now every missionary that ever went out from Iona, had taught that to reduce Christians to slavery was wholly inconsistent with a belief in the doctrines of the Gospel. St. Aidan, the Apostle of Northumbria, had refused the late Egfrid's father absolution, on one occasion, until he solemnly promised to restore their freedom to certain captives of this description. In the same spirit Adamnan voluntarily undertook a journey to York, where Aldfrid (a Prince educated in Ireland, and whose "Itinerary" of Ireland we still have) now reigned. The Abbot of Iona succeeded in his humane mission, and crossing over to his native land, he restored sixty of the captives to their homes and kindred. While the liberated exiles rejoiced in the plain of Meath, the tent of the Abbot of Iona was pitched on the rath of Tara—a fact which would seem to indicate that already, in little more than a century since the interdict had fallen on it, the edifices which made so fine a show in the days of Patrick were ruined and uninhabitable. Either at Tara, or some other of the royal residences, Adamnan on this visit procured the passing of a law, (A. D. 684,) forbidding women to accompany an army to battle, or to engage personally in the conflict. The mild maternal genius of Christianity is faithfully exhibited in such a law, which consummates the glory of the worthy successor of Columbkill. It is curious here to observe that it was not until another hundred years had past—not till the beginning of the ninth century—that the clergy were "exempt" from military service. So slow and patient is the process by which Christianity infuses itself into the social life of a converted people!

The long reign of FINNACTA, the hospitable, who may, for his many other virtues, be called also the pious, was rendered farther remarkable in the annals of the country by the formal abandonment of the special tax, so long levied upon, and so long and desperately resisted by, the men of Leinster. The all-powerful intercessor in this case, was Saint Moling, of the royal house of Leinster, and Bishop of Fernamore (now Ferns). In the early part of his reign Finnacta seems not to have been disposed to collect this invidious tax by force; but, yielding to other motives, he afterwards took a different view of his duty, and marched into Leinster to compel its payment. Here the holy Prelate of Ferns met him, and related a Vision in which he had been instructed to demand the abolition of the impost. The abolition, he contended, should not be simply a suspension, but final and forever. The tribute was, at this period, enormous; 15,000 head of cattle annually. The decision must have been made about the time that Abbot Adamnan was in Ireland, (A. D. 684,) and that illustrious personage is said to have been opposed to the abolition. Abolished it was, and though its re-enactment was often attempted, the authority of Saint Moling's solemn settlement, prevented it from being re-enforced for any length of time, except as a political or military infliction.

Finnacta fell in battle in the 20th year of his long and glorious reign; and is commemorated as a saint in the Irish calendar. St. Moling survived him three years, and St. Adamnan, so intimately connected with his reign, ten years. The latter revisited Ireland in 697, under the short reign of Loingsech, and concerned himself chiefly in endeavoring to induce his countrymen to adopt the Roman rule, as to the tonsure, and the celebration of Easter. On this occasion there was an important Synod of the Clergy, under the presidency of Flan, Archbishop of Armagh, held at Tara. Nothing could be more natural than such an assembly in such a place, at such a period. In every recorded instance the power of the clergy had been omnipotent in politics for above a century. St. Patrick had expurgated the old constitution; St. Ruadan's curse drove the kings from Tara; St. Columbkill had established the independence of Alba, and preserved the Bardic Order; St. Moling had abolished the Leinster tribute. If their power was irresistible in the sixth and especially in the seventh centuries, we must do these celebrated Abbots and Bishops the justice to remember that it was always exercised against the oppression of the weak by the strong, to mitigate the horrors of war, to uphold the right of sanctuary (the *Habeus Corpus* of that rude age), and for the maintenance and spread of sound Christian principles.

CHAPTER VII.

KINGS OF THE EIGHTH CENTURY.

THE kings of the eighth century are Congall II. (surnamed Kenmare), who reigned seven years; Feargal, who reigned ten years; Forgartah, Kenneth, Flaherty, respectively one, four, and seven years; Hugh V. (surnamed Allan), nine years; Donald III., who reigned (A. D. 739-759) twenty years; Nial II. (surnamed Nial of the Showers), seven years; and Donough I., who reigned thirty-one years, A. D. 766-797. The obituaries of these kings show that we have fallen on a comparatively peaceful age, since of the entire nine but three perished in battle. One retired to Armagh and one to Iona, where both departed in the monastic habit; the others died either of sickness or old age.

Yet the peaceful character of this century is but comparative, for in the first quarter (A. D. 722), we have the terrible battle of Almain, between Leinster and the Monarch, in which 30,000 men were stated to have engaged, and 7,000 to have fallen. The monarch, who had double the number of the Leinster Prince, was routed and slain, *apropos* of which we have a Bardic tale told, which almost transports one to the far East, the simple lives and awful privileges of the Hindoo Brahmins. It seems that some of King FEARGAL'S army, in foraging for their fellows, drove off the only cow of a hermit, who lived in seclusion near a solitary little chapel called Killin. The enraged recluse, at the very moment the armies were about to engage, appeared between them, regardless of personal danger, denouncing ruin and death to the monarch's forces. And in this case, as in others, to be found in every history, the prophecy, no doubt, helped to produce its own fulfilment. The malediction of men, dedicated to the service of God, has often routed hosts as gallant as were marshalled on the field of Almain.

FEARGAL'S two immediate successors met a similar fate—death in the field of battle—after very brief reigns, of which we have no great events to record.

FLAHERTY, the next who succeeded, after a vigorous reign of seven years, withdrew from the splendid cares of a crown, and passed the long remainder of his life—thirty years—in the habit of a monk at Armagh. The heavy burthen which he had cheerfully laid down, was taken up by a Prince, who combined the twofold character of poet and hero. HUGH THE VTH (surnamed Allan), the son of FEARGAL, of whom we have just spoken, was the very opposite of his father, in his veneration for the privileges of holy persons and places. His first military achievement was undertaken in vindication of the rights of those, who were unable by arms to vindicate their own. Hugh Roin, Prince of the troublesome little principality of Ulidia (Down), though well stricken in years and old enough to know better, in one of his excursions had forcibly compelled the clergy of the country through which he passed to give him free quarters, contrary to to the law everywhere existing. Congus, the Primate, jealous of the exemptions of his order, complained of this sacrilege in a poetic message addressed to Hugh Allan, who, as a Christian and a Prince, was bound to espouse his quarrels. He marched into the territory of the offender, defeated him in battle, cut off his head on the threshold of the Church of Faughard, and marched back again, his host chanting a war song composed by their leader.

In this reign died Saint Gerald of Mayo, an Anglo-Saxon Bishop, and apparently the head of a colony of his countrymen, from whom that district is ever since called "Mayo of the Saxons." The name, however, being a general one for strangers from Britain about that period, just as Dane became for foreigners from the Baltic in the next century, is supposed to be incorrectly applied: the colony being, it is said, really from Wales, of old British stock, who had migrated rather than live under the yoke of their victorious Anglo-Saxon Kings. The descendants of these Welshmen are still to be traced, though intimately intermingled with the original Belgic and later Milesian settlers in Mayo, Sligo, and Galway—thus giving a peculiar character to that section of the country, easily dististinguishable from all the rest.

Although Hugh Allan did not imitate his father's conduct toward's ecclesiastics, he felt bound by all-ruling custom to avenge his father's death. In all ancient countries the kinsmen of a murdered man were both by law and custom the avengers of his blood. The members of the Greek *phratry* of the Roman *fatria*, or *gens*, of the Germanic and Anglo-Saxon *guild*, and of the mediæval sworn *commune*, were all solemnly bound to avenge the blood of any of their brethren, unlawfully slain. So that the repulsive repetition of reprisals, which so disgusts the modern reader in our old annals, is by no means a phenomenon peculiar to the Irish state of society. It was in the middle age and in early times common to all Europe, to Britain and Germany, as well as to Greece and Rome. It was, doubtless, under a sense of duty of this sort, that Hugh V. led into Leinster a large army (A. D. 733), and the day of Ath-Senaid fully atoned for the day of Almain. Nine thousand of the men of Leinster were left on the field, including most of their chiefs; the victorious monarch losing a son, and other near kinsmen. Four years later, he himself fell in an obscure contest near Kells, in the plain of Meath. Some of his quatrains have come down to us, and they breathe a spirit at once religious and heroic—such as must have greatly endeared the Prince who possessed it to his companions in arms. We are not surprised, therefore, to find his reign a favorite epoch with subsequent Bards and Story-tellers.

The long and prosperous reign of Donald III. succeeded (A. D. 739 to 759). He is almost the only one of this series of Kings of whom it can be said that he commanded in no notable battle. The annals of his reign are chiefly filled with ordinary accidents, and the obits of the learned. But its literary and religious record abounds with bright names and great achievements, as we shall find when we come to consider the educational and missionary fruits of Christianity in the eight century. While on a pilgrimage to Durrow, a famous Columbian foundation in Meath, and present King's County, Donald III. departed this life, and in Durrow, by his own desire, his body was interred.

Nial II. (surnamed of the Showers), son to FEARGAL and brother of the warrior-Bard, Hugh V., was next invested with the white wand of sovereignty. He was a prince less warlike and more pious than his elder brother. The *soubriquet* attached to his name is accounted for by a Bardic tale, which represents him as another Moses, at whose prayer food fell from heaven, in time of famine. Whatever "showers" fell or wonders were wrought in his reign, it is certain that after enjoying the kingly office for seven years, Nial resigned, and retired to Iona, there to pass the remainder of his days in penance and meditation. Eight years he led the life of a monk in that sacred Isle, where his grave is one of those of "the three Irish Kings," still pointed out in the cemetery of the Kings. He is but one among several Princes, his cotemporaries, who had made the same election. We learn in this same century, that Cellach, son of the King of Connaught, died in Holy Orders, and that Bec, Prince of Ulidia, and Ardgall, son of a later King of Connaught, had taken the "crostaff" of the pilgrim, either for Iona or Armagh, or some more distant shrine. Pilgrimages to Rome and to Jerusalem seem to have been begun even before this time, as we may infer from St. Adamnan's work on the situation of the Holy Places, of which Bede gives an abstract.

The reign of Donogh I. is the longest and the last among the Kings of the eighth century (A. D. 776 to 797). The Kings of Ireland had now not only abandoned Tara, but one by one, the other royal residences in Meath as their usual place of abode. As a consequence a local sovereignty sprung up in the family of O'Melaghlin, a minor branch of the ruling race. This house developing its power so unexpectedly, and almost always certain to have the national forces under the command of a Patron Prince at their back, were soon involved in quarrels about boundaries, both with Leinster and Munster. King Donogh, at the outset of his reign, led his forces into both principalities, and without battle

eceived their hostages. Giving hostages—generally the sons of
he chiefs—was the usual form of ratifying any treaty. Generally
lso, the Bishop of the district, or its most distinguished eccle-
iastic, was called in as witness of the terms, and both parties were
olemnly sworn on the relics of Saints—the Gospels of the Monas-
eries or Cathedrals—or the croziers of their venerated founders.
he breach of such a treaty was considered "a violation of the
elics of the saint," whose name had been invoked, and awful pen-
lties were expected to follow so heinous a crime. The hostages
rere then carried to the residence of the King, to whom they
vere entrusted, and while the peace lasted, enjoyed a parole free-
om, and every consideration due to their rank. If of tender
ge they were educated with the same care as the children of
he household. But when war broke out their situation was
lways precarious, and sometimes dangerous. In a few instances
hey had even been put to death, but this was considered a
iolation of all the laws both of hospitality and chivalry; usually
hey were removed to some strong secluded fort, and carefully
;uarded as pledges to be employed, according to the chances
nd changes of the war. That Donogh preferred negotiation to
var, we may infer by his course towards Leinster and Munster,
n the beginning of his reign, and his "kingly parlee" at a later
eriod (A. D. 783) with FIACHNA, of Ulidia, son of that over-
xacting Hugh Roin, whose head was taken from his shoulders at
he Church door of Faughard. This "kingly parlee" was held on
n island off the Methian shore, called afterwards "King's Island."
But little good came of it. Both parties still held their own
iews, so that the satirical poets asked what was the use of the
sland, when one party "would not come upon the land, nor the
ther upon the sea?" However, we needs must agree with King
)onogh, that war is the last resort, and is only to be tried when
ll other means have failed.

Twice during this reign, the whole island was stricken with
)anic, by extraordinary signs in the heavens, of huge serpents
coiling themselves through the stars, of fiery bolts flying like
huttles from one side of the horizon to the other, or shooting
lownward directly to the earth. These atmospheric wonders
vere accompanied by thunder and lightning so loud and so pro-

longed that men hid themselves for fear in the caverns of the earth. The fairs and markets were deserted by buyers and sellers; the fields were abandoned by the farmers; steeples were rent by lightning, and fell to the ground; the shingled roofs of churches caught fire and burned whole buildings. Shocks of earthquake were also felt, and round towers and cyclopean masonry were strewn in fragments upon the ground. These visitations first occurred in the second year of Donogh, and returned again in 786. When, in the next decade, the first Danish descent was made on the coast of Ulster (A. D. 794), these signs and wonders were superstitiously supposed to have been the precursors of that far more terrible and more protracted visitation.

The Danes at first attracted little notice, but in the last year of Donogh (A. D. 797) they returned in greater force, and swept rapidly along the coast of Meath; it was reserved for his successors of the following centuries to face the full brunt of this new national danger.

But before encountering the fierce nations of the north, and the stormy period they occupy, let us cast back a loving glance over the world-famous schools and scholars of the last two centuries. Hitherto we have only spoken of certain saints, in connection with high affairs of state. We must now follow them to the college and the cloister, we must consider them as founders at home, and as missionaries abroad: otherwise how could we estimate all that is at stake for Erin and for Christendom, in the approaching combat with the devotees of Odin,—the deadly enemies of all Christian institutions?

CHAPTER VIII.

WHAT THE IRISH SCHOOLS AND SAINTS DID IN THE THREE FIRST CHRISTIAN CENTURIES.

WE have now arrived at the close of the third century, from the death of Saint Patrick, and find ourselves on the eve of a protracted struggle with the heathen warriors of Scandinavia: it is time, therefore, to look back on the interval we have passed, and see what changes have been wrought in the land, since its kings, instead of waiting to be attacked at home, had made the surrounding sea "foam with the oars" of their outgoing expeditions.

The most obvious change in the condition of the country is traceable in its constitution and laws, into every part of which, as was its wont from the beginning, the spirit of Christianity sought patiently to infuse itself. We have already spoken of the expurgation of the constitution, which prohibited the observance of Pagan rites to the kings, and imposed on them instead, certain social obligations. This was a first change suggested by Saint Patrick, and executed mainly by his disciple, Saint Benignus. We have seen the legislative success which attended the measures of Columbkill, Moling, and Adamnan; in other reforms of minor importance the paramount influence of the clerical order may be easily traced.

But it is in their relation as teachers of human and divine science that the Irish Saints exercised their greatest power, not only over their own countrymen, but over a considerable part of Europe. The intellectual leadership of western Europe—the glorious ambition of the greatest nations—has been in turn obtained by Italy, France, Britain and Germany. From the middle of the sixth to the middle of the eighth century, it will hardly be disputed that that leadership devolved on Ireland. All the circumstances of the sixth century helped to confer it upon the newly converted western isle; the number of her schools, and the wisdom, energy, and zeal of her masters, retained for her the proud distinction for two hundred years. And when it passed away from her grasp, she might still console herself with the grateful reflection, that the power she had founded and exercised, was divided among British and continental schools, which her own *alumni* had largely contributed to form and establish. In the northern Province, the schools most frequented were those of Armagh, and of Bangor, on Belfast lough; in Meath, the school of Clonard, and that of Clonmacnoise, (near Athlone); in Leinster, the school of Taghmon (*Ta-mun*), and Beg-Erin, the former near the banks of the Slaney, the latter in Wexford harbor; in Munster, the school of Lismore on the Blackwater, and of Mungret (now Limerick), on the Shannon; in Connaught, the school of "Mayo of the Saxons," and the schools of the isles of Aran. These seats of learning were almost all erected on the banks of rivers, in situations easy of access, to the native or foreign student; a circumstance which proved most disastrous to them, when the sea kings of the north began to find their way to the shores of the island. They derived their maintenance—not from taxing their pupils—but in the first instance from public endowments. They were essentially free schools; not only free as to the lessons given, but the venerable Bede tells us they supplied free bed and board and books to those who resorted to them from abroad. The Prince and the Clansmen of every principality in which a school was situated, endowed it with a certain share— often an ample one—of the common land of the clan. Exclusive rights of fishery, and exclusive mill-privileges seem also to have been granted. As to timber for building purposes and for fuel, it was to be had for carrying and cutting. The right of quarry went with the soil, wherever building stone was found. In addition to these means of sustenance, a portion of the collegiate clergy appeared to have discharged missionary duty, and received offerings of the produce of the land. We hear of periodical *quests* or collections, made for the sustenance of these institutions, wherein the learned Lectors and Doctors, no doubt, pleaded their claims, to popular favor, with irresistible eloquence. Individuals, anxious to promote the spread of religion and of science, endowed particular institutions out of their personal means; Princes, Bishops, and pious ladies, contributed to enlarge the bounds and increase the income of their favorite foundations, until a generous emulation seems to have seized on all the great families as well as on the different Provinces, as to which could boast the most largely attended schools, and the greatest number of distinguished scholars. The love of the *alma mater*—that college patriotism which is so sure a sign of the noble-minded scholar—never received more striking illustration than among the graduates of those schools. Columbkill, in his new home among the Hebrides, invokes blessings on blessings on "the angels" with whom it was once his happiness to walk in Aran, and Columbanus, beyond the Alps, remembers with pride the school of Bangor—the very name of which inspires him with poetic rapture.

The buildings, in which so many scholars were housed and taught, must have been extensive. Some of the schools we have mentioned were, when most flourishing, frequented by one, two, three, and even, at some periods, as many as seven thousand scholars. Such a population was alone sufficient to form a large village; and if we add the requisite number of teachers and attendants, we will have an addition of at least one-third to the total. The buildings seem to have been separately of no great size, but were formed into streets, and even into something like wards. Armagh was divided into three parts—*trianmore* (or the town proper), *trian-Patrick*, the Cathedral close, and *trian-Sassenagh*, the Latin quarter, the home of the foreign students. A tall sculptured Cross, dedicated to some favorite saint, stood at the bounds of these several wards, reminding the anxious student to invoke their spiritual intercession as he passed by. Early hours and vigilant night watches had to be exercised to prevent conflagrations in such village-seminaries, built almost wholly of wood, and roofed with reeds or shingles. A Cathedral, or an Abbey Church, a round tower, or a cell of some of the ascetic masters, would probably be the only stone structure within the limits. To the students, the evening star gave the signal for retirement, and the morning sun for awaking. When, at the sound of the early bell, two or three thousand of them poured into the silent streets and made their way towards the lighted Church, to join in the service of matins, mingling, as they went or returned, the tongues of the Gael, the Cimbri, the Pict, the Saxon, and the Frank, or hailing and answering each other in the universal language of the Roman Church, the angels in Heaven must have loved to contemplate the union of so much perseverance with so much piety.

The lives of the masters, not less than their lessons, were studied and observed by their pupils. At that time, as we gather from every authority, they were models of simplicity. One Bishop is found, erecting with his own hands, the *cashel* or stone enclosure which surrounded his cell; another is laboring in the field, and gives his blessing to his visitors, standing between the stilts of the plough. Most ecclesiastics work occasionally either in wood, in bronze, in leather, or as scribes. The decorations of the Church, if not the entire structure, was the work of those who served at the altar. The tabernacle, the rood-screen, the ornamental font; the vellum on which the Psalms and Gospels were written; the ornamented case which contained the precious volume, were often of their making. The music which made the vale of Bangor resound as if inhabited by angels, was their composition; the hymns that accompanied it were their own. "It is a poor Church that has no music," is one of the oldest Irish proverbs; and the *Antiphonarium* of Bangor, as well as that of Armagh, remains to show that such a want was not left unsupplied in the early Church.

All the contemporary schools were not of the same grade nor of equal reputation. We constantly find a scholar, after passing years in one place, transferring himself to another, and sometimes to a third and a fourth. Some masters were, perhaps, more distinguished in human Science; others in Divinity. Columbkill studied in two or three different schools, and *visited* others, perhaps as disputant or lecturer—a common custom in later years. Nor should we associate the idea of under-age with the students of whom we speak. Many of them, whether as teachers or learners, or combining both characters together, reached middle life before they ventured as instructors upon the world. Forty years is no uncommon age for the graduate of those days, when as yet the discovery was unmade, that all-sufficient wisdom comes with the first trace of down upon the chin of youth.

The range of studies seems to have included the greater part of the collegiate course of our own times. The language of the country, and the language of the Roman Church; the languages of Scripture—Greek and Hebrew; the logic of Aristotle, the writings of the Fathers, especially of Pope Gregory the Great—who appears to have been a favorite author with the Irish Church; the defective Physics of the period; Mathematics, Music, and Poetical composition went to complete the largest course. When we remember that all the books were manuscripts; that even paper had not yet been invented; that the best parchment was equal to so much beaten gold, and a perfect MS. was worth a king's ransom, we may better estimate the difficulties in the way of the scholar of the seventh century. Knowing these facts, we can very well credit that part of the story of St. Columbkill's banishment into Argyle, which turns on what might be called a copyright dispute, in which the monarch took the side of St. Finian of Clonard, (whose original MSS. his pupil seems to have copied without permission,) and the Clan-Conal stood up, of course, for their kinsman. This dispute is even said to have led to the affair of Culdrum, in Sligo, which is sometimes mentioned as "the battle of the book." The same tendency of the national character which overstocked the Bardic Order, becomes again visible in its Christian schools; and if we could form anything like an approximate census of the population, anterior to the northern invasions, we would find that the proportion of ecclesiastics was greater than has existed either before or since in any Christian country. The vast designs of missionary zeal drew off large bodies of those who had entered Holy Orders; still the numbers engaged as teachers in the great schools, as well as of those who passed their lives in solitude and contemplation, must have been out of all modern proportion to the lay inhabitants of the Island.

The most eminent Irish Saints of the fifth century were St. Ibar, St. Benignus and St. Kieran, of Ossory; in the sixth, St. Brendan, of Clonfert; St. Brendan, of Birr; St. Maccartin, of Clogher; St. Finian, of Moville; St. Finbar, St. Cannice, St. Finian, of Clonard; and St. Jarlath, of Tuam; in the seventh century, St. Fursey, St. Laserian, Bishop of Leighlin; St. Kieran, Abbot of Clonmacnoise; St. Comgall, Abbot of Bangor; St. Carthage, Abbot of Lismore; St. Colman, Bishop of Dromore; St. Moling, Bishop of Ferns; St. Colman Ela, Abbot; St. Cumnian, "the White;" St. Fintan, Abbot; St. Gall, Apostle of Switzerland; St. Fridolin, "the Traveller;" St. Columbanus, Apostle of Burgundy and Lombardy; St. Killian, Apostle of Franconia; St. Columbkill, Apostle of the Picts; St. Cormac, called "the Navigator;" St. Cuthbert; and St. Aidan, Apostle of Northumbria. In the eighth century the most illustrious names are St. Catablus, Bishop of Tarentum; St. Adamnan, Abbot of Iona; St. Rumold, Apostle of Brabant; Clement and Albinus, "the Wisdom-seekers;" and St. Feargal or Virgilius, Bishop of Saltzburgh. Of holy women in the same ages, we have some account of St. Samthan, in the eighth century; of St. Bees, St. Dympna and St. Syra, in the seventh century; and of St. Monina, St. Ita of Desies, and St. Bride, or Bridget, of Kildare, in the sixth. The number of conventual institutions for women established in those ages, is less easily ascertained than the number of monastic houses for men; but we may suppose them to have borne some proportion to each other, and to have even counted by hundreds. The veneration in which St. Bridget was held during her life, led many of her countrywomen to embrace the religious state, and no less than fourteen *Saints*, her namesakes, are recorded. It was the custom of those days to call all holy persons who died in the odor of sanctity *Saints*, hence national or provincial tradition venerates very many names, which the reader may look for in vain, in the Roman calendar.

The intellectual labors of the Irish schools, besides the task of teaching such immense numbers of men of all nations on their own soil, and the missionary conquests to which I have barely alluded, were diversified by controversies, partly scientific and partly theological—such as the "Easter Controversy," the "Tonsure Controversy," and that maintained by "Feargal the Geometer," as to the existence of the Antipodes.

The discussion, as to the proper time of observing Easter, which had occupied the doctors of the Council of Nice in the fourth century, was raised in Ireland and in Britain early in the sixth, and complete uniformity was not established till far on in the eighth. It occupied the thoughts of several generations of the chief men of the Irish Church, and some of their arguments still fortunately survive, to attest their learning and tolerance, as well as their zeal. St. Patrick had introduced in the fifth century the computation of time then observed in Gaul, and to this custom many of the Irish doctors rigidly adhered, long after the rest of Christendom had agreed to adopt the Alexandrian computation. Great names were found on both sides of the controversy: Columbanus, Fintan, and Aidan, for adhering exactly to the rule of St. Patrick; Cummian the White, Laserian and Adamnan, in favor of strict agreement with Rome and the East. Monks of the same Monastery and Bishops of the same Province maintained opposite opinions with equal ardor, and mutual charity. It was a question of discipline not a matter of faith; but it involved a still greater question, whether national churches were to plead the inviolability of their local usages, even on points of discipline, against the sense and decision of the Universal Church.

In the year of our Lord 630, the Synod of Leighlin was held, under the shelter of the ridge of Leinster, and the presidency of St. Laserian. Both parties at length agreed to send deputies to Rome, as "children to their mother," to learn her decision. Three years later, that decision was made known, and the midland and southern dioceses at once adopted it. The northern churches, however, still held out, under the lead of Armagh and the influence of Iona, nor was it till a century later that this scandal of celebrating Easter on two different days in the same church was entirely removed. In justification of the Roman rule, St. Cummian, about the middle of the seventh century, wrote his famous epistle to Segenius, Abbot of Iona, of the ability and learning of which all modern writers from Archbishop Usher to Thomas Moore, speak in terms of the highest praise. It is one of the few remaining documents of that controversy. A less vital question of discipline arose about the tonsure. The Irish shaved the head in a semicircle from temple to temple, while the Latin usage was to shave the crown, leaving an external circle of hair to typify the crown of thorns. At the conference of Whitby (A. D. 664) this was one of the subjects of discussion between the clergy of Iona, and those who followed the Roman method—but it never assumed the importance of the Easter controversy.

In the following century an Irish Missionary, Virgilius, of Saltzburgh, (called by his countrymen "Feargal the Geometer,") was maintaining in Germany against no less an adversary than St. Boniface, the sphericity of the earth and the existence of antipodes. His opponents endeavored to represent him, or really believed him to hold, that there were other men, on our earth, for whom the Redeemer had not died; on this ground they appealed to Pope Zachary against him; but so little effect had this gross distortion of his true doctrine at Rome, when explanations were given, that Feargal was soon afterwards raised to the See of Saltzburgh, and subsequently canonized by Pope Gregory IX. In the ninth century we find an Irish geographer and astronomer of something like European reputation in Dicuil and Dungal, whose treatises and epistles have been given to the press. Like their compatriot, Columbanus, these accomplished men had passed their youth and early manhood in their own country, and to its schools are to be transferred the compliments paid to their acquirements by such competent judges as Muratori, Latronne, and Alexander von Humboldt. The origin of the scholastic philosophy—which pervaded Europe for nearly ten centuries—has been traced by the learned Mosheim to the same insular source. Whatever may now be thought of the defects or shortcomings of that system, it certainly was not unfavorable either to wisdom or eloquence, since among its professors may be reckoned the names of St. Thomas and St. Bernard.

We must turn away our eyes from the contemplation of those days in which were achieved for Ireland the title of the land of saints and doctors. Another era opens before us, and we can already discern the longships of the north, their monstrous beaks turned towards the holy Isle, their sides hung with glittering shields and their benches thronged with fair-haired warriors, chanting as they advance the fierce war songs of their race. Instead of the monk's familiar voice on the river banks we are to hear the shouts of strange warriors from a far-off country; and for matin hymn and vesper song, we are to be beset through a long and stormy period, with sounds of strife and terror, and deadly conflict.

BOOK II.

CHAPTER I.

THE DANISH INVASION.

Hugh VI., surnamed Ornie, succeeded to the throne vacant by the death of Donogh I. (A. D. 797), and reigned twenty-two years; Conor II. succeeded (A. D. 819), and reigned fourteen years; Nial III. (called from the place of his death Nial of Callan), reigned thirteen years; Malachy I. succeeded (A. D. 845), and reigned fifteen years; Hugh VII., succeeded and reigned sixteen years, (dying A. D. 877); Flan (surnamed Flan of the Shannon), succeeded at the latter date, and reigned for thirty-eight years, far into the tenth century. Of these six kings, whose reigns average twenty years each, we may remark that not one died by violence, if we except perhaps Nial of Callan, drowned in the river of that name in a generous effort to save the life of one of his own servants. Though no former princes had ever encountered dangers equal to these—yet in no previous century was the person of the ruler so religiously respected. If this was evident in one or two instances only, it would be idle to lay much stress upon it; but when we find the same truth holding good of several successive reigns, it is not too much to attribute it to that wide diffusion of Christian morals, which we have pointed out as the characteristic of the two preceding centuries. The kings of this age owed their best protection to the purer ethics which overflowed from Armagh and Bangor and Lismore; and if we find hereafter the regicide habits of former times partially revived, it will only be after the new Paganism—the Paganism of interminable anti-Christian invasions—had recovered the land, and extinguished the beacon lights of the three first Christian centuries.

The enemy, who were now to assault the religious and civil institutions of the Irish, must be admitted to possess many great military qualities. They certainly exhibit, in the very highest degree, the first of all military virtues—unconquerable courage. Let us say cheerfully, that history does not present in all its volumes a braver race of men than the Scandinavians of the ninth century. In most respects they closely resembled the Gothic tribes, who, whether starting into historic life on the Euxine or the Danube, or faintly heard of by the Latins from the far off Baltic, filled with constant alarm the Roman statesmen of the fourth century: nor can the invasions of what we may call the maritime Goths be better introduced to the reader than by a rapid sketch of the previous triumphs of their kindred tribes over the Roman Empire.

It was in the year of Our Lord 378 that these long-dreaded barbarians defeated the Emperor Valens in the plain of Adrianople, and as early as 404—twenty-six years after their first victory in Eastern Europe—they had taken and burned great Rome herself. Again and again—in 410, in 455 and in 472—they captured and plundered the Imperial City. In the same century they had established themselves in Burgundy, in Spain, and in Northern Africa; in the next, another branch of the Gothic stock twice took Rome; and yet another founded the Lombard Kingdom in Northern Italy. With these Goths thus for a time masters of the Roman Empire, whose genius and temper has entered so deeply into all subsequent civilization, war was considered the only pursuit worthy of men. According to their ideas of human freedom, that sacred principle was supposed to exist only in force and by force; they had not the faintest conception, and at first received with unbounded scorn the Christian doctrine of the unity of the human race, the privileges and duties annexed to Christian baptism, and the sublime ideal of the Christian republic. But they were very far from being so cruel or so faithless as their enemies represented them; they were even better than they cared to represent themselves. And they had amongst them men of the highest capacity and energy, well worthy to be the founders of new nations. Alaric, Attila, and Genseric, were fierce and unmerciful it is true; but their acts are not all written in blood; they had their better moments and higher purposes in the intervals of battle; and the genius for civil government of the Gothic race was in the very beginning demonstrated by such rulers as Theodoric in Italy, and Clovis in Gaul. The rear guard of this irresistible barbaric invasion was now about to break in upon Europe by a new route; instead of the long land marches by which they had formerly concentrated from the distant Baltic and from the tributaries of the Danube, on the capital of the Roman empire; instead of the tedious expeditions striking across the Continent, hewing their paths through dense forests, arrested by rapid rivers and difficult mountains, the last northern invaders of Europe had sufficiently advanced in the arts of ship-building and navigation to strike boldly into the open sea and commence their new conquests among the Christian islands of the West. The defenders of Roman power and Christian civilization in the fifth and sixth centuries, were arrayed against a warlike but pastoral people encumbered with their women and children; the defenders of the same civilization, in the British Islands in the ninth and tenth centuries, were contending with kindred tribes, who had substituted maritime arts and habits for the pastoral arts and habits of the companions of Attila and Theodoric. The Gothic invasions of Roman territory in the earlier period was, with the single exception of the naval expeditions of Genseric from his new African Kingdom, a continental war; and notwithstanding the partiality of Genseric for his fleet, as an arm of offence and defence, his companions and successors abandoned the ocean as an uncongenial element. The only parallel for the new invasion, of which we are now to speak, is to be found in the history and fortunes of the Saxons of the fifth century, first the allies and afterwards the conquerors of part of Britain. But even their descendants in England had not kept pace, either in the arts of navigation or in thirst for adventure, with their distant relatives, who remained two centuries later among the friths and rocks of Scandinavia.

The first appearance of these invaders on the Irish and British coasts occurred in 794. Their first descent on Ireland was at Rathlin island, which may be called the outpost of Erin, towards the north; their second attempt (A. D. 797) was at a point much more likely to arouse attention—at Skerries, off the coast of Meath, (now Dublin); in 803, and again in 806, they attacked and plundered the holy Iona; but it was not until a dozen years later they became really formidable. In 818 they landed at Howth; and the same year, and probably the same party, sacked the sacred edifices in the estuary of the Slaney, by them afterwards called Wexford; in 820 they plundered Cork, and in 824—most startling blow of all—they sacked and burned the schools of Bangor. The same year they revisited Iona; and put to death many of its inmates; destroyed Moville; received a severe check in Lecale, near Strangford lough, (one of their favorite stations). Another party fared better in a land foray into Ossory, where they defeated those who endeavored to arrest their progress, and carried off a rich booty. In 830 and 831, their ravages were equally felt in Leinster, in Meath, and in Ulster, and besides many prisoners of princely rank, they plundered the primatial city of Armagh for the first time, in the year 832. The names of their chief captains, at this period, are carefully preserved by those who had so many reasons to remember them; and we now begin to hear of the Ivars, Olafs, and Sitricks, strangely intermingled with the Hughs, Nials, Connors, and Felims, who contended with them in battle or in diplomacy. It was not till the middle of this century (A. D. 837) that they undertook to fortify Dublin, Limerick, and some other harbors which they had seized, to winter in Ireland, and declare their purpose to be the complete conquest of the country.

The earliest of these expeditions seem to have been annual visitations; and as the northern winter sets in about October, and the Baltic is seldom navigable before May, the summer was the season of their depredations. Awaiting the breaking up of the ice, the intrepid adventurers assembled annually upon the islands in the Cattegat or on the coast of Norway, awaiting the favorable moment of departure. Here they beguiled their time between the heathen rites they rendered to their gods, their wild bacchanal festivals, and the equipment of their galleys. The largest ship built in Norway, and probably in the north, before the eleventh century, had 34 banks of oars. The largest class of vessel carried from 100 to 120 men. The great fleet which invaded Ireland in 837 counted 120 vessels, which, if of average size for such long voyages, would give a total force of some 6,000 men. As the whole population of Denmark, in the reign of Canute who died in 1035, is estimated at 800,000 souls, we may judge from their fleets how large a portion of the men were engaged in these piratical pursuits. The ships on which they prided themselves so highly were flat-bottomed craft, with little or no keel, the sides of wicker work, covered with strong hides. They were impelled either by sails or oars as the changes of the weather allowed; with favorable winds they often made the voyage in three days. As if to favor their designs, the north and north-west blast blows for a hundred days of the year over the sea they had to traverse. When land was made, in some safe estuary, their galleys were drawn up on shore, a convenient distance beyond highwater mark, where they formed a rude camp, watch-fires were lighted, sentinels set, and the fearless adventurers slept as soundly as if under their own roofs, in their own country. Their revels after victory, or on returning to their homes, were as boisterous as their lives. In food they looked more to quantity than quality, and one of their most determined prejudices against Christianity was that it did not sanction the eating of horse flesh. An exhilerating beer, made from heath, or from the spruce tree, was their principal beverage, and the recital of their own adventures, or the national songs of the Scalds, were their most cherished amusement. Many of the Vikings were themselves Scalds, and excelled, as might be expected, in the composition of war songs.

The Pagan belief of this formidable race was in harmony with all their thoughts and habits, and the exact opposite of Christianity. In the beginning of time, according to their tradition, there was neither heaven nor earth, but only universal chaos and a bottomless abyss, where dwelt Surtur in an element of unquenchable fire. The generation of their gods proceeded amid the darkness and void, from the union of heat and moisture, until Odin and the other children of Asa-Thor, or the Earth, slew Ymer, or the Evil One, and created the material universe out of his lifeless remains. These heroic conquerors also collected the sparks of eternal fire flying about in the abyss and fixed them as stars in the firmament. In addition, they erected in the far

East, Asgard, the City of the Gods; on the extreme shore of the ocean stood Utgard, the City of Nor and his giants, and the wars of these two cities, of their gods and giants, fill the first and most obscure ages of the Scandinavian legend. The human race had as yet no existence until Odin created a man and woman, Ask and Embla, out of two pieces of wood (ash and elm), thrown upon the beach by the waves of the sea.

Of all the gods of Asgard, Odin was the first in place and power; from his throne he saw everything that happened on the earth; and lest anything should escape his knowledge, two ravens, Spirit and Memory, sat on his shoulders, and whispered in his ears whatever they had seen in their daily excursions round the world. Night was a divinity and the father of Day, who travelled alternately throughout space, with two celebrated steeds called Shining-mane and Frost-mane. Friga was the daughter and wife of Odin; the mother of Thor, the Mars, and of the beautiful Balder, the Apollo, of Asgard. The other gods were of inferior rank to these, and answered to the lesser divinities of Greece and Rome. Niord was the Neptune, and Frega, daughter of Niord, was the Venus of the North. Heimdall, the watchman of Asgard, whose duty it was to prevent the rebellious giants scaling by surprise the walls of the celestial city, dwelt under the end of the rainbow; his vision was so perfect he could discern objects 100 leagues distant, either by night or day, and his ear was so fine he could hear the wool growing on the sheep, and the grass springing in the meadows.

The hall of Odin which had 540 gates, was the abode of heroes who had fought bravest in battle. Here they were fed with the lard of a wild boar, which became whole every night, though devoured every day, and drank endless cups of hydromel, drawn from the udder of an inexhaustible she-goat, and served out to them by the Nymphs, who had counted the slain, in cups which were made of the skulls of their enemies. When they were wearied of such enjoyments, the sprites of the Brave exercised themselves in single combat, hacked each other to pieces on the floor of Valhalla, resumed their former shape, and returned to their lard and their hydromel.

Believing firmly in this system—looking forward with undoubting faith to such an eternity—the Scandinavians were zealous to serve their gods according to their creed. Their rude hill altars gave way as they increased in numbers and wealth, to spacious temples, at Upsala, Ledra, Tronheim, and other towns and ports. They had three great festivals, one at the beginning of February, in honor of Thor, one in Spring, in honor of Odin, and one in Summer, in honor of the fruitful daughter of Niord. The ordinary sacrifices were animals and birds; but, every ninth year, there was a great festival at Upsala, at which the kings and nobles were obliged to appear in person, and to make valuable offerings. Wizards and sorcerers, male and female, haunted the temples, and good and ill winds, length of life, and success in war, were spiritual commodities bought and sold. Ninety-nine human victims were offered at the great Upsala festival, and in all emergencies, such sacrifices were considered most acceptable to the gods. Captives and slaves were at first selected; but, in many cases, princes did not spare their subjects, nor fathers their own children. The power of a Priesthood who could always enforce such a system, must have been unbounded and irresistible.

The active pursuits of such a population were necessarily maritime. In their short summer, such crops as they planted ripened rapidly, but their chief sustenance was animal food and the fish that abounded in their waters. The artizans in highest repute among them were the shipwrights and smiths. The hammer and anvil were held in the highest honor; and of this class, the armorers held the first place. The kings of the North had no standing armies, but their lieges were summoned to war by an arrow in Pagan times, and a cross after their conversion. Their chief dependence was in infantry, which they formed into wedge-like columns, and so, clashing their shields and singing hymns to Odin, they advanced against their enemies. Different divisions were differently armed; some with a short two-edged sword and a heavy battle-axe; others with the sling, the javelin, and the bow. The shield was long and light, commonly of wood and leather, but for the chiefs, ornamented with brass, with silver, and even with gold. Locking the shields together formed a rampart which it was not easy to break; in bad weather the concave shield seems to have served the purpose of our umbrella; in sea-fights the vanquished often escaped by swimming ashore on their shields. Armor, many of them wore; the Bersærkers, or champions, were so called from always engaging, *bare* of defensive armor.

Such were the men, the arms, and the creed, against which the Irish of the ninth age, after three centuries of exemption from foreign war, were called upon to combat. A people, one-third of whose youth and manhood had embraced the ecclesiastical state, and all whose tribes now professed the religion of peace, mercy, and forgiveness, were called to wrestle with a race whose religion was one of blood, and whose beatitude was to be in proportion to the slaughter they made while on earth. The Northman hated Christianity as a rival religion, and despised it as an effeminate one. He was the soldier of Odin, the elect of Valhalla; and he felt that the offering most acceptable to his sanguinary gods was the blood of those religious who denied their existence and execrated their revelation. The points of attack, therefore, were almost invariable the great seats of learning and religion. There, too, was to be found the largest bulk of the portable wealth of the country, in richly adorned altars, jewelled chalices, and shrines of saints. The ecclesiastical map is the map of their campaigns in Ireland. And it is to avenge or save these innumerable sacred places—as countless as the Saints of the last three centuries—that the Christian population have to rouse themselves year after year, hurrying to a hundred points at the same time. To the better and nobler spirits the war becomes a veritable crusade, and many of those slain in single-hearted defence of their altars may well be accounted martyrs—but a war so protracted and so devastating will be found, in the sequel, to foster and strengthen many of the worst vices as well as some of the best virtues of our humanity.

The early events are few and ill known. During the reign of Hugh VI., who died in 819, their hostile visits were few and far between; his successors, Conor II. and Nial III., were destined to be less fortunate in this respect. During the reign of Conor, Cork, Lismore, Dundalk, Bangor and Armagh, were all surprised, plundered, and abandoned by "the Gentiles," as they are usually called in Irish annals; and with the exception of two skirmishes in which they were worsted on the coasts of Down and Wexford, they seem to have escaped with impunity. At Bangor they shook the bones of the revered founder out of the costly shrine before carrying it off; on their first visit to Kildare they contented themselves with taking the gold and silver ornaments of the tomb of St. Bridget, without desecrating the relics; their main attraction at Armagh was the same, but there the relics seem to have escaped. When, in 830, the brotherhood of Iona apprehended their return, they carried into Ireland, for greater safety, the relics of St. Columbkill. Hence it came that most of the memorials of SS. Patrick, Bridget, and Columbkill, were afterwards united at Downpatrick.

While these deplorable sacrileges, too rapidly executed perhaps to be often either prevented or punished, were taking place, Conor the King had on his hand a war of succession, waged by the ablest of his cotemporaries, Felim, King of Munster, who continued during this and the subsequent reign to maintain a species of rival monarchy in the South. It seems clear enough that the abandonment of Tara, as the seat of authority, greatly aggravated the internal weakness of the Milesian constitution. While over-centralization is to be dreaded as the worst tendency of imperial power, it is certain that the want of a sufficient centralization has proved as fatal, on the other hand, to the independence of many nations. And anarchical usages once admitted, we see from the experience of the German Empire, and the Italian republics, how almost impossible it is to apply a remedy. In the case before us, when the Irish Kings abandoned the old mensal domain and betook themselves to their own patrimony, it was inevitable that their influence and authority over the southern tribes should diminish and disappear. Aileach, in the far North, could never be to them what Tara had been. The charm of conservatism, the halo of ancient glory, could not be transferred. Whenever, therefore, ambitious and able Princes arose in the South, they found the border tribes rife for backing their pretensions against the Northern dynasty. The Bards, too, plied their craft, reviving the memory of former times, when Heber the Fair divided Erin equally with Heremon, and when Eugene More divided it a second time with Con of the Hundred Battles. Felim, the son of Crimthan, the contemporary of Conor II. and Nial

III., during the whole term of their rule, was the resolute assertor of these pretensions, and the Bards of his own Province do not hesitate to confer on him the high title of *Ard-righ*. As a punishment for adhering to the Hy-Nial dynasty, or for some other offence, this Christian king, in rivalry with "the Gentiles," plundered Kildare, Durrow, and Clonmacnoise—the latter perhaps for siding with Connaught in the dispute as to whether the present county of Clare belonged to Connaught or Munster. Twice he met in conference with the monarch at Birr and at Cloncurry—at another time he swept the plain of Meath, and held temporary court in the royal rath of Tara. With all his vices he united an extraordinary energy, and during his time, no Danish settlement was established on the Southern rivers. Shortly before his decease (A.D. 846) he resigned his crown and retired from the world, devoting the short remainder of his days to penance and mortification. What we know of his ambition and ability makes us regret that he ever appeared upon the scene, or that he had not been born of that dominant family, who alone were accustomed to give kings to the whole country.

King Conor died A. D. 833, and was succeeded by Nial III., surnamed Nial of Callan. The military events of this last reign are so intimately bound up with the more brilliant career of the next ruler—Melaghlin, or Malachy I.—that we must reserve them for the introduction to the next chapter.

CHAPTER II.

KINGS OF THE NINTH CENTURY (CONTINUED) — NIAL III.— MALACHY I.—HUGH VII.

WHEN, in the year 833, Nial III. received the usual homage and hostages, which ratified his title of *Ard-Righ*, the northern invasion had clearly become the greatest danger that ever yet had threatened the institutions of Erin. Attacks at first predatory and provincial had so encouraged the Gentile leaders of the second generation that they began to concert measures and com-

bine plans for conquest and colonization. To the Vikings of
Norway the fertile Island with which they were now so familiar,
whose woods were bent with the autumnal load of acorns, mast,
and nuts, and filled with numerous herds of swine—their favorite
food—whose pleasant meadows were well stored with beeves and
oxen, whose winter was often as mild as their northern summer,
and whose waters were as fruitful in fish as their own Lofoden
friths; to these men, this was a prize worth fighting for; and for
it they fought, long and desperately.

King Nial inherited a disputed sovereignty from his predecessor, and the Southern annalists say he did homage to Felim of
Munster, while those of the North—and with them the majority
of historians—reject this statement as exaggerated and untrue.
He certainly experienced continual difficulty in maintaining his
supremacy, not only from the Prince of Cashel, but from lords
of lesser grade—like those of Ossory and Ulidia; so that we may
say, while he had the title of King of Ireland, he was, in fact,
King of no more than Leath-Con, or the Northern half. The
central Province, Meath, long deserted by the monarchs, had run
wild into independence, and was parcelled out between two or
three chiefs, descendants of the same common ancestor as the
kings, but distinguished from them by the tribe-name of "the
Southern Hy-Nial." Of these heads of new houses, by far the
ablest and most famous was Melaghlin, who dwelt near Mullingar, and lorded it over western Meath; a name with which we
shall become better acquainted presently. It does not clearly
appear that Melaghlin was one of those who actively resisted the
prerogatives of this monarch, though others of the Southern Hy-Nial did at first reject his authority, and were severely punished
for their insubordination, the year after his assumption of power.

In the fourth year of Nial III. (A. D. 837), arrived the great Norwegian fleet of 120 sail, whose commanders first attempted, on a
combined plan, the conquest of Erin. Sixty of the ships entered
the Boyne; the other sixty the Liffey. This formidable force,
according to all Irish accounts, was soon after united under one
leader, who is known in our Annals as *Turgeis* or *Turgesius*,
but of whom no trace can be found, under that name, in the
chronicles of the Northmen. Every effort to identify him in the

records of his native land has hitherto failed—so that we are forced to conclude that he must have been one of those wandering sea-kings whose fame was won abroad, and whose story, ending in defeat, yet entailing no dynastic consequences on his native land, possessed no national interest for the authors of the old Norse Sagas. To do all the Scandinavian chroniclers justice, in cases which come directly under their notice, they acknowledge defeat as frankly as they claim victory proudly. Equal praise may be given to the Irish annalists in recording the same events, whether at first or second-hand. In relation to the campaigns and sway of Turgesius, the difficulty we experience in separating what is true from what is exaggerated or false, is not created for us by the annalists, but by the bards and storytellers, some of whose inventions, adopted by *Cambrensis*, have been too readily received by subsequent writers. For all the acts of national importance with which his name can be intelligibly associated, we prefer to follow in this as in other cases, the same sober historians who condense the events of years and generations into the shortest space and the most matter of fact expression.

If we were to receive the chronology while rejecting the embellishments of the Bards, Turgesius must have first come to Ireland with one of the expeditions of the year 820, since they speak of him as having been "the scourge of the country for seventeen years," before he assumed the command of the forces landed from the fleet of 837. Nor is it unreasonable to suppose that an accurate knowledge of the country, acquired by years of previous warfare with its inhabitants, may have been one of the grounds upon which the chief command was conferred on Turgesius. This knowledge was soon put to account; Dublin was taken possession of, and a strong fort, according to the Scandinavian method, was erected on the hill where now stands the Castle. This fort and the harbor beneath it were to be the *rendezvous* and arsenal for all future operations against Leinster, and the foundation of foreign power then laid, continued in foreign hands, with two or three brief intervals, until transferred to the Anglo-Norman chivalry, three centuries and a half later. Similar lodgment was made at Waterford, and a third was attempted at

Limerick, but at this period without success; the Danish fort at the latter point is not thought older than the year 855. But Turgesius—if, indeed, the independent acts of cotemporary and even rival chiefs be not too often attributed to him—was not content with fortifying the estuaries of some principal rivers; he established inland centres of operation, of which the cardinal one was on Lough Ree, the expansion of the Shannon, north of Athlone; another was at a point called Lyndwachill, on Lough Neagh. On both these waters were stationed fleets of boats, constructed for that service, and communicating with the forts on shore. On the eastern border of Lough Ree, in the midst of its meadows, stood Clonmacnoise, rich with the offerings and endowments of successive generations. Here, three centuries before, in the heart of the desert, St. Kieran had erected with his own hands a rude sylvan cell, where, according to the allegory of tradition, "the first monks who joined him," were the fox, the wolf, and the bear; but time had wrought wonders on that hallowed ground, and a group of churches—at one time, as many as ten in number—were gathered within two or three acres, round its famous schools, and presiding Cathedral. Here it was Turgesius made his usual home, and from the high altar of the Cathedral his unbelieving Queen was accustomed to issue her imperious mandates in his absence. Here, for nearly seven years, this conqueror and his consort, exercised their far-spread and terrible power. According to the custom of their own country—a custom attributed to Odin as its author—they exacted from every inhabitant subject to their sway—a piece of money annually, the forfeit for the non-payment of which was the loss of the nose, hence called "nose-money." Their other exactions were a union of their own northern imposts, with those levied by the chiefs whose authority they had superseded, but whose prerogatives they asserted for themselves. Free quarters for their soldiery, and a system of inspection extending to every private relation of life, were the natural expedients of a tyranny so odious. On the ecclesiastical order especially their yoke bore with peculiar weight, since, although avowed Pagans, they permitted no religious house to stand, unless under an Abbot, or at least an *Erenach* (or Treasurer) of their approval.

Such is the complete scheme of oppression presented to us, that it can only be likened to a monstrous spider-web spread from the centre of the Island over its fairest and most populous districts. Glendalough, Ferns, Castle-Dermid, and Kildare in the east; Lismore, Cork, Clonfert, in the southern country; Dundalk, Bangor, Derry, and Armagh in the north; all groaned under this triumphant despot, or his colleagues. In the meanwhile King Nial seems to have struggled resolutely with the difficulties of his lot, and in every interval of insubordination to have struck boldly at the common enemy. But the tide of success for the first few years after 837 ran strongly against him. The joint hosts from the Liffey and the Boyne swept the rich plains of Meath, and in an engagement at Invernabark (the present Bray) gave such a complete defeat to the southern Hy-Nial clans as prevented them making head again in the field, until some summers were past and gone. In this campaign Saxolve, who is called "the chief of the foreigners," was slain; and to him, therefore, if to any commander-in-chief, Turgesius must have succeeded. The shores of all the inland lakes were favorite sites for Raths and Churches, and the beautiful country around Lough Erne shared the fiery ordeal which blazed on Lough Ree and Lough Neagh. In 839 the men of Connaught also suffered a defeat equal to that experienced by those of Meath in the previous campaign; but more unfortunate than the Methians, they lost their leader and other chiefs on the field. In 840, Ferns and Cork were given to the flames, and the fort at Lyndwachill, or Magheralin, poured out its ravagers in every direction over the adjacent country, sweeping off flocks, herds, and prisoners, laymen and ecclesiastics, to their ships. The northern depredators counted among their captives "several Bishops and learned men," of whom the Abbot of Clogher and the Lord of Galtrim are mentioned by name. Their equally active colleagues of Dublin and Waterford took captive, Hugh, Abbot of Clonenagh, and Foranan, Archbishop of Armagh, who had fled southwards with many of the relics of the Metropolitan Church, escaping from one danger only to fall into another a little farther off. These prisoners were carried into Munster, where Abbot Hugh suffered martyrdom at their hands, but the Archbishop, after being carried to their fleet at Limerick, seems to have been rescued or ransomed, as we find him dying in peace at Armagh in the next reign. The martyrs of these melancholy times were very numerous, but the exact particulars being so often unrecorded it is impossible to present the reader with an intelligible account of their persons and sufferings. When the Anglo-Normans taunted the Irish that their Church had no martyrs to boast of, they must have forgotten the exploits of their Norse kinsmen about the middle of this century.

But the hour of retribution was fast coming round, and the native tribes, unbound, divided, confused, and long unused to foreign war, were fast recovering their old martial experience, and something like a politic sense of the folly of their border feuds. Nothing perhaps so much tended to arouse and combine them together as the capture of the successor of Saint Patrick, with all his relics, and his imprisonment among a Pagan host, in Irish waters. National humiliation could not much farther go, and as we read we pause, prepared for either alternative—mute submission or a brave uprising. King Nial seems to have been in this memorable year, 843, defending as well as he might his ancestral province—Ulster—against the ravagers of Lough Neagh, and still another party whose ships flocked into Lough Swilly. In the ancient plain of Moynith, watered by the little river Finn, (the present barony of Raphoe,) he encountered the enemy, and according to the Annals, "a countless number fell"—victory being with Nial. In the same year, or the next, Turgesius was captured by Melaghlin, Lord of Westmeath, apparently by stratagem, and put to death by the rather novel process of drowning. The Bardic tale told to *Cambrensis*, or parodied by him from an old Greek legend, of the death by which Turgesius died, is of no historical authority. According to this tale, the tyrant of Lough Ree conceived a passion for the fair daughter of Melaghlin, and demanded her of her father, who, fearing to refuse, affected to grant the infamous request, but despatched in her stead, to the place of assignation, twelve beardless youths, habited as maidens, to represent his daughter and her attendants; by these maskers the Norwegian and his boon companions were assassinated, after they had drank to excess and laid aside their arms and armor.

For all this superstructure of romance there is neither groundwork nor license in the facts themselves, beyond this, that Turgesius was evidently captured by some clever stratagem. We hear of no battle in Meath or elsewhere against him immediately preceding the event; nor, is it likely that a secondary Prince, as Melaghlin then was, could have hazarded an engagement with the powerful master of Lough Ree. If the local traditions of Westmeath may be trusted, where *Cambrensis* is rejected, the Norwegian and Irish principals in the tragedy of Lough Owel were on visiting terms just before the denouement, and many curious particulars of their peaceful but suspicious intercourse used to be related by the modern story-tellers around Castlepollard. The anecdote of the rookery, of which Melaghlin complained, and the remedy for which his visitor suggested to be "to cut down the trees and the rooks would fly," has a suspicious look of the "tall poppies" of the Roman and Grecian legend; two things only do we know for certain about the matter: *firstly*, that Turgesius was taken and drowned in Lough Owel in the year 843 or 844; and *secondly*, that this catastrophe was brought about by the agency and order of his neighbor, Melaghlin.

The victory of Moynith and the death of Turgesius were followed by some local successes against other fleets and garrisons of the enemy. Those of Lough Ree seem to have abandoned their fort, and fought their way (gaining in their retreat the only military advantage of that year) towards Sligo, where some of their vessels had collected to bear them away. Their colleagues of Dublin, undeterred by recent reverses, made their annual foray southward into Ossory, in 844, and immediately we find King Nial moving up from the north to the same scene of action. In that district he met his death in an effort to save the life of a *gilla*, or common servant. The river of Callan being greatly swollen, the *gilla*, in attempting to find a ford, was swept away in its turbid torrent. The King entreated some one to go to his rescue, but as no one obeyed he generously plunged in himself and sacrificed his own life in endeavoring to preserve one of his humblest followers. He was in the 55th year of his age and the 13th of his reign, and in some traits of character reminded men of his grandfather, the devout Nial "of the Showers." The

Bards have celebrated the justice of his judgments, the goodness of his heart, and the comeliness of his "brunette-bright face." He left a son of age to succeed him, (and who ultimately did become *Ard-Righ*,) yet the present popularity of Melaghlin of Meath triumphed over every other interest, and he was raised to the monarchy—the first of his family who had yet attained that honor. Hugh, the son of Nial, sank for a time into the rank of a Provincial Prince, before the ascendant star of the captor of Turgesius, and is usually spoken of during this reign as "Hugh of Aileach." He is found towards its close, as if impatient of the succession, employing the arms of the common enemy to ravage the ancient mensal land of the kings of Erin, and otherwise harassing the last days of his successful rival.

Melaghlin, or Malachy I. (sometimes called "of the Shannon," from his patrimony along that river), brought back again the sovereignty to the centre, and in happier days might have become the second founder of Tara. But it was plain enough then, and it is tolerably so still, that this was not to be an age of restoration. The kings of Ireland after this time, says the quaint old translator of the Annals of Clonmacnoise, "had little good of it," down to the days of King Brian. It was, in fact, a perpetual struggle for self-preservation—the first duty of all governments, as well as the first law of all nature. The powerful action of the Gentile forces, upon an originally ill-centralized and recently much abused Constitution, seemed to render it possible that every new Ard-Righ would prove the last. Under the pressure of such a deluge all ancient institutions were shaken to their foundations; and the venerable authority of Religion itself, like a Hermit in a mountain torrent, was contending for the hope of escape or existence. We must not, therefore, amid the din of the conflicts through which we are to pass, condemn without stint or qualification those Princes who were occasionally driven —as some of them *were* driven—to that last resort, the employment of foreign mercenaries, (and those mercenaries often anti-Christians,) to preserve some show of native government and kingly authority. Grant that in some of them the use of such allies and agents cannot be justified on any plea or pretext of state necessity; where base ends or unpatriotic motives are clear or credible, such treason to country cannot be too heartily condemned; but it is indeed far from certain that such were the motives in *all* cases, or that such ought to be our conclusion in any, in the absence of sufficient evidence to that effect.

Though the Gentile power had experienced towards the close of the last reign such severe reverses, yet it was not in the nature of the men of Norway to abandon a prize which was once so nearly being their own. The fugitives who escaped, as well as those who remained within the strong ramparts of Waterford and Dublin, urged the fitting out of new expeditions, to avenge their slaughtered countrymen and prosecute the conquest. But defeat still followed on defeat; in the first year of Malachy, they lost 1,200 men in a disastrous action near Castle Dermot, with Olcobar the Prince-bishop of Cashel; and in the same or the next season, they were defeated with the loss of 700 men, by Malachy, at Fore, in Meath. In the third year of Malachy, however, a new Northern expedition arrived in 140 vessels, which, according to the average capacity of the long-ships of that age, must have carried with them from 7,000 to 10,000 men. Fortunately for the assailed, this fleet was composed of what they called *Black*-Gentiles, or Danes, as distinguished from their predecessors, the *Fair*-Gentiles, or Norwegians. A quarrel arose between the adventurers of the two nations as to the possession of the few remaining fortresses, especially of Dublin; and an engagement was fought along the Liffey, which "lasted for three days;" the Danes finally prevailed, driving the Norwegians from their stronghold, and cutting them off from their ships. The new Northern leaders are named Anlaf, or Olaf, Sitrick (Sigurd?) and Ivar; the first of the Danish Earls, who established themselves at Dublin, Waterford and Limerick respectively. Though the immediate result of the arrival of the great fleet of 847 relieved for the moment the worst apprehensions of the invaded, and enabled them to rally their means of defence, yet as Denmark had more than double the population of Norway, it brought them into direct collision with a more formidable power than that from which they had been so lately delivered. The tactics of both nations were the same. No sooner had they established themselves on the ruins of their predecessors in Dublin, than the

Danish forces entered East-Meath, under the guidance of Kenneth, a local lord, and overran the ancient mensal, from the sea to the Shannon. One of their first exploits was burning alive 260 prisoners in the tower of Treoit, in the island of Lough Gower, near Dunshaughlin. The next year, his allies having withdrawn from the neighborhood, Kenneth was taken by King Malachy's men, and the traitor himself drowned in a sack, in the little river Nanny, which divides the two baronies of Duleek. This death-penalty by drowning seems to have been one of the useful hints which the Irish picked up from their invaders.

During the remainder of this reign the Gentile war resumed much of its old local and guerrilla character, the Provincial chiefs, and the Ard-Righ, occasionally employing bands of one nation of the invaders to combat the other, and even to suppress their native rivals. The only pitched battle of which we hear is that of "the Two Plains" (near Coolestown, King's County), in the second last year of Malachy (A. D. 859), in which his usual good fortune attended the king. The greater part of his reign was occupied, as always must be the case with the founder of a new line, in coercing into obedience his former peers. On this business he made two expeditions into Munster, and took hostages from all the tribes of the Eugenian race. With the same object he held a conference with all the chiefs of Ulster, Hugh of Aileach only being absent, at Armagh, in the fourth year of his reign, and a General *Feis*, or Assembly of all the Orders of Ireland, at Rathugh, in West-Meath, in his thirteenth year (A. D. 857). He found, notwithstanding his victories and his early popularity, that there are always those ready to turn from the setting to the rising sun, and towards the end of his reign he was obliged to defend his camp, near Armagh, by force, from a night assault of the discontented Prince of Aileach; who also ravaged his patrimony, almost at the moment he lay on his death-bed. Malachy I. departed this life on the 13th day of November, A. D. 860, having reigned sixteen years. "Mournful is the news to the Gael!" exclaims the elegiac Bard! "Red wine is spilled into the valley! Erin's monarch has died!" And the lament contrasts his stately form as "he rode the white stallion," with the striking reverse when, "his only horse this day"—that is the bier on which his body was borne to the churchyard—" is drawn behind two oxen."

The restless Prince of Aileach now succeeded as Hugh VII., and possessed the perilous honor, he so much coveted, for sixteen years, the same span that had been allotted to his predecessor. The beginning of this reign was remarkable for the novel design of the Danes, who marched out in great force, and set themselves busily to breaking open the ancient mounds in the cemetery of the Pagan kings, beside the Boyne, in hope of finding buried treasure. The three Earls, Olaf, Sitrick, and Ivar are said to have been present, while their gold-hunters broke into in succession the mound-covered cave of the wife of Goban, at Drogheda, the cave of "the Shepherd of Elcmar," at Dowth, the cave of the field of Aldai, at New Grange, and the similar cave at Knowth. What they found in these huge cairns of the old *Tuatha* is not related; but Roman coins of Valentinian and Theodosius, and torques and armlets of gold, have been discovered by accident within their precincts, and an enlightened modern curiosity has not explored them in vain, in the higher interests of history and science.

In the first two years of his reign, Hugh VII. was occupied in securing the hostages of his suffragans; in the third he swept the remaining Danish and Norwegian garrisons out of Ulster, and defeated a newly arrived force on the borders of Lough Foyle; the next the Danish Earls went on a foray into Scotland, and no exploit is to be recorded; in his sixth year, Hugh, with 1,000 chosen men of his own tribe and the aid of the Sil-Murray (O'Conor's) of Connaught, attacked and defeated a force of 5,000 Danes with their Leinster allies, near Dublin, at a place supposed to be identical with Killaderry. Earl Olaf lost his son, and Erin her *Roydamna*, or heir-apparent on this field, which was much celebrated by the Bards of Ulster and of Connaught. Amongst those who fell was Flan, son of Conaing, chief of the district which included the plundered cemeteries, fighting on the side of the plunderers. The mother of Flan was one of those who composed quatrians on the event of the battle, and her lines are a natural and affecting alternation from joy to grief—joy for the triumph of her brother and her country, and grief for the loss of her self-willed, warlike son. Olaf, the Danish leader, avenged in the next campaign the loss of his son, by a successful descent on Armagh, once again rising from its ruins. He put to the sword 1,000 persons, and left the primatial city lifeless, charred, and desolate. In the next ensuing year the monarch chastised the Leinster allies of the Danes, traversing their territory with fire and sword from Dublin to the border town of Gowran. This seems to have been the last of his notable exploits in arms. He died on the 20th of November, 876, and is lamented by the Bards as "a generous, wise, staid man." These praises belong—if at all deserved—to his old age.

Flan, son of Malachy I. (and surnamed like his father "of the Shannon"), succeeded in the year 877, of the Annals of the Four Masters, or more accurately the year 879 of our common era. He enjoyed the very unusual reign of thirty-eight years. Some of the domestic events of his time are of so unprecedented a character, and the period embraced is so considerable, that we must devote to it a separate chapter.

CHAPTER III.

REIGN OF FLAN "OF THE SHANNON" (A. D. 879 TO 916).

MIDWAY in the reign we are called upon to contemplate, falls the centenary of the first invasion of Ireland by the Northmen. Let us admit that the scenes of that century are stirring and stimulating; two gallant races of men, in all points strongly contrasted, contend for the most part in the open field, for the possession of a beautiful and fertile island. Let us admit that the Milesian-Irish, themselves invaders and conquerors of an older date, may have had no right to declare the era of colonization closed for their country, while its best harbors were without ships, and leagues of its best land were without inhabitants; yet what gives to the contest its lofty and fearful interest, is, that the foreigners who come so far and fight so bravely for the prize, are a Pagan people, drunk with the evil spirit of one of the most anti-Christian forms of human error. And what is still worse, and still more to be lamented, it is becoming, after the experience of a century, plainer and plainer, that the Christian natives, while defending with unfaltering courage their beloved country, are yet descending more and more to the moral level of their assailants, without the apology of their Paganism. Degenerate civilization may be a worse element for truth to work in than original barbarism; and therefore, as we enter on the second century of this struggle, we begin to fear for the Christian Irish, *not* from the arms or the valor, but from the contact and example, of the unbelievers. This it is necessary to premise, before presenting to the reader a succession of Bishops who lead armies to battle, of Abbots whose voice is still for war, of treacherous tactics and savage punishments; of the almost total disruption of the last links of that federal bond, which, "though light as air were strong as iron," before the charm of inviolability had been taken away from the ancient constitution.

We begin to discern in this reign that royal marriages have much to do with war and politics. Hugh, the late king, left a widow, named Maelmara ("follower of Mary"), daughter to Kenneth McAlpine, King of the Caledonian Scots: this lady, Flan married. The mother of Flan was the daughter of Dungal, Prince of Ossory, so that to the cotemporary lords of that border-land the monarch stood in the relation of cousin. A compact seems to have been entered into in the past reign, that the *Roydamna*, or successor, should be chosen alternately from the Northern and Southern Hy-Nial; and subsequently, when Nial, son of his predecessor, assumed that onerous rank, Flan gave him his daughter Gormley, celebrated for her beauty, her talents, and her heartlessness, in marriage. From these several family ties, uniting him so closely with Ossory, with the Scots, and with his successor, much of the wars and politics of Flan Siona's reign take their cast and complexion. A still more fruitful source of new complications was the coequal power, acquired through a long series of aggressions, by the kings of Cashel. Their rivalry with the monarchy, from the beginning of the eighth till the end of the tenth century, was a constant cause of intrigues, coalitions, and wars, reminding us of the constant rivalry of Athens with Sparta, of Genoa with Venice. This kingship of Cashel, according to the Munster law of succession, "the will of Olild" ought to have alternated regularly between the descendants of his sons, Eugene More and Cormac Cas—the Eugenians and Dalcassians. But the families of the former kindred were for many centuries the more powerful of the two, and frequently set at nought the testamentary law of their common ancestor, leaving the tribe of Cas but the border-land of Thomond, from which they had sometimes to pay tribute to Cruachan, and at others to Cashel. In the ninth century the competition among the Eugenian houses—of which too many were of too nearly equal strength—seems to have suggested a new expedient, with the view of permanently setting aside the will of Olild. This was, to confer the kinship when vacant, on whoever happened to be Bishop of Emly or of Cashel, or on some other leading ecclesiastical dignitary, always provided that he was of Eugenian descent; a qualification easily to be met with, since the great sees and abbacies were now filled, for the most part, by the sons of the neighboring chiefs. In this way we find Cenfalad, Felim, and Olcobar, in this century, styled Prince-Bishops or Prince-Abbots. The principal domestic difficulty of Flan Siona's reign followed from the elevation of Cormac, son of Cuillenan, from the see of Emly to the throne of Cashel.

Cormac, a scholar, and, as became his calling, a man of peace, was thus, by virtue of his accession, the representative of the old quarrel between his predecessors and the dominant race of kings. All Munster asserted that it was never the intention of their common ancestors to subject the southern half of Erin to the sway of the north; that Eber and Owen More had resisted such pretensions when advanced by Eremhon and Conn of the Hundred Battles; that the *esker* from Dublin to Galway was the true division, and that, even admitting the title of the Hy-Nial king as Ard-Righ, all the tribes south of the *esker*, whether in Leinster or Connaught, still owed tribute by ancient right to Cashel. Their antiquaries had their own version of "the Book of Rights," which countenanced these claims to coequal dominion, and their Bards drew inspiration from the same high pretensions. Party spirit ran so high that tales and prophecies were invented to show

how St. Patrick had laid his curse on Tara, and promised dominion to Cashel and to Dublin in its stead. All Leinster, except the lordship of Ossory—identical with the present diocese of the same name—was held by the *Brehons* of Cashel to be tributary to their king; and this *Borooa* or tribute, abandoned by the monarchs at the intercession of Saint Moling, was claimed for the Munster rulers as an inseparable adjunct of their southern kingdom.

The first act of Flan Siona, on his accession, was to dash into Munster, demanding hostages at the point of the sword, and sweeping over both Thomond and Desmond with irresistible force, from Clare to Cork. With equal promptitude he marched through every territory of Ulster, securing, by the pledges of their heirs and *Tanists*, the chiefs of the elder tribes of the Hy-Nial. So effectually did he consider his power established over the provinces, that he is said to have boasted to one of his hostages, that he would, with no other attendants than his own servants, play a game of chess on Thurles Green, without fear of interruption. Carrying out this foolish wager, he accordingly went to his game at Thurles, and was very properly taken prisoner for his temerity, and made to pay a smart ransom to his captors. So runs the tale, which, whether true or fictitious, is not without its moral. Flan experienced greater difficulty with the tribes of Connaught, nor was it till the thirteenth year of his reign (892) that Cathal, their Prince, "came into his house," in Meath, "under the protection of the clergy" of Clonmacnoise, and made peace with him. A brief interval of repose seems to have been vouchsafed to this Prince, in the last years of the century; but a storm was gathering over Cashel, and the high pretensions of the Eugenian line were again to be put to the hazard of battle.

Cormac, the Prince-Bishop, began his rule over Munster in the year 900 of our common era, and passed some years in peace, after his accession. If we believe his panegyrists, the land over which he bore sway, "was filled with divine grace and worldly prosperity," and with order so unbroken, "that the cattle needed no cowherd, and the flocks no shepherd, so long as he was king." Himself an antiquary and a lover of learning, it seems but natural, that "many books were written, and many schools opened," by his liberality. During this enviable interval, councillors of less pacific mood than their studious master, were not wanting to stimulate his sense of kingly duty, by urging him to assert the claim of Munster, to the tribute of the southern half of Erin. As an antiquary himself, Cormac must have been bred up in undoubting belief in the justice of that claim, and must have given judgment in favor of its antiquity and validity, before his accession. These *dicta* of his own were now quoted with emphasis, and he was besought to enforce by all the means within his reach the learned judgments he himself had delivered. The most active advocate of a recourse to arms was Flaherty, Abbot of Scattery, in the Shannon, himself an Eugenian, and the kinsman of Cormac. After many objections, the peaceful Prince-Bishop allowed himself to be persuaded, and in the year 907, he took up his line of march, "in the fortnight of the harvest," from Cashel toward Gowran, at the head of all the armament of Munster. Lorcan, son of Lactna, and grandfather of Brian, commanded the Dalcassians, under Cormac; and Oliol, lord of Desies, and the warlike Abbot of Scattery, led on the other divisions. The monarch marched southward to meet his assailants, with his own proper troops, and the contingents of Connaught under Cathal, Prince of that Province, and those of Leinster under the lead of Kerball, their king. Both armies met at Ballaghmoon, in the southern corner of Kildare, not far from the present town of Carlow, and both fought with most heroic bravery. The Munster forces were utterly defeated; the Lords of Desies, of Fermoy, of Kinalmeaky, and of Kerry, the Abbots of Cork and Kennity, and Cormac himself, with 6,000 men, fell on the ensanguined field. The losses of the victors are not specified, but the 6,000, we may hope, included the total of the slain on both sides. Flan at once improved the opportunity of victory by advancing into Ossory, and establishing his cousin Dermid, son of Kerball, over that territory. This Dermid, who appears to have been banished by Munster intrigues, had long resided with his royal cousin, previous to the battle, from which he was probably the only one that derived any solid advantage. As to the Abbot Flaherty, the instigator of this ill-fated expedition, he escaped from the conquerors, and safe in his island sanctuary gave himself up for a while to penitential rigors. The worldly spirit, however, was not dead in his breast, and after the decease of Cormac's next successor, he emerged from his cell, and was elevated to the kingship of Cashel.

In the earlier and middle years of this long reign, the invasions from the Baltic had diminished both in force and in frequency. This is to be accounted for from the fact, that during its entire length, it was cotemporaneous with the reign of Harold, "the Fair-haired" King of Norway, the scourge of the sea-kings. This more fortunate Charles XII., born in 853, died at the age of 81, after sixty years of almost unbroken successes, over all his Danish, Swedish, and insular enemies. It is easy to comprehend by reference to his exploits upon the Baltic, the absence of the usual northern force from the Irish waters, during his lifetime, and that of his cotemporary, Flan of the Shannon. Yet the race of the sea-kings was not extinguished by the fair-haired Harold's victories over them, at home. Several of them permanently abandoned their native coasts never to return, and recruited their colonies, already so numerous, in the Orkneys, Scotland, England, Ireland, and the Isle of Man. In 885, Flan was repulsed in an attack on Dublin, in which repulse the Abbots of Kildare and Kildalkey were slain; in the year 890 Aileach was surprised and plundered by Danes, for the first time, and Armagh shared its fate; in 887, 888, and 891, three minor victories were gained over separate hordes, in Mayo, at Waterford, and in Ulidia (Down). In 897, Dublin was taken for the first time in sixty years, its chiefs put to death, while its garrison fled in their ships beyond sea. But in the first quarter of the tenth century, better fortune begins to attend the Danish cause. A new generation enters on the scene, who dread no more the long arm of the age-stricken Harold, nor respect the treaties which bound their predecessors in Britain to the great Alfred. In 912, Waterford received from sea a strong reinforcement, and about the same date, or still earlier, Dublin, from which they had been expelled in 897, was again in their possession. In 913, and for several subsequent years, the southern garrisons continued their ravages in Munster, where the warlike Abbot of Scattery found a more suitable object for the employment of his valor than that which brought him, with the studious Cormac, to the fatal field of Ballaghmoon.

The closing days of Flan of the Shannon were embittered and darkened by the unnatural rebellion of his sons, Connor and Donogh, and his successor, Nial, surnamed *Black-Knee (Glun-dubh)*, the husband of his daughter, Gormley. These children were by his second marriage with Gormley, daughter of that son of Conaing, whose name has already appeared in connection with the plundered sepulchres upon the Boyne. At the age of three score and upwards Flan is frequently obliged to protect by recourse to arms his mensal lands in Meath—their favorite point of attack—or to defend some faithful adherent whom these unnatural Princes sought to oppress. The daughter of Flan, thus wedded to a husband in arms against her father, seems to have been as little dutiful as his sons. We have elegiac stanzas by her on the death of two of her husbands and of one of her sons, but none on the death of her father: although this form of tribute to the departed, by those skilled in such compositions, seems to have been as usual as the ordinary prayers for the dead.

At length, in the 37th year of his reign, and the 68th of his age, King Flan was at the end of his sorrows. As became the prevailing character of his life, he died peacefully, in a religious house, at Kyneigh, in Kildare, on the 8th of June, in the year 916, of the common era. The Bards praise his "fine shape" and "august mien," as well as his "pleasant and hospitable" private habits. Like all the kings of his race he seems to have been brave enough: but he was no lover of war for war's-sake, and the only great engagement in his long reign was brought on by enemies who left him no option but to fight. His munificence rebuilt the Cathedral of Clonmacnoise, with the co-operation of Colman, the Abbot, the year after the battle of Ballaghmoon (908); for which age, it was the largest and finest stone Church in Ireland. His charity and chivalry both revolted at the cruel excesses of war, and when the head of Cormac of Cashel was presented to him after his victory, he rebuked those who rejoiced over his rival's fall, kissed reverently the lips of the dead, and ordered the relics to be delivered, as Cormac had himself willed it, to the Church of Castledermot, for Christian burial. These traits of character, not less than his family afflictions, and the generally peaceful tenor of his long life, have endeared to many the memory of Flan of the Shannon.

CHAPTER IV.

KINGS OF THE TENTH CENTURY; NIAL IV.; DONOGH II.; CONGAL III.; DONALD IV.

Nial IV. (surnamed *Black-Knee*) succeeded his father-in-law, Flan of the Shannon, A. D. 916, and in the third year of his reign fell in an assault on Dublin; Donogh II., son of Flan Siona, reigned for twenty-five years; Congal III. succeeded, and was slain in an ambush by the Dublin Danes, in the twelfth year of his reign (A. D. 956); Donald IV., in the twenty-fourth year of his reign, died at Armagh, A. D. 979: which four reigns bring us to the period of the accession of Malachy II. as *Ard-Righ*, and the entrance of Brian Boru, on the national stage, as King of Cashel, and competitor for the monarchy.

The reign of Nial *Black-Knee* was too brief to be memorable for any other event than his heroic death in battle. The Danes having recovered Dublin, and strengthened its defences, Nial, it is stated, was incited by his confessor, the Abbot of Bangor, to attempt their re-expulsion. Accordingly, in October, 919, he marched towards Dublin, with a numerous host; Conor, son of the late king and *Roydamna;* the lords of Ulidia (Down), Oriel (Louth), Breagh (East-Meath), and other chiefs with their clans accompanying him. Sitrick and Ivar, sons of the first Danish leaders in Ireland, marched out to meet them, and near Rathfarnham, on the Dodder, a battle was fought, in which the Irish were utterly defeated and their monarch slain. This Nial left a son named Murkertach, who, according to the compact entered into between the Northern and Southern Hy-Nial, became the *Roydamna* of the next reign, and the most successful leader against the Danes, since the time of Malachy I. He was the step-son of the poetic Lady Gormley, whose lot it was to have been married in succession to the King of Munster, the King of Leinster, and the Monarch. Her first husband was Cormac, son of Cuilenan, before he entered holy orders; her second, Kerball of Leinster, and her third, Nial *Black-Knee*. She was an accomplished poetess, besides being the daughter, wife, and mother of kings, yet after the death of Nial she " begged from door to door," and no one had pity on her fallen state. By what vices she had thus estranged from her every kinsman, and every dependant, we are left to imagine; but that such was her misfortune, at the time her brother was monarch, and her step-son successor, we learn from the annals, which record her penance and death, under the date of 946.

The defeat sustained near Rathfarnham, by the late king, was amply avenged in the first year of the new *Ard-Righ* (A. D. 920), when the Dublin Danes having marched out, taken and burned Kells, in Meath, were on their return through the plain of Breagh, attacked and routed with unprecedented slaughter. " There fell of the nobles of the Norsemen here," say the old Annalists, " as many as fell of the nobles and plebeians of the Irish, at Ath-Cliath" (Dublin). The Northern Hydra, however, was not left headless. Godfrey, grandson of Ivar, and Tomar, son of Algi, took command at Dublin, and Limerick, infusing new life into the remnant of their race. The youthful son of the late king, soon after at the head of a strong force (A. D. 921), compelled Godfrey to retreat from Ulster, to his ships, and to return by sea to Dublin. This was Murkertach, fondly called by the elegiac Bards, " the Hector of the West," and for his heroic achievements, not undeserving to be named after the gallant defender of Troy. Murkertach first appears in our annals at the year 921, and disappears in the thick of the battle in 938. His whole career covers seventeen years; his position throughout was subordinate and expectant—for King Donogh outlived his heir: but there are few names in any age of the history of his country more worthy of historical honor than his. While Donogh was king in name, Murkertach was king in fact; on him devolved the burden of every negotiation, and the brunt of every battle. Unlike his ancestor, Hugh of Aileach, in his opposition to Donogh's ancestor, Malachy I., he never attempts to counteract the king, or to harass him in his patrimony. He rather does what is right and needful himself leaving Donogh to claim the credit, if he be so minded. True, a coolness and a quarrel arises between them, and even "a challenge of battle" is exchanged, but better councils prevail, peace is restored, and the king and the *Roydamna* march as one man against the common enemy. It has been said of another but not wholly dissimilar form of government, that Crown-Princes are always in opposition; if this saying holds good of father and son, as occupant and expectant of a throne, how much more likely is it to be true of a successor and a principal, chosen from different dynasties, with a view to combine, or at worst to balance, conflicting hereditary interests? In the conduct of Murkertach, we admire, in turn, his many shining personal qualities, which even tasteless panegyric cannot hide, and the prudence, self-denial, patience, and perseverance with which he awaits his day of power. Unhappily, for one every way so worthy of it, that day never arrived!

At no former period,—not even at the height of the tyranny of Turgesius,—was a capable Prince more needed in Erin. The new generation of Northmen were again upon all the estuaries and inland waters of the Island. In the years 923-4 and 5, their light armed vessels swarmed on Lough Erne, Lough Ree, and other lakes, spreading flame and terror on every side. Clonmacnoise and Kildare, slowly recovering from former pillage, were again left empty and in ruins. Murkertach, the base of whose early operations was his own patrimony in Ulster, attacked near Newry a Northern division under the command of the son of Godfrey (A. D. 926), and left 800 dead on the field. The escape of the remnant was only secured by Godfrey marching rapidly to their relief and covering the retreat. His son lay with the dead. In the years 933, at Slieve Behma, in his own Province, Murkertach won a third victory; and in 936, taking politic advantage of the result of the great English battle of Brunanburgh, which had so seriously diminished the Danish strength, the *Roydamna* in company with the King assaulted Dublin, expelled its garrison, levelled its fortress, and left the dwellings of the Northmen in ashes. From Dublin they proceeded southward, through

Leinster and Munster, and after taking hostages of every tribe, Donogh returned to his Methian home and Murkertach to Aileach. While resting in his own fort (A. D. 939), he was surprised by a party of Danes, and carried off to their ships, but says the old translator of the Annals of Clonmacnoise, "he made a good escape from them, as it was God's will." The following season he redoubled his efforts against the enemy. Attacking them on their own element he ravaged their settlements on the Scottish coasts and among the isles of Insi-Gall (the Hebrides), returned laden with spoils, and hailed with acclamations as the liberator of his people.

Of the same age with Murkertach, the reigning Prince at Cashel, was Kellachan, one of the heroes of the latter Bards and Story-tellers of the South. The romantic tales of his capture by the Danes, and captivity in their fleet at Dundalk, of the love which Sitricks' wife bore him, and of his gallant rescue by the Dalcassians and Eugenians, have no historical sanction. He was often both at war and at peace with the foreigners of Cork and Limerick, and did not hesitate more than once to employ their arms for the maintenance of his own supremacy; but his only authentic captivity was, as a hostage, in the hands of Murkertach. While the latter was absent, on his expedition to Insi-Gall, Kellachan fell upon the Deisi and Ossorians, and inflicted severe chastisement upon them—alleging, as his provocation, that they had given hostages to Murkertach, and acknowledged him as *Roydamna* of all Erin, in contempt of the coequal rights of Cashel. When Murkertach returned from his Scotch expedition, and heard what had occurred, and on what pretext Kellachan had acted, he assembled at Aileach all the branches of the Northern Hy-Nial, for whom this was cause, indeed. Out of these he selected 1,000 chosen men, whom he provided, among other equipments, with those "leathern coats," which lent a *soubriquet* to his name; and with these "ten hundred heroes," he set out—strong in his popularity and his alliances—to make a circuit of the entire island (A. D. 940). He departed from Aileach, says his Bard, whose Itinerary we have, "keeping his left hand to the sea;" Dublin, once more rebuilt, acknowledged his title, and Sitrick, one of its lords, went with him as hostage for Earl Blacair and his countrymen; Leinster surrendered him Lorcan, its King; Kellachan, of Cashel, overawed by his superior fortune, advised his own people not to resist by force, and consented to become himself the hostage for all Munster. In Connaught, Conor, (from whom the O'Conors take their family name,) son of the Prince, came voluntarily to his camp, and was received with open arms. Kellachan alone was submitted to the indignity of wearing a fetter. With these distinguished hostages, Murkertach and his leather cloaked " ten hundred" returned to Aileach, where, for five months, they spent a season of unbounded rejoicing. In the following year, the *Roydamna* transferred the hostages to King Donogh, as his *suzerain*, thus setting the highest example of obedience from the highest place. He might now look abroad over all the tribes of Erin, and feel himself without a rival among his countrymen. He stood at the very summit of his good fortune, when the Danes of Dublin, reinforced from abroad, after his " Circuit," renewed their old plundering practises. They marched north, at the close of winter, under Earl Blacair, their destination evidently being Armagh. Murkertach, with some troops hastily collected, disputed their passage at the ford of Ardee. An engagement ensued on Saturday, the 4th of March, 913, in which the noble *Roydamna* fell. King Donogh, to whose reign his vigorous spirit has given its main historical importance, survived him but a twelvemonth; the Monarch died in the bed of repose; his destined successor in the thick of the battle.

The death of the brave and beloved Murkertach filled all Erin with grief and rage, and as King Donogh was too old to avenge his destined successor, that duty devolved on Congal, the new *Roydamna*. In the year after the fatal action at Ardee, Congal, with Brann, King of Leinster, and Kellach, heir of Leinster, assaulted and took Dublin, and wreaked a terrible revenge for the nation's loss. The " women, children, and plebeians," were carried off captive; the greater part of the garrison were put to the sword; but a portion escaped in their vessels to their fortress on Dalkey, an island in the bay of Dublin. This was the third time within a century that Dublin had been rid of its foreign yoke, and yet as the Gaelic-Irish would not themselves dwell in fortified towns, the site remained open and unoccupied, to be rebuilt as often as it might be retaken. The gallant Congal, the same year, succeeded on the death of Donogh to the sovereignty, and, so soon as he had secured his seat, and surrounded it with sufficient hostages, he showed that he could not only avenge the death, but imitate the glorious life of him whose place he held. Two considerable victories in his third and fourth years increased his fame, and rejoiced the hearts of his countrymen: the first was won at Slane, aided by the Lord of Breffni (O'Ruarc), and by Olaf the Crooked, a northern chief. The second was fought at Dublin (947), in which Blacair, the victor at Ardee, and 1,600 of his men were slain. Thus was the death of Murkertach finally avenged.

It is very remarkable that the first conversions to Christianity among the Danes of Dublin should have taken place immediately after these successive defeats—in 948. Nor, although quite willing to impute the best and most disinterested motives to these first neophytes, can we shut our eyes to the fact that no change of life, such as we might reasonably look for, accompanied their change of religion. Godfrid, son of Sitrick, and successor of Blacair, who professed himself a Christian in 948, plundered and destroyed the churches of East-Meath in 949, burnt 150 persons in the oratory of Drumree, and carried off as captives 3,000 persons. If the tree is to be judged by its fruits, this first year's growth of the new faith is rather alarming. It compels us to disbelieve the sincerity of Godfrid, at least, and the fighting men who wrought these outrages and sacrileges. It forces us to rank them with the incorrigible heathens who boasted that they had twenty times received the Sacrament of Baptism, and valued it for the twenty white robes which had been presented to them on those occasions. Still, we must endeavor hereafter, when we can, to distinguish Christian from Pagan Danes, and those of Irish birth, sons of the first comers, from the foreign-born kinsmen of their ancestors. Between these two classes there grew a gulf of feeling and experience, which a common language and common dangers only partially bridged over. Not seldom the interests and inclinations of the Irish-born Dane, especially if a true Christian, were at open variance with the interests and designs of the new arrivals from Denmark, and it is generally, if not invariably, with the former, that the Leinster and other Irish Princes enter into coalitions for common political purposes. The remainder of the reign of Congal is one vigorous battle. The Lord of Breffni, who had fought beside him on the hill of Slane, advanced his claim to be recognized *Roydamna*, and this being denied, broke out into rebellion and harassed his patrimony. Donald, son of Murkertach, and grandson of Nial, (the first who took the name of *Uai*-Nial, or O'Neill,) disputed these pretensions of the Lord of Breffni; carried his boats overland from Aileach to Lough Erne in Fermanagh, and Lough Oughter in Cavan; attacked the lake-islands, where the treasure and hostages of Breffni were kept, and carried them off to his own fortress. The warlike and indefatigable king was in the field summer and winter enforcing his authority on Munster and Connaught, and battling with the foreign garrisons between times. No former Ard-Righ had a severer struggle with the insubordinate elements which beset him from first to last. His end was sudden, but not inglorious. In returning from the chariot-races at the Curragh of Kildare, he was surprised and slain in an ambuscade laid for him by Godfrid at a place on the banks of the Liffey called Tyraris or Tecraris house. By his side, fighting bravely, fell the lords of Teffia and Ferrard, two of his nephews, and others of his personal attendants and companions. The Dublin Danes had in their turn a day of rejoicing and of revenge for the defeats they had suffered at Congal's hands.

This reign is not only notable for the imputed first conversion of the Danes to Christianity, but also for the general adoption of family names. Hitherto, we have been enabled to distinguish clansmen only by tribe-names formed by prefixing *Hy*, *Kinnel*, *Sil*, *Muintir*, *Dal*, or some synonymous term, meaning race, kindred, sept, district, or part, to the proper name of a remote common ancestor, as Hy-Nial, Kinnel-Connel, Sil-Murray, Muintir-Eolais, Dal-g Cais, and Dal-Riada. But the great tribes now begin to break into families, and we are hereafter to know particular houses, by distinct hereditary surnames, as O'Neill, O'Conor, MacMurrough, and McCarthy. Yet, the whole body of relatives are often spoken of by the old tribal title, which, unless exceptions are named, is supposed to embrace all the descendants of the old connexion to whom it was once common. At first this alternate use of tribe and family names may confuse the reader—for it *is* rather puzzling to find a MacLoughlin with the same paternal ancestor as an O'Neill, and a McMahon of Thomond as an O'Brien, but the difficulty disappears with use and familiarity, and though the number and variety of newly-coined names cannot be at once committed to memory, the story itself gains in distinctness by the change.

In the year 955, Donald O'Neill, son of the brave and beloved Murkertach, was recognized as Ard-Righ, by the required number of Provinces, without recourse to coercion. But it was not to be expected that any Ard-Righ should, at this period of his country's fortunes, reign long in peace. War was then the business of the King; the first art he had to learn, and the first to practise. Warfare in Ireland had not been a stationary science since the arrival of the Norwegians and their successors, the Danes. Something they may have acquired from the natives, and in turn the natives were not slow to copy whatever seemed most effective in their tactics. Donald IV. was the first to imitate their habit of employing armed boats on the inland lakes. He even improved on their example, by carrying these boats with him overland, and launching them wherever he needed their co-operation; as we have already seen him do in his expedition against Breffni, while *Roydamna*, and as we find him doing again, in the seventh year of his reign, when he carried his boats overland from Armagh to Westmeath in order to employ them on Loch Ennell, near Mullingar. He was at this time engaged in making his first royal visitation of the Provinces, upon which he spent two months in Leinster, with all his forces, coerced the Munster chiefs by fire and sword into obedience, and severely punished the insubordination of Fergal O'Ruarc, King of Connaught. His fleet upon Loch Ennell, and his severities generally while in their patrimony, so exasperated the powerful families of the Southern Hy-Nial (the elder of which was now known as O'Melaghlin), that on the first opportunity they leagued with the Dublin Danes, under their leader, Olaf "the Crooked" (A. D. 966), and drove King Donald out of Leinster and Meath, pursuing him across Slieve-Fuaid, almost to the walls of Aileach. But the brave tribes of Tyrconnell and Tyrowen rallied to his support, and he pressed south upon the insurgents of Meath and Dublin; West-Meath he rapidly overran, and "planted a garrison in every cantred from the Shannon to Kells." In the campaigns which now succeeded each other, without truce or pause, for nearly a dozen years, the Leinster people generally sympathized with, and assisted those of West-Meath, and Olaf, of Dublin, who recruited his ranks by the junction of the Lagmans, a warlike tribe, from Insi-Gall (the Hebrides). Ossory, on the other hand, acted with the monarch, and the son of its Tanist (A. D. 974) was slain before Dublin, by Olaf and his Leinster allies, with 2,600 men, of Ossory and Ulster. The campaign of 978 was still more eventful: the Leinstermen quarrelled with their Danish allies, who had taken their king captive, and in an engagement at Belan, near Athy, defeated their forces, with the loss of the heir of Leinster, the lords of Kinsellagh, Lea and Morett, and other chiefs. King Donald had no better fortune at Killmoon, in Meath, the same season, where he was utterly routed by the same force with the loss of Ardgal, heir of Ulidia, and Kenneth, Lord of Tyrconnell. But for the victories gained about the same period in Munster, by Mahon and Brian, the sons of Kennedy, over the Danes of Limerick, of which we shall speak more fully hereafter, the balance of victory would have strongly inclined towards the Northmen at this stage of the contest.

A leader, second in fame and in services only to Brian, was now putting forth his energies against the common enemy, in Meath. This was Melaghlin, better known afterwards as Malachy II., son of Donald, son of King Donogh, and, therefore, great-grandson to his namesake, Malachy I. He had lately attained to the command of his tribe—and he resolved to earn the honors which were in store for him, as successor to the sovereignty. In the year 979, the Danes of Dublin and the Isles marched in unusual strength into Meath, under the command of Rannall, son of Olaf the Crooked, and Connail, "the Orator of Ath-Cliath," (Dublin.) Malachy, with his allies, gave them battle near Tara, and achieved a complete victory. Earl Rannall and the Orator were left dead on the field, with, it is reported, 5,000 of the foreigners. On the Irish side fell the heir of Leinster, the lord of Morgallion and his son; the lords of Fertullagh and Cremorne, and a host of their followers. The engagement, in true Homeric spirit, had been suspended on three successive nights, and renewed three successive days. It was a genuine pitched battle—a trial of main strength, each party being equally confident of victory. The results were most important, and most gratifying to the national pride. Malachy, accompanied by his friend, the lord of Ulidia (Down), moved rapidly on Dublin, which, in its panic, yielded to all his demands. The King of Leinster and 2,000 other prisoners were given up to him without ransom. The Danish Earls solemnly renounced all claims to tribute or fine from any of the dwellers without their own walls. Malachy remained in the city three days, dismantled its fortresses, and carried off its hostages and treasure. The unfortunate Olaf the Crooked fled beyond seas, and died at Iona, in exile, and a Christian. In the same year, and in the midst of universal rejoicing, Donald IV. died peacefully and piously at Armagh, in the 24th year of his reign. He was succeeded by Malachy, who was his sister's son, and in whom all the promise of the lamented Murkertach seemed to revive.

The story of Malachy II. is so interwoven with the still more illustrious career of Brian *Borooa*, that it will not lose in interest by being presented in detail. But before entering on the rivalry of these great men, we must again remark on the altered position which the Northmen of this age hold to the Irish from that which existed formerly. A century and a half had now elapsed since their first settlement in the seaports, especially of the eastern and southern Provinces. More than one generation of their descendants had been born on the banks of the Liffey, the Shannon and the Suir. Many of them had married into Irish families, had learned the language of the country, and embraced its religion. When Limerick was taken by Brian, Ivor its Danish lord fled for sanctuary to Scattery Island, and when Dublin was taken by Malachy II., Olaf the Crooked fled to Iona. Intermarriages with the highest Gaelic families became frequent, after their conversion to Christianity. The mother of Malachy, after his father's death, had married Olaf of Dublin, by whom she had a son, named *Gluniarran*, (*Iron-Knee*, from his armor,) who was thus half-brother to the King. It is natural enough to find him the ally of Malachy, a few years later, against Ivar of Waterford; and curious enough to find Ivar's son called Gilla-Patrick—servant of Patrick. Kellachan of Cashel had married a Danish, and Sitrick, "of the Silken beard," an Irish lady. That all the Northmen were not, even in Ireland, converted in one generation, is evident. Those of Insi-Gall were still, perhaps, Pagans; those of the Orkneys and of Denmark, who came to the battle of Clontarf in the beginning of the next century, chose to fight on Good Friday under the advice of their heathen Oracles. The first half of the XIth century, the age of Saint Olaf and of Canute, is the era of the establishment of Christianity among the Scandinavians, and hence the necessity for distinguishing between those who came to Ireland, direct from the Baltic, from those who, born in Ireland and bred up in the Christian faith, had as much to apprehend from such an invasion, as the Celts themselves.

CHAPTER V.

REIGN OF MALACHY II. AND RIVALRY OF BRIAN.

MELAGHLIN, or Malachy II., fifth in direct descent from Malachy I. (the founder of the Southern Hy-Nial dynasty), was in his thirtieth year, when (A.D. 980) he succeeded to the monarchy. He had just achieved the mighty victory of Tara when the death of his predecessor opened his way to the throne; and seldom did more brilliant dawn usher in a more eventful day than that which Fate held in store for this victor-king. None of his predecessors, not even his ancestor and namesake, had ever been able to use the high language of his "noble Proclamation," when he announced on his accession—"Let all the Irish who are suffering servitude in the land of the stranger return home to their respective houses and enjoy themselves in gladness and in peace." In obedience to this edict, and the power to enforce it established by the victory at Tara, 2,000 captives, including the King of Leinster and the Prince of Aileach, were returned to their homes.

The hardest task of every Ard-Righ of this and the previous century had been to circumscribe the ambition of the kings of Cashel within Provincial bounds. Whoever ascended the southern throne—whether the warlike Felim or the learned Cormac—we have seen the same policy adopted by them all. The descendants of Heber had tired of the long ascendancy of the race of Heremon, and the desertion of Tara, by making that ascendancy still more strikingly Provincial, had increased their antipathy. It was a struggle for supremacy between north and south; a contest of two geographical parties; an effort to efface the real or fancied dependency of one-half the island on the will of the other. The Southern Hy-Nial dynasty, springing up as a third power upon the Methian bank of the Shannon, and balancing itself between the contending parties, might perhaps have given a new centre to the whole system; Malachy II. was in the most favorable position possible to have done so had he not had to contend with a rival, his equal in battle and superior in council, in the person of Brian, the son of Kennedy, of Kincorra.

The rise to sovereign rank of the house of Kincorra (the O'Briens), is one of the most striking episodes of the tenth century. Descending, like most of the leading families of the South, from Olild, the Clan Dalgais had long been excluded from the throne of Cashel, by successive coalitions of their elder brethren, the Eugenians. Lactna and Lorcan, the grandfather and father of Kennedy, intrepid and able men, had strengthened their tribe by wise and vigorous measures, so that the former was able to claim the succession, apparently with success. Kennedy had himself been a claimant for the same honor, the alternate provision in the will of Olild, against Kellachan Cashel (A. D. 940-2), but at the convention held at Glanworth, on the river Funcheon, for the selection of king, the aged mother of Kellachan addressed his rival in a quatrain, beginning—

"Kennedy Cas revere the law!"

which induced him to abandon his pretensions. This Prince, usually spoken of by the Bards as "the chaste Kennedy," died in the year 950, leaving behind him four or five out of twelve sons, with whom he had been blessed. Most of the others had fallen in Danish battles—three in the same campaign (943), and probably in the same field. There appear in after scenes, Mahon, who became King of Cashel; Echtierna, who was chief of Thomond, under Mahon; Marcan, an ecclesiastic, and Brian, born in 941, the Benjamin of the household. Mahon proved himself, as Prince and Captain, every way worthy of his inheritance. He advanced from victory to victory over his enemies, foreign and domestic. In 960 he claimed the throne of Munster, which claim he enforced by royal visitation five years later. In the latter year he rescued Clonmacnoise from the Danes, and in 968 defeated the same enemy, with a loss of several thousand men, at Sulchoid. This great blow he followed up, by the sack of Limerick, from which " he bore off a large quantity of gold, and silver, and jewels." In these and all his expeditions, from a very early age, he was attended by Brian, to whom he acted not only as a brother and prince, but as a tutor in arms. Fortune had accompanied him in all his undertakings. He had expelled his most intractable rival — Molloy, son of Bran, Lord of Desmond; his rule was acknowledged by the Northmen of Dublin and Cork, who opened their fortresses to him, and served under his banner; he carried " all the hostages of Munster to his house," which had never before worn so triumphant an aspect. But family greatness begets family pride, and pride begets envy and hatred. The Eugenian families who now found themselves overshadowed by the brilliant career of the sons of Kennedy, conspired against the life of Mahon, who, from his too confiding nature, fell easily into their trap. Molloy, son of Bran, by the advice of Ivor, the Danish lord of Limerick, proposed to meet Mahon in friendly conference at the house of Donovan, an Eugenian chief, whose rath was at Bruree, on the river Maigue. The safety of each person was guaranteed by the Bishop of Cork, the mediator on the occasion. Mahon proceeded unsuspiciously to the conference, where he was suddenly seized by order of his treacherous host, and carried into the neighboring mountains of Knocinreorin. Here a small force, placed for the purpose by the conspirators, had orders promptly to dispatch their victim. But the foul deed was not done unwitnessed. Two priests of the Bishop of Cork followed the Prince, who, when arrested, snatched up "the Gospel of St. Barry," on which Molloy was to have sworn his fealty. As the swords of the assassins were aimed at his heart, he held up the Gospel for a protection, and his blood spouting out, stained the Sacred Scriptures. The priests, taking up the blood-stained volume, fled to their Bishop, spreading the horrid story as they went. The venerable successor of St. Barry "wept bitterly and uttered a prophecy concerning the future fate of the murderers;" a prophecy which was very speedily fulfilled.

This was in the year 976, three or four years before the battle of Tara and the accession of Malachy. When the news of his noble-hearted brother's murder was brought to Brian, at Kinkora, he was seized with the most violent grief. His favorite harp was taken down, and he sang the death-song of Mahon, recounting all the glorious actions of his life. His anger flashed out through his tears, as he wildly chanted

> "My heart shall burst within my breast,
> Unless I avenge this great king;
> They shall forfeit life for this foul deed
> Or I must perish by a violent death."

But the climax of his lament was, that Mahon "had not fallen in battle behind the shelter of his shield, rather than trust in the treacherous words of Donovan." Brian was now in his thirty-fifth year, was married and had several children. Morrogh, his eldest, was able to bear arms, and shared in his ardor and ambition. "His first effort," says an old Chronicle, "was directed against Donovan's allies, the Danes of Limerick, and he slew Ivor their king, and two of his sons." These conspirators, foreseeing their fate, had retired into the holy isle of Scattery, but Brian slew them between "the horns of the altar." For this violation of the sanctuary, considering his provocation, he was little blamed. He next turned his rage against Donovan, who had called to his aid the Danish townsmen of Desmond. "Brian," says the Annalist of Innisfallen, "gave them battle where Auliffe and his Danes, and Donovan and his Irish forces, were all cut off." After that battle, Brian sent a challenge to Molloy, of Desmond, according to the custom of that age, to meet him in arms near Macroom, where the usual coalition, Danes and Irish, were against him. He completely routed the enemy, and his son Morrogh, then but a lad, "killed the murderer of his uncle Mahon with his own hand." Molloy was buried on the north side of the mountain where Mahon was murdered and interred; on Mahon the southward sun shone full and fair; but on the grave of his assassin, the black shadow of the northern sky rested always. Such was the tradition which all Munster piously believed. After this victory over Molloy, son of Bran (A. D. 978), Brian was universally acknowledged King of Munster, and until Malachy had won the battle of Tara, was justly considered the first Irish captain of his age.

Malachy, in the first year of his reign, having received the hostages of the Danes of Dublin, having liberated the Irish prisoners and secured the unity of his own territory, had his attention drawn, naturally enough, towards Brian's movements. Whether Brian had refused him homage or that his revival of the old claim to the half-kingdom was his offence, or from whatever immediate cause, Malachy marched southwards, enforcing homage as he went. Entering Thomond he plundered the Dalcassians, and marching to the mound at Adair, where, under an old oak, the kings of Thomond had long been inaugurated, he caused it to be "dug from the earth with its roots," and cut into pieces. This act of Malachy's certainly bespeaks an embittered and aggressive spirit, and the provocation must, indeed, have been grievous to palliate so barbarous an action. But we are not informed what the provocation was. At the time Brian was in Ossory enforcing his tribute; the next year we find him seizing the person of Gilld-Patrick, Lord of Ossory, and soon after he burst into Meath, avenging with fire and sword the wanton destruction of his ancestral oak.

Thus were these two powerful Princes openly embroiled with each other. We have no desire to dwell on all the details of their struggle, which continued for full twenty years. About the year 987, Brian was practically king of half Ireland, and having the power, (though not the title,) he did not suffer any part of it to lie waste. His activity was incapable of exhaustion; in Ossory, in Leinster, in Connaught, his voice and his arm were felt everywhere. But a divided authority was of necessity so favorable to invasion, that the Danish power began to loom up to its old proportions. Sitrick, "with the silken beard," one of the ablest of Danish leaders, was then at Dublin, and his occasional incursions were so formidable, that they produced (what probably nothing else could have done) an alliance between Brian and Malachy, which lasted for three years, and was productive of the best consequences. Thus, in 997, they imposed their yoke on Dublin, taking "hostages and jewels," from the foreigners. Reinforcements arriving from the North, the indomitable Danes proceeded to plunder Leinster, but were routed by Brian and Malachy at Glen-Mama, in Wicklow, with the loss of 6,000 men and all their chief captains. Immediately after this victory the two kings, according to the Annals, "entered into Dublin, and the fort thereof, and there remained seven nights, and at their departure took all the gold, silver, hangings and other precious things that were there with them, burnt the town, broke down the fort, and banished Sitrick from thence" (A.D. 999).

The next three years of Brian's life are the most complex in his career. After resting a night in Meath, with Malachy, he proceeded with his forces towards Armagh, nominally on a pilgrimage, but really, as it would seem, to extend his party. He remained in the sacred city a week, and presented ten ounces of gold, at the Cathedral altar. The Archbishop Marian received him with the distinction due to so eminent a guest, and a record of his visit, in which he is styled "Imperator of the Irish," was entered in the Book of St. Patrick. He, however, got no hostages in the North, but on his march southward, he learned that the Danes had returned to Dublin, were rebuilding the City and Fort, and were ready to offer submission and hostages to him, while refusing both to Malachy. Here Brian's eagerness for supremacy misled him. He accecpted the hostages, joined the foreign forces to his own, and even gave his daughter in marriage, to Sitrick of "the silken beard." Immediately he broke with Malachy, and with his new allies and son-in-law, marched into Meath in hostile array. Malachy, however, stood to his defence; attacked and defeated Brian's advance guard of Danish horse, and the latter, unwilling apparently to push matters to extremities, retired as he came, without "battle, or hostage, or spoil of any kind."

But his design of securing the monarchy was not for an instant abandoned, and, by combined diplomacy and force, he effected his end. His whole career would have been incomplete without that last and highest conquest over every rival. Patiently but surely he had gathered influence and authority, by arms, by gifts, by connexions on all sides. He had propitiated the chief families of Connaught by his first marriage with More, daughter of O'Heyne, and his second marriage with Duvchalvay, daughter of O'Connor. He had obtained one of the daughters of Godwin, the powerful Earl of Kent, for his second son; had given a daughter to the Prince of Scots, and another to the Danish King of Dublin.

Malachy, in diplomatic skill, in foresight, and in tenacity of purpose, was greatly inferior to Brian, though in personal gallantry and other princely qualities, every way his equal. He was of a hospitable, out-spoken, enjoying disposition, as we gather from many characteristic anecdotes. He is spoken of as "being generally computed the best horseman in those parts of Europe;" and as one who, "delighted to ride a horse that was never broken, handled or ridden, until the age of seven years." From an ancient story, which represents him as giving his revenues for a year to one of the Court Poets and then fighting him with "a headless staff" to compel the Poet to return them, it would appear that his good humor and profusion were equal to his horsemanship. Finding Brian's influence still on the increase west of the Shannon, Malachy, in the year of our Lord 1000, threw two bridges across the Shannon, one at Athlone, the other at the present Lanesborough. This he did with the consent and assistance of O'Connor, but the issue was as usual—he made the bridges, and Brian profited by them. While Malachy was at Athlone superintending the work, Brian arrived with a great force recruited from all quarters (except Ulster), including Danish men-in-armor. At Athlone was held the conference so memorable in our annals, in which Brian gave his rival the alternative of a pitched battle, within a stated time, or abdication. According to the Southern Annalists first a month, and afterwards a year, were allowed the Monarch to make his choice. At the expiration of the time Brian marched into Meath, and encamped at Tara, where Malachy, having vainly endeavored to secure the alliance of the Northern Hy-Nial in the interval, came and submitted to Brian without safeguard or surety. The unmade monarch was accompanied by a guard "of twelve score horsemen," and on his arrival, proceeded straight to the tent of his successor. Here the rivals contended in courtesy, as they had often done in arms, and when they separated, Brian, as Lord Paramount, presented Malachy as many horses as he had horsemen in his train when he came to visit him. This event happened in the year 1001, when Brian was in his 60th and Malachy in his 53d year. There were present at the Assembly all the princes and chiefs of the Irish, except the Prince of Aileach, and the Lords of Oriel, Ulidia, Tirowen and Tirconnell, who were equally unwilling to assist Malachy or to acknowledge Brian. What is still more remarkable is, the presence in this national assembly of the Danish Lords of Dublin, Carmen (Wexford), Waterford and Cork, whom Brian, at this time, was trying hard to conciliate by gifts and alliances.

CHAPTER VI.

BRIAN, ARD-RIGH—BATTLE OF CLONTARF.

By the deposition of Malachy II., and the transfer of supreme power to the long-excluded line of Heber, Brian completed the revolution which Time had wrought in the ancient Celtic constitution. He threw open the sovereignty to every great family as a prize to be won by policy or force, and no longer an inheritance to be determined by usage and law. The consequences were what might have been expected. After his death the O'Conors of the west competed with both O'Neills and O'Briens for supremacy, and a chronic civil war prepared the path for Strongbow and the Normans. The term "Kings with Opposition" is applied to nearly all who reigned between Brian's time and Roderick O'Conor's, meaning, thereby, kings who were unable to secure general obedience to their administration of affairs.

During the remainder of his life, Brian wielded with accustomed vigor the supreme power. The Hy-Nials were, of course, his chief difficulty. In the year 1002, we find him at Ballysadare, in Sligo, challenging their obedience; in 1004, we find him at Armagh "offering twenty ounces of gold on Patrick's altar," staying a week there, and receiving hostages; in 1005, he marched through Connaught, crossed the river Erne at Ballyshannon, proceeded through Tyrconnell and Tyrowen, crossed the Bann into Antrim, and returned through Down and Dundalk, "about Lammas," to Tara. In this and the two succeeding years, by taking similar "circuits," he subdued Ulster, without any pitched battle, and caused his authority to be feared and obeyed nearly as much at the Giant's Causeway as at the bridge of Athlone. In his own house of Kinkora, Brien entertained at Christmas 3,000 guests, including the Danish lords of Dublin and Man, the fugitive Earl of Kent, the young King of Scots, certain Welsh Princes, and those of Munster, Ulster, Leinster and Connaught, beside his hostages. At the same time Malachy, with the shadow of independence, kept his unfrequented court in West-Meath, amusing himself with wine and chess and the taming of unmanageable horses, in which last pursuit, after his abdication, we hear of his breaking a limb. To support the hospitalities of Kinkora, the tributes of every province were rendered in kind at his gate, on the first day of November. Connaught sent 800 cows and 800 hogs; Ulster alone 500 cows, and as many hogs, and "sixty loads of iron;" Leinster 300 bullocks, 300 hogs, and 300 loads of iron; Ossory, Desmond, and the smaller territories, in proportion; the Danes of Dublin 150 pipes of wine, and the Danes of Limerick 365 of red wine. The Dalcassians, his own people, were exempt from all tribute and taxation—while the rest of Ireland was thus catering for Kinkora.

The lyric Poets, in their nature courtiers and given to enjoyment, flocked, of course, to this bountiful palace. The harp was seldom silent night or day, the strains of panegyric were as prodigal and incessant as the falling of the Shannon over Killaloe. Among these eulogiums none is better known than that beautiful allegory of the poet McLaig, who sung that "a young lady of great beauty, adorned with jewels and costly dress, might perform unmolested a journey on foot through the Island, carrying a straight wand, on the top of which might be a ring of great value." The name of Brian was thus celebrated as in itself a sufficient protection of life, chastity, and property, in every corner of the Island. Not only the Poets, but the more exact and simple Annalists applaud Brian's administration of the laws, and his personal virtues. He labored hard to restore the Christian civilization, so much defaced by two centuries of Pagan warfare. To facilitate the execution of the laws he enacted the general use of surnames, obliging the clans to take the name of a common ancestor, with the addition of "Mac," or "O"—words which signify "of," or "son of," a forefather. Thus, the Northern Hy-Niais, divided into O'Neils, O'Donnells, McLaughlins, &c.; the Sil-Murray took the name of O'Conor, and Brian's own posterity became known as O'Briens. To justice he added munificence, and of this the Churches and Schools of the entire Island were the recipients. Many a desolate shrine he adorned, many a bleak chancel he hung with lamps, many a long silent tower had its bells restored. Monasteries were rebuilt, and the praise of God was kept up perpetually by a devoted brotherhood. Roads and bridges were repaired, and several strong stone fortresses were erected, to command the passes of lakes and rivers. The vulnerable points along the Shannon, and the Suir, and the lakes, as far north as the Foyle, were secured by forts, of clay and stone. Thirteen "royal houses" in Munster alone are said to have been by him restored to their original uses. What increases our respect for the wisdom and energy thus displayed, is, the fact, that the author of so many improvements, enjoyed but five short years of peace, after his accession to the Monarchy. His administrative genius must have been great when, after a long life of warfare, he could apply himself to so many works of internal improvement and external defence.

In the five years of peace just spoken of (from 1005 to 1010), Brian lost by death his second wife, a son called Donald, and his brother Marcan, called in the annals "head of the clergy of Munster;" Hugh, the son of Mahon, also died about the same period. His favorite son and heir, Morrogh, was left, and Morrogh had, at this time, several children. Other sons and daughters were also left him, by each of his wives, so that there was every prospect that the posterity for whom he had so long sought the sovereignty of Ireland, would continue to possess it, for countless generations. But God disposes of what man only proposes!

The Northmen had never yet abandoned any soil on which they had once set foot, and the policy of conciliation which the veteran King adopted in his old age, was not likely to disarm men of their stamp. Every intelligence of the achievements of their race in other realms stimulated them to new exertions and shamed them out of peaceful submission. Rollo and his successors had, within Brian's lifetime, founded in France the great dukedom of Normandy; while Sweyn had swept irresistibly over England and Wales, and prepared the way for a Danish dynasty. Pride and shame alike appealed to their warlike compatriots not to allow the fertile Hibernia to slip from their grasp, and the great age of its long-dreaded king seemed to promise them an easier victory than heretofore was possible. In 1012 we find Brian at Lough Foyle repelling a new Danish invasion, and giving "freedom to Patrick's Churches;" the same year, an army under Morrogh and another under Malachy was similarly engaged in Leinster and Meath; the former carrying his arms to Kilmainham, on the south side of Dublin, the other to Howth, on the north; in this year also "the Gentiles," or Pagan Northmen, made a descent on Cork, and burned the city, but were driven off by the neighboring chiefs.

The great event, however, of the long war which had now been waged for full two hundred years between the men of Erin and the men of Scandinavia was approaching. What may fairly be called the last field day of Christianity and Paganism on Irish soil, was near at hand. A taunt thrown out over a game of chess, at Kinkora, is said to have hastened this memorable day. Maelmurra, Prince of Leinster, playing or advising on the game, made, or recommended, a false move, upon which Morrogh, son of Brian, observed, it was no wonder his friends, the Danes, (to whom he owed his elevation,) were beaten at Glen-Mama, if he gave them advice like that. Maelmurra, highly incensed by this allusion—all the more severe for its bitter truth—arose, ordered his horse, and rode away in haste. Brian, when he heard it, despatched a messenger after the indignant guest, begging him to return, but Maelmurra was not to be pacified, and refused. We next hear of him as concerting with certain Danish agents, always open to such negotiations, those measures which led to the great invasion of the year 1014, in which the whole Scanian race, from Anglesea and Man, north to Norway, bore an active share.

These agents passing over to England and Man, among the Scottish isles and even to the Baltic, followed up the design of an invasion on a gigantic scale. Suibne, Earl of Man, entered warmly into the conspiracy, and sent "the war arrow" through all those "out-islands" which obeyed him as Lord. A yet more formidable potentate, Sigurd, of the Orkneys, next joined the league. He was the fourteenth Earl of Orkney of Norse origin, and his power was, at this period, a balance to that of his nearest neighbor, the King of Scots. He had ruled since the year 996, not only over the Orkneys, Shetland, and Northern Hebrides, but the coasts of Caithness and Sutherland, and even Ross and Moray rendered him homage and tribute. Eight years before the battle of Clontarf, Malcolm II., of Scotland, had been feign to purchase his alliance, by giving him his daughter in marriage, and the Kings of Denmark and Norway treated with him on equal terms. The hundred inhabited isles which lie between Yell and Man,—isles which after their conversion contained "three hundred churches and chapels"—sent in their contingents, to swell the following of the renowned Earl Sigurd. As his fleet bore southward from Kirkwall it swept the subject coast of Scotland, and gathered from every lough its galleys and its fighting men. The rendezvous was the Isle of Man, where Suibne had placed his own forces, under the command of Brodar or Broderick, a famous leader against the Britons of Wales and Cornwall. In conjunction with Sigurd, the Manxmen sailed over to Ireland, where they were joined, in the Liffey, by Carl Canuteson, Prince of Denmark, at the head of 1,400 champions clad in armor. Sitrick of Dublin stood, or affected to stand, neutral in these preparations, but Maelmurra of Leinster had mustered all the forces he could command for such an expedition. He was himself the head of the powerful family of O'Byrne, and was followed in his alliances by others of the descendants of Cahir More. O'Nolan and O'More, with a truer sense of duty, fought on the patriotic side.

Brian had not been ignorant of the exertions which were made during the summer and winter of the year 1013, to combine an overwhelming force against him. In his exertions to meet force with force, it is gratifying to every believer in human excellence to find him actively supported by the Prince whom he had so recently deposed. Malachy, during the summer of 1013, had, indeed, lost two sons in skirmishes with Sitrick and Maelmurra, and had therefore his own personal wrongs to avenge; but he cordially co-operated with Brian before those occurrences, and now loyally seconded all his movements. The lords of the southern half-kingdom—the lords of Desies, Fermoy, Inchiquin, Corca-Baskin, Kinalmeaky, Kerry, and the lords of Hy-Many and Hy-Fiachra, in Connaught, hastened to his standard. O'More and O'Nolan of Leinster, and Donald, Steward of Marr, in Scotland, were the other chieftains who joined him before Clontarf, besides those of his own kindred. None of the Northern Hy-Nial took part in the battle—they had submitted to Brian, but they never cordially supported him.

Clontarf, the lawn or meadow of bulls, stretches along the crescent-shaped north strand of Dublin harbor, from the ancient salmon weir at Ballyboght bridge, towards the promontory of Howth. Both horns of the crescent were held by the enemy, and communicated with his ships: the inland point terminating in the roofs of Dublin, and the seaward marked by the lion-like head of Howth. The meadow land between sloped gently upward and inward from the beach, and for the myriad duels which formed the ancient battle, no field could present less positive vantage ground to combatants on either side. The invading force had possession of both wings, so that Brian's army which had first encamped at Kilmainham must have crossed the Liffey higher up, and marched round by the present Drumcondra in order to reach the appointed field. The day seems to have been decided on by formal challenge, for we are told Brian did not wish to fight in the last week of Lent, but a Pagan oracle having assured victory to Brodar, one of the northern leaders, if he engaged on a Friday, the invaders insisted on being led to battle on that day. And it so happened that, of all Fridays in the year, it fell on the Friday before Easter: that awful anniversary when the altars of the Church are veiled throughout Christendom, and the dark stone is rolled to the door of the mystic sepulchre.

The forces on both sides could not have fallen short of twenty thousand men. Under Carl Canuteson fought "the ten hundred in armor," as they are called in the Irish annals, or "the fourteen hundred," as they are called in northern chronicles; under Broder, the Manxmen and the Danes of Anglesea and Wales; under Sigurd, the men of Orkney and its dependencies; under Maelmurra, of Leinster, his own tribe, and their kinsmen of Offally and Cullen—the modern Kildare and Wicklow; under Brian's son, Morrogh, were the tribes of Munster; under the command of Malachy, those of Meath; under the lord of Hy-Many, the men of Connaught; and the Stewart of Marr had also his command. The engagement was to commence with the morning, so that, as soon as it was day, Brian, Crucifix in hand, harangued his army. "On this day Christ died for *you!*" was the spirit-stirring appeal of the venerable Christian King. At the entreaty of his friends, after this review, he retired to his tent, which stood at some distance, and was guarded by three of his aids. Here, he alternately prostrated himself before the Crucifix, or looked out from the tent door upon the dreadful scene that lay beyond. The sun rose to the zenith and took his way towards the west, but still the roar of the battle did not abate. Sometimes as their right hands swelled with the sword-hilts, well-known warriors might be seen falling back to bathe them, in a neighboring spring, and then rushing again into the melee. The line of the engagement extended from the salmon-weir towards Howth, not less than a couple of miles, so that it was impossible to take in at a glance the probabilities of victory. Once during the heat of the day one of his servants said to Brian, "a vast multitude are moving towards us." "What sort of people are they?" inquired Brian. "They are green-naked people," said the attendant. "Oh!" replied the king, "they are the Danes in armor!" The utmost fury was displayed on all sides. Sigurd, Earl of Orkney, fell by Thurlogh, grandson of Brian; and Anrud, one of the captains of the men in armor, by the hand of his father, Morrogh; but both father and son perished in the dreadful conflict: Maelmurra, of Leinster, with his lords, fell on one side, and Conaing, nephew of Brian, O'Kelly, O'Heyne, and the Stewart of Marr, on the other. Hardly a nobly born man escaped, or sought to escape. The ten hundred in armor, and three thousand others of the enemy, with about an equal number of the men of Ireland, lay dead upon the field. One division of the enemy were, towards sunset, retreating to their ships, when Brodar, the Viking, perceiving the tent of Brian, standing apart, without a guard, and the aged king on his knees before the Crucifix, rushed in, cut him down with a single blow, and then continued his flight. But he was overtaken by the guard, and despatched by the most cruel death they could devise. Thus, on the field of battle, in the act of prayer, on the day of our Lord's Crucifixion, fell the Christian King in the cause of native land and Holy Cross. Many elegies have been dedicated to his memory, and not the least noble of these strains belong to his enemies. In death as in life he was still Brian " of the tributes."

The deceased hero took his place at once in history, national and foreign. On hearing of his death, Maelmurra, Archbishop of Armagh, came with his clergy to Swords, in Meath, and conducted the body to Armagh, where, with his son and nephew and the Lord of Desies, he was solemnly interred "in a new tomb." The fame of the event went out through all nations. The chronicles of Wales, of Scotland, and of Man; the annals of Ademar and Marianus; the Sagas of Denmark and the Isles all record the event. In " the Orcades" of Thormodus Torfæus, a wail over the defeat of the Islesmen is heard, which they call

"Orkney's woe and Randver's bane."

The Norse settlers in Caithness saw terrific visions of Valhalla "the day after the battle." In the NIALA SAGA a Norwegian prince is introduced as asking after his men, and the answer is, "they were all killed." Malcolm of Scotland rejoiced in the defeat and death of his dangerous and implacable neighbor. "Brian's battle," as it is called in the Sagas, was, in short, such a defeat as prevented any general northern combination for the subsequent invasion of Ireland. Not that the country was entirely free from their attacks till the end of the eleventh century, but from the day of Clontarf forward, the long cherished Northern idea of a conquest of Ireland, seems to have been gloomily abandoned by that indomitable people.

CHAPTER VII.

EFFECTS OF THE RIVALRY OF BRIAN AND MALACHY ON THE ANCIENT CONSTITUTION.

If a great battle is to be acccounted lost or won, as it affects principles rather than reputations, then Brian lost at Clontarf. The leading ideas of his long and politic life were, evidently, centralization and an hereditary monarchy. To beat back foreign invasion, to conciliate and to enlist the Irish-born Danes under his standard, were preliminary steps. For Morrogh, his first-born, and for Morrogh's descendants, he hoped to found an hereditary kinship after the type universally copied throughout Christendom. He was not ignorant of what Alfred had done for England, Harold for Norway, Charlemagne for France, and Otho for Germany; and it was inseparable from his imperial genius to desire to reign in his posterity, long after his own brief term of sway should be forever ended. A new centre of royal authority should be established on the banks of the great middle river of the island—itself the best bond of union, as it was the best highway of intercourse; the Dalgais dynasty should there flourish for ages, and the descendants of Brian of the Tributes, through after centuries, eclipse the glory of the descendants of

Nial of the Hostages. It is idle enough to call the projector of such a change an usurper and a revolutionist. Usurper he clearly was not, since he was elevated to power by the action of the old legitimate electoral principle; revolutionist he was not, because his design was defeated at Clontarf, in the death of his eldest son and grandson. Not often have three generations of Princes of the same family been cut off on the same field; yet at Clontarf it so happened. Hence, when Brian fell, and his heir with him, and his heir's heir, the projected Dalgais dynasty, like the Royal Oak at Adair, was cut down and its very roots destroyed. For a new dynasty to be left suddenly without indisputable heirs is ruinous to its pretensions and partizans. And in this the event of the battle proved destructive to the Celtic Constitution. Not from the Anglo-Norman invasion, but from the day of Clontarf we may date the ruin of the old electoral monarchy. The spell of ancient authority was effectually broken and a new one was to be established. Time, which was indispensable, was not given. No Prince of the blood of Brian succeeded immediately to himself. On Clontarf Murrogh, and Murrogh's heir fell, in the same day and hour. The other sons of Brian had no direct title to the succession, and, naturally enough, the deposed Malachy resumed the rank of monarch, without the consent of Munster, but *with* the approval of all the Princes, who had witnessed with ill-concealed envy the sudden ascendancy of the sons of Kennedy. While McLaig was lamenting for Brian, by the cascade of Killaloe, the Laureat of Tara, in an elegy over a lord of Breffni, was singing—

> "Joyful are the race of Conn after Brian's
> Fall, in the battle of Clontarf."

A new dynasty is rarely the work of one able man. Designed by genius, it must be built up by a succession of politic Princes, before it becomes an essential part of the framework of the State. So all history teaches—and Irish history, after the death of Brian, very clearly illustrates that truth. Equally true is it that when a nation breaks up of itself, or from external forces, and is not soon consolidated by a conqueror, the most natural result is the aggrandizement of a few great families. Thus it was in Rome when Julius was assassinated, and in Italy, when the empire of the west fell to pieces of its own weight. The kindred of the late sovereign will be sure to have a party, the chief innovators will have a party, and there is likely to grow up a third, or moderate party. So it fell out in Ireland. The Hy-Nials of the north, deprived of the succession, rallied about the Princes of Aileach as their head. Meath, left crownless, gave room to the ambition of the sons of Malachy, who, under the name of O'Melaghlin, took provincial rank. Ossory, like Issachar, long groaning beneath the burdens of Tara and of Cashel, cruelly revenged on the Dalgais, returning from Clontarf, the subjection to which Mahon and Brian had forcibly reduced that borderland. The Eugenians of Desmond withdrew in disgust from the banner of Donogh O'Brien, because he had openly proclaimed his hostility to the alternate succession, and left his surviving clansmen an easy prey to the enraged Ossorians. Leinster soon afterwards passed from the house of O'Byrne to that of McMurrogh. The O'Briens maintained their dominant interest in the south, as, after many local struggles, the O'Conors did in the west. For a hundred and fifty years, after the death of Malachy II., the history of Ireland is mainly the history of those five families, O'Neils, O'Melaghlins, McMurroghs, O'Briens and O'Conors. And for ages after the Normans enter on the scene, the same provincialized spirit, the same family ambitions, feuds, hates, and coalitions, with some exceptional passages, characterize the whole history. Not that there will be found any want of heroism, or piety, or self-sacrifice, or of any virtue or faculty, necessary to constitute a state, save and except the *power of combination*, alone. Thus, judged by what came after him, and what was happening in the world abroad, Brian's design to re-centralize the island, seems the highest dictate of political wisdom, in the condition to which the Norwegian and Danish wars had reduced it, previous to his elevation to the monarchy.

Malachy II.—of the events of whose second reign some mention will be made hereafter—held the sovereignty after Brian's death, until the year 1023, when he died an edifying death in one of the islands of Lough Ennel, near the present Mullingar.

He is called in the annals of Clonmacnoise, "the last king of Ireland, of Irish blood, that had the crown." An ancient quatrain, quoted by Geoffrey Keating, is thus literally translated·

> "After the happy Melaghlin
> Son of Donald, son of Donogh,
> Each noble king ruled his own tribe
> But Erin owned no sovereign Lord."

The annals of the eleventh and twelfth centuries curiously illustrate the workings of this "anarchical constitution"—to employ a phrase first applied to the Germanic Confederation. "After Malachy's death," says the quaint old Annalist of Clonmacnoise, " this kingdom was without a king 20 years, during which time the realm was governed by two learned men; the one called Con O'Lochan, a well learned temporal man, and chief poet of Ireland ; the other Corcran Claireach, a devout and holy man that was anchorite of all Ireland, whose most abiding was at Lismore. The land was governed like a free state, and not like a monarchy by them." Nothing can show the headlessness of the Irish Constitution in the eleventh century clearer than this interregnum. No one Prince could rally strength enough to be elected, so that two Arbitrators, an illustrious Poet, and a holy Priest, were appointed to take cognizance of national causes. The associating together of a Priest and a layman, a southerner and a northerner, is conclusive proof that the bond of Celtic unity, frittered away during the Danish period, was never afterwards entirely restored. Con O'Lochan having been killed in Teffia, after a short jurisdiction, the holy Corcran exercised his singular jurisdiction, until his decease, which happened at Lismore, (A.D. 1040.) His death produced a new paroxysm of anarchy, out of which a new organizer arose, among the tribes of Leinster. This was Dermid, son of Donogh, who died (A D. 1005), when Dermid must have been a mere infant, as he does not figure in the annals till the year 1032, and the acts of young Princes are seldom overlooked in Gaelic Chronicles. He was the first McMurrogh who became King of Leinster, that royalty having been in the O'Byrne family, until the son of Maelmurra, of Clontarf, was deposed by O'Neil in 1035, and retired to a monastery in Cologne, where he died in 1052. In 1036 or 1037 Dermid captured Dublin and Waterford, married the granddaughter of Brian, and by '41 was strong enough to assume the rank of ruler of the southern half-kingdom. This dignity he held with a strong and warlike hand thirty years, when he fell in battle, at Ova, in Meath. He must have been at that time full threescore years and ten. He is described by the elegiac Bards as of "ruddy complexion," "with teeth laughing in danger," and possessing all the virtues of a warrior-king; "whose death," adds the lamentation, "brought scarcity of peace" with it, so that "there will not be peace," "there will not be armistice," between Meath and Leinster. It may well be imagined that every new resort to the two-third test, in the election of Ard-Righ, should bring "scarcity of peace" to Ireland. We can easily understand the ferment of hope, fear, intrigue, and passion, which such an occasion caused among the great rival families. What canvassing there was in Kincora and Cashel, at Cruachan and Aileach, and at Fernamore! What piecing and patching of interests, what libels on opposing candidates, what exultation in the successful, what discontent in the defeated camp!

The successful candidate for the southern half-kingdom after Dermid's death was Thorlogh, grandson of Brian, and foster-son of the late ruler. In his reign, which lasted thirty-three years, the political fortunes of his house revived. He died in peace at Kinkora, A. D. 1087, and the war of succession again broke out. The rival candidates at this period were Murrogh O'Brien, son of the late king, whose ambition was to complete the design of Brian, and Donald, Prince of Aileach, the leader of the Northern Hy-Nials. Two abler men seldom divided a country by their equal ambition. Both are entered in the annals as "Kings of Ireland," but it is hard to discover that, during all the years of their contest, either of them submitted to the other. To chronicle all the incidents of the struggle would take too much space here; and, as was to be expected, a third party profited most by it; the West came in, in the person of O'Conor, to lord it over both North and South, and to add another element to the dynastic confusion.

This brief abstract of our civil affairs after the death of Brian, presents us with the extraordinary spectacle of a country without a constitution working out the problem of its stormy destiny in despite of all internal and external dangers. Everything now, depended on individual genius and energy; nothing on system, usage, or prescription. Each leading family and each province became, in turn, the head of the State. The supreme title seems to have been fatal for a generation to the family that obtained it, for in no case is there a lineal descent of the crown. The Prince of Aileach or Kinkora naturally preferred his permanent patrimony to an uncertain tenure of Tara; an office not attached to a locality became, of course, little more than an arbitrary title. Hence, the titular King of Ireland might for one lifetime reign by the Shannon, in the next by the Bann, in a third, by Lough Corrib. The supremacy, thus came to be considered a merely personal appurtenance, was carried about in the old King's tent, or on the young King's crupper, deteriorating and decaying by every transposition it underwent. Herein, we have the origin of Irish disunion with all its consequences, good bad and indifferent.

Are we to blame Brian for this train of events against which he would have provided a sharp remedy in the hereditary principle? Or, on the other hand, are we to condemn Malachy, the possessor of legitimate power, if he saw in that remedy only the ambition of an aspiring family already grown too great? Theirs was in fact the universal struggle of reform and conservatism; the reformer and the heirs of his work were cut off on Clontarf; the abuses of the elective principle continued unrestrained by ancient salutary usage and prejudice, and the land remained a tempting prey to such Adventurers, foreign or native, as dare undertake to mould power out of its chaotic materials.

CHAPTER VIII.

LATTER DAYS OF THE NORTHMEN IN IRELAND.

Though Ireland dates the decay of Scandinavian power from Good Friday, 1014, yet the North did not wholly cease to send forth its warriors, nor were the shores of the western Island less tempting to them than before. The second year after the battle of Clontarf, Canute founded his Danish dynasty in England, which existed in no little splendor during thirty-seven years. The Saxon line was restored by Edward " the Confessor," in the forty-third year of the century, only to be extinguished forever by the Norman conquest twenty-three years later. Scotland, during the same years, was more than once subject to invasion from the same ancient enemy. Malcolm II., and the brave usurper Macbeth, fought several engagements with the northern leaders, and generally with brilliant success. By a remarkable coincidence, the Scottish chronicles also date the decadence of Danish power on their coasts from 1014, though several engagements were fought in Scotland after that year.

Malachy II. had promptly followed up the victory of Clontarf by the capture of Dublin, the destruction of its fort, and the exemplary chastisement of the tribes of Leinster, who had joined Maelmurra as allies of the Danes. Sitrick himself seems to have eluded the suspicions and vengeance of the conquerors by a temporary exile, as we find in the succession of the Dublin Vikings, " one Hyman, an usurper," entered as ruling " part of a year while Sitrick was in banishment." His family interest, however, was strong among the native Princes, and whatever his secret sympathies may have been he had taken no active part against them in the battle of Clontarf. By his mother, the Lady Gormley of Offally, he was a half O'Conor ; by marriage he was son-in-law of Brian, and uterine brother of Malachy. After his return to Dublin, when, in 1018, Bran, son of Maelmurra, fell prisoner into his hands, as if to clear himself of any lingering suspicion of an understanding with that family, he caused his eyes to be put out—a cruel but customary punishment in that age. This act procured for him the deadly enmity of the warlike mountaineers of Wicklow, who, in the year 1022, gave him a severe defeat at Delgany. Even this he outlived, and died seven years later, the acknowledged lord of his town and fortress, forty years after his first accession to that title. He was succeeded by his son, grandson, and great-grandson during the remaining half century.

The kingdom of Leinster, in consequence of the defeat of Maelmurra, the incapacity of Brian, and the destruction of other claimants of the same family, passed to the family of McMurrogh, another branch of the same ancestry. Dermid, the first and most distinguished King of Leinster of this house, took Waterford (A.D. 1037) and so reduced its strength, that we find its hosts no longer formidable in the field. Those of Limerick continued their homage to the house of Kinkora, while the descendants of Sitrick recognized Dermid of Leinster as their sovereign. In short, all the Dano-Irish from thenceforward began to knit themselves kindly to the soil, to obey the neighboring Princes, to march with them to battle, and to pursue the peaceful calling of merchants, upon sea. The only peculiarly *Danish* undertaking we hear of again, in our Annals, was the attempt of a united fleet, equipped by Dublin, Wexford and Waterford, in the year 1088, to retake Cork from the men of Desmond when they were driven with severe loss to their ships. Their few subsequent expeditions were led abroad, into the Hebrides, the Isle of Man, or Wales, where they generally figure as auxiliaries or mercenaries in the service of local Princes. They appear in Irish battles only as contingents to the native armies—led by their own leaders and recognized as a separate, but subordinate force. In the year 1073, the Dublin Danes did homage to the monarch Thorlogh, and from 1095, until his death (A.D. 1119), they recognized no other lord but Murkertach More O'Brien; this king, at their own request, had also nominated one of his family as Lord of the Danes and Welsh of the Isle of Man.

The wealth of these Irish-Danes, before and after the time of

Brian, may be estimated by the annual tribute which Limerick paid to that Prince—a pipe of red wine for every day in the year. In the year 1029, Olaf, son of Sitrick, of Dublin, being taken prisoner by O'Regan, the lord of East-Meath, paid for his ransom—"twelve hundred cows, seven score British horses, three score ounces of gold!" sixty ounces of white silver as his "fetter-ounce;" the sword of Carlus, besides the usual legal fees, for recording these profitable formalities.

Being now Christians, they also began to found and endow churches, with the same liberality with which their Pagan fathers had once enriched the temples of Upsala and Trondheim. The oldest religious foundations in the seaports they possessed owe their origin to them; but even as Christians, they did not lose sight of their nationality. They contended for, and obtained Dano-Irish Bishops, men of their own race, speaking their own speech, to preside over the sees of Dublin, Waterford and Limerick. When the Irish Synods or Primates asserted over them any supervision which they were unwilling to admit—except in the case of Saint Malachy—they usually invoked the protection of the See of Canterbury, which, after the Norman conquest of England, became by far the most powerful Archbishopric in either island.

In the third quarter of this century there arose in the Isle of Man a fortunate leader, who may almost be called the last of the sea kings. This was Godard *Crovan* (the white-handed), son of an Icelandic Prince, and one of the followers of Harald Harfagar and Earl Tosti, in their invasion of Northumbria (A. D. 1066). Returning from the defeat of his chiefs, Godard saw and seized upon Man as the centre of future expeditions of his own, in the course of which he subdued the Hebrides, divided them with the gallant Somerled, (ancestor of the MacDonalds of the Isles,) and established his son Lagman (afterwards put to death by King Magnus *Barefoot*) as his viceroy in the Orkneys and Shetlands. The weakened condition of the Danish settlement at Dublin attracted his ambition, and where he entered as a mediator he remained as a master. In the succession of the Dublin Vikings he is assigned a reign of ten years, and his whole course of conquest seems to have occupied some twenty years (A. D. 1077 to 1098).

At length the star of this Viking of the Irish sea, paled before the mightier name of a king of Norway, whose more brilliant ambition had a still shorter span. The story of this *Magnus* (called, it is said, from his adoption of the Scottish kilt, Magnus *Barefoot*) forms the eleventh Saga in "the Chronicles of the Kings of Norway." He began to reign in the year 1093, and soon after undertook an expedition to the south, "with many fine men, and good shipping." Taking the Orkneys on his way he sent their Earls prisoners to Norway, and placed his own son, Sigurd, in their stead. He overran the Hebrides, putting Lagman, son of Godard Crovan, to death. He spared only "the holy Island," as Iona was now called, even by the Northmen, and there, in after years, his own bones were buried. The Isles of Man and Angleasea, and the coast of Wales, shared the same fate, and thence he retraced his course to Scotland, where, borne in his galley across the Isthmus of Cantire, to fulfil an old prophecy, he claimed possession of the land, on both shores of Loch Awe. It was while he wintered in the Southern Hebrides, according to the Saga, that he contracted his son Sigurd with the daughter of Murkertach O'Brien, called by the Northmen "Biadmynia." In summer he sailed homeward, and did not return southward till the ninth year of his reign (A. D. 1102), when his son, Sigurd, had come of age, and bore the title of "King of the Orkneys and Hebrides." "He sailed into the west sea," says the Saga, "with the finest men who could be got in Norway. All the powerful men of the country followed him, such as Sigurd Hranesson, and his brother Ulf, Vidkunner Johnsson, Dag Eliffsson, Sorker of Sogn, Eyvind Olboge, the king's marshal, and many other great men." On the intelligence of this fleet having arrived in Irish waters, according to the annals, Murkertach and his allies marched in force to Dublin, where, however, Magnus "made peace with them for one year," and Murkertach "gave his daughter to Sigurd, with many jewels and gifts." That winter Magnus spent with Murkertach at Kinkora, and "towards Spring both kings went westward with their army all the way to Ulster." This was one of those annual visitations which kings, whose authority was not yet established, were accustomed to make. The circuit, as usual, was performed in about six weeks, after which the Irish monarch returned home, and Magnus went on board his fleet at Dublin, to return to Norway, According to the Norse account he landed again on the coast of Ulidia (Down), where he expected "cattle for ship-provision" which Murkertach had promised to send him, but the Irish version would seem to imply that he went on shore to seize the cattle perforce. It certainly seems incredible that Murkertach should send cattle to the shore of Strangford Lough, from the pastures of Thomond, when they might be more easily driven to Dublin, or the mouth of the Boyne. "The cattle had not made their appearance on the eve of Bartholomew's Mass" (August 23 1, A.D. 1103), says the Saga, so "when the sun rose in the sky, King Magnus himself went on shore with the greater part of his men. King Magnus," continues the scald, "had a helmet on his head; a red shield, in which was inlaid a gilded lion; and was girt with the sword Legbiter, of which the hilt was of ivory, and the hand grip wound about with gold thread; and the sword was extremely sharp. In his hand he had a short spear, and a red silk short cloak over his coat, on which both before and behind was embroidered a lion, in yellow silk; and all men acknowledged that they had never seen a brisker, statelier man." A dust cloud was seen far inland, and the Northmen fell into order of battle. It proved, however, by their own account to be the messengers with the promised supply of cattle; but, after they came up, and while returning to the shore, they were violently assailed on all sides by the men of Down. The battle is described, with true Homeric vigor, by Sturleson. "The Irish," he says, "shot boldly; and although they fell in crowds, there came always two in place of one." Magnus, with most of his nobles, were slain on the spot, but Vidkunner Johnsson escaped to the shipping, "with the King's banner and the sword Legbiter." And the Saga of Magnus Barefoot concludes thus: "Now when King Sigurd heard that his father had fallen, he set off immediately, leaving the Irish King's daughter behind, and proceeded in autumn, with the whole fleet directly to Norway." The annalists of Ulster barely record the fact, that "Magnus, King of Lochlan and the Isles, was slain by the Ulidians, with a slaughter of his people about him, while on a predatory excursion." They place the event in the year 1104.

Our account with the Northmen may here be closed. Borne along by the living current of events, we leave them behind, high up on the remoter channels of the stream. Their terrible ravens shall flit across our prospect no more. They have taken wing to their native north, where they may croak yet a little while over the cold and crumbling altars of Odin and Asa Thor. The bright light of the Gospel has penetrated even to those last haunts of Paganism, and the fierce but not ungenerous race with which we have been so long familiar begin to change their natures, under its benign influence.

Although both the scalds and chroniclers of the North frequently refer to Ireland as a favorite theatre of their heroes, we derive little light from those of their works which have yet been made public. All connexion between the two races had long ceased, before the first scholars of the North began to investigate the earlier annals of their own country, and then they were content with a very vague and general knowledge of the western Island, for which their ancestors had so fiercely contended throughout so many generations. The oldest maps, known in Scandinavia, exhibit a mere outline of the Irish coast, with a few points in the interior; flords, with Norse names, are shown, answering to Loughs Foyle, Swilly, Larne, Strang*ford*, and Carling*ford;* the Provincial lines of Ulster and of Connaught are rudely traced; and the situation of Enniskillen, Tara, Dublin, Glendaloch, Water*ford*, Limer*ick*, and Swer*wick*, accurately laid down. It is thought that all those places ending in *wick* or *ford*, on the Irish map, are of Scandinavian origin; as well as the names of the islets, Skerries, Lambey, and Saltees. Many noble families, as the Plunkets, McIvers, Archbolds, Harolds, Stacks, Skiddies, Cruises, and McAuliffes, are derived from the same origin.

During the contest we have endeavored to describe, three hundred and ten years had passed since the warriors of Lochlin first landed on the shores of Erin. Ten generations, according to the measured span of adult life, were born, and trained to arms and marshalled in battle, since the enemy, "powerful on sea," first burst upon the shield-shaped Isle of Saints. At the close of the eighth century we cast back a grateful retrospect on the Christian ages of Ireland. Can we do so now, at the close of the eleventh? Alas! far from it. Bravely and in the main successfully as the Irish have borne themselves, they come out of that cruel, treacherous, interminable war with many rents and stains in that vesture of innocence in which we saw them arrayed at the close of their third Christian century. Odin has not conquered, but all the worst vices of warfare—its violence, its impiety, discontent, self-indulgence, and contempt for the sweet paths of peace and mild counsels of religion—these must and did remain, long after Dane and Norwegian have forever disappeared!

BOOK III.

WAR OF SUCCESSION.

CHAPTER I.

THE FORTUNES OF THE FAMILY OF BRIAN.

THE last scene of the Irish monarchy, before it entered on the anarchical period, was not destitute of an appropriate grandeur. It was the death-bed scene of the second Malachy, the rival, ally, and successor of the great Brian. After the eventful day of Clontarf he resumed the monarchy, without opposition, and for eight years he continued in its undisturbed enjoyment. The fruitful land of Meath again gave forth its abundance, unscourged by the spoiler, and beside its lakes and streams the hospitable Ard-Righ had erected, or restored, three hundred fortified houses, where, as his poets sung, shelter was freely given to guests from the king of the elements. His own favorite residence was at Dunnasciath ("the fort of shields"), in the northwest angle of Lough Ennel, in the present parish of Dysart. In the eighth year after Clontarf—the summer of 1022—the Dublin Danes once again ventured on a foray into Eastmeath, and the aged monarch marched to meet them. At Athboy he encountered the enemy, and drove them, routed and broken, out of the ancient mensal land of the Irish kings.

Thirty days after that victory he was called on to confront the conqueror of all men, even Death. He had reached the age of seventy-three, and he prepared to meet his last hour with the zeal and humility of a true Christian. To Dunnasciath repaired Amalgaid, Archbishop of Armagh, the Abbots of Clonmacnoise and of Durrow, with a numerous train of the clergy. For greater solitude, the dying king was conveyed into an island of the lake opposite his fort—then called Inis-Cro, now Cormorant Island—and there, "after intense penance," on the fourth of the Nones of September precisely, died Malachy, son of Donald, son of Donogh, in the fond language of the bards, "the pillar of the dignity and nobility of the western world:" and "the seniors of all Ireland sung masses, hymns, psalms, and canticles for the welfare of his soul."

"This," says the old Translator of the Clonmacnoise Annals, "was the last king of Ireland of Irish blood, that had the crown; yet there were seven kings after without crown, before the coming in of the English." Of these seven subsequent kings we are to write under the general title of "the War of Succession." They are called Ard-Righ *go Fresabra*, that is, kings opposed, or unrecognized, by certain tribes, or Provinces. For it was essential to the completion of the title, as we have before seen, that when the claimant was of Ulster, he should have Connaught and Munster, or Leinster and Munster, in his obedience: in other words, he should be able to command the allegiance of two-thirds of his suffragans. If of Munster, he should be equally potent in the other Provinces, in order to rank among the recognized kings of Erin. Whether some of the seven kings subsequent to Malachy II., who assumed the title, were not fairly entitled to it, we do not presume to say; it is our simpler task to narrate the incidents of that brilliant war of succession, which occupies almost all the interval between the Danish and Anglo-Norman invasions. The chaunt of the funeral Mass of Malachy was hardly heard upon Lough Ennel, when Donogh O'Brien despatched his agents, claiming the crown from the Provincial Princes. He was the eldest son of Brian by his second marriage, and his mother was an O'Conor, an additional source of strength to him, in the western Province. It had fallen to the lot of Donogh and his elder brother, Teigue or Thaddeus, to conduct the remnant of the Dalcassians from Clontarf to their home. Marching through Ossory, by the great southern road they were attacked in their enfeebled state by the lord of that brave little border territory, on whom Brian's hand had fallen with heavy displeasure. Wounded as many of them were, they fought their way desperately towards Cashel, leaving 150 men dead in one of their skirmishes. Of all who had left the Shannon side to combat with the enemy, but 850 men lived to return to their homes

No sooner had they reached Kinkora, than a fierce dispute arose, between the friends of Teigue and Donogh, as to which should reign over Munster. A battle ensued, with doubtful result, but by the intercession of the Clergy this unnatural feud was healed, and the brothers reigned conjointly for nine years afterwards, until Teigue fell in an engagement in Ely (Queen's County), as was charged and believed, by the machinations of his colleague and brother. Thorlogh, son of Teigue, was the foster-son, and at this time the guest or hostage of Dermid of Leinster, the founder of the McMurrogh family, which had now risen into the rank, justly forfeited by the traitor, Maelmurra. When he reached man's age he married the daughter of Dermid, and we shall soon hear of him again asserting in Munster the pretensions of the eldest surviving branch of the O'Brien family.

The death of his brother and of Malachy, within the same year, proved favorable to the ambition of Donogh O'Brien. All Munster submitted to his sway; Connaught was among the first to recognize his title as Ard-Righ. Ossory and Leinster, though, unwillingly, gave in their adhesion. But Meath refused to recognize him, and placed its government in commission, in the hands of Con O'Lochan, the arch-poet, and Corcran, the priest, already more than once mentioned. The country, north of Meath, obeyed Flaherty O'Neil, of Aileach, whose ambition, as well as that of all his house, was to restore the northern supremacy, which had continued unbroken, from the fourth to the ninth century. This Flaherty was a vigorous, able, and pious Prince, who held stoutly on to the northern half-kingdom. In the year 1030 he made the frequent but adventurous pilgrimage to Rome, from which he is called, in the pedigree of his house, *an Trostain*, or the cross-bearer.

The greatest obstacle, however, to the complete ascendency of Donogh, arose in the person of his nephew, now advanced to manhood. Thorlogh O'Brien possessed much of the courage and ability of his grandfather, and he had at his side a faithful and powerful ally in his foster-father, Dermid, of Leinster. Rightly or wrongly, on proof or on suspicion, he regarded his uncle as his father's murderer, and he pursued his vengeance with a skill and constancy worthy of *Hamlet*. At the time of his father's death he was a mere lad—in his fourteenth year. But, as he grew older, he accompanied his foster-father in all his expeditions, and rapidly acquired a soldier's fame. By marriage with Dervorgoil, daughter of the Lord of Ossory, he strengthened his influence at the most necessary point; and what with so good a cause and such fast friends as he made in exile, his success against his uncle is little to be wondered at. Leinster and Ossory, which had temporarily submitted to Donogh's claim, soon found good pretexts for refusing him tribute, and a border war, marked by all the usual atrocities, raged for several successive seasons. The contest is relieved, however, of its purely civil character by the capture of Waterford, still Danish, in 1037, and of Dublin in 1051. On this occasion, Dermid, of Leinster, bestowed the city on his son Morrogh, (grandfather of Strongbow's ally,) to whom the remnant of its inhabitants, as well as their kinsmen in Man, submitted for the time, with what grace they could.

The position of Donogh O'Brien became yearly weaker. His rival had youth, energy and fortune on his side. The Prince of Connaught finally joined him, and thus a league was formed, which overcame all opposition. In the year 1058, Donogh received a severe defeat at the base of the Galtees; and although he went into the house of O'Conor the same year, and humbly submitted to him, it only postponed his day of reckoning. Three years after O'Conor took Kincorra, and Dermid, of Leinster, burned Limerick, and took hostages as far southward as Saint Brendan's hill (Tralee). The next year Donogh O' Brien, then fully fourscore years of age, weary of life and of the world, took the cross-staff, and departed on a pilgrimage to Rome, where he died soon after, in the monastery of St. Stephen. It is said by some writers that Donogh brought with him to Rome and presented to the Pope, Alexander II., the crown of his father—and from this tradition many theories and controversies have sprung. It is not unlikely that a deposed monarch should have carried into exile whatever portable wealth he still retained, nor that he should have presented his crown to the Sovereign Pontiff before finally quitting the world. But as to conferring with the crown, the sovereignty of which it was once an emblem, neither reason nor religion obliges us to believe any such hypothesis.

Dermid, of Leinster, upon the banishment of Donogh, son of Brian (A. D. 1063), became actual ruler of the southern half-kingdom and nominal Ard-Righ, "with opposition." The two-fold antagonism to this Prince came as might be expected from Conor, son of Malachy, the head of the Southern Hy-Nial dynasty, and from the chiefs of the elder dynasty of the North. Thorlogh O'Brien, now King of Cashel, loyally repaid by his devoted adherence, the deep debt he owed in his struggles and his early youth to Dermid. There are few instances in our Annals of a more devoted friendship than existed between these brave and able Princes through all the changes of half a century. No one act seems to have broken the life-long intimacy of Dermid and Thorlogh; no cloud ever came between them; no mistrust, no distrust. Rare and precious felicity of human experience! How many myriads of men have sighed out their souls in vain desire for that best blessing which Heaven can bestow, a true, unchanging, unsuspecting friend!

To return: Conor O Melaghlin could not see, without deep-seated discontent, a Prince of Leinster assume the rank which his father and several of his ancestors had held. A border strife between Meath and Leinster arose not unlike that which had been waged a few years before for the deposition of Donogh, between Leinster and Ossory on the one part, and Munster on the other. Various were the encounters, whose obscure details are seldom preserved to us. But the good fortune of Dermid prevailed in all, until, in the year 1070, he lost Morrogh, his heir, by a natural death at Dublin, and Gluniarn, another son, fell in battle with the men of Meath. Two years later, in the battle of Ova, in the same territory, and against the same enemy, Dermid himself fell, with the lord of Forth, and a great host of Dublin Danes and Leinstermen. The triumph of the son of Malachy, and the sorrow and anger of Leinster, were equally great. The Bards have sung the praise of Dermid in strains which history accepts: they praise his ruddy aspect and laughing teeth; they remember how he upheld the standard of war, and none dared contend with him in battle; they denounce vengeance on Meath as soon as his death-feast is over—a vengeance too truly pursued.

As a picture of the manners and habits of thought in those times, the fate of Conor, son of Melaghlin, and its connection with the last illness and death of Thorlogh O'Brien, are worthy of mention. Conor was treacherously slain, the year after the battle of Ova, in a parley with his own nephew, though the parley was held under the protection of the *Bachall-Isa*, or Staff of Christ, the most revered relic of the Irish Church. After his death, his body was buried in the great Church of Clonmacnoise, in his own patrimony. But Thorlogh O'Brien perhaps, from his friendship for Dermid, carried off his head, as the head of an enemy, to Kincorra. When it was placed in his presence in his palace, a mouse ran out from the dead man's head, and under the king's mantle, which occasioned him such a fright that he grew suddenly sick, his hair fell off, and his life was despaired of. It was on Good Friday that the buried head was carried away, and on Easter Sunday it was tremblingly restored again, with two rings of gold as a peace offering to the Church. Thus were God and Saint Kieran vindicated. Thorlogh O'Brien slowly regained his strength, though Keating, and the authors he followed, think he was never the same man again, after the fright he received, from the head of Conor O Melaghlin. He died peaceably and full of penitence, at Kincorra, on the eve of the Ides of July, A. D. 1086, after severe physical suffering. He was in the 77th year of his age, the 32d of his rule over Munster, and the 13th—since the death of Dermid, of Leinster—in his actual sovereignty of the southern half, and nominal rule of the whole kingdom He was succeeded by his son Murkertach, or Murtogh, afterwards called *More*, or the great.

We have thus traced to the third generation the political fortunes of the family of Brian, which includes so much of the history of those times. That family had become, and was long destined to remain, the first in rank and influence in the southern half-kingdom. But internal discord in a great house, as in a great state, is fatal to the peaceable transmission of power. That "acknowledged right of birth" to which a famous historian attributes "the peaceful successions" of modern Europe, was too little respected in those ages, in many countries of Christendom —and had no settled prescription in its favor among the Irish. Primogeniture and the whole scheme of feudal dependence seems to have been an essential preparative for modern civilization: but as Ireland had escaped the legions of Rome, so she existed without the circle of feudal organization. When that system did at length appear upon her soil it was embodied in an invading host, and patriot zeal could discern nothing good, nothing imitable in the laws and customs of an enemy, whose armed presence in the land was an insult to its inhabitants. Thus did our Island twice lose the discipline which elsewhere laid the foundation of great states: once in the Roman, and again in the Feudal era.

CHAPTER II.

THE CONTEST BETWEEN THE NORTH AND SOUTH—RISE OF THE FAMILY OF O'CONOR.

FOUR years before the death of Thorlogh O'Brien, a Prince destined to be the life-long rival of his great son, had succeeded to the kingship of the northern tribes. This was Donald, son of Ardgall, Prince of Aileach, sometimes called "O" and sometimes "Mac" Laughlin. Donald had reached the mature age of forty when he succeeded in the course of nature to his father, Ardgall, and was admitted the first man of the North, not only in station but for personal graces and accomplishments; for wisdom, wealth, liberality, and love of military adventure.

Murkertach, or Murtogh O'Brien, was of nearly the same age as his rival, and his equal, if not superior in talents, both for peace and war. During the last years of his father's reign and illness, he had been the real ruler of the south, and had enforced the claims of Cashel on all the tribes of Leath Mogha, from Dublin to Galway. In the year 1094, by mutual compact, brought about through the intercession of the Archbishop of Armagh and the great body of the clergy, north and south—and still more perhaps by the pestilence and famine which raged at intervals during the last years of the eleventh century—this ancient division of the midland *esker*, running east and west, was solemnly restored by consent of both parties, and Leath Mogha and Leath Conn became for the moment independent territories. So thoroughly did the Church enter into the arrangement, that, at the Synod of Rath-Brazil, held a few years later, the seats of the twelve Bishops of the southern half were grouped round the Archbishop of Cashel, while the twelve of the northern half were ranged round the Archbishop of Armagh. The Bishops of Meath, the ancient mensal of the monarchy, seem to have occupied a middle station between the benches of the north and south.

Notwithstanding the solemn compact of 1094, Murtogh did not long cease to claim the title, nor to seek the hostages of all Ireland. As soon as the fearful visitations with which the century had closed were passed over, he resumed his warlike forays, and found Donald of Aileach nothing loath to try again the issue of arms. Each prince, however, seems to have been more anxious to coerce or interest the secondary chiefs in his own behalf than to meet his rival in the old-style pitched battle. Murtogh's annual march was usually along the Shannon, into Leitrim, thence north by Sligo, and across the Erne and Finn into Donegal and Derry. Donald's annual excursion led commonly along the Bann, into Dalriada and Ulidia, thence by way of Newry, across the Boyne, into Meath, and from Westmeath into North Munster. In one of these forays, at the very opening of the twelfth century, Donald surprised Kincorra in the absence of its lord, razed the fort and levelled the buildings to the earth. But the next season the southern king paid him back in kind, when he attacked and demolished Aileach, and caused each of his soldiers to carry off a stone of the ruin in his knapsack. "I never heard of the billeting of grit stones," exclaims a bard of those days, "though I have heard of the billeting of soldiers·

but now we see the stones of Aileach billeted on the horses of the King of the West!"

Such circuits of the Irish kings, especially in days of opposition, were repeated with much regularity. They seem to have set out commonly in May—or soon after the festival of Easter—and when the tour of the island was made, they occupied about six weeks in duration. The precise number of men, who took part in these visitations, is nowhere stated, but in critical times no prince, claiming the perilous honor of *Ard-Righ*, would be likely to march with less than from five to ten thousand men. The movements of such a multitude must have been attended with many oppressions and inconveniences; their encampment for even a week in any territory must have been a serious burthen to the resident inhabitants, whether hostile or hospitable. Yet this was one inevitable consequence of the breaking up of the federal centre at Tara. In earlier days, the *Ard-Righ*, on his election, or in an emergency, made an armed procession through the island. Ordinarily, however, his suffragans visited him, and not he them; all Ireland went up to Tara to the *Feis*, or to the festivals of Baaltine and Samhain. Now that there was no Tara to go to, the monarch, or would-be monarch, found it indispensable to show himself often, and to exercise his authority in person, among every considerable tribe in the island. To do justice to Murtogh O'Brien, he does not appear to have sought occasions of employing force when on these expeditions, but rather to have acted the part of an armed negotiator. On his return from the demolition of Aileach (A.D. 1101), among other acts of munificence, he, in an assembly of the clergy of Leath Mogha, made a solemn gift of the city of Cashel, free of all rents and dues, to the Archbishop and the Clergy, forever. His munificence to churches, and his patronage of holy men, were eminent traits in this Prince's character. And the clergy of that age were eminently worthy of the favors of such Princes. Their interposition frequently brought about a truce between the northern and southern kings. In the year 1103, the hostages of both were placed in custody with Donald, Archbishop of Armagh, to guarentee a twelvemonth's peace. But the next season the contest was renewed. Murtogh besieged Armagh for a week, which

Donald of Aileach successfully defended, until the siege was abandoned. In a subsequent battle the northern force defeated one division of Murtogh's allies in Iveagh, under the Prince of Leinster, who fell on the field, with the lords of Idrone, Ossory, Desies, Kerry, and the Dublin Danes. Murtogh himself, with another division of his troops, was on an incursion into Antrim when he heard of this defeat. The northern visitors carried off among other spoils the royal tent and standard, a trophy which caused new bitterness on the one side, and new confidence on the other. Donald, the good Archbishop, the following year (A.D. 1105) proceeded to Dublin, where Murtogh was, or was soon expected, to renew the previous peace between North and South, but he fell suddenly ill soon after his arrival, and caused himself to be carried homewards in haste. At a church by the wayside, not far from Dublin, he was anointed and received the viaticum. He survived, however, to reach Armagh, where he expired on the 12th day of August. Kellach, latinized Celsus, his saintly successor, was promoted to the Primacy, and solemnly consecrated on Saint Adamnan's day following—the 23d of September, 1105.

Archbishop Celsus, whose accession was equally well received in Munster as in Ulster, followed in the footsteps of his pious predecessor, in taking a decided part with neither Leath Mogha nor Leath Conn. When, in the year 1110, both parties marched to Slieve-Fuaid, with a view to a challenge of battle, Celsus interposed between them the *Bachall-Isa*—and a solemn truce followed; again, three years later, when they confronted each other in Iveagh, in Down, similar success attended a similar interposition. A few years later Murtogh O'Brien was seized with so severe an illness, that he became like to a living skeleton, and though he recovered sufficiently to resume the exercise of authority he never regained his full health. He died on a spiritual retreat, at Lismore, on the 4th of the Ides of March, A.D. 1119, and was buried at Killaloe. His great rival, Donald of Leath Conn, did not long survive him: he died at Derry, also in a religious house, on the 5th of the Ides of February, A.D. 1121.

While these two able men were thus for more than a quarter of a century struggling for the supremacy, a third power was gradually strengthening itself west of the Shannon, destined to profit by the contest, more than either of the principals. This was the family of O'Conor, of Roscommon, who derived their pedigree from the same stock as the O'Neils, and their name from Conor, an ancestor, who ruled over Connaught, towards the end of the ninth century. Two or three of their line before Conor had possessed the same rank and title, but it was by no means regarded as an adjunct of the house of Rathcrogan, before the time at which we have arrived. Their co-relatives, sometimes their rivals, but oftener their allies, were the O'Ruarcs of Breffny, McDermots of Moylurg, the O'Flahertys of *Iar* or West Connaught, the O'Shaughnessys, O'Heynes, and O'Dowdas. The great neighboring family of O'Kelly had sprung from a different branch of the far-spreading Gaelic tree. At the opening of the twelfth century, Thorlogh More O'Conor, son of Ruari of the Yellow Hound, son of Hugh of the Broken Spear, was the recognized head of his race, both for valor and discretion. By some historians he is called the half-brother of Murtogh O'Brien, and it is certain that he was the faithful ally of that powerful prince. In the early stages of the recent contest between North and South, Donald of Aileach had presented himself at Rathcrogan, the residence of O'Conor, who entertained him for a fortnight, and gave him hostages; but Connaught finally sided with Munster, and thus, by a decided policy, escaped being ground to powder, as corn is ground between the mill stones. But the nephew and successor of Murtogh was not prepared to reciprocate to Connaught the support it had rendered to Munster, but rather looked for its continuance to himself. Conor O'Brien, who became King of Munster in 1120, resisted all his life the pretensions of any house but his own to the southern half-kingdom, and against a less powerful or less politic antagonist, his energy and capacity would have been certain to prevail. The posterity of Malachy in Meath, as well as the Princes of Aileach, were equally hostile to the designs of the new aspirant. One line had given three, another seven, another twenty kings to Erin—but who had ever heard of an *Ard-Righ* coming out of Connaught? 'Twas so, they reasoned, in those days of fierce family pride, and so they acted. Yet Thorlogh, son of Ruari, son of Hugh, proved himself in the fifteen years' war, previous to his accession (1021 to 1136), more than a match for all his enemies. He had been chief of his tribe since the year 1106, and from the first had begun to lay his far forecasting plans for the sovereignty. He had espoused the cause of the house of O'Brien, and had profited by that alliance. Nor were all his thoughts given to war. He had bridged the river Suca at Ballinasloe, and the Shannon at Athlone and Shannon harbor, and the same year these works were finished (1120 or '21) he celebrated the ancient games at Tailtean, in assertion of his claim to the monarchy. His main difficulty was the stubborn pride of Munster, and the valor and enterprize of Conor O'Brien, surnamed Conor "of the fortresses." Of the years following his assertion of his title, few passed without war between those Provinces. In 1121 and 1127, Thorlogh triumphed in the south, took hostages from Lismore to Tralee, and returned home exultingly; a few years later the tide turned, and Conor O'Brien was equally victorious against him, in the heart of his own country. Thorlogh played off in the south the ancient jealousy of the Eugenian houses against the Dalcassians, and thus weakened both, to his own advantage. In the year 1126 he took Dublin and raised his son to the lordship, as Dermid of Leinster, and Thorlogh O'Brien had done formerly: marching southward he encamped in Ormond, from Lammas to St. Bridget's day, and overran Munster with his troops in all directions, taking Cork, Cashel, Ardfinnan, and Tralee. Celsus, the holy Primate of Armagh, deploring the evils of this protracted war, left his peaceful city, and spent thirteen months in the south and west, endeavoring to reconcile, and bind over to the peace the contending kings. In these days the Irish hierarchy performed, perhaps, their highest part—that of peace-makers and preachers of good will to men. When in 1132 and '33 the tide had temporarily turned against Thorlogh, and Conor O'Brien had united Munster, Leinster and Meath, against him, the Archbishop of Tuam performed effectually the office of mediator, preserving not only his own Province, but the whole country, from the most sanguinary consequences. In the year 1130, the holy Celsus had rested from his labors, and Malachy, the illustrious friend of St. Bernard, was nominated as his successor. At the time he was absent in Munster, as the Vicar of the aged Primate, engaged in a mission of peace, when the crozier and the dying message of his predecessor were delivered to him. He returned to Armagh, where he found that Maurice, son of Donald, had been intruded as Archbishop in the *interim;* to this city peace, order, and unity, were not even partially restored, until two years later—A. D. 1132.

The reign of Thorlogh O'Conor over Leath Mogha, or as Ard-Righ "with opposition," is dated by the best authorities from the year 1136. He was then in his forty-eighth year, and had been chief of his tribe from the early age of eighteen. He afterwards reigned for twenty years, and as those years, and the early career of his son Roderick, are full of instruction, in reference to the events which follow—we must relate them somewhat in detail. We again beg the reader to observe the consequences of the destruction of the federal bond among the Irish; how every Province has found an ambitious dynasty of its own, which each contends shall be supreme; how the ambition of the great families grows insatiable as the ancient rights and customs decay; how the law of Patrick enacted in the fifth century is no longer quoted or regarded; how the law of the strong hand alone decides the quarrel of these proud, unyielding Princes.

CHAPTER III.

THORLOGH MORE O'CONOR—MURKERTACH OF AILEACH—ACCESSION OF RODERICK O'CONOR.

THE successful ambition of Thorlogh O'Conor had thus added, as we have seen in the last chapter, a fifth dynasty to the number of competitors for the sovereignty. And if great energy and various talents could alone entitle a chief to rule over his country, this Prince well merited the obedience of his cotemporaries. He is the first of the latter kings who maintained a regular fleet at sea; at one time we find these Connaught galleys doing service on the coast of Cork, at another co-operating with his land forces, in the harbor of Derry. The year of his greatest power was the fifteenth of his reign (A. D. 1151), when his most signal success was obtained over his most formidable antagonists. Thorlogh O'Brien, King of Munster, successor to Conor of the fortresses, had on foot, in that year, an army of three battalions (or *caths*), each battalion consisting of 3,000 men, with which force he overawed some, and compelled others of the southern chiefs to withdraw their homage from his western namesake. The latter, uniting to his own the forces of Meath, and those of Leinster, recently reconciled to his supremacy, marched southward, and, encamping at Glanmire, received the adhesion of such Eugenian families as still struggled with desperation against the ascendancy of the O'Briens. With these forces he encountered, at Moanmore, the army of the south, and defeated them, with the enormous loss of 7,000 men—a slaughter unparalleled throughout the war of succession. Every leading house in North Munster mourned the loss of either its chief or its tanist; some great families lost three, five, or seven brothers on that sanguinary day. The household of Kinkora was left without an heir, and many a near kinsman's seat was vacant in its hospitable hall. The O'Brien himself was banished into Ulster, where, from Murkertach, Prince of Aileach, he received the hospitality due to his rank and his misfortunes, not without an ulterior politic view on the part of the Ulster Prince. In this battle of Moanmore, Dermid McMurrogh, King of Leinster, of whom we shall hear hereafter, fought gallantly on the side of the victor. In the same year,—but whether before or after the Munster campaign is uncertain—an Ulster force having marched into Sligo, Thorlogh met them near the Curlew mountains, and made peace with their king. A still more important interview took place the next year in the plain, or *Moy*, between the rivers Erne and Drowse, near the present Ballyshannon. On the *Bacchal-Isa* and the relics of Columbkill, Thorlogh and Murkertach made a solemn peace, which is thought to have included the recognition of O'Conor's supremacy. A third meeting was had during the summer in Meath, where were present, beside the Ard-Righ, the Prince of Aileach, Dermid of Leinster, and other chiefs and nobles. At this conference they divided Meath into east and west, between two branches of the family of Melaghlin. Part of Longford and South Leitrim were taken from Tiernan O'Ruarc, lord of Breffni, and an angle of Meath, including Athboy and the hill of Ward, was given him instead. Earlier in the same year, King Thorlogh had divided Munster into three parts, giving Desmond to MacCarthy, Ormond to Thaddeus O'Brien, who had fought under him at Moanmore, and leaving the remainder to the O'Brien, who had only two short years before competed with him for the sovereignty. By these subdivisions the politic monarch expected to weaken to a great degree the power of the rival families of Meath and Munster. It was an arbitrary policy which could originate only on the field of battle, and could be enforced only by the sanction of victory. Thorlogh O'Brien, once King of all Munster, refused to accept a mere third, and carrying away his jewels and valuables, including the drinking horn of the great Brian, he threw himself again on the protection of Murkertach of Aileach. The elder branch of the family of O'Melaghlin were equally indisposed to accept half of Meath, where they had claimed the whole from the Shannon to the sea. To complicate still more this tangled web, Dermid, King of Leinster, about the same time, (A. D. 1153,) eloped with Dervorgoil, wife of O'Ruarc of Breffni, and daughter of O'Melaghlin, who both appealed to the monarch for vengeance on the ravager. Up to this date Dermid had acted as the steadfast ally of O'Conor, but when compelled by the presence of a powerful force on his borders to restore the captive, or partner of his guilt, he conceived an enmity for the aged king which he extended, with increased virulence, to his son and successor.

What degree of personal criminality to attach to this elopement it is hard to say. The cavalier in the case was on the wintry side of fifty, while the lady had reached the mature age of forty-four. Such examples have been, where the passions of youth, surviving the period most subject to their influence, have broken out with renewed frenzy on the confines of old age. Whether the flight of Dermid and Dervorgoil arose from a mere criminal passion, is not laid down with certainty in the old Annals, though national and local tradition strongly point to that conclusion. The Four Masters indeed state that after the restoration of the lady she "returned to O'Ruarc," another point wanting confirmation. We know that she soon afterwards retired to the shelter of Mellifont Abbey, where she ended her days towards the close of the century, in penitence and alms-deeds.

Murtogh of Aileach now became master of the situation. Thorlogh was old and could not last long; Dermid of Leinster was forever estranged from him; the new arbitrary divisions, though made with the general consent, satisfied no one. With a powerful force he marched southward, restored to the elder branch of the O'Melaghlins the whole of Meath, defeated Thaddeus O'Brien, obliterated Ormond from the map, restored the old bounds of Thomond and Desmond, and placed his guest, the banished O'Brien, on the throne of Cashel. A hostile force, under Roderick O'Conor, was routed, and retreated to their own territory. The next year (A. D. 1154) was signalized by a fierce naval engagement between the galleys of King Thorlogh and those of Murtogh, on the coast of Innishowen. The latter, recruited by vessels hired from the Gael and Galls of Cantire, the Arran isles, and Man, were under the command of MacScellig; the Connaught fleet was led by O'Malley and O'Dowda. The engagement, which lasted from the morning till the evening, ended in the repulse of the Connaught fleet, and the death of O'Dowda. The occurrence is remarkable as the first general sea-fight between vessels in the service of native Princes, and as reminding us forcibly of the lessons acquired by the Irish during the Danish period.

During the two years of life which remained to King Thorlogh O'Conor, he had the affliction of seeing the fabric of power, which had taken him nearly half a century to construct, abridged at many points, by his more vigorous northern rival. Murtogh gave law to territories far south of the ancient *esker*. He took hostages from the Danes of Dublin, and interposed in the affairs of Munster. In the year 1156, the closing incidents which signalized the life of Thorlogh More, was a new peace which he made between the people of Breffni, Meath, and Connaught, and the reception of hostages from his old opponent, the restored O'Brien. While this new light of prosperity was shining on his house, he passed away from this life, on the 13th of the Kalends of June, in the 68th year of his age, and the 50th of his government. By his last will he bequeathed to the clergy numerous legacies, which are thus enumerated by Geoffrey Keating: "namely, four hundred and forty ounces of gold, and forty marks of silver; and all the other valuable treasures he possessed, both cups and precious stones, both steeds and cattle and robes, chess-boards, bows, quivers, arrows, equipments, weapons, armor, and utensils." He was interred beside the high altar of the Cathedral of Clonmacnoise, to which he had been in life and in death a munificent benefactor.

The Prince of Aileach now assumed the title of Monarch, and after some short-lived opposition from Roderick O'Conor, his sovereignty was universally acknowledged. From the year 1161 until his death, he might fairly be called Ard-Righ, without opposition, since the hostages of all Ireland were in those last five years in his hands. These hostages were retained at the chief seat of power of the northern dynasty, the fortress of Aileach, which crowns a hill nearly a thousand feet high, at the head of Lough Swilly. To this stronghold the ancestor of Murtogh had removed early in the Danish period, from the more exposed and more ancient Emania, beside Armagh. On that hill-summit the ruins of Aileach may still be traced with its inner wall twelve feet thick, and its three concentric ramparts, the first enclosing one acre, the second four, and the last five acres. By what remains we can still judge of the strength of the stronghold which watched over the waters of Lough Swilly like a sentinel on an outpost. No Prince of the Northern Hy-Nial had for two centuries entered Aileach in such triumph or with so many nobles in his train, as did Murtogh in the year 1161. But whether the supreme power wrought a change for the worse in his early character, or that the lords of Ulster had begun to consider the line of Conn as equals rather than sovereigns, he was soon involved in quarrels with his own Provincial suffragans which ended in his defeat and death. Most other kings of whom we have read found their difficulties in rival dynasties and provincial prejudices; but this ruler, when most freely acknowledged abroad, was disobeyed and defeated at home. Having taken prisoner the lord of Ulidia (Down), with whom he had previously made a solemn peace, he ordered his eyes to be put out, and three of his principal relatives to be executed. This and other arbitrary acts so roused the lords of Leath Conn, that they formed a league against him, at the head of which stood Donogh O'Carroll, lord of Oriel, the next neighbor to the cruelly ill-treated chief of Ulidia. In the year 1166, this chief, with certain tribes of Tyrone and North Leitrim, to the number of three battalions, (9,000 men,) attacked the patrimony of the monarch—that last menace and disgrace to an Irish king. Murtogh with his usual valor, but not his usual fortune, encountered them in the district of the Fews, with an inferior force, chiefly his own tribesmen. Even these deserted him on the eve of the battle, so that he was easily surprised and slain, only thirteen men falling in the affray. This action, of course, is unworthy the name of a battle, but resulting in the death of the monarch, it became of high political importance.

Roderick O'Conor, son of Thorlogh More, was at this period in the tenth year of his reign over Connaught, and the fiftieth year of his age. Rathcrogan, the chief seat of his jurisdiction, had just attained to the summit of its glory. The site of this now almost forgotten palace is traceable in the parish of Elphin, within three miles of the modern village of Tulsk. Many objects contributed to its interest and importance in Milesian times. There were the *Naasteaghna*, or place of assembly of the clans of Connaught, "the Sacred Cave," which in the Druidic era was supposed to be the residence of a god, and the *Relig na Righ* —the venerable cemetery of the Pagan kings of the West, where still the red pillar stone stood over the grave of Dathy, and many another ancient tomb could be as clearly distinguished. The relative importance of Rathcrogan we may estimate by the more detailed descriptions of the extent and income of its rivals— Kincorra and Aileach. In an age when Roscommon alone contained 470 fortified *duns*, over all which the royal rath presided; when half the tributes of the island were counted at its gate, it must have been the frequent *rendezvous* of armies, the home of many guests, the busy focus of intrigue, and the very elysium of bards, story-tellers, and mendicants. In an after generation, Cathal, the red-handed O'Conor, from some motive of policy or pleasure, transferred the seat of government to the newly-founded Ballintober: in the lifetime of Thorlogh More, and the first years of Roderick, when the fortunes of the O'Conors were at their full, Rathcrogan was the coequal in strength and in splendor of Aileach and Kincorra.

Advancing directly from this family seat, on the first tidings of Murtogh's death, Roderick presented himself before the walls of Dublin, which opened its gates, accepted his stipend of four thousand head of cattle, and placed hostages for its fidelity in his hands. He next marched rapidly to Drogheda, with an auxiliary force of Dublin Danes, and there O'Carroll, lord of Oriel (Louth), came into his camp, and rendered him homage. Retracing his steps he entered Leinster, with an augmented force, and demanded hostages from Dermid McMurrogh. Thirteen years had passed since his father had taken up arms to avenge the rape of Dervorgoil, and had earned the deadly hatred of the abductor. That hatred, in the interim, had suffered no decrease, and sooner than submit to Roderick, the ravager, burned his own city of Ferns to the ground, and retreated into his fastnesses. Roderick proceeded southward, obtained the adhesion of Ossory and Munster; confirming Desmond to McCarthy, and Thomond to O'Brien. Returning to Leinster, he found that Tiernan O'Ruarc had entered the province, at the head of an auxiliary army, and Dermid, thus surrounded, deserted by most of his own followers, outwitted and overmatched, was feign to seek safety in flight beyond seas (A. D. 1168). A solemn sentence of banishment was publicly pronounced against him by the assembled Princes, and Morrogh, his cousin, commonly called Morrogh *na Gael*, or "of the Irish," to distinguish him from Dermid *na Gall*, or "of the Stranger," was inaugurated in his stead. From Morrogh *na Gael* they took seventeen hostages, and so Roderick returned rejoicing to Rathcrogan, and O'Ruarc to Breffni, each vainly imagining that he had heard the last of the dissolute and detested King of Leinster.

CHAPTER IV.

STATE OF RELIGION AND LEARNING AMONG THE IRISH, PREVIOUS TO THE ANGLO-NORMAN INVASION.

At the end of the eighth century, before entering on the Norwegian and Danish wars, we cast a backward glance on the Christian ages over which we had passed; and now again we have arrived at the close of an era, when a rapid retrospect of the religious and social condition of the country requires to be taken.

The disorganization of the ancient Celtic constitution has already been sufficiently described. The rise of the great families and their struggles for supremacy have also been briefly sketched. The substitution of the clan for the race, of pedigree for patriotism, has been exhibited to the reader. We have now to turn to the inner life of the people, and to ascertain what substitutes they found in their religious and social condition, for the absence of a fixed constitutional system, and the strength and stability which such a system confers.

The followers of Odin, though they made no proselytes to their horrid creed among the children of St. Patrick, succeeded in inflicting many fatal wounds on the Irish Church. The schools, monasteries, and nunneries, situated on harbors or rivers, or within a convenient march of the coast, were their first objects of attack; teachers and pupils were dispersed, or, if taken, put to death, or, escaping, were driven to resort to arms in self-defence. Bishops could no longer reside in their sees, nor anchorites in their cells, unless they invited martyrdom; a fact which may, perhaps, in some degree, account for the large number of Irish ecclesiastics, many of them in episcopal orders, who are found, in the ninth century, in Gaul and Germany, at Rheims, Mentz, Ratisbon, Fulda, Cologne, and other places, already Christian. But it was not in the banishment of masters, the destruction of libraries and school buildings, the worst consequences of the Gentile war were felt. Their ferocity provoked retaliation in kind, and effaced, first among the military class, and gradually from among all others, that growing gentleness of manners and clemency of temper, which we can trace in such princes as Nial of the Showers and Nial of Callan. "A change in the national spirit is the greatest of all revolutions;" and this change the Danish and Norwegian wars had wrought, in two centuries, among the Irish.

The number of Bishops in the early Irish Church was greatly in excess of the number of modern dioceses. From the eighth to the twelfth century we hear frequently of *Episcopi Vagantes*, or itinerant, and *Episcopi Vacantes*, or unbeneficed Bishops; the Provincial Synods of England and France frequently had to complain of the influx of such Bishops into their country. At the Synod held near the Hill of Usny, in the year 1111, fifty Bishops attended, and at the Synod of Rath-Brazil, seven years later, according to Keating, but twenty-five were present. To this period, then, when Celsus was Primate and Legate of the Holy See, we may attribute the first attempted reduction of the Episcopal body to something like its modern number, but so far was this salutary restriction from being universally observed that, at the Synod of Kells (A. D. 1152), the hierarchy had again risen to thirty-four, exclusive of the four Archbishops. Three hundred priests, and three thousand ecclesiastics are given as the number present at the first-mentioned Synod.

The religious orders, probably represented by the above proportion of three thousand ecclesiastics to three hundred [secular] priests had also undergone a remarkable revolution. The rule of all the early Irish monasteries and convents was framed upon an original constitution, which St. Patrick had obtained in France from St. Martin of Tours, who in turn had copied after the monachism of Egypt and the East. It is called by ecclesiastical writers the Columban rule, and was more rigid in some particulars than the rule of St. Benedict, by which it was afterwards supplanted. Amongst other restrictions it prohibited the admission of all unprofessed persons within the precincts of the monastery—a law as regards females incorporated in the Benedictine Constitution; and it strictly enjoined silence on the professed—a discipline revived by the brethren of La Trappe. The primary difference between the two orders lay perhaps in this, that the Benedictine made study and the cultivation of the intellect subordinate to manual labor and implicit obedience, while the Columban Order attached more importance to the acquisition of knowledge and missionary enterprize. Not that this was their invariable, but only their peculiar characteristic: a deep-seated love of seclusion and meditation often intermingled with this fearless and experimental zeal. It was not to be expected in a century like the ninth, especially when the Benedictine Order was overspreading the West, that its milder spirit should not act upon the spirit of the Columban rule. It was, in effect, more social, and less scientific, more a wisdom to be acted than to be taught. Armed with the syllogism, the Columbites issued out of their remote island, carrying their strongly marked personality into every controversy and every correspondence. In Germany and Gaul, their system blazed up in Virgilius, in Erigena, and Macarius, and then disappeared in the calmer, slower, but safer march of the Benedictine discipline. By a reform of the same ancient order, its last hold on native soil was loosened when, under the auspices of St. Malachy, the Cistercian rule was introduced into Ireland the very year of his first visit to Clairvaux (A. D. 1139). St. Mary's Abbey, Dublin, was the first to adopt that rule, and the great monastery of Mellifont, placed under the charge of the brother of the Primate, sprung up in Meath three years later. The Abbeys of Bective, Boyle, Baltinglass, and Monasternenagh, date from the year of Malachy's second journey to Rome, and death at Clairvaux—A. D. 1148. Before the end of the century the rule was established at Fermoy, Holycross, and Odorney; at Athlone and Knockmoy; at Newry and Assaroe, and in almost every tribe-land of Meath and Leinster. It is usually, but erroneously supposed that the Cistercian rule came in with the Normans; for although many houses owed their foundation to that race, the order itself had been naturalized in Ireland a generation before the first landing of the formidable allies of Dermid on the coast of Wexford. The ancient native order had apparently fulfilled its mission, and long rudely lopped and shaken by civil commotions and Pagan war, it was prepared to give place to a new and more vigorous organization of kindred holiness and energy.

As the horrors of war disturbed continually the clergy from their sacred calling, and led many of them, even Abbots and Bishops, to take up arms, so the yoke of religion gradually loosened and dropped from the necks of the people. The awe of the eighth century for a Priest or Bishop had already disappeared in the tenth, when Christian hands were found to decapitate Cormac of Cashel, and offer his head as a trophy to the Ard-Righ. In the twelfth century the Archbishop and Bishops of Connaught, bound to the Synod of Trim, were fallen upon by the Kern of Carbre the Swift, before they could cross the Shannon, their people beaten and dispersed and two of them killed. In the time of Thorlogh More O'Conor, a similar outrage was offered by Tiernan O'Ruarc to the Archbishop of Armagh, and one of his ecclesiastics was killed in the assault. Not only for the persons of ministers of religion had the ancient awe and reverence disappeared, but even for the sacred precincts of the Sanctuary. In the second century of the war with the Northmen we begin to hear of churches and cloisters plundered by native chiefs, who yet called themselves Christians, though in every such instance our annalists are careful to record the vengeance of Heaven following swift on sacrilege. Clonmacnoise, Kildare, and Lismore, were more than once rifled of their wealth by impious hands, and given over to desolation and burning by so-called Christian nobles and soldiers! It is some mitigation of the dreadful record thus presented to be informed—as we often are—especially in the annals of the twelfth century, that the treasures so pillaged were not the shrines of saints nor the sacred ornaments of the altar, but the temporal wealth of temporal proprietors, laid up in churches as places of greatest security.

The estates of the Church were, in most instances, farmed by laymen, called *Erenachs*, who, in the relaxation of all discipline, seem to have gradually appropriated the lands to themselves, leaving to the Clergy and Bishops only periodical dues and the actual enclosure of the Church. This office of Erenach was hereditary, and must have presented many strong temptations to its occupants. It is indeed certain that the Irish Church was originally founded on the broadest voluntaryism, and that such was the spirit of all its most illustrious fathers. "Content with food and raiment," says an ancient Canon attributed to St. Patrick, "reject the gifts of the wicked beside, seeing that the lamp takes only that with which it is fed." Such, to the letter, was the maxim which guided the conduct of Colman and his brethren, of whom Bede makes such honorable mention, in the third century after the preaching of St. Patrick. But the munificence of tribes and Princes was not to be restrained, and to obviate any violation of the revered canons of the apostle, laymen, as treasurers and stewards over the endowments of the Church, were early appointed. As those possessions increased, the desire of family aggrandizement proved too much for the Erenachs not only of Armagh, but of most other sees, and left the clergy as practically dependent on free-will offerings, as if their Cathedrals or Convents had never been endowed with an acre, a mill, a ferry, or a fishery. The free offerings were, however, always generous and sometimes munificent. When Celsus, on his elevation to the Primacy, made a tour of the southern half-kingdom, he received "seven cows and seven sheep, and half an ounce of silver from every cantred [hundred] in Munster." The bequests were also a fruitful source of revenue to the principal foundations; of the munificence of the monarchs we may form some opinion by what has been already recorded of the gifts left to churches by Thorlogh More O'Conor.

The power of the clerical order, in these ages of Pagan warfare, had very far declined from what it was, when Adamnan caused the law to be enacted to prevent women going to battle, when Moling obtained the abolition of the Leinster tribute, and Columbkill the recognition of Scottish independence. Truces made in the presence of the highest dignitaries, and sworn to on the most sacred relics, were frequently violated, and often with impunity. Neither excommunication nor public penance were latterly inflicted as an atonement for such perjury: a fine or offering to the Church was the easy and only mulct on the offender. When we see the safeguard of the Bishop of Cork so flagrantly disregarded by the assassins of Mahon, son of Kennedy, and the solemn peace of the year 1094 so readily broken by two such men as the Princes of the North and the South, we need no other proofs of the decadence of the spiritual authority in that age of Irish history.

And the morals of private life tell the same sad tale. The facility with which the marriage tie was contracted and dissolved is the strongest evidence of this degeneracy. The worst examples were set in the highest stations, for it is no uncommon incident, from the ninth century downwards, to find our Princes with more than one wife living, and the repudiated wife married again to a person of equal or superior rank. We have the authority of Saint Anselm and Saint Bernard, for the existence of grave scandal and irregularities of life among the clergy and we can well believe that it needed a generation of Bishops, with all the authority and all the courage of Saint Celsus, Saint Malachy, and Saint Lawrence, to rescue from ruin a Priesthood and a people, so far fallen from the bright example of their ancestors. That the reaction towards a better life had strongly set in, under their guidance, we may infer from the horror with which, in the third quarter of the twelfth century, the elopement of Dermid and Dervorgoil was regarded by both Princes and People. A hundred years earlier, that event would have been hardly noticed in the general disregard of the marriage tie, but the frequent Synods, and the holy lives of the reforming Bishops, had already revived the zeal that precedes and ensures reformation.

Primate Malachy died at Clairvaulx, in the arms of Saint Bernard, in the year 1148, after having been fourteen years Archbishop of Armagh and ten years Bishop of Down and Connor. His episcopal life, therefore, embraced the history of that remarkable second quarter of the century, in which the religious reaction fought its first battles against the worst abuses. The attention of Saint Bernard, whose eyes nothing escaped, from Jerusalem to the farthest west, was drawn ten years before to the Isle of Saints, now, in truth, become an Isle of Sinners. The death of his friend, the Irish Primate, under his own roof, gave him a fitting occasion for raising his accusing voice—a voice that thrilled the Alps and filled the Vatican—against the fearful degeneracy of that once fruitful mother of holy men and women. The attention of Rome was thoroughly aroused, and immediately after the appearance of the Life of Saint Malachy, Pope Eugenius III.—himself a monk of Clairvaulx—despatched Cardinal Papiron, with legantine powers, to correct abuses, and establish a stricter discipline. After a tour of great part of the Island, the Legate, with whom was associated Gilla-Criost, or Christianus, Bishop of Lismore, called the great Synod of Kells, early in the year after his arrival (March, 1152), at which simony, usury, concubinage, and other abuses, were formally condemned, and tythes were first decreed to be paid to the secular clergy. Two new Archbishoprics, Dublin and Tuam, were added to Armagh and Cashel, though not without decided opposition from the Primates, both of Leath Mogha and Leath Conn, backed by those stern conservatives of every national usage, the Abbots of the Columban Order. The *pallium*, or Roman cape, was, by this Legate, presented to each of the Archbishops, and a closer conformity with the Roman ritual was enacted. The four ecclesiastical Provinces thus created were in outline nearly identical with the four modern Provinces. Armagh was declared the metropolitan over all; Dublin, which had been a mere Danish borough-see, gained most in rank and influence by the new arrangement, as Glendalough, Ferns, Ossory, Kildare and Leighlin, were declared subject to its presidency.

We must always bear in mind the picture drawn of the Irish Church by the inspired orator of Clairvaulx, when judging of the conduct of Pope Adrian IV., who, in the year 1155—the second of his Pontificate—granted to King Henry II. of England, then newly crowned, his Bull, authorizing the invasion of Ireland. The authenticity of that Bull is now universally admitted; and both its preamble and conditions show how strictly it was framed in accordance with St. Bernard's accusation. It sets forth that for the eradication of vice, the implanting of virtue and the spread of the true faith, the Holy Father solemnly sanctions the projected invasion; and it attaches as a condition, the payment of Peter's pence, for every house in Ireland. The bearer of the Bull, John of Salisbury, carried back from Rome a gold ring, set with an emerald stone, as a token of Adrian's friendship, or it may be, his subinfeudation of Henry. As a title, however powerless in modern times such a Bull might prove, it was a formidable weapon of invasion with a Catholic people, in the twelfth century. We have mainly referred to it here, however, as an illustration of how entirely St. Bernard's impeachment of the Irish Church and nation was believed at Rome, even after the salutary decrees of the Synod of Kells had been promulgated.

The restoration of religion which was making such rapid progress previous to the Norman invasion, was accompanied by a relative revival of learning. The dark ages of Ireland are not those of the rest of Europe—they extend from the middle of the ninth century to the age of Brian and Malachy II. This darkness came from the North, and cleared away rapidly after the eventful day of Clontarf. The first and most natural direction which the revival took was historical investigation, and the composition of Annals. Of these invaluable records, the two of highest reputation are those of Tigernach (Tiernan) O'Broin, brought down to the year of his own death, A. D. 1088, and the chronicle of Marianus Scotus, who died at Mentz, A. D. 1086. Tiernan was abbott of Clonmacnoise, and Marian is thought to have been a monk of that monastery, as he speaks of a superior called Tigernach, under whom he had lived in Ireland. Both these learned men quote accurately the works of foreign writers; both give the dates of eclipses, in connection with historical events for several centuries before their own time; both show a familiarity with Greek and Latin authors. *Marianus* is the first writer by whom the name *Scotia Minor* was given to the Gaelic settlement in Caledonia, and his chronicle was an authority mainly relied on in the disputed Scottish succession in the time of Edward I. of England. With *Tigernach*, he may be considered the founder of the school of Irish Annalists, which flourished in the shelter of the great monasteries, such as Innisfallen, Boyle and Multifernan; and culminated in the great compilation made by " the Four Masters" in the Abbey of Donegal.

Of the Gaelic metrical chroniclers, Flann of the Monastery, and Gilla-Coeman ; of the Bards McLiag and McCoisse; of the learned professors and lectors of Lismore and Armagh—now restored for a season to studious days and peaceful nights, we must be content with the mention of their names. Of Lismore, after its restoration, an old British writer has left us this pleasant and happy picture. "It is," he says, "a famous and holy city, half of which is an asylum, into which no woman dares enter; but it is full of cells and monasteries; and religious men in great abundance abide there."

Such was the promise of better days, which cheered the hopes of the Pastors of the Irish, when the twelfth century had entered on its third quarter. The pious old Gaelic proverb, which says, "on the Cross the face of Christ was looking westwards ——," was again on the lips and in the hearts of men, and though much remained to be done, much had been already done, and done under difficulties greater than any that remained to conquer.

CHAPTER V.

SOCIAL CONDITION OF THE IRISH PREVIOUS TO THE NORMAN INVASION.

THE total population of Ireland, when the Normans first entered it, can only be approximated by conjecture. Supposing the whole force with which Roderick and his allies invested the Normans in Dublin, to be, as stated by a cotemporary writer, some 50,000 men, and that that force included one-fourth of all the men of the military age in the country; and further supposing the men of military age to bear the proportion of one-fifth to the whole number of inhabitants, this would give a total population of about one million. Even this conjecture is to be taken with great diffidence and distrust, but, for the sake of clearness, it is set down as a possible Irish census, towards the close of the twelfth century.

This population was divided into two great classes, the *Saer-Clanna*, or free tribes, chiefly, if not exclusively, of Milesian race; and the *Daer-Clanna*, or unfree tribes, consisting of the descendants of the subjugated older races, or of clans once free, reduced to servitude by the sword, or of the posterity of foreign mercenary soldiers. Of the free clans, the most illustrious were those of whose Princes we have traced the record—the descendants of Nial in Ulster and Meath, of Cathaeir More in Leinster, of Oliold in Munster, and of Eochaid in Connaught. An arbitrary division once limited the free clans to six in the southern half-kingdom, and six in the north; and the unfree also to six. But Geoffrey Keating, whose love of truth was quite as strong as his credulity in ancient legends—and that is saying much—disclaimed that classification, and collected his genealogies from principal heads—branching out into three families of tribes, descended from Heber Finn, one from Ir, and four from Heremhon, sons of Milesians of Spain; and a ninth tribe sprung from Ith, granduncle to the sons of Milesius. The principal Heberian families' names were McCarthy, O'Sullivan, O'Mahony, O'Donovan, O'Brien, O'Dea, O'Quin, McMahon (of Clare), McNamara, O'Carroll (of Ely), and O'Gara; the Irian families were Magennis, O'Farrall, and O'Conor (of Kerry); the posterity of Heremhon branched out into the O'Neils, O'Donnells, O'Doherty's O'Gallahers, O'Boyles, McGeoghegans, O Conors (of Connaught), O'Flahertys, O'Heynes, O'Shaughnessys, O'Clerys, O'Dowdas, McDonalds (of Antrim), O'Kellys, Maguires, Kavanaghs, Fitzpatricks, O'Dwyers, and O'Conors (of Offally). The chief families of Ithian origin were the O'Driscolls, O'Learys, Coffeys, and Clancys. Out of the greater tribes many subdivisions arose from time to time, when new names were coined from some intermediate ancestor; but the farther enumeration of these may be conveniently dispensed with.

The *Daer-Clanna*, or unfree tribes, have left no history. Under the despotism of the Milesian kings it was high treason to record the actions of the conquered race; so that the Irish Belgæ fared as badly in this respect, at the hands of the Milesian historians, as the latter fared in after times from the chroniclers of the Normans. We only know that such tribes were, and that their numbers and physical force more than once excited the apprehension of the children of the conquerors. What proportion they bore to the *Saer-Clanna* we have no positive data to determine. A fourth, a fifth, or a sixth, they may have been; but one thing is certain, the jealous policy of the superior race never permitted them to reascend the plane of equality, from which they had been hurled, at the very commencement of the Milesian ascendancy.

In addition to the enslaved by conquest and the enslaved from crime, there were also the enslaved by purchase. From the earliest period, slave dealers from Ireland had frequented Bristol, the great British slave market, to purchase human beings. Christian morality, though it may have mitigated the horrors of this odious traffic, did not at once lead to its abolition. In vain Saint Wulfstan preached against it in the South, as Saint Aidan had done long before in the North of England. Files of fair-haired Saxon slaves, of both sexes, yoked together with ropes, continued to be shipped at Bristol, and bondmen and bondwomen continued to be articles of value—exchanged between the Prince and his subordinates, as stipend or tribute. The King of Cashel alone gave to the chief of the Eugenians, as part of his annual stipend, ten bondmen and ten women; to the lord of Bruree, seven pages and seven bondwomen; to the lord of the Deisi, eight slaves of each sex, and seven female slaves to the lord of Kerry; among the items which make up the tribute from Ossory to Cashel are ten bondmen and ten grown women; and from the Deisi, eight bondmen and eight "brown-haired" women. The annual exchanges of this description, set down as due in the Book of Rights, would require the transfer of several hundreds of slaves yearly, from one set of masters to another. Cruelties and outrages must have been inseparable from the system, and we can hardly wonder at the sweeping decree by which the Synod of Armagh (A. D. 1171) declared all the English slaves in Ireland free to return to their homes, and anathematized the whole inhuman traffic. The fathers of that council looked upon the Norman invasion as a punishment from Heaven on the slave trade; for they believed in their purity of heart, that power *is* transferred from one nation to another, because of injustices, oppressions, and divers deceits.

The purchased slaves and unfree tribes tilled the soil, and practised the mechanic arts. Agriculture seems first to have been lifted into respectability by the Columban Monks, while spinning, weaving, and almost every mechanic calling, if we except the scribe, the armorer, and the bell-founder, continued down to very recent times to be held in contempt among the Gael. A brave man is mentioned as having been a "weaving woman's son," with much the same emphasis as Jeptha is spoken of as the son of an Harlot. Mechanic wares were disposed of at those stated gatherings, which combined popular games, chariot races for the nobles, and markets for the merchants. A Bard of the tenth or eleventh century, in a desperate effort to vary the usual high-flown descriptions of the country, calls it "Erin of the hundred fair greens,"—a very graphic, if not a very poetic illustration.

The administration of justice was an hereditary trust, committed to certain judicial families, who held their lands, as the Monks did, by virtue of their profession. When the posterity of the Brehon, or Judge, failed, it was permitted to adopt from the class of students, a male representative, in whom the judicial authority was perpetuated: the families of O'Gnive and O'Clery in the North, of O Daly in Meath, O'Doran in Leinster, McEgan in Munster, Mulconry or Conroy in Connaught, were the most distinguished Brehon houses. Some peculiarities of the Brehon law, relating to civil succession and sovereignty, such as the institution of Tanistry, and the system of stipends and tributes, have been already explained; parricide and murder were in latter ages punished with death; homicide and rape by *eric* or fine. There were besides the laws of gavel-kind or division of property among the members of the clan; laws relating to boundaries; sumptuary laws regulating the dress of the various castes into which society was divided; laws relating to the planting of trees, the trespass of cattle, and billeting of troops. These laws were either written in detail, or consisted of certain acknowledged ancient maxims of which the Brehon made the application in each particular case, answering to what we call "Judge-made law." Of such ancient tracts as composed the Celtic code, an immense number have fortunately survived, even to this late day, and we may shortly expect a complete digest of all that are now known to exist, in a printed and imperishable form, from the hands of native scholars, every way competent to the task.

The commerce of the country, in the eleventh and twelfth centuries, was largely in the hands of the Christian Hiberno-Danes, of the eastern and southern coast. By them the slave trade with Bristol was mostly maintained, and the Irish oak, with which William Rufus roofed Westminster Abbey, was probably rafted by them in the Thames. The English and Welsh coasts, at least, were familiar to their pilots, and they combined, as was usual in that age, the military with the mercantile character. In 1142, and again in 1165, a troop of Dublin Danes fought under Norman banners against the brave Britons of Cambria, and in the camps of their allies sung the praises of the fertile island of the west. The hundred fairs of Erin—after their conversion and submission to native authority—afforded them convenient markets for disposing of the commodities they imported from abroad.

The Gaelic mind, long distracted by the din of war from the purifying and satisfying influences of a Christian life, naturally fell back upon the abandoned, half-forgotten superstitions of the Pagan period. Preceding every fresh calamity we hear of signs and wonders, of migratory lakes disappearing in a night, of birds and wolves speaking with human voices, of showers of blood falling in the fields, of a whale with golden teeth stranded at Carlingford, of cloud ships, with their crews, seen plainly sailing in the sky. One of the marvels of this class is thus gravely entered in our Annals, under the year 1054—" A steeple of fire was seen in the air over Rossdala, on the Sunday of the festival of St. George, for the space of five hours; innumerable black birds passed into and out of it, and one large bird in the middle of them; and the little birds went under his wings when they went into the steeple. They came out and raised up a greyhound that was in the middle of the town aloft in the air, and let it drop down again, so that it died immediately; and they took up three cloaks and two shirts, and let them drop down in the same manner. The wood on which these birds perched fell under them; and the oak tree on which they perched shook with its roots in the earth." In many other superstitions of the same age we see the latent moral sentiment, as well as the over-excited imagination of the people. Such is the story of the stolen jewels of Clonmacnoise, providentially recovered in the year 1130. The thief in vain endeavored to escape out of the country, from Cork,

Lismore, and Waterford, "but no ship into which he entered found a wind to sail, while all the other ships did." And the conscience striken thief declared, in his dying confession, that he used to see Saint Kieran "stopping, with his crozier, every ship into which he entered." It was also an amiable popular illusion that abundant harvests followed the making of peace, the enacting of salutary laws, and the accession of a King who loved justice; and careful entry is made in our chronicles of every evidence of this character.

The literature of the masses of the people was pretty equally composed of the legends of the Saints and the older Ossianic legend, so much misunderstood and distorted by modern criticism. The legends of the former class were chiefly wonders wrought by the favorite Saints of the district or the island, embellished with many quaint fancies and tagged out with remnants of old Pagan superstition. St. Columbkill and St. Kieran were, most commonly, the heroes of those tales, which, perhaps, were never intended by their authors to be seriously believed. Such was the story of the great founder of Iona having transformed the lady and her maid, who insulted him on his way to Drom-Keth, into two herons, who are doomed to hover about the neighboring ford till the day of doom; and such that other story of "the three first monks" who joined St. Kieran in the desert, being a fox, a badger, and a bear, all endowed with speech, and all acting a part in the legend true to their own instincts. Of higher poetic merit is the legend of the voyage of St. Brendan over the great sea, and how the birds which sung vespers for him in the groves of the Promised Land were inhabited by human souls, as yet in a state of probation waiting for their release!

In the Ossianic legend we have the common stock of Oriental ideas—the metamorphosis of guilty wives and haughty concubines into dogs and birds; the speaking beasts and fishes; the enchanted swans, originally daughters of Lir; the boar of Ben Bulben, by which the champion, Diarmid, was slain; the Phœnix in the stork of Inniskea, of which there never was but one, yet that one perpetually reproduced itself; the spirits of the wood, and the spirits inhabiting springs and streams; the fairy horse; the sacred trees; the starry influences. Monstrous and gigantic human shapes, like the Jinns of the Arabian tales, occasionally enter into the plot and play a midnight part, malignant to the hopes of good men. At their approach the earth is troubled, the moon is overcast, gusts of storm are shaken out from the folds of their garments, the watch dogs and the war dogs cower down, in camp and rath, and whine piteously, as if in pain.

The variety of grace, and peculiarities of organization, with which, if not the original, certainly the Christianized Irish imagination, endowed and equipped the personages of the fairy world, were of almost Grecian delicacy. There is no personage who rises to the sublime height of Zeus, or the incomparable union of beauty and wisdom in Pallas Athene: what forms Bel, or Crom, or Bride, the queen of Celtic song, may have worn to the pre-Christian ages we know not, nor can know; but the minor creations of Grecian fancy, with which they peopled their groves and fountains, are true kindred of the brain, to the innocent, intelligent, and generally gentle inhabitants of the Gaelic Fairyland. The *Sidhe*, a tender, tutelary spirit, attached herself to heroes, accompanied them in battle, shrouded them with invisibility, dressed their wounds with more than mortal skill, and watched over them with more than mortal love; the *Banshee*, a sad, Cassandra-like spirit, shrieked her weird warning in advance of death, but with a prejudice eminently Milesian, watched only over those of pure blood, whether their fortunes abode in hovel or hall. The more modern and grotesque personages of the Fairy world are sufficiently known to render description unnecessary.

Two habitual sources of social enjoyment and occupation with the Irish of those days were music and chess. The harp was the favorite instrument, but the horn or trumpet, and the pibroch or bagpipe, were also in common use. Not only professional performers, but men and women of all ranks, from the humblest to the highest, prided themselves on some knowledge of instrumental music. It seems to have formed part of the education of every order, and to have been cherished alike in the palace, the shieling, and the cloister. "It is a poor church that has no music," is a Gaelic proverb, as old, perhaps, as the establishment of Christianity in the land; and no house was considered furnished without at least one harp. Students from other countries, as we learn from *Giraldus*, came to Ireland for their musical education in the twelfth century, just as our artists now visit Germany and Italy with the same object in view.

. The frequent mention of the game of chess, in ages long before those at which we have arrived, shows how usual was that most intellectual amusement. The chess board was called in Irish *fithcheall*, and is described in the Glossary of Cormac, of Cashel, composed towards the close of the ninth century, as quadrangular, having straight spots of black and white. Some of them were inlaid with gold and silver, and adorned with gems. Mention is made in a tale of the twelfth century of a " man-bag of woven brass wire." No entire set of the ancient men is now known to exist, though frequent mention is made of " the brigade or family of chessmen," in many old manuscripts. Kings of bone, seated in sculptured chairs, about two inches in height, have been found, and specimens of them engraved in recent antiquarian publications.

It only remains to notice, very briefly, the means of locomotion which bound and brought together this singular state of society. Five great roads, radiating from Tara, as a centre, are mentioned in our earliest record; the road *Dala* leading to Ossory, and so on into Munster; the road *Assail*, extending western through Mullingar towards the Shannon; the road *Cullin*, extending towards Dublin and Bray; the exact route of the northern road, *Midhluachra*, is undetermined; *Slighe Mor*, the great western road, followed the course of the *esker*, or hill-range, from Tara to Galway. Many cross-roads are also known as in common use from the sixth century downwards. Of these, the Four Masters mention, at various dates, not less than forty, under their different local names, previous to the Norman invasion. These roads were kept in repair, according to laws enacted for that purpose, and were traversed by the chiefs and ecclesiastics in *carbads*, or chariots; a main road was called a *slighe* (*sleigh*), because it was made for the free passage of two chariots—"i. e. the chariot of a King and the chariot of a Bishop." Persons of that rank were driven by an *ara*, or charioteer, and, no doubt, made a very imposing figure. The roads were legally to be repaired at three seasons, namely, for the accommodation of those going to the national games, at fair-time, and in time of war. Weeds and brushwood were to be removed, and water to be drained off;. items of road-work which do not give us a very high idea of the comfort or finish of those ancient highways.

Such, faintly seen from afar, and roughly sketched, was domestic life and society among our ancestors, previous to the Anglo-Norman invasion, in the reign of King Roderick O'Conor.

CHAPTER VI.

FOREIGN RELATIONS OF THE IRISH PREVIOUS TO THE ANGLO-NORMAN INVASION.

THE relations of the Irish with other nations, notwithstanding the injurious effects of their War of Succession on national unity and reputation, present several points of interest. After the defeat of Magnus Barefoot, we may drop the Baltic countries out of the map of the relations of Ireland. Commencing, therefore, at the north of the neighboring island—which, in its entirety, they sometimes called *Inismore*—the most intimate and friendly intercourse was always upheld with the kingdom of Scotland. Bound together by early ecclesiastical and bardic ties, confronting together for so many generations a common enemy, those two countries were destined never to know an international quarrel. About the middle of the ninth century (A. D. 843), when the Scoto-Irish in Caledonia had completely subdued the Picts and other ancient tribes, the first national dynasty was founded by Kenneth McAlpine. The constitution given by this Prince to the whole country seems to have been a close copy of the Irish—it embraced the laws of Tanistry and succession, and the whole Brehon code, as administered in the parent state. The line of Kenneth may be said to close with Donald Bane, brother of Malcolm III., who died in 1094, and not only his dynasty but his system ended with that century. Edgar, Alexander I., and David I., all sons of Malcolm III., were educated in England among the victorious Normans, and in the first third of the twelfth century, devoted themselves with the inauspicious aid of Norman allies, to the introduction of Saxon settlers and the feudal system, first into the lowlands, and subsequently into Moray-shire. This innovation on their ancient system, and confiscation of their lands, was stoutly resisted by the Scottish Gael. In Somerled, lord of the isles, and ancestor of the Macdonalds, they found a powerful leader, and Somerled found Irish allies always ready to assist him, in a cause which appealed to all their national prejudices. In the year 1134, he led a strong force of Irish and Islesmen to the assistance of the Gaelic insurgents, but was defeated and slain, near Renfrew, by the royal troops, under the command of the Steward of Scotland. During the reigns of William the Lion, Alexander II., and Alexander III., the war of systems raged with all its fierceness, and in nearly all the great encounters Irish auxiliaries, as was to be expected, were found on the side of the Gaelic race and Gaelic rights. Nor did this contest ever wholly cease in Scotland, until the last hopes of the Stuart line were extinguished on the fatal field of Culloden, where Irish captains formed the battle, and Irish blood flowed freely, intermingled with the kindred blood of Highlanders and Islesmen.

The adoption of Norman usages, laws, and tactics, by the Scottish dynasties of the twelfth and succeeding centuries, did not permanently affect the national relations of Ireland and Scotland. It was otherwise with regard to England. We have every reason to believe—we have the indirect testimony of every writer from Bede to Malmsbury—that the intercourse between the Irish and Saxons, after the first hostility engendered by the cruel treatment of the Britons had worn away, became of the most friendly character. The "Irish" who fought at Brunanburgh against Saxon freedom were evidently the natural allies of the Northmen, the Dano-Irish of Dublin and the southern seaports. The commerce of intelligence between the islands was long maintained; the royalty of Saxon England had more than once, in times of domestic revolution, found a safe and desired retreat in the western island. The fair Elgiva and the gallant Harold had crossed the western waves in their hour of need. The fame of Edward the Confessor took such deep hold on the Irish mind that, three centuries after his death, his banner was unfurled and the royal leopards laid aside to facilitate the march of an English King, through the fastnesses of Leinster. The Irish, therefore, were not likely to look upon the establishment of a Norman dynasty, in lieu of the old Saxon line, as a matter of indifference. They felt that the Norman was but a Dane disguised in armor. It was true he carried the cross upon his banner, and claimed the benediction of the successor of St. Peter; true also he spoke the speech of France, and claimed a French paternity; but the lust for dominion, the iron self-will, the wily devices of strategy, bespoke the Norman of the twelfth, the lineal descendant of the Dane of the tenth century. When, therefore, tidings reached Ireland of the battle of Hastings and the death of Harold, both the apprehensions and the sympathies of the country were deeply excited. Intelligence of the coronation of William the Conqueror quickly followed, and emphatically announced to the Irish the presence of new neighbors, new dangers, and new duties.

The spirit with which our ancestors acted towards the defeated Saxons, whatever we may think of its wisdom, was, at least, respectable for decision and boldness. Godwin, Edmund, and Magnus, sons of Harold, had little difficulty in raising in Ireland a numerous force to co-operate with the Earls Edwin and Morcar, who still upheld the Saxon banner. With this force, wafted over in sixty-six vessels, they entered the Avon, and besieged Bristol, then the second commercial city of the kingdom. But Bristol held out, and the Saxon Earls had fallen back into Northumberland, so the sons of Harold ran down the coast, and tried their luck in Somersetshire with a better prospect. Devonshire and Dorsetshire favored their cause; the old Britons of Cornwall swelled their ranks, and the rising spread like flame over the west. Eadnoth, a renegade Saxon, formerly Harold's Master of Horse, despatched by William against Harold's sons, was defeated and slain. Doubling the Land's End, the victorious force entered the Tamar, and overran South Devon. The united garrisons of London, Winchester, and Salisbury, were sent against them, under the command of the martial Bishop of Coutances; while a second force advanced along the Tamar, under Brian, heir of the Earl of Brittany, who routed them with a loss of 2,000 men, English, Welsh, and Irish. The sons of Harold retreated to their vessels with all their booty, and returned again into Ireland, where they vanish from history. Such, in the vale of Tamar, was the first collision of the Irish and Normans; and as the race of Rolla never forgot an enemy, nor forewent a revenge, we may well believe that, even thus early, the invasion of Ireland was decided upon. Meredith Hanmer relates in his Chronicle that William Rufus, standing on a high rock, and looking towards Ireland, said: "I will bring hither my ships, and pass over and conquer that land;" and on these words of the son of the Conqueror being repeated to Murkertach O'Brien, he replied: "Hath the King in his great threatening said *if it please God;*" and when answered "no," "then," said the Irish monarch, "I fear him not, since he putteth his trust in man and not in God."

Ireland, however, was destined to be reached through Wales, along whose mountain coast we early find Norman castles and Norman ships. It was the special ambition of William Rufus to add the principality to the conquests of his father, and the active sympathy of the Welsh with the Saxons on their inland border gave him pretexts enough. A bitter feud between North and South Wales hastened an invasion, in which Robert Fitz-Aymon and his companions played, by anticipation, the parts of Strongbow and Fitz-Stephen in the invasion of Ireland.

The struggle, commenced under them, was protracted through the reign of Rufus, who led an army in person (A. D. 1095) against the Welsh, but with little gain and less glory. As an afterthought he adopted the device of his father, (followed, too, in Ireland by Henry II.,) of partitioning the country among the most enterprizing nobles, gravely accepting their homage in advance of possession, and authorizing them to maintain troops at their own charges, for making good his grant of what never belonged to him. Robert Fitz-Aymon did homage for Glamorgan, Bernard Newmarch for Brecknock, Roger de Montgomery for Cardigan, and Gilbert de Clare for Pembroke: the best portions of North Wales were partitioned between the Mortimers, Latimers, De Lacys, Fitz-Alans, and Montgomerys. Rhys, Prince of Cambria, with many of his nobles, fell in battle defending bravely his native hills; but Griffith, son of Rhys, escaped into Ireland, from which he returned some twenty years later, and recovered by arms and policy a large share of his ancestral dominions. In the reign of Henry I. (A. D. 1110), a host of Flemings, driven from their own country by an inundation of the sea, were planted upon the Welsh marches, from which they soon swarmed into all the Cambrian glens and glades. The industry and economy of this new people, in peaceful times, seemed almost inconsistent with their stubborn bravery in battle; but they demonstrated to the Welsh, and afterwards to the Irish, that they could handle the halbert as well as throw the shuttle; that men of trade may on occasion prove themselves capable men of war.

The Norman Kings of England were not insensible to the fact that the Cymric element in Wales, the Saxon element in England, and the Gaelic element in Scotland, were all more agreeable to the Irish than the race of Rollo and William. They were not ignorant that Ireland was a refuge for their victims and a recruiting ground for their enemies. They knew, furthermore, that most of the strong points on the Irish coast, from the Shannon to the Liffey, were possessed by Christian Northmen kindred to themselves. They knew that the land was divided within itself, weakened by a long war of succession; groaning under the ambition of five competitors for the sovereignty; and suffering in reputation abroad under the invectives of Saint Bernard and the displeasure of Rome. More tempting materials for intrigue, or fairer opportunities of aggrandizement, nowhere presented themselves, and it was less want of will than of leisure from other and nearer contests, which deferred this new invasion for a century after the battle of Hastings.

While that century was passing over their heads, an occasional intercourse, not without its pleasing incidents, was maintained between the races. In the first year of the twelfth, Arnulph de Montgomery, Earl of Chester, obtained a daughter of Murkertach O'Brien in marriage; the proxy on the occasion being Gerald, son of the Constable of Windsor, and ancestor of the Geraldines. Murkertach, according to Malmsbury, maintained a close correspondence with Henry I., for whose advice he professed great deference. He was accused of aiding the rebellion of the Montgomerys against that Prince; and if at one time he did so, seems to have abandoned their alliance, when threatened with reprisals on the Irish engaged in peaceful commerce with England. The argument used on this occasion seems to be embodied in the question of Malmsbury—and has since become familiar—"What would Ireland do," says the old historian, "if the merchandize of England were not carried to her shores?"

The estimation in which the Irish Princes were held in the century preceding the invasion, at the Norman Court, may be seen in the style of Lanfranc and Anselm, when addressing—the former King Therlogh, and the latter King Murkertach O'Brien. The first generation of the conquerors had passed away before the second of these epistles was written. In the first the address runs—"Lanfrancus, a sinner, and the unworthy Bishop of the Holy Church of Dover, to the illustrious Terdelvacus, King of Ireland, blessing," &c., &c.; and the epistle of Anselm is addressed—"To Muriardachus, by the grace of God, glorious King of Ireland, Anselm, servant of the Church of Canterbury, greeting health, and salvation," &c., &c. This was the tone of the highest ecclesiastics in England towards the rulers of Ireland, in the reigns of William I. and Henry I., and equally obsequious were the replies of the Irish Princes.

After the death of Henry I., nineteen years of civil war and anarchy diverted the Anglo-Normans from all other objects. In the year 1154, however, Henry of Anjou succeeded to the throne, on which he was destined to act so important a part. He was born in Anjou, in the year 1133, and married at eighteen the divorced wife of the King of France. Uniting her vast dominions to his own patrimony, he became the lord of a larger part of France than was possessed by the titular king. In his twenty-first year he began to reign in England, and in his thirty-fifth he received the fugitive Dermid of Leinster, in some camp or castle of Aquitaine, and took, that outlaw by his own act, under his protection. The centenary of the victory of Hastings had just gone by, and it needed only this additional agent to induce him to put into execution a plan which he must have formed in the first months of his reign, since the Bull he had procured from Pope Adrian bears the date of that year—1154. The return from exile and martyrdom of Beckett, disarranged and delayed the projects of the English King; nor was he able to lead an expedition into Ireland until four years after his reception of the Leinster fugitive in France.

Throughout the rest of Christendom—if we except Rome—the name of Ireland was comparatively little known. The commerce of Dublin, Limerick and Galway, especially in the article of wine, which was already largely imported, may have made those ports and their merchants somewhat known on the coasts of France and Spain. But we have no statistics of Irish commerce at that early period. Along the Rhine, and even upon the Danube, the Irish missionary and the Irish schoolmaster were still sometimes found. The chronicle of Ratisbon records with gratitude the munificence of Conor O'Brien, King of Munster, whom it considers the founder of the Abbey of St. Peter in that city. The records of the same Abbey credit its liberal founder with having sent large presents to the Emperor Lothaire, in aid of the second crusade for the recovery of the Holy Land. Some Irish adventurers joined in the general European hosting to the plains of Palestine, but though neither numerous nor distinguished enough to occupy the page of history, their *glibs* and *cooluns* did not escape the studious eye of him who sang Jerusalem Delivered and Regained.

BOOK IV.

THE NORMANS IN IRELAND.

CHAPTER I.

DERMID M'MURROGH'S NEGOTIATIONS AND SUCCESS—THE FIRST EXPEDITION OF THE NORMANS INTO IRELAND.

The result of Dermid McMurrogh's interview with Henry II., in Aquitaine, was a royal letter, addressed to all his subjects, authorizing such of them as would, to enlist in the service of the Irish Prince. Armed alone with this, the expelled adulterer, chafing for restoration and revenge, retraced his course to England. He was at this time some years beyond three score, but the snows of age had no effect in cooling his impetuous blood; his stature is described as almost gigantic; his voice loud and harsh; his features stern and terrible. His cruel and criminal character we already know. Yet it is but just here to recall that much of the horror and odium which has accumulated on his memory is posthumous and retrospective. Some of his cotemporaries were no better in their private lives than he was; but then they had no part in bringing in the Normans. Talents both for peace and war he certainly had, and there was still a feeling of attachment, or at least of regret, cherished towards him among the people of his patrimony.

Dermid proceeded at once to seek the help he so sorely needed, upon the marches of Chester, in the city of Bristol, and at the court of the Prince of North Wales. At Bristol he caused

King Henry's letter to be publicly read, and each reading was accompanied by ample promises of land and recompense to those disposed to join in the expedition—but all in vain. From Bristol he proceeded to make the usual pilgrimage to the shrine of St. David, the Apostle of Wales, and then he visited the Court of Griffith ap Rhys, Prince of North Wales, whose family ties formed a true Welsh triad among the Normans, the Irish, and the Welsh.. He was the nephew of the celebrated Nest or Nesta, the Helen of the Welsh, whose blood flowed in the veins of almost all the first Norman adventurers in Ireland, and whose story is too intimately interwoven with the origin of many of the highest names of the Norman-Irish to be left untold.

She was, in her day, the loveliest woman of Cambria, and perhaps of Britain, but the fabled mantel of Tregau, which, according to her own mythology, will fit none but the chaste, had not rested on the white shoulders of Nesta, the daughter of Rhys ap Tudor. Her girlish beauty had attracted the notice of Henry I., to whom she bore Robert Fitz-Roy and Henry Fitz-Henry, the former the famous Earl of Gloucester, and the latter the father of two of Strongbow's most noted companions. Afterwards, by consent of her royal paramour, she married Gerald, constable of Pembroke, by whom she had Maurice Fitzgerald, the common ancestor of the Kildare and Desmond Geraldines. While living with Gerald at Pembroke, Owen, son of Cadogan, Prince of Powis, hearing of her marvellous beauty at a banquet given by his father at the Castle of Abertelvi, came by night to Pembroke, surprised the Castle and carried off Nesta and her children into Powis. Gerald, however, had escaped, and by the aid of his father-in-law, Rhys, recovered his wife and rebuilt his castle (A. D. 1105). The lady survived this husband, and married a second time, Stephen, constable of Cardigan, by whom she had Robert Fitzstephen, and probably other children. One of her daughters, Angharad, married David de Barri, the father of Giraldus and Robert de Barri; another, named after herself, married Bernard of Newmarch, and became the father of the Fitz-Bernard, who accompanied Henry II. In the second and third generations this fruitful Cambrian vine, grafted on the Norman stock, had branched out into the great families of the Carews, Gerards, Fitzwilliams, and Fitzroys, of England and Wales, and the Geraldines, Graces, Fitz-Henries, and Fitz-Maurices, of Ireland. These names will show how entirely the expeditions of 1169 and 1170 were joint-stock undertakings with most of the adventurers; Cambria, not England, sent them forth; it was a family compact; they were brothers in blood as well as in arms, those comely and unscrupulous sons, nephews, and grandsons of Nesta!

When the Leinster King reached the residence of Griffith ap Rhys, near St. David's, he found that for some personal or political cause he held in prison his near kinsman, Robert, son of Stephen, who had the reputation of being a brave and capable knight. Dermid obtained the release of Robert, on condition of his embarking in the Irish enterprize, and he found in him an active recruiting agent, alike among Welsh, Flemings, and Normans. Through him Maurice Fitzgerald, the de Barris, and Fitz-Henrys, and their dependants, were soon enlisted in the adventure. The son of Griffith ap Rhys, may be mentioned along with the knights, his kinsmen, as one whom the Irish annalists consider the most important person of the first expedition —their pillar of battle—also resolved to accompany them, with such forces as he could enlist.

But a still more important ally waited to treat with Dermid, on his return to Bristol. This was Richard de Clare, called variously from his castles or his county, Earl of Strigul and Chepstow, or Earl of Pembroke. From the strength of his arms he was nicknamed Strongbow, and in our Annals he is usually called Earl Richard, by which title we prefer hereafter to distinguish him. His father, Gilbert de Clare, was descended from Richard, of Normandy, and stood no farther removed in degree from that Duke than the reigning Prince. For nearly forty years under Henry I. and during the stormy reign of King Stephen, he had been Governor of Pembroke, and like all the great Barons played his game chiefly to his own advantage. His castle at Chepstow was one of the strongest in the west, and the power he bequeathed to his able and ambitious son excited the apprehensions of the astute and suspicious Henry II. Fourteen years of this King's reign had passed away, and Earl Richard had received no great employments, no new grants of land, no personal favors from his Sovereign. He was now a widower, passed middle age, condemned to a life of inaction such as no true Norman could long endure. Arrived at Bristol, he read the letter of Henry, and heard from Dermid the story of his expulsion and the grounds on which he vested his hopes of restoration. A consultation ensued, at which it is probable the sons of Nesta assisted, as it was there agreed that the town of Wexford, with two cantreds of land adjoining it, should be given to them. The pay of the archers and men-at-arms, and the duration of their service, were also determined. Large grants of land were guaranteed to all adventurers of knightly rank, and Earl Richard was to marry the King's daughter and succeed him in the sovereignty of Leinster.

Having by such lavish promises enlisted this powerful Earl and those adventurous Knights, Dermid resolved to pass over in person with such followers as were already equipped, in order to rally the remnant of his adherents. The Irish Annals enter this return under the year 1167, within twelvemonths or thereabouts from the time of his banishment; by their account he came back, accompanied by a fleet of strangers whom they call Flemings, and who were probably hired soldiers of that race, then easily to be met with in Wales. The Welsh Prince already mentioned seems to have accompanied him personally, as he fell by his side in a skirmish the following year. Whatever this force may have amounted to, they landed at Glascarrig point, and wintered—probably spent the Christmas—at Ferns. The more generally received account of Dermid's landing alone, and disguised, and secretly preparing his plans, under shelter of the Austin Friary at Ferns, must be rejected, if we are still to follow those trite but trustworthy guides, whom we have so many reasons to confide in. Their details differ in many very important particulars from those usually received, as we shall endeavor to make clear in a few words.

Not only do they bring Dermid over with a fleet of Flemings, of whom the natives made "small account," but dating that event before the expiration of the year 1167, at least sixteen months must have elapsed between the return of the outlaw and the arrival of the Normans. By allowing two years instead of one for the duration of his banishment, the apparent difficulty as to time would be obviated, for his return and Fitzstephen's arrival would follow upon each other in the spring and winter of the same year. The difficulty, however, is more apparent than real. A year sufficed for the journey to Aquitane and the Welsh negotiations. Another year seems to have been devoted with equal art and success to resuscitating a native Leinster party favorable to his restoration. For it is evident from our Annals that when Dermid showed himself to the people after his return, it was simply to claim his partrimony—Hy-Kinsellagh—and not to dispute the Kingdom of Leinster with the actual ruler, *Murrogh na Gael*. By this pretended moderation and humility, he disarmed hostility and lulled suspicion asleep. Roderick and O'Ruarc did indeed muster a host against him, and some of their cavalry and Kernes skirmished with the troops in his service at Kellistown, in Carlow, when six were killed on one side and twenty-five on the other, including the Welsh Prince already mentioned; afterwards Dermid emerged from his fastnesses, and entering the camp of O'Conor, gave him seven hostages for the ten cantreds of his patrimony; and to O'Ruarc he gave "'one hundred ounces of gold for his *eineach*"—that is, as damages for his criminal conversation with Devorgoil. During the remainder of the year 1168, Dermid was left to enjoy unmolested the moderate territory which he claimed, while King Roderick was engaged in enforcing his claims on the North and South, founding lectorships at Armagh, and partitioning Meath between his inseparable colleague, O'Ruarc, and himself. He celebrated, in the midst of an immense multitude, the ancient national games at Tailtin, he held an assembly at Tara, and distributed magnificent gifts to his suffragaus. Roderick might have spent the festival of Christmas, 1168, or of Easter, 1169, in the full assurance that his power was firmly established, and that a long succession of peaceful days were about to dawn upon Erin. But he was destined to be soon and sadly undeceived.

In the month of May, a little fleet of Welsh vessels, filled with armed men, approached the Irish shore, and Robert Fitzstephen ran into a creek of the bay of Bannow, called by the adventurers, from the names of two of their ships, Bag-and-Bun. Fitzstephen had with him thirty knights, sixty esquires, and three hundred footmen. The next day he was joined by Maurice de Prendergast, a Welsh gentleman, with ten knights and sixty archers. After landing they reconnoitered cautiously, but saw neither ally nor enemy—the immediate coast seemed entirely deserted. Their messenger despatched to Dermid, then probably at Ferns, in the northern extremity of the county, must have been absent several anxious days, when, much to their relief, he returned with Donald, the son of Dermid, at the head of 500 horsemen. Uniting their troops, Donald and Fitzstephen set out for Wexford, about a day's march distant, and the principal town in that angle of the island which points towards Wales. The tradition of the neighborhood says they were assailed upon the way by a party of the native population, who were defeated and dispersed. Within ten days or a fortnight of their landing, they were drawn up within sight of the walls of Wexford, where they were joined by Dermid, who obviously did not come unattended to such a meeting. What additional force he may have brought up is nowhere indicated; that he was not without followers or mercenaries, we know from the mention of the Flemings in his service, and the action of Kellistown in the previous year. The force that had marched from Bannow consisted, as we have seen, of 500 Irish horse under his son Donald, surnamed *Kavanagh;* 30 knights, 60 esquires, and 300 men-at-arms under Fitzstephen; 10 knights and 60 archers under Prendergast; in all, nobles or servitors, not exceeding 1,000 men. The town, a place of considerable strength, could muster 2,000 men capable of bearing arms, nor is it discreditable to its Dano-Irish artizans and seamen that they could boast no captain equal to Fitzstephen or Donald Kavanagh. What a town multitude could do they did. They burned down an exposed suburb, closed their gates, and manned their walls. The first assault was repulsed with some loss on the part of the assailants, and the night passed in expectation of a similar conflict on the morrow. In the early morning the townsmen could discern that the Holy Sacrifice of the Mass was being offered in the camp of their besiegers as a preparative for the dangers of the day. Within the walls, however, the clergy exercised all their influence to spare the effusion of blood, and to bring about an accommodation. Two Bishops who were in the town especially advised a surrender on honorable terms, and their advice was taken. Four of the principal citizens were deputed to Dermid, and Wexford was yielded on condition of its rights and privileges, hitherto existing, being respected. The cantreds immediately adjoining the town on the north and east were conferred on Fitzstephen according to the treaty made at Bristol, and he at once commenced the erection of a fortress on the rock of Carrig, at the narrowest pass on the river Slaney. Strongbow's uncle, Herve, was endowed with two other cantreds, to the south of the town, now known as the baronies of Forth and Bargy, where the descendants of the Welsh and Flemish settlers then planted are still to be found in the industrious and sturdy population, known as Flemings, Furlongs, Waddings, Prendergasts, Barrys, and Walshes. Side by side with them now dwell in peace the Kavanaghs, Murphys, Conors, and Breens, whose ancestors so long and so fiercely disputed the intrusion of these strangers amongst them.

With some increase of force derived from the defenders of Wexford, Dermid, at the head of 3,000 men, including all the Normans, marched into the adjoining territory of Ossory, to chastise its chief, Donogh Fitzpatrick, one of his old enemies. This campaign appears to have consumed the greater part of the summer of the year, and ended with the submission of Ossory, after a brave but unskilful resistance. The tidings of what was done at Wexford and in Ossory had, however, roused the apprehension of the monarch Roderick, who appointed a day for a national muster "of the Irish" at the Hill of Tara. Thither repaired accordingly the monarch himself, the lords of Meath, Oriel, Ulidia, Breffni, and the chiefs of the farther north. With this host they proceeded to Dublin, which they found as yet in no immediate danger of attack; and whether on this pretext or some other, the Ulster chiefs returned to their homes, leaving Roderick to pursue, with the aid of Meath and Breffni only, the footsteps of McMurrogh. The latter had fallen back upon Ferns, and had, under the skilful directions of Fitzstephen, strengthened the naturally difficult approaches to that ancient capital, by digging artificial pits, by felling trees, and other devices of Norman strategy. The season, too, must have been drawing nearly to a close, and the same amiable desire to prevent the shedding of Christian blood, which characterized all the clergy of this age, again subserved the unworthy purposes of the traitor and invader. Roderick, after a vain endeavor to detach Fitzstephen from Dermid and to induce him to quit the country, agreed to a treaty with the Leinster King, by which the latter acknowledged his supremacy as monarch, under the ancient conditions, for the fulfilment of which he surrendered to him his son Conor as hostage. By a secret and separate agreement Dermid bound himself to admit no more of the Normans into his service—an engagement which he kept as he did all others, whether of a public or a private nature. After the usual exchange of stipends and tributes, Roderick returned to his home in the west; and thus, with the treaty of Ferns, ended the comparatively unimportant but significant campaign of the year 1169.

CHAPTER II.

THE ARMS, ARMOR AND TACTICS OF THE NORMANS AND IRISH.

This would seem to be the proper place to point out the peculiarities in arms, equipment, and tactics, which gave the first Normans those military advantages over the Irish and Dano-Irish, which they had hitherto maintained over the Saxons, Welsh and Scots. In instituting such a comparison, we do not intend to confine it strictly to the age of Strongbow and Dermid; the description will extend to the entire period from the arrival of Fitzstephen to the death of Richard, Earl of Ulster—from 1169 to 1333—a period of five or six generations, which we propose to treat of in the present book. After this Earl's decease, the Normans and Irish approximated more closely in all their customs, and no longer presented those marked contrasts which existed in their earlier intercourse and conflicts with each other. The armor of the first adventurers, both for man and horse, excited the wonder, the sarcasms, and the fears of the Irish. No such equipments had yet been seen in that country, nor indeed in any other, where the Normans were still strangers. As the Knights advanced on horseback, in their metal coating, they looked more like iron cylinders filled with flesh and blood, than like lithe and limber human combatants. The man-at-arms, whether Knight or Squire, was almost invariably mounted; his war-horse was usually led, while he rode a hackney, to spare the *destrier*. The body armor was a hauberk of netted iron or steel, to which were joined a hood, sleeves, breeches, hose and sabatons, or shoes, of the same material. Under the hauberk was worn a quilted gambeson of silk or cotton, reaching to the knees; over armor, except when actually engaged, all men of family wore costly coats of satin, velvet, cloth of gold or cloth of silver, emblazoned with their arms. The shields of the thirteenth century were of tri-angular form, pointed at the bottom; the helmet conical, with or without bars; the beaver, vizor and plate armor, were inventions of a later day. Earls, Dukes, and Princes, wore small crowns upon their helmets; lovers wore the favors of their mistresses; and victors the crests of champions they had overthrown. The ordinary weapons of these cavaliers were sword, lance, and knife; the demi-launce, or light horsemen, were similarly armed; and a force of this class, common in the Irish wars, was composed of mounted cross-bow men, and called from the swift, light *hobbies* they rode, Hobiler-Archers. Besides many improvements in arms and manual exercise, the Normans perfected the old Roman machines and engines used in sieges. The scorpion was a huge cross-bow, the balista showered stones to a great distance; the catapulta discharged flights of darts and arrows. There were many other varieties of stone-throwing machinery; "the war-wolf" was long the chief of projectile machines, as the ram was of manual forces. The power of a battering ram of the largest size, worked by a thousand men, has been proven to be equal to a point-blank shot from a thirty-six pounder. There were **moveable towers of all sizes and of many names: "the sow" was a variety** which continued in use in England and Ireland till the middle of the seventeenth century. The divisions of the cavalry were: first, the *Constable's* command, some twenty-five men; next, the *Banneret* was entitled to unfurl his own colors with consent of the Marshal, and might unite under his pennon one or more constabularies; the *Knight* led into the field all his retainers who held of him by feudal tenure, and sometimes the retainers of his squires, wards or valets, and kinsmen. The laws of chivalry were fast shaping themselves into a code complete and coherent in all its parts, when these iron-clad, inventive and invincible masters of the art of war first entered on the invasion of Ireland.

The body of their followers in this enterprize, consisting of Flemish, Welsh, and Cornish archers, may be best described by the arms they carried. The irresistible cross-bow was their main reliance. Its shot was so deadly that the Lateran Council, in 1139, strictly forbade its employment among Christian enemies. It combined with its stock, or bed, wheel, and trigger, almost all the force of the modern musket, and discharged square pieces of iron, leaden balls, or, in scarcity of ammunition, flint stones. The common cross-bow would kill, point blank, at forty or fifty yards distance, and the best improved, at fully one hundred yards. The manufacture of these weapons must have been profitable, since their cost was equal, in the relative value of money, to that of the rifle, in our times. In the reign of Edward II. each cross-bow, purchased for the garrison of Sherborne Castle, cost 3s. and 8d.; and every hundred of *quarrels*—the ammunition just mentioned—1s. and 6d. Iron, steel, and wood, were the materials used in the manufacture of this weapon.

The long-bow had been introduced into England by the Normans, who are said to have been more indebted to that arm than any other, for their victory at Hastings. To encourage the use of the long-bow many statutes were passed, and so late as the time of the Stuarts, royal commissions were issued for the promotion of this national exercise. Under the early statutes no archer was permitted to practise at any standing mark at less than "eleven score yards distant;" no archer under twenty-four years of age was allowed to shoot twice from the same standpoint; parents and masters were subject to a fine of 6s. and 8d. if they allowed their youth, under the age of seventeen, "to be without a bow and two arrows for one month together;" the walled towns were required to set up their butts, to keep them in repair, and to turn out for target-practice on holidays and at other convenient times. Aliens residing in England were forbidden the use of this weapon—a jealous precaution, showing the great importance attached to its possession. The usual length of the bow—which was made of yew, witch-hazel, ash, or elm—was about six feet; and the arrow, about half that length. Arrows were made of ash, feathered with part of a goose's wing, and barbed with iron or steel. In the reign of Edward III., a painted bow cost 1s. and 6d., a white bow, 1s.; a sheaf of steel-tipped arrows (24 to the sheaf), 1s. and 2d., and a sheaf of *non accerata* (the blunt sort), 1s. The range of the long-bow, at its highest perfection, was, as we have seen, "eleven score yards," more than double that of the ordinary cross-bow. The common sort of both these weapons carried about the same distance—nearly 100 yards.

The natural genius of the Normans for war had been sharpened and perfected by their campaigns in France and England, but more especially in the first and second Crusades. All that was to be learned of military science in other countries—all that Italian skill, Greek subtlety, or Saracen invention, could teach, they knew and combined into one system. Their feudal discipline moreover, in which the youth who entered the service of a veteran as page, rose in time to the rank of esquire and bachelor-at-arms, and finally won his spurs on some well-contested field, was eminently favorable to the training and proficiency of military talents. Not less remarkable was the skill they displayed in seizing on the strong and commanding points of communication, within the country, as we see at this day, from the sites of their old Castles, many of which must have been, before the invention of gunpowder, all but impregnable.

The art of war, if art it could in their case be called, was in a much less forward stage among the Irish in the twelfth and thirteenth centuries than amongst the Normans. Of the science of fortification they perhaps knew no more than they had learned in their long struggle with the Danes and Norwegians. To render roads impassible, to strengthen their islands by stockades, to hold the naturally difficult passes which connect one province or one district with another—these seem to have been their chief ideas of the aid that valor may derive from artificial appliances. The fortresses of which we hear so frequently, during and after the Danish period, and which are erroneously called *Danes'-forts*, were more numerous than formidable to such enemies as the Normans. Some of these earth-and-stone-works are older than the Milesian invasion, and of Cyclopean style and strength. Those of the Milesians are generally of larger size, contain much more earth, and the internal chambers are of less massive masonry. They are almost invariably of circular form, and the largest remaining specimens are the Giant's Ring near Belfast, the fort at Netterville, which measures 300 paces in circumference round the top of the embankment; the Black Rath, on the Boyne, which measures 321 paces round the outer wall of circumvallation; and the King's Rath at Tara, upwards of 280 in length. The height of the outer embankment in forts of this size varied from fifteen to twenty feet; this embankment was usually surrounded by a fosse; within the embankment there was a platform, depressed so as to leave a circular parapet above its level. Many of these military raths have been found to contain subterranean chambers and circular winding passages, supposed to be used as granaries and armories. They are accounted capable of containing garrisons of from 200 to 500 men; but many of the fortresses mentioned from age to age in our annals were mere private residences, enclosing within their outer and inner walls space enough for the immediate retainers and domestics of the chief. Although coats of mail are mentioned in manuscripts long anterior to the Norman invasion, the Irish soldiers seem seldom or never to have been completely clothed in armor. Like the northern *Berserkers*, they prided themselves in fighting, if not naked, in their orange colored shirts, dyed with saffron. The helmet and the shield were the only defensive articles of dress; nor do they seem to have had trappings for their horses. Their favorite missile weapon was the dart or javelin, and in earlier ages the sling. The spear or lance, the sword, and the sharp, short-handled battle axe, were their **favor-**

lte manual weapons. Their power with the battle-axe was prodigious; *Giraldus* says they sometimes lopped off a horseman's leg at a single blow, his body falling over on the other side. Their bridle-bits and spurs were of bronze, as were generally their spear heads and short swords. Of siege implements, beyond the torch and the scaling-ladder, they seem to have had no knowledge, and to have desired none. The Dano-Irish alone were accustomed to fortify and defend their towns, on the general principles, which then composed the sum of what was known in Christendom of military engineering. Quick to acquire in almost every department of the art, the native Irish continued till the last, obstinately insensible to the absolute necessity of learning how modern fortifications are constructed, defended, and captured; a national infatuation, of which we find melancholy evidence in every recurring native insurrection.

The two divisions of the Irish infantry were the *galloglass*, or heavily armed foot soldier, called *gall*, either as a mercenary, or from having been equipped after the Norman method, and the *kerne*, or light infantry. The horsemen were men of the free tribes, who followed their chiefs on terms almost of equality, and who, except his immediate retainers, equipped and foraged for themselves. The highest unit of this force was a *Cath*, or battalion of 3,000 men; but the subdivision of command and the laws which established and maintained discipline have yet to be recovered and explained. The old Spanish "right of insurrection" seems to have been recognized in every chief of a free tribe, and no Hidalgo of old Spain, for real or fancied slight, was ever more ready to turn his horse's head homeward than were those refractory lords, with whom Roderick O'Conor and his successors, in the front of the national battle, had to contend or to co-operate.

CHAPTER III.

THE FIRST CAMPAIGN OF EARL RICHARD—SIEGE OF DUBLIN—DEATH OF KING DERMID M'MURROGH.

The campaigns of 1168 and 1169 had ended prosperously for Dermid in the treaty of Ferns. By that treaty he had bound himself to bring no more Normans into the country, and to send those already in his service back to their homes. But in the course of the same autumn or winter, in which this agreement was solemnly entered into, he welcomed the arrival at Wexford—of Maurice Fitzgerald—son of the fair Nesta by her first husband —and immediately employed this fresh force, consisting of ten knights, 30 esquires, and 100 footmen, upon a hosting which harried the open country about Dublin, and induced the alarmed inhabitants to send hostages into his camp, bearing proffers of allegiance and amity. As yet he did not feel in force sufficient to attack the city, for, if he had been, his long cherished vengeance against its inhabitants would not have been postponed till another season.

In the meantime he had written most urgent letters to Earl Richard to hasten his arrival, according to the terms agreed upon at Bristol. That astute and ambitious nobleman had been as impatiently biding his time as Dermid had been his coming. Knowing the jealous sovereign under whom he served, he had gone over to France to obtain Henry's sanction to the Irish enterprize, but had been answered by the monarch, in oracular phrases, which might mean anything or nothing. Determined, however, to interpret these doubtful words in his own sense, he despatched his vanguard early in the spring of the year 1170 under the command of his uncle Herve and a company of 10 knights and 70 archers, under Raymond, son of William, lord of Carew, elder brother of Maurice Fitzgerald, and grandson of

Nesta. In the beginning of May, Raymond, nicknamed *le grôs*, or the Fat, entered Waterford harbor, and landed eight miles below the city, under the rock of Dundonolf, on the east, or Wexford side. Here they rapidly threw up a camp to protect themselves against attack, and to hold the landing place for the convenience of the future expedition. A tumultuous body of natives, amounting, according to the Norman account, to 3,000 men, were soon seen swarming across the Suir to attack the foreigners. They were men of Idrone and Desies, under their chiefs, O'Ryan and O'Phelan, and citizens of Waterford, who now rushed towards the little fortress, entirely unprepared for the long and deadly range of the Welsh and Flemish cross-bows. Thrown into confusion by the unexpected discharge, in which every shot from behind the ramparts of turf brought down its man, they wavered and broke; Raymond and Hervy then sallied out upon the fugitives who were fain to escape, as many as could, to the other side of the river, leaving 500 prisoners, including 70 chief citizens of Waterford behind them. These were all inhumanly massacred, according to *Giraldus*, the eulogist of all the Geraldines, by the order of Hervy, contrary to the entreaties of Raymond. Their legs were first violently broken, and they were then hurled down the rocks into the tide. Five hundred men could not well be so captured and put to death by less than an equal number of hands, and we may, therefore, safely set down that number as holding the camp of Dundonolf during the summer months of the year.

Earl Richard had not completed his arrangements until the month of August—so that his uncle and lieutenant had to hold the post they had seized for fully three months, awaiting his arrival in the deepest anxiety. At last, leaving his castle in Pembroke, he marched with his force through North Wales, by way of St. David's to Milford Haven—"and still as he went he took up all the best chosen and picked men he could get." At Milford, just as he was about to embark, he received an order from King Henry forbidding the expedition. Wholly disregarding this missive he hastened on board with 200 knights and 1,200 infantry in his company, and on the eve of St. Bartholomew's Day (August 23d), landed safely under the earthwork of

Dundonolf, where he was joyfully received by Raymond at the head of 40 knights, and a corresponding number of men-at-arms. The next day the whole force, under the Earl, "who had all things in readiness" for such an enterprize, proceeded to lay siege to Waterford. Malachy O'Phelan, the brave lord of Desies, forgetting all ancient enmity against his Danish neighbors, had joined the townsmen to assist in the defence. Twice the besieged beat back the assailants, until Raymond perceiving at an angle of the wall the wooden props upon which a house rested, ordered them to be cut away, on which the house fell to the ground, and a breach was effected. The men-at-arms then burst in, slaughtering the inhabitants without mercy. In the tower, long known as Reginald's, or the ring tower, O'Phelan and Reginald, the Dano-Irish chief, held out until the arrival of King Dermid, whose intercession procured them such terms as led to their surrender. Then, amid the ruins of the burning city, and the muttered malediction of its surviving inhabitants, the ill-omened marriage of Eva McMurrogh with Richard de Clare was gaily celebrated, and the compact entered into at Bristol three years before was perfected.

The marriage revelry was hardly over when tidings came from Dublin that Asculph Mac Torcall, its Danish lord, had, either by the refusal of the annual tribute, or in some other manner, declared his independence of Dermid, and invoked the aid of the monarch Roderick, in defence of that city. Other messengers brought news that Roderick had assumed the protection of Dublin, and was already encamped at the head of a large army at Clondalkin, with a view of intercepting the march of the invaders from the south. The whole Leinster and Norman force, with the exception of a troop of archers left to garrison Waterford, were now put in motion for the siege of the chief city of the Hibernicized descendants of the Northmen. Informed of Roderick's position which covered Dublin on the south and west, Dermid and Richard followed boldly the mountain paths and difficult roads which led by the secluded city of Glendalough, and thence along the coast road from Bray towards the mouth of the Liffey, until they arrived unexpectedly within the lines of Roderick, to the amazement and terror of the townsmen.

The force which now, under the command-in-chief of Dermid, sat down to the siege of Dublin, was far from being contemptible. For a year past he had been recognized in Leinster as fully as any of his predecessors, and had so strengthened his military position as to propose nothing short of the conquest of the whole country. His choice of a line of march sufficiently shows how thoroughly he had overcome the former hostility of the stubborn mountaineers of Wicklow. The exact numbers which he encamped before the gates of Dublin are nowhere given, but on the march from Waterford, the vanguard, led by Milo de Cogan, consisted of 700 Normans and "an Irish battalion," which, taken literally, would mean 3,000 men, under Donald *Kavanagh;* Raymond the Fat followed "with 800 British;" Dermid led on "the chief part of the Irish" (number not given), in person; Richard commanded the rear-guard, "300 British and 1,000 Irish soldiers." Altogether, it is not exorbitant to conjecture that the Leinster Prince led to the siege of Dublin an army of about 10,000 native troops, 1,500 Welsh and Flemish archers, and 250 knights. Except the handful who remained with Fitzstephen to defend his fort at Carrick, on the Slaney, and the archers left in Waterford, the entire Norman force in Ireland, at this time, were united in the siege. Of the foreign knights, many were eminent for courage and capacity, both in peace and war. The most distinguished among them were Maurice Fitzgerald, the common ancestor of the Geraldines of Desmond and Kildare; Raymond the Fat, ancestor of the Graces of Ossory; the two Fitz-Henries, grandsons of Henry I., and the fair Nesta; Walter de Riddlesford, first Baron of Bray; Robert de Quincy, son-in-law and standard-bearer to Earl Richard; Herve, uncle to the Earl, and Gilbert de Clare, his son; Milo de Cogan, the first who entered Dublin by assault, and its first Norman governor; the de Barries, and de Prendergast. Other founders of Norman-Irish houses, as the de Lacies, de Courcies, le Poers, de Burgos, Butlers, Birminghams, came not over until the landing of Henry II., or still later, with his son John.

The townsmen of Dublin had every reason, from their know-lodge of Dermid's cruel character, to expect the worst at his hands and those of his allies. The warning of Waterford was before them, but besides this they had a special cause of apprehension, Dermid's father having been murdered in their midst, and his body ignominiously interred with the carcase of a dog. Roderick having failed to intercept him, the citizens, either to gain time or really desiring to arrive at an accommodation, entered into negotiations. Their ambassador for this purpose was Lorcan, or Lawrence O'Toole, the first Archbishop of the city, and its first prelate of Milesian origin. This illustrious man, canonized both by sanctity and patriotism, was then in the thirty-ninth year of his age, and the ninth of his episcopate. His father was lord of Imayle and chief of his clan; his sister had been wife of Dermid and mother of Eva, the prize-bride of Earl Richard. He himself had been a hostage with Dermid in his youth, and afterwards Abbot of Glendalough, the most celebrated monastic city of Leinster. He stood, therefore, to the besieged, being their chief pastor, in the relation of a father; to Dermid, and strangely enough to Strongbow also, as brother-in-law and uncle by marriage. A fitter ambassador could not be found.

Maurice Regan, the "*Latiner*," or Secretary of Dermid, had advanced to the walls, and summoned the city to surrender, and deliver up "30 pledges" to his master, their lawful Prince. Asculph, son of Torcall, was in favor of the surrender, but the citizens could not agree among themselves as to hostages. No one was willing to trust himself to the notoriously untrustworthy Dermid. The Archbishop was then sent out on the part of the citizens to arrange the terms in detail. He was received with all reverence in the camp, but while he was deliberating with the commanders without, and the townsmen were anxiously awaiting his return, Milo de Cogan and Raymond the Fat, seizing the opportunity, broke into the city at the head of their companies, and began to put the inhabitants ruthlessly to the sword. They were soon followed by the whole force eager for massacre and pillage. The Archbishop hastened back to endeavor to stay the havoc which was being made of his people. He threw himself before the infuriated Irish and Normans, he threatened, he denounced, he bared his own breast to the swords of the assassins. All to little purpose; the blood fury exhausted itself before peace settled over the city. Its Danish chief, Asculph, with many of his followers, escaped to their ships, and fled to the Isle of Man and the Hebrides in search of succor and revenge. Roderick, unprepared to besiege the enemy who had thus outmarched and outwitted him at that season of the year—it could not be earlier than October—broke up his encampment at Clondalkin, and retired to Connaught. Earl Richard having appointed de Cogan his governor of Dublin, followed on the rear of the retreating *Ard-Righ*, at the instigation of McMurrogh, burning and plundering the churches of Kells, Clonard and Slane, and carrying off the hostages of East-Meath.

Though Dermid seemed to have forgotten altogether the conditions of the treaty of Ferns, yet not so Roderick. When he reached Athlone he caused Conor, son of Dermid, and the son of Donald *Kavanagh*, and the son of Dermid's fosterer, who had been given him as hostages for the fulfilment of that treaty, so grossly violated in every particular, to be beheaded. Dermid indulged in impotent vows of vengeance against Roderick, when he heard of these executions which his own perjuries had provoked; he swore that nothing short of the conquest of Connaught in the following spring would satisfy his revenge, and he sent the Ard-Righ his defiance to that purport. Two other events of military consequence marked the close of the year 1170. The foreign garrison of Waterford was surprised and captured by Cormac McCarthy, Prince of Desmond, and Henry II. having prohibited all intercourse between his lieges and his disobedient subject, Earl Richard, the latter had despatched Raymond the Fat, with the most humble submission of himself and his new possessions to his Majesty's decision. And so with Asculph, son of Torcall, recruiting in the isles of Insi-Gall, Lawrence, the Archbishop, endeavoring to unite the proud and envious Irish lords into one united phalanx, and Roderick, preparing for the new year's campaign, the winter of 1170–'71, came, and waned, and went.

One occurrence of the succeeding spring may most appropriately be dismissed here—the death of the wretched and odious

McMurrogh. This event happened, according to *Giraldus*, in the kalends of May. The Irish Annals surround his death-bed with all the horrors appropriate to such a scene. He became, they say, " putrid while living," through the miracles of St. Columbcille and St. Finian, whose churches he had plundered; " and he died at Fernamore, without making a will, without penance, without the body of Christ, without unction, as his evil deeds deserved." We have no desire to meditate over the memory of such a man. He far more than his predecessor, whatever that predecessor's crimes might have been, deserved to have been buried with a dog.

CHAPTER IV.

SECOND CAMPAIGN OF EARL RICHARD—HENRY II. IN IRELAND.

The campaign of the year 1171 languished from a variety of causes. At the very outset, the invaders lost their chief patron, who had been so useful to them. During the siege of Dublin, in the previous autumn, the townsmen of Wexford, who were in revolt, had, by stratagen, induced Robert Fitzstephen to surrender his fort, at Carrick, and had imprisoned him in one of the islands of their harbor. Waterford had been surprised and taken by Cormac McCarthy, Prince of Desmond, and Strongbow, alarmed by the proclamation of Henry, knew hardly whether to consider himself outlaw, subject or independent sovereign.

Raymond the Fat had returned from his embassy to King Henry, with no comfortable tidings. He had been kept day after day waiting the pleasure of the King, and returned with sentences as dubious in his mouth, as those on which Earl Richard had originally acted. It was evidently not the policy of Henry to abandon the enterprize already so well begun, but neither was it his interest or desire that any subject should reap the benefit, or erect an independent power, upon his mere permission to embark in the service of McMurrough. Herve, the Earl's uncle, had been despatched as embassador in Raymond's place, but with no better success. At length, Richard himself, by the advice of all his councillors, repaired to England, and waited on Henry at Newenham, in Gloucestershire. At first he was ignominiously refused an audience, but after repeated solicitations he was permitted to renew his homage. He then yielded in due form the city of Dublin, and whatever other conquests he claimed, and consented to hold his lands in Leinster, as chief tenant from the crown: in return for which he was graciously forgiven the success that had attended his adventure, and permitted to accompany the King's expedition, in the ensuing autumn.

Before Strongbow's departure for England three unsuccessful attempts had been made for the expulsion of the Norman garrison from Dublin. They were unfortunately not undertaken in concert; but rather in succession. The first was an attempt at surprising the city by Asculph MacTorcall, probably relying on the active aid of the inhabitants of his own race. He had but "a small force," chiefly from the isles of Insi-Gall and the Orkneys. The Orcadians were under the command of a warrior called John the Furious or Mad, the last of those wild Berserkers of the North, whose valor was regarded in Pagan days as a species of divine frenzy. This redoubted champion, after a momentary success, was repulsed by Milo and Richard de Cogan, and finally fell by the hand of Walter de Riddlesford. Asculph was taken prisoner, and, avowing boldly his intention never to desist from attempting to recover the place, was put to death. The second attack has been often described as a regular investment by Roderick O'Connor, at the head of all the forces of the Island, which was only broken up in the ninth week of its duration, by a desperate sally on the part of the famished garrison. Many details and episodes, proper to so long a beleaguerment, are given by *Giraldus*, and reproduced by his copyists. We find, however, little warrant for these passages in our native annals, any more than for the antithetical speeches which the same partial historian places in the mouths of his heroes. The Four Masters limit the time to "the course of a fortnight." Roderick, according to their account, was accompanied by the lords of Breffni and Oriel only; frequent skirmishes and conflicts took place;

an excursion was made against the Leinster Allies of the Normans, "to cut down and burn the corn of the Saxons." The surprise by night of the monarch's camp is also duly recorded; and that the enemy carried off "the provisions, armor, and horses of Roderick." By which sally, according to *Giraldus*, Dublin having obtained provisions enough for a year, Earl Richard marched to Wexford, "taking the higher way by Idrone," with the hope to deliver Fitzstephen. But the Wexford men having burned their suburbs, and sent their goods and families into the stockaded island, sent him word that at the first attack they would put Fitzstephen and his companions to death. The Earl, therefore, held sorrowfully on his way to Waterford, where, leaving a stronger force than the first garrison, to which he had entrusted it, he sailed for England to make his peace with King Henry. The third attempt on Dublin was made by the lord of Breffni during the Earl's absence, and when the garrison were much reduced; it was equally unsuccessful with those already recorded. De Cogan displayed his usual courage, and the Lord of Breffni lost a son and some of his best men in the assault.

It was upon the marches of Wales that the Earl found King Henry busily engaged in making preparations for his own voyage into Ireland. He had levied on the landholders throughout his dominions an escutage or commutation for personal service, and the Pipe roll, which contains his disbursements for the year, has led an habitually cautious writer to infer "that the force raised for the expedition was much more numerous than has been represented by historians." During the muster of his forces he visited Pembroke, and made a progress through North Wales, severely censuring those who had enlisted under Strongbow, and placing garrisons of his own men in their castles. At Saint David's he made the usual offering on the shrine of the Saint and received the hospitalities of the Bishop. All things being in readiness, he sailed from Milford Haven, with a fleet of 400 transports, having on board many of the Norman nobility, 500 knights, and an army usually estimated at 4,000 men at arms. On the 18th of October, 1171, he landed safely at Crook, in the county of Waterford, being unable, according to an old local tradition, to sail up the river from adverse winds. As one headland of that harbor is called *Hook*, and the other *Crook*, the old adage " by hook or by crook," is thought to have arisen on this occasion.

In Henry's train, beside Earl Richard, there came over Hugh de Lacy, some time Constable of Chester; William, son of Aldelm, ancestor of the Clanrickards; Theobald Walter, ancestor of the Butlers; Robert le Poer, ancestor of the Powers; Humphrey de Bohun, Robert Fitz-Barnard, Hugh de Gundeville, Philip de Hastings, Philip de Braos, and many other cavaliers whose names were renowned throughout France and England. As the imposing host formed on the sea side, a white hare, according to an English chronicler, leapt from a neighboring hedge, and was immediately caught and presented to the King as an omen of victory. Prophecies, pagan and christian—quatrains fathered on Saint Moling and triads attributed to Merlin—were freely showered in his path. But the true omen of his success he might read for himself, in a constitution which had lost its force, in laws which had ceased to be sacred, and in a chieftain race, brave indeed as mortal men could be, but envious, arrogant, revengeful and insubordinate. For their criminal indulgence of these demoniacal passions a terrible chastisement was about to fall on them, and not only on them, but also, alas! on their poor people.

The whole time passed by Henry II. in Ireland was from the 18th October, 1171, till the 17th of April following, just seven months. For the first politician of his age, with the command of such troops, and so much treasure, these seven months could not possibly be barren of consequences. Winter, the season of diplomacy, was seldom more industriously or expertly employed. The townsmen of Wexford, aware of his arrival as soon as it had taken place, hastened to make their submission and to deliver up to him their prisoner, Robert Fitzstephen, the first of the invaders. Henry, affecting the same displeasure towards Fitzstephen he did for all those who had anticipated his own expedition, ordered him to be fettered and imprisoned in Reginald's tower. At Waterford he also received the friendly overtures of the lords of Desies and Ossory, and probably some form of feudal submission was undergone by those chiefs. Cormac, Prince of Desmond, followed their example, and soon afterwards Donald O'Brien of Thomond met him on the banks of the Suir, not far from Cashel, made his peace, and agreed to receive a Norman garrison in his Hiberno-Danish city of Limerick. Having appointed commanders over these and other southern garrisons Henry proceeded to Dublin, where a spacious cage-work palace, on a lawn without the city, was prepared for winter quarters. Here he continued those negotiations with the Irish chiefs, which we are told were so generally successful. Amongst others whose adhesion he received, mention is made of the lord of Breffni, the most faithful follower the Monarch Roderick could count. The chiefs of the Northern Hy-Nial remained deaf to all his overtures, and though Fitz-Aldelm and de Lacy, the commissioners despatched to treat with Roderick, are said to have procured from the deserted *Ard-Righ* an act of submission, it is incredible that a document of such consequence should have been allowed to perish. Indeed most of the confident assertions about submissions to Henry are to be taken with great caution; it is quite certain he himself, though he lived nearly twenty years after his Irish expedition, never assumed any Irish title whatever. It is equally true that his successor Richard I. never assumed any such title, as an incident of the English crown. And although Henry in the year 1185 created his youngest son, John *Lackland*, "lord of Ireland," it was precisely in the same spirit and with as much ground of title as he had for creating Hugh de Lacy, Lord of Meath, or John de Courcy, Earl of Ulster. Of this question of title we shall speak more fully hereafter, for we do not recognize any English sovereign as *King* of Ireland, previous to the year 1541; but it ought surely be conclusive evidence, that neither had Henry claimed the crown, nor had the Irish chiefs acknowledged him as their *Ard-Righ*, that in the two authentic documents from his hand which we possess, he neither signs himself *Rex* nor *Dominus Hiberniæ*. These documents are the Charter of Dublin, and the Concession of Glendalough, and their authenticity has never been disputed.

After spending a right merry Christmas with Norman and Milesian guests in abundance at Dublin, Henry proceeded to that work of religious reformation, under plea of which he had obtained the Bill of Pope Adrian, seventeen years before, declaring such an expedition, undertaken with such motives, lawful and praiseworthy. Early in the new year, by his desire, a synod was held at Cashel, where many salutary decrees were enacted. These related to the proper solemnization of marriage; the catechising of children before the doors of churches; the administration of baptism in baptismal or parish churches; the abolition of *Erenachs* or lay Trustees of church property, and the imposition of tithes, both of corn and cattle. By most English writers this synod is treated as a National Council, and inferences are thence drawn of Henry's admitted power over the clergy of the nation. There is, however, no evidence that the Bishops of Ulster or Connaught were present at Cashel, but strong negative testimony to the contrary. We read under the date of the same year in the Four Masters, that a synod of the clergy and laity of Ireland was convened at Tuam by Roderick O'Conor and the Archbishop Catholicus O'Duffy. It is hardly possible that this meeting could be in continuation or in concord with the assembly convoked at the instance of Henry.

Following quickly upon the Cashel Synod, Henry held a "Curia Regis" or Great Court at Lismore, in which he created the offices of Marshal, Constable, and Seneschal for Ireland. Earl Richard was created the first lord Marshal; de Lacy, the first lord Constable. Theobald, ancestor of the Ormond family, was already chief Butler, and de Vernon was created the first high Steward or Seneschal. Such other order as could be taken for the preservation of the places already captured, was not neglected. The surplus population of Bristol obtained a charter of Dublin to be held of Henry and his heirs, "with all the same liberties and free customs which they enjoyed at Bristol." Wexford was committed to the charge of Fitz-Aldelm, Waterford to de Bohun, and Dublin to de Lacy. Castles were ordered to be erected in the towns and at other points, and the politic King, having caused all those who remained behind to renew their homage in the most solemn form, sailed on Easter Monday from Wexford Haven, and on the same day landed at Port-Finan, in Wales. Here he assumed the Pilgrim's staff, and proceeded humbly on foot to St. David's, preparatory to meeting the Papal Commissioners appointed to inquire into Beckett's murder.

It is quite apparent that had Henry landed in Ireland at any other period of his life except in the year of the martyrdom of the renowned Archbishop of Canterbury, while the wrath of Rome was yet hanging poised in the air ready to be hurled against him, he would not have left the work he undertook but half begun. The nett result of his expedition, of his great fleet, mighty army, and sagacious counsels, was the infusion of a vast number of new adventurers (most of them of higher rank and better fortunes than their precursors), into the same old field. Except the garrisons admitted into Limerick and Cork, and the displacing of Strongbow's commandants by his own at Waterford, Wexford, and Dublin, there seems to have been little gained in a military sense. The decrees of the Synod of Cashel would, no doubt, stand him in good stead with the Papal legates as evidences of his desire to enforce strict discipline, even on lands beyond those over which he actually ruled. But, after all, harassed as he was with apprehensions of the future, perhaps no other Prince could have done more in a single winter in a strange country than Henry II. did for his seven months' sojourn in Ireland.

CHAPTER V.

FROM THE RETURN OF HENRY II. TO ENGLAND TILL THE DEATH OF EARL RICHARD AND HIS PRINCIPAL COMPANIONS.

THE Ard-Righ Roderick, during the period of Henry the Second's stay in Ireland, had continued west of the Shannon. Unsupported by his suffragans, many of whom made peace with the invader, he attempted no military operation, nor had Henry time sufficient to follow him into his strongholds. It was reserved for this ill-fated, and, we cannot but think, harshly judged monarch, to outlive the first generation of the invaders of his country, and to close a reign which promised so brightly at the beginning, in the midst of a distracted, war-spent people having preserved through all vicissitudes the title of sovereign, but little else that was of value to himself or others.

Among the guests who partook of the Christmas cheer of King Henry at Dublin, we find mention of Tiernan O'Ruarc, the the lord of Breffni and East-Meath. For the Methian addition to his possessions, Tiernan was indebted to his early alliance with Roderick, and the success of their joint arms. Anciently the east of Meath had been divided between the four families called "the four tribes of Tara," whose names are now anglicized O'Hart, O'Kelly, O'Connelly and O'Regan. Whether to balance the power of the great Westmeath family of O'Melaghlin, or because these minor tribes were unable to defend themselves successfully, Roderick, like his father, had partitioned Meath, and given the seaward side a new master in the person of O'Ruarc. The investiture of Hugh de Lacy by King Henry with the seignory of the same district, led to a tragedy, the first of its kind in our annals, but destined to be the prototype of an almost indefinite series, in which the gainers were sometimes natives, but much oftener Normans.

O'Ruarc gave de Lacy an appointment at the hill of Ward, near Athboy, in the year 1173, in order to adjust their conflicting claims upon East-Meath. Both parties naturally guarded against surprise, by having in readiness a troop of armed retainers. The principals met apart on the summit of the hill, amid the circumvallations of its ancient fort; a single unarmed interpreter only was present. An altercation having arisen between them, O'Ruarc lost his temper and raised the battle-axe, which all our warriors carried in those days, as the gentlemen of the last century did their swords; this was the signal for both troops of guards to march towards the spot. De Lacy, in attempting to fly, had been twice felled to the earth, when his followers, under Maurice Fitzgerald and Griffith, his nephew, came to his rescue, and assailed the chief of Breffini. It was now Tiernan's turn to attempt escaping, but as he mounted his horse the spear of Griffith brought him to the earth mortally wounded, and his followers fled. His head was carried in triumph to Dublin, where it was spiked over the northern gate, and his body was gibbeted on the northern wall, with the feet uppermost. Thus a spectacle of intense pity to the Irish did these severed members of one of their most famous nobles remain exposed on that side of the stronghold of the stranger which looks towards the pleasant plains of Meath and the verdant uplands of Cavan

The administration of de Lacy was now interrupted by a summons to join his royal master, sore beset by his own sons in Normandy. The Kings of France and Scotland were in alliance with those unnatural Princes, and their mother, Queen Eleanor, might be called the author of their rebellion. As all the force that could be spared from Ireland was needed for the preservation of Normandy, de Lacy hastened to obey the royal summons, and Earl Richard, by virtue of his rank of Marshal, took for the moment the command in chief. Henry, however, who never cordially forgave that adventurer, first required his presence in France, and when, alarmed by ill news from Ireland, he sent him back to defend the conquests already made, he associated with him in the supreme command—though not apparently in the civil administration—the gallant Raymond *le gros*. And it was full time for the best head and the bravest sword among the first invaders to return to their work—a task not to be so easily achieved as many confident persons then believed, and as many ill-informed writers have since described it.

During the early rule of de Lacy, Earl Richard had established himself at Ferns, assuming, to such of the Irish as adhered to him, the demeanor of a king. After Dermid's death he styled himself, in utter disregard of Irish law, "Prince of Leinster," in virtue of his wife. He proceeded to create feudal dignitaries, placing at their head, as Constable of Leinster, Robert de Quincy, to whom he gave his daughter, by his first wife, in marriage. At this point the male representatives of King Dermid came to open rupture with the Earl. Donald *Kavanagh*, surnamed "the Handsome," and by the Normans usually spoken of as "Prince" Donald, could scarcely be expected to submit to an arrangement, so opposed to all ancient custom, and to his own interests. He had borne a leading part in the restoration of his father, but surely not to this end—the exclusion of the male succession. He had been one of King Henry's guests during the Christmas holidays of the year 1172, and had rendered him some sort of homage, as Prince of Leinster. Henry, ever ready to raise up rivals to Strongbow, seems to have received him into favor until Eva, the Earl's wife, proved, both in Ireland and England, that Donald and his brother Enna were born out of wedlock, and that there was no direct male heir of Dermid left, after the execution of Conor, the hostage put to death by King Roderick. To English notions this might have been conclusive against Donald's title, but to the Irish, among whom the electoral principle was the source of all chieftainry, it was not so. A large proportion of the patriotic Leinstermen—what might be called the native party—adhered to Donald *Kavanagh*, utterly rejecting the title derived through the lady Eva.

Such conflicting interests could only be settled by a resort to force, and the bloody feud began by the Earl executing at Ferns one of Donald's sons, held by him as a hostage. In an expedition against O'Dempsey, who also refused to acknowledge his title, the Earl lost in the campaign of 1173 his son-in-law, de Quincy, several other knights, and the "banner of Leinster." The following year we read in the Anglo-Irish Annals of Leinster, that King Donald's men being moved against the Earl's men, made a great slaughter of English. Nor was this the worst defeat he suffered in the same year—1174. Marching into Munster he was encountered in a pitched battle at Thurles by the troops of the monarch Roderick, under command of his son, Conor, surnamed *Moinmoy*, and by the troops of Thomond, under Donald More O'Brien. With Strongbow were all who could be spared of the garrison of Dublin, including a strong detachment of Danish origin. Four knights and seven hundred (or, according to other accounts, seventeen hundred) men of the Normans were left dead on the field. Strongbow retreated with the remnant of his force to Waterford, but the news of the defeat having reached that city before him, the townspeople ran to arms and put his garrison of two hundred men to the sword. After encamping for a month on an island without the city, and hearing that Kilkenny Castle was taken and raised by O'Brien, he was feign to return to Dublin as best he could.

His fortunes at the close of this campaign were at their lowest ebb. The loss of de Quincy and the defeat of Thurles had sorely shaken his military reputation. His jealousy of that powerful family connexion, the Geraldines, had driven Maurice Fitzgerald and Raymond the Fat to retire in disgust into Wales. Donald Kavanagh, O'Dempsey, and the native party in Leinster, set him at defiance, and his own troops refused to obey the orders of his uncle Hervey, demanding to be led by the more popular and youthful Raymond. To add to his embarrassments, Henry summoned him to France in the very crisis of his troubles, and he dared not disobey that jealous and exacting master. He was, however, not long detained by the English King. Clothed with supreme authority, and with Raymond for his lieutenant, he returned to resume the work of conquest. To conciliate the Geraldines, he at last consented to give his sister Basilia in marriage to the brilliant captain, on whose sword so much depended. At the same time Alina, the widow of de Quincy, was married to the second son of Fitzgerald, and Nesta Fitzgerald was united to Raymond's former rival, Hervey. Thus, bound together, fortune returned in full tide to the adventurers. Limerick, which had been taken and burned to the water's edge by Donald O'Brien after the battle of Thurles, was recaptured and fortified anew; Waterford was more strongly garrisoned than ever; Donald *Kavanagh* was taken off, apparently by treachery (A. D. 1175), and all seemed to promise the enjoyment of uninterrupted power to the Earl. But his end was already come. An ulcer in his foot brought on a long and loathsome illness which terminated in his death, in the month of May, 1176, or 1177. He was buried in Christ Church, Dublin, which he had contributed to enlarge, and was temporarily succeeded in the government of the Normans by his lieutenant and brother-in-law, Raymond. By the Lady Eva he left one daughter, Isabel, married at the age of fourteen to William Marshall, Earl of Pembroke, who afterwards claimed the proprietary of Leinster, by virtue of this marriage. Lady Isabel left again five daughters, who were the ancestresses of the Mortimers, Bruces, and other historic families of England and Scotland. And so the blood of Earl Richard and his Irish Princess descended for many generations to enrich other houses and ennoble other names than his own.

Strongbow is described by *Giraldus*, whose personal sketches, of the leading invaders form the most valuable part of his book, as less a statesman than a soldier, and more a soldier than a general. His complexion was freckled, his neck slender, his voice feminine and shrill, and his temper equable and uniform. His career in Ireland was limited to seven years in point of time, and his resources were never equal to the task he undertook. Had they been so, or had he not been so jealously counteracted by his suzerain, he might have founded a new Norman dynasty on as solid a basis as William, or as Rollo himself had done.

Raymond and the Geraldines had now, for a brief moment, the supreme power, civil and military, in their own hands. In his haste to take advantage of the Earl's death, of which he had privately been informed by a message from his wife, Raymond left Limerick in the hands of Donald More O'Brien, exacting, we are told, a solemn oath from the Prince of Thomond to protect the city, which the latter broke before the Norman garrisons were out of sight of its walls. This story, like many others of the same age, rests on the uncertain authority of the vain, impetuous and passionate *Giraldus*. Whether the loss of Limerick discredited him with the king, or the ancient jealousy of the first adventurers prevailed in the royal councils, Henry, on hearing of Strongbow's death, at once despatched as Lord Justice, William Fitz-Aldelm de Burgo, first cousin to Hubert de Burgo, Chief Justiciary of England, and, like Fitz-Aldelm, descended from Arlotta, mother of William the Conqueror, by Harlowen de Burgo, her first husband. From him have descended the noble family of de Burgo, or Burke, so conspicuous in the after annals of our island. In the train of the new Justiciary came John de Courcy, another name destined to become historical, but before relating his achievements, we must conclude the narrative so far as regards the first set of adventurers.

Maurice Fitzgerald, the common ancestor of the Earls of Desmond and Kildare, the Knights of Glyn, of Kerry, and of all the Irish Geraldines, died at Wexford in the year 1177. Raymond the Fat, superceded by Fitz-Aldelm, and looked on coldly by the King, retired to his lands in the same county, and appears only once more in arms—in the year 1182—in aid of his uncle, Robert Fitzstephen. This premier invader had been entrusted by the new ruler with the command of the garrison of Cork, as Milo de Cogan had been with that of Waterford, and both had been invested with equal halves of the principality of Desmond. De Cogan, Ralph, son of Fitzstephen, and other knights had been cut off by surprise, at the house of one McTire near Lismore, in 1182, and all Desmond was up in arms for the expulsion of the foreign garrisons. Raymond sailed from Wexford to the aid of his uncle and succeeded in relieving the city from the sea. But Fitzstephen, afflicted with grief for the death of his son, and worn down with many anxieties, suffered the still greater loss of his reason. From thenceforth, we hear no more of either uncle or nephew, and we may therefore account this the last year of Robert Fitzstephen, Milo de Cogan and Raymond *le gros*. Hervey de Montmorency, the ancient rival of Raymond, had three years earlier retired from the world, to become a brother in the Monastery of the Holy Trinity at Canterbury. His Irish estates passed to his brother Geoffrey, who subsequently became Justiciary of the Normans in Ireland, the successful rival of the Marshals, and founder of the Irish title of Mountmorres. The posterity of Raymond survived in the noble family of Grace, Barons of Courtstown, in Ossory. It is not, therefore, strictly true, what Geoffrey Keating and the authors he followed have asserted —that the first Normans were punished by the loss of posterity for the crimes and outrages they had committed, in their various expeditions.

Let us be just even to these spoilers of our race. They were fair specimens of the prevailing type of Norman character. Indomitable bravery was not their only virtue. In patience, in policy, and in rising superior to all obstacles and reverses, no group of conquerors ever surpassed Strongbow and his companions. Ties of blood and brotherhood in arms were strong between them, and whatever unfair advantages they allowed themselves to take of their enemy, they were in general constant and devoted in their friendships towards each other. Rivalries and intrigues were not unknown among them, but generous self-denial and chivalrous self-reliance were equally as common. If it had been the lot of our ancestors to be effectually conquered they could hardly have yielded to nobler foes. But as they proved themselves able to resist successfully the prowess of this hitherto invincible race, their honor is augmented in proportion to the energy and genius, both for government and war, brought to bear against them.

Neither should we overstate the charge of impiety. If the invaders broke down and burned churches in the heat of battle, they built better and costlier temples out of the fruits of victory. Christ Church, Dublin, Dunbrody Abbey, on the estuary of Waterford, the Grey Friars' Abbey at Wexford, and other religious houses long stood, or still stand, to show that although the first Norman, like the first Dane, thirsted after spoil, and lusted after land, unlike the Dane, he created, he enriched, he improved, wherever he conquered.

CHAPTER VI.

THE LAST YEARS OF THE ARD-RIGH, RODERICK O'CONOR.

THE victory of Thurles, in the year 1174, was the next important military event, as we have seen, after the raising of the second siege of Dublin, in the first campaign of Earl Richard. It seems irreconcileable with the consequences of that victory, that Ambassadors from Roderick should be found at the Court of Henry II. before the close of the following year: but events personal to both sovereigns will sufficiently explain the apparent anomaly.

The campaign of 1174, so unfavorable to Henry's subjects in Ireland, had been most fortunate for his arms in Normandy. His rebellious sons, after severe defeats, submitted, and did him homage; the King of France had gladly accepted his terms of peace; the King of Scotland, while in duress, had rendered him fealty as his liege man; and Queen Eleanor, having fallen into his power, was a prisoner for life. Tried by a similar unnatural conspiracy in his own family, Roderick O'Conor had been less fortunate in coercing them into obedience. His oldest son, Muray, claimed, according to ancient custom, that his father should resign in his favor the patrimonial Province, contenting himself with the higher rank of King of Ireland. But Roderick well understood that in his days, with a new and most formidable enemy established in the old Danish strongholds, with the Constitution torn to shreds by the war of succession, his only real power was over his patrimony; he refused, therefore, the unreasonable request, and thus converted some of his own children into enemies. Nor were there wanting Princes, themselves fathers, who abetted this household treason, as the Kings of France and Scotland had done among the sons of Henry II. Soon after the battle of Thurles, the recovery of Limerick, and the taking of Kilkenny, Donald More O'Brien, lending himself to this odious intrigue, was overpowered and deposed by Roderick, but the year next succeeding having made submission he was restored by the same hand which had cast him down. It was, therefore, while harassed by the open rebellion of his eldest son, and while Henry was rejoicing in his late success, that Roderick despatched to the Court of Windsor Catholicus, Archbishop of Tuam, Concors, Abbot of St. Brendan's, and Laurence, Archbishop of Dublin, who is styled in these proceedings, "Chancellor of the Irish King," to negotiate an alliance with Henry, which would leave him free to combat against his domestic enemies. An extraordinary treaty, agreed upon at Windsor, about the feast of Michaelmas, 1175, recognized Roderick's sovereignty over Ireland, the cantreds and cities actually possessed by the subjects of Henry excepted; it subinfeudated his authority to that of Henry, after the manner lately adopted towards William, King of Scotland; the payment of a merchantable hide of every tenth hide of cattle was agreed upon as an annual tribute, while the minor chiefs were to acknowledge their dependence by annual presents of hawks and hounds. This treaty, which proceeded on the wild assumption that the feudal system was of force among the free clans of Erin, was probably the basis of Henry's grant of the Lordship of Ireland to his son, John *Lackland*, a few years later: it was solemnly approved by a special Council, or Parliament, and signed by the representatives of both parties.

Among the signors we find the name of the Archbishop of

Dublin, who, while in England, narrowly escaped martyrdom from the hands of a maniac, while celebrating Mass at the tomb of St. Thomas. Four years afterwards this celebrated ecclesiastic attended at Rome, with Catholicus of Tuam, and the Prelates of Lismore, Limerick, Waterford and Killaloe, the third general council of Lateran, where they were received with all honor by Pope Alexander III. From Rome he returned with legantine powers which he used with great energy during the year 1180. In the autumn of that year, he was entrusted with the delivery to Henry II. of the son of Roderick O'Conor, as a pledge for the fulfilment of the treaty of Windsor, and with other diplomatic functions. On reaching England, he found the king had gone to France, and following him thither, he was seized with illness as he approached the Monastery of Eu, and with a prophetic foretaste of death, he exclaimed as he came in sight of the towers of the Convent, "here shall I make my resting place." The Abbot Osbert and the monks of the Order of St. Victor, received him tenderly and watched his couch for the few days he yet lingered. Anxious to fulfil his mission he despatched David, tutor of the son of Roderick, with messages to Henry, and awaited his return with anxiety. David brought him a satisfactory response from the English King, and the last anxiety only remained. In death, as in life, his thoughts were with his country. "Ah, foolish and insensible people!" he exclaimed in his latest hours, "what will become of you? Who will relieve your miseries? Who will heal you?" When recommended to make his last will, he answered with apostolic simplicity—"God knows out of all my revenues I have not a single coin to bequeath." And thus on the 11th day of November, 1180, in the 48th year of his age, under the shelter of a Norman roof, surrounded by Norman mourners, the Gaelic statesman-saint departed out of this life, bequeathing one more canonized memory to Ireland and to Rome.

The prospects of his native land were, at that moment, of a cast which might well disturb the death-bed of the sainted Laurence. Fitz-Aldelm, advanced to the command at Dublin in 1177, had shown no great capacity for following up the conquest. But there was one among his followers who, unaffected by his sluggish example, and undeterred by his jealous interference, resolved to push the outposts of his race into the heart of Ulster. This was John de Courcy, Baron of Stoke Courcy, in Somersetshire, a cavalier of fabulous physical strength, romantic courage, and royal descent. When he declared his settled purpose to be the invasion of Ulster, he found many spirits as discontented with Fitz-Aldelm's inaction as himself ready to follow his banner. His inseparable brother-in-arms, Sir Almaric of St. Laurence, his relative, Jourdain de Courcy, Sir Robert de la Poer, Sir Geoffrey and Walter de Marisco, and other Knights to the number of twenty, and five hundred men at arms, marched with him out of Dublin. Hardly had they got beyond sight of the city, when they were attacked by a native force, near Howth, where Saint Laurence laid in victory the foundation of that title still possessed by his posterity. On the fifth day, they came by surprise upon the famous ecclesiastical city of Downpatrick, one of the first objects of their adventure. An ancient prophecy had foretold that the place would be taken by a chief with birds upon his shield, the bearings of de Courcy, mounted on a white horse, which de Courcy happened to ride. Thus the terrors of superstition were added to the terrors of surprise, and the town being entirely open, the Normans had only to dash into the midst of its inhabitants. But the free clansmen of Ulidia, though surprised, were not intimidated. Under their lord Rory, son of Dunlevy, they rallied to expel the invader. Cardinal Vivian, the Papal Legate, who had just arrived from Man and Scotland, on the neighboring coast, proffered his mediation, and besought de Courcy to withdraw from Down. His advice was peremptorily rejected, and then he exhorted the Ulidians to fight bravely for their rights. Five several battles are enumerated as being fought, in this and the following year, between de Courcy and the men of Down, Louth, and Antrim, sometimes with success, at others without it, always with heavy loss and obstinate resistance.

The barony of Lecale in which Downpatrick stands is almost a peninsula, and the barony of the Ardes on the opposite shore of Strangford Lough is nearly insulated by Belfast Lough, the Channel, and the tides of Strangford. With the active co-operation from the sea of Godred, King of Man, (whose daughter

Africa he had married,) de Courcy's hold on that coast became an exceedingly strong one. A ditch and a few towers would as effectually enclose Lecale and the Ardes from any landward attack, as if they were a couple of well-walled cities. Hence, long after "the Pale" ceased to extend beyond the Boyne, and while the mountain passes from Meath into Ulster were all in native hands, these two baronies continued to be succored and strengthened by sea, and retained as English possessions. Reinforced from Dublin and from Man after their first success, de Courcy's companions stuck to their castle-building about the shores of Strangford Lough, while he himself made incursions into the interior, by land or by sea, fighting a brisk succession of engagements at Newry, in Antrim, at Coleraine, and on the eastern shore of Lough Foyle.

At the time these operations were going forward in Ulster, Milo de Cogan quitted Dublin on a somewhat similar expedition. We have already said that Murray, eldest son of Roderick, had claimed, according to ancient usage, the O'Conor patrimony, his father being Ard-Righ; and had his claim refused. He now entered into a secret engagement with de Cogan, whose force is stated by *Giraldus* at 500 men-at-arms; and by the Irish annalists as "a great army." With the smaller force he left Dublin, but, marching through Meath, was joined at Trim by men from the garrisons de Lacy had planted in East-Meath. So accompanied, de Cogan advanced on Roscommon, where he was received by the son of Roderick during the absence of the Ard-Righ on a visitation among the glens of Connemara. After three days spent in Roscommon, these allies marched across the plain of Connaught, directed their course on Tuam, burning as they went Elphin, Roskeen, and many other churches. The western clansmen everywhere fell back before them, driving off their herds and destroying whatever they could not remove. At Tuam they found themselves in the midst of a solitude without food or forage, with an eager enemy swarming from the west and the south to surround them. They at once decided to retreat, and no time was to be lost, as the Kern were already at their heels. From Tuam to Athleague and from Athleague to their castles in East-Meath, fled the remnant of de Cogan's inglorious expedition. Murray O'Conor being taken prisoner by his own kinsmen, his eyes were plucked out as the punishment of his treason, and Conor Moinmoy, the joint-victor, with Donald O'Brien over Strongbow at Thurles, became the *Roydamna* or successor of his father.

But fresh dissensions soon broke out between the sons and grandsons of Roderick, and the sons of his brother Thurlogh, in one of whose deadly conflicts sixteen Princes of the Sil-Murray fell. Both sides looked beyond Connaught for help; one drew friends from the northern O'Neills, another relied on the aid of O'Brien. Conor Moinmoy, in the year 1186, according to most Irish accounts, banished his father into Munster, but at the intercession of the Sil-Murray, his own clan, allowed him again to return, and assigned him a single cantred of land for his subsistence. From this date we may count the unhappy Roderick's retirement from the world.

Near the junction of Lough Corrib with Lough Mask, on the boundary line between Mayo and Galway, stands the ruins of the once populous monastery and village of Cong. The first Christian kings of Connaught had founded the monastery, or enabled St. Fechin to do so by their generous donations. The father of Roderick had enriched its shrine by the gift of a particle of the true Cross, reverently enshrined in a reliquary, the workmanship of which still excites the admiration of the antiquaries. Here Roderick retired in the 70th year of his age, and for twelve years thereafter—until the 29th day of November, 1198, here he wept and prayed, and withered away. Dead to the world, as the world to him, the opening of a new grave in the royal corner at Clonmacnoise was the last incident connected with his name, which reminded Connaught that it had lost its once prosperous Prince, and Ireland, that she had seen her last Ard-Righ, according to the ancient Milesian Constitution. Powerful Princes of his own and other houses the land was destined to know for many generations, before its sovereignty was merged in that of England, but none fully entitled to claim the high-sounding, but often fallacious title, of Monarch of all Ireland.

The public character of Roderick O'Conor has been hardly dealt with by most modern writers. He was not like his father, like Murkertach O'Brien, Malachy II., Brian, Murkertach of the leathern cloaks, or Malachy I., eminent as a lawgiver, a soldier, or a popular leader. He does not appear to have inspired love, or awe, or reverence, into those of his own household and patrimony, not to speak of his distant cotemporaries. He was probably a man of secondary qualities, engulped in a crisis of the first importance. But that he is fairly chargeable with the success of the invaders—or that there was any very overwhelming success to be charged up to the time of his enforced retirement from the world—we have failed to discover. From Dermid's return until his retreat to Cong, seventeen years had passed away. Seventeen campaigns, more or less energetic and systematic, the Normans had fought. Munster was still in 1185 —when John Lackland made his memorable exit and entrance on the scene—almost wholly in the hands of the ancient clans. Connaught was as yet without a single Norman garrison. Hugh de Lacy returning to the government of Dublin, in 1179, on Fitz-Aldelm's recall, was more than half *Hibernicized* by marriage with one of Roderick's daughters, and the Norman tide stood still in Meath. Several strong fortresses were indeed erected in Desmond and Leinster, by John Lackland and by de Courcy, in his newly won northern territory. Ardfinan, Lismore, Leighlin, Carlow, Castledermot, Leix, Delvin, Kilkay, Maynooth and Trim, were fortified; but considering who the Anglo-Normans were, and what they had done elsewhere, even these very considerable successes may be corrrectly accounted for without overcharging the memory of Roderick with folly and incapacity. That he was personally brave has not been questioned. That he was politic—or at least capable of conceiving the politic views of such a statesman as St. Laurence O'Toole, we may infer from the rank of Chancellor which he conferred, and the other negotiations which he entrusted to that great man. That he maintained his self-respect as a sovereign, both in abstaining from visiting Henry II. under pretence of hospitality at Dublin and throughout all his difficult diplomacy with the Normans, we are free to conclude. With the Normans for foes—with a decayed and obselete national constitution to patch up—with nominal subordinates more powerful than himself—with rebellion staring him in the face out of the eyes of his own children—Roderick O'Conor had no ordinary part to play in history. The fierce family pride of our fathers and the vices of their political system are to be deplored and avoided; let us not make the last of their national kings the scape-goat for all his cotemporaries and all his predecessors.

CHAPTER VII.

ASSASSINATION OF HUGH DE LACY—JOHN "LACKLAND" IN IRELAND—VARIOUS EXPEDITIONS OF JOHN DE COURCY—DEATH OF CONOR MOINMOY, AND RISE OF CATHAL, "THE RED-HANDED" O'CONOR—CLOSE OF THE CAREER OF DE COURCY AND DE BURGH.

HUGH DE LACY, restored to the supreme authority on the recall of Fitz-Aldelm in 1179, began to conceive hopes, as Strongbow had done, of carving out for himself a new kingdom. After the assassination of O'Ruarc, already related, he assumed without further parley the titles of lord of Meath and Breffni. To these titles he added that of Oriel, or Louth, but his real strength lay in Meath, where his power was enhanced by a politic second marriage with Rose, daughter of O'Conor. Among the Irish he now began to be known as King of the foreigners, and some such assumption of royal authority caused his recall for a few months in the year 1180, and his substitution by de Courcy and Philip de Broasa, in 1184. But his great qualities caused his restoration a third time to the rank of Justiciary for Henry, or Deputy for John, whose title of "Lord of Ireland" was bestowed by his father, at a Parliament held at Oxford, in 1177.

This founder of the Irish de Lacys is described by *Giraldus*, who knew him personally, as a man of Gallic sobriety, ambitious, avaricious, and lustful; of small stature, and deformed shape, with repulsive features, and dark, deep-set eyes. By the Irish of the midland districts he was bitterly detested as a sacrilegious spoiler of their churches and monasteries, and the most powerful among their invaders. The murder of O'Ruarc, whose title of Breffni he had usurped, was attributed to a deep-laid design; he certainly shared the odium with the advantage that ensued from it. Nor was his own end unlike that of his rival. Among other sites for castles, he had chosen the foundations of the ancient and much venerated monastery of Durrow, planted by Columbcille, seven centuries before, in the midst of the fertile region, watered by the Brosna. This act of profanity was fated to be his last, for, while personally superintending the work, O'Meyey, a young man of good birth, and foster-brother to a neighboring chief of Teffia, known as *Sionnach*, or "the Fox," struck off his head with a single blow of his axe and escaped into the neighboring forest of Kilclare during the confusion which ensued. De Lacy left issue—two sons, Hugh and Walter, by his first wife, and a third, William *Gorm*, by his second—of whom, and of their posterity, we shall have many occasions to make mention.

In one of the intervals of de Lacy's disfavor Prince John, surnamed *Sans-terre*, or "lack-land," was sent over by his father to strengthen the English interest in Ireland. He arrived in Waterford, accompanied by a fleet of sixty ships, on the last of March, 1185, and remained in the country till the following November. If anything could excuse the levity, folly and misconduct of the Prince on this expedition, it would be his youth;—he was then only eighteen. But Henry had taken every precaution to ensure success to his favorite son. He was preceded into Ireland by Archbishop Cuming, the English successor of St. Laurence; the learned Glanville was his legal adviser; John de Courcy was his lieutenant, and the eloquent, but passionate and partial *Giraldus Cambrensis*, his chaplain and tutor. He had, however, other companions more congenial to his age and temper, young noblemen as froward and as extravagant as himself; yet as he surpassed them all in birth and rank, so he did in wickedness and cruelty of disposition. For age he had no reverence, for virtue no esteem, neither truth towards man, nor decency towards woman. On his arrival at Waterford, the new Archbishop of Dublin, John de Courcy, and the principal Norman nobles, hastened to receive him. With them came also certain Leinster chiefs, desiring to live at peace with the new Galls. When, according to the custom of the country, the chiefs advanced to give John the kiss of peace, their venerable age was made a mockery by the young Prince, who met their proffered salutations by plucking at their beards. This appears to have been as deadly an insult to the Irish as it is to the Asiatics, and the deeply offended guests instantly quitted Waterford. Other follies and excesses rapidly transpired, and the native nobles began to discover that a royal army encumbered, rather than led by such a Prince, was not likely to prove itself invincible. In an idle parade from the Suir to the Liffey, from the Liffey to the Boyne, and in issuing orders for the erection of castles, (some of which are still correctly and others erroneously called King John's Castles,) the campaign months of the year were wasted by the King of England's son. One of these castles, to which most importance was attached, Ardfinan on the Suir, was no sooner built than taken by Donald More O'Brien, on midsummer day, when four knights and its other defenders were slain. Another was rising at Lismore, on the Blackwater, under the guardianship of Robert Barry, one of the brood of Nesta, when it was attacked and Barry slain. Other knights and castellans were equally unfortunate; Raymond Fitz-Hugh fell at Leighlin, another Raymond in Idrone, and Roger le Poer in Ossory. In Desmond, Cormac McCarthy besieged Theobald, ancestor of the Butlers in Cork, but this brave Prince—the worthy compeer of O Brien—was cut off "in a parlee by them of Cork." The Clan-Colman, or O'Melaghlins, had risen in Westmeath to reclaim their own, when Henry, not an hour too soon, recalled his reckless son, and entrusted, for the last time, the command to Hugh de Lacy, whose fate has been already related.

In the fluctuations of the power of the invaders after the death of de Lacy, and during the next reign in England, one steadfast name appears foremost among the adventurers—that of the gallant giant, de Courcy, the conqueror of the Ards of Down. Not only in prowess, but also in piety, he was the model of all the knighthood of his time. We are told that he always carried about his person a copy of the prophecies attributed to Columbcille, and when, in the year 1186, the relics of the three great saints, whose dust sanctifies Downpatrick, were supposed to be discovered by the Bishop of Down in a dream, he caused them to be translated to the altar-side with all suitable reverence. Yet all his devotions and pilgrimages did not prevent him from pushing on the work of conquest whenever occasion offered. His plantation in Down had time to take root from the unexpected death of Donald, Prince of Aileach, in an encounter with the garrison of one of the new castles, near Newry. (A. D. 1188.) The same year he took up the enterprize against Connaught, in which Milo de Cogan had so signally failed, and from which even de Lacy had, for reasons of his own, refrained. The feuds of the O'Conor family were again the pretext and the ground of hope with the invaders, but Donald More O'Brien, victorious on the Suir and the Shannon, carried his strong succors to Conor *Moinmoy* on the banks of the Suca, near the present Ballinasloe, and both powers combined marched against de Courcy. Unprepared for this junction, the Norman retreated towards Sligo, and had reached Ballysadare, when Flaherty, Lord of Tyrconnel (Donegal), came against them from the opposite point, and thus placed between two fires, they were forced to fly through the rugged passes of the Curlieu mountains, skirmishing as they went. The only incidents which signalized this campaign on their side was the burning of Ballysadare and the plunder of Armagh; to the Irish it was creditable for the combinations it occasioned. It is cheering in the annals of those desultory wars to find a national advantage gained by the joint action of a Munster, a Connaught, and an Ulster force.

The promise of national unity held out by the alliance of O'Brien and O'Conor, in the years 1188-'89, had been followed up by the adhesion of the lords of Breffni, Ulidia, or Down, the chiefs of the Clan-Colman, and McCarthy, Prince of Desmond. But the assassination of Conor Moinmoy, by the partizans of his cousins, extinguished the hopes of the country, and the peace of his own province. The old family feuds broke out with new fury. In vain the aged Roderick emerged from his convent, and sought with feeble hand to curb the fiery passions of his tribe; in vain the Archbishops of Armagh and of Tuam interposed their spiritual authority. A series of fratricidal contests, for which history has no memory and no heart, were fought out between the waring branches of the family during the last ten years of the century, until by virtue of the strong arm, Cathal *Crovdearg*, son of Turlogh More, and younger brother of Roderick, assumed the sovereignty of Connaught about the year 1200.

In the twelve years which intervened between the death of *Moinmoy* and the establishment of the power of Cathal *Crovdearg* O'Conor, the Normans had repeated opportunities for intervention in the affairs of Connaught. William de Burgh, a powerful Baron of the family of Fitz-Aldelm, the former Lord Justice, sided with the opponents of Cathal, while de Courcy, and subsequently the younger de Lacy, fought on his side. Once at least these restless Barons changed allies, and fought as desperately against their former candidate for the succession as they had before fought for him. In one of these engagements, the date assigned to which is the year 1190, Sir Armoric St. Laurence, founder of the Howth family, at the head of a numerous division, is said to have been cut off with all his troop. But the fortune of war frequently shifted during the contest. In the year 1199, Cathal *Crovdearg*, with his allies de Lacy and de Courcy, was utterly defeated at Kilmacduagh, in the present county of Galway, and were it not that the rival O'Conor was sorely defeated, and trodden to death in the route which ensued, three years later, Connaught might never have known the vigorous administration of her "red-handed" hero.

The early career of this able and now triumphant Prince, as preserved to us by history and tradition, is full of romantic incidents. He is said to have been born out of wedlock, and that his mother, while pregnant of him, was subject to all the cruel persecutions and magical torments the jealous wife of his father could invent. No sooner was he born than he became an object of hatred to the Queen, so that mother and child, after being concealed for three years in the sanctuaries of Connaught, had to fly for their lives into Leinster. In this exile, though early informed of his origin, he was brought up among the laborers in the field and was actually engaged, sickle in hand, cutting the harvest, when a travelling *Bollscaire*, or newsman from the west, related the events which enabled him to return to his native province. "Farewell sickle," he exclaimed, casting it from him—"now for the sword." Hence "Cathal's farewell to the rye" was long a proverbial expression for any sudden change of purpose or of condition. Fortune seems to have favored him in most of his undertakings. In a storm upon Lough Ree, when a whole fleet foundered and its warrior crew perished, he was one of seven who was saved. Though in some of his early battles unsuccessful, he always recovered his ground, kept up his alliances, and returned to the contest. After the death of the celebrated Donald More O'Brien (A. D. 1194) he may certainly be considered the first soldier and first diplomatist among the Irish. Nor was his lot cast on more favored days, nor was he pitted against less able men than those with whom the brave King of Munster—the stoutest defender of his fatherland—had so honorably striven. Fortunate it was for the renown of the Gael, that as one star of the race set over Thomond, another of equal brilliancy rose to guide them in the west.

With the end of the century, the career of Cathal's allies, de Courcy and de Burgh, may be almost said to have ended. The obituary of the latter bears the date of 1204. He had obtained large grants from King John of lands in Connaught—if he could conquer them—which his vigorous descendants, the Burkes of Clanrickarde, did their best to accomplish. De Courcy, waring with the sons of de Lacy and seeking refuge among the clansmen of Tyrone, disappears from the stage of Irish affairs. He is said to have passed on to England, and ended his days in prison, a victim to the caprice or jealousy of King John. Many tales are told of his matchless intrepidity. His indirect descendants, the Barons of Kinsale, claim the right to wear their hats before the King in consequence of one of these legends, which represents him as the champion Knight of England, taken from a dungeon to uphold her honor against a French challenger. Other tales as ill authenticated are founded on his career, which, however, in its literal truth, is unexcelled for hardihood and adventure, except, perhaps, by the cotemporaneous story of the lion-hearted Richard, whom he closely resembled. The title of Earl of Ulster, created for de Courcy in 1181, was transferred in 1205, by royal patent, to Walter de Lacy, whose only daughter

Maud brought it in the year 1264 to Walter de Burgh, lord of Connaught, from whose fourth female descendant it passed in 1354, by her marriage with Lionel, Duke of Clarence, into the royal family of England.

CHAPTER VIII.

EVENTS OF THE THIRTEENTH CENTURY — THE NORMANS IN CONNAUGHT.

IRELAND, during the first three quarters of the thirteenth century, produced fewer important events, and fewer great men, than in the thirty last years of the century preceding. From the side of England, she was subjected to no imminent danger, in all that interval. The reign of John ending in 1216, and that of Henry III. extending till 1271, were fully occupied with the insurrections of the Barons, with French, Scotch, and Welsh wars, family feuds, the rise and fall of royal favorites, and all those other incidents which naturally befal in a state of society where the King is weak, the aristocracy strong and insolent, and the commons disunited and despised. During this period the fusion of Norman, Saxon and Briton went slowly on, and the next age saw for the first time a population which could be properly called English. "Do you take me for an Englishman?" was the last expression of Norman arrogance in the reign of King John; but the close of the reign of Henry III., through the action of commercial and political causes, saw a very different state of feeling growing up between the descendants of the races which contended for mastery under Harold and William. The strongly marked Norman characteristics lingered in Ireland half a century later, for it is usually the case that traits of caste survive longest in colonies and remote provinces. In Richard de Burgo, commonly called the Red Earl of Ulster, all the genius and the vices of the race of Rollo blazed out over Ireland for the last time, and with terrible effect.

During the first three quarters of the century, our history, like

that of England, is the history of a few great houses; nation
there is, strictly speaking, none. It will be necessary, therefore,
to group together the acts of two or three generations of
men of the same name, as the only method of finding our way
through the shifting scenes of this stormy period.

The power of the great Connaught family of O'Conor, so
terribly shaken by the fratricidal wars and unnatural alliances
of the sons and grandsons of Roderick, was in great part restored by the ability and energy of Cathal *Crovdearg*. In his
early struggles for power he was greatly assisted by the anarchy
which reigned among the English nobles. Mayler Fitz-Henry,
the last of Strongbow's companions, who rose to such eminence,
being justiciary in the first six years of the century, was aided
by O'Conor to besiege William de Burgo in Limerick, and to
cripple the power of the de Lacy's in Meath. In the year 1207,
John Gray, Bishop of Norwich, was sent over, as more likely to
be impartial than any ruler personally interested in the old quarrels, but during his first term of office, the interdict with which
Innocent III. had smitten England, hung like an Egyptian darkness over the Anglo-Norman power in Ireland. The native Irish,
however, were exempt from its enervating effects, and Cathal
O'Conor, by the time King John came over in person—in the
year 1210—to endeavor to retrieve the English interest, had
warred down all his enemies, and was of power sufficient to treat
with the English sovereign as independently as Roderick had
done with Henry II. thirty-five years before. He personally
conferred with John at Dublin, as the O'Neil and other native
Princes did; he procured from the English King the condemna-
tion of John de Burgo, who had maintained his father's claims
on a portion of Connaught, and he was formally recognized,
according to the approved forms of Norman diplomacy, as seized
of the whole of Connaught, in his own right.

The visit of King John, which lasted from the 20th of June
till the 25th of August, was mainly directed to the reduction of
those intractable Anglo-Irish Barons whom Fitz-Henry and Gray
had proved themselves unable to cope with. Of these the de
Lacys of Meath were the most obnoxious. They not only
assumed an independent state, but had sheltered de Braos, Lord

of Brecknock, one of the recusant Barons of Wales, and refused to surrender him on the royal summons. To assert his authority and to strike terror into the nobles of other possessions, John crossed the channel with a prodigious fleet—in the Irish annals said to consist of 700 sail. He landed at Crook, reached Dublin, and prepared at once to subdue the Lacys. With his own army, and the co-operation of Cathal O'Conor, he drove out Walter de Lacy, Lord of Meath, who fled to his brother, Hugh de Lacy, since de Courcy's disgrace, Earl of Ulster. From Meath into Louth John pursued the brothers, crossing the lough at Carlingford with his ships, which must have coasted in his company. From Carlingford they retreated, and he pursued to Carrickfergus, and from that fortress, unable to resist a royal fleet and navy, they fled into Man or Scotland, and thence escaped in disguise into France. With their guest de Braos, they wrought as gardeners in the grounds of the Abbey of Saint Taurin Evreux, until the Abbot, having discovered by their manners the key to their real rank, negotiated successfully with John for their restoration to their estates. Walter agreed to pay a fine of 2,500 marks for his lordship in Meath, and Hugh 4,000 marks for his possessions in Ulster. Of de Braos we have no particulars; his high-spirited wife and children were thought to have been starved to death by order of the unforgiving tyrant in one of his castles. The de Lacys, on their restoration, were accompanied to Ireland by a nephew of the Abbot of St. Taurin, on whom they conferred an estate and the honor of knighthood.

The only other acts of John's sojourn in Ireland, was his treaty with O'Conor, already mentioned, and the mapping out, on paper, of the intended counties of Oriel (or Louth), Meath, Dublin, Kildare, Kilkenny, Katherlough (or Carlow), Wexford, Waterford, Cork, Kerry, Limerick, and Tipperary, as the only districts in which those he claimed as his subjects had any possessions. He again installed the Bishop of Norwich as his justiciary or lieutenant, who, three years later, was succeeded by Henry de Londres, the next Archbishop of Dublin, and he again (A. D. 1215), by Geoffrey de Marisco, the last of John's deputies. In the year 1216, Henry III., an infant ten years of age, succeeded to the English throne, and the next dozen years the history of the two islands is slightly connected, except by the fortunes of the family of de Burgh, whose head, Hubert de Burgh, the Chief Justiciary, from the accession of the new King, until the first third of the century had closed, was in reality the Sovereign of England. Among his other titles he held that of Lord of Connaught, which he conveyed to his relative, Richard de Burgo, the son or grandson of William Fitz-Aldelm de Burgo, about the year 1225. And this brings us to relate how the house of Clanrickard rose upon the flank of the house of O'Conor, and after holding an almost equal front for two generations, finally overshadowed its more ancient rival.

While Cathal *Crovdearg* lived, the O'Conors held their own, and rather more than their own, by policy or arms. Not only did his own power suffer no diminution, but he more than once assisted the Dalgais and the Eugenians to expel their invaders from North and South Munster, and to uphold their ancient rights and laws. During the last years of John's reign that King and his Barons were mutually too busy to set aside the arrangement entered into in 1210. In the first years of Henry it was also left undisturbed by the English court. In 1221 we read that the de Lacys, remembering, no doubt, the part he had played in their expulsion, endeavored to fortify Athleague against him, but the veteran King, crossing the Shannon farther northward, took them in the rear, compelled them to make peace, and broke down their Castle. This was almost the last of his victories. In the year 1213 we read in the Annals of "an awful and heavy shower which fell over Connaught," and was held to presage the death of its heroic King. Feeling his hour had come, this Prince, to whom are justly attributed the rare union of virtues, ardor of mind, chastity of body, meekness in prosperity, fortitude under defeat, prudence in civil business, undaunted bravery in battle, and a piety of life beyond all his cotemporaries — feeling the near approach of death retired to the Abbey of Knockmoy, which he had founded and endowed, and there expired in the Franciscan habit, at an age which must have bordered on fourscore. He was succeeded by his son, Hugh O'Conor, "the hostages of Connaught being in his house" at the time of his illustrious father's death.

No sooner was Cathal *Crovdearg* deceased than Hubert de Burgo procured the grants of the whole Province, reserving only five cantreds about Athlone for a royal garrison to be made to Richard de Burgo, his nephew. Richard had married Hodierna, granddaughter to Cathal, and thus like all the Normans, though totally against the Irish custom, claimed a part of Connaught in right of his wife. But in the sons of Cathal he found his equal both in policy and arms, and with the fall of his uncle at the English court, (about the year 1233,) Feidlim O'Conor, the successor of Hugh, taking advantage of the event, made interest at the Court of Henry III. sufficient to have his overgrown neighbor stripped of some of his strongholds by royal order. The King was so impressed with O'Conor's representations that he wrote peremptorily to Maurice Fitzgerald, second Lord Offally, then his deputy, " to root out that barren tree planted in Offally by Hubert de Burgh, in the madness of his power, and not to suffer it to shoot forth." Five years later, Feidlim. in return, carried some of his force, in conjunction with the deputy, to Henry's aid in Wales, though, as their arrival was somewhat tardy, Fitzgerald was soon after dismissed on that account.

Richard de Burgo died in attendance on King Henry in France (A. D. 1243), and was succeeded by his son, Walter de Burgo, who continued, with varying fortunes, the contest for Connaught with Feidlim, until the death of the latter, in the Black Abbey of Roscommon, in the year 1265. Hugh O'Conor, the son and successor of Feidlim, continued the intrepid guardian of his house and province during the nine years he survived his father. In the year 1254, by marriage with the daughter of de Lacy, Earl of Ulster, that title had passed into the family of de Burgh, bringing with it, for the time, much substantial, though distant, strength. It was considered only a secondary title, and as the eldest son of the first de Lacy remained Lord of Meath, while the younger took de Courcy's forfeited title of Ulster, so, in the next generation, did the sons of this Walter de Burgh, until death and time reunited both titles in the same person. Walter de Burgh died in the year 1271, in the Castle of Galway; his great rival, Feidlim O'Conor, in 1274, was buried in the Abbey of Boyle.

The former is styled King of the English of Connaught by the Irish Aonalists, who also speak of Feidlim as "the most triumphant and the most feared (by the invaders) of any King that had been in Connaught before his time." The relative position of the Irish and English in that Province, towards the end of this century may be judged by the fact, that of the Anglo-Normans summoned by Edward I. to join him in Scotland in 1299, but two, Richard de Burgo and Piers de Bermingham, Baron of Athenry, had then possessions in Connaught. There were Norman Castles at Athlone, at Athenry, at Galway, and perhaps at other points; but the natives still swayed supreme over the plains of Rathcrogan, the plains of Boyle, the forests and lakes of Roscommon, and the whole of *Iar*, or West Connaught, from Lough Corrib to the ocean, with the very important exception of the castle, and port of Galway. A mightier de Burgo than any that had yet appeared was to see in his house, in the year 1286, "the hostages of all Connaught;" but his life and death form a distinct epoch in our story and must be treated separately.

CHAPTER IX.

EVENTS OF THE THIRTEENTH CENTURY—THE NORMANS IN MUNSTER AND LEINSTER.

WE have already told the tragic fate of the two adventurers—Fitzstephen and de Cogan—between whom the whole of Desmond was first partitioned by Henry II. But there were not wanting other claimants, either by original grant from the crown, by intermarriage with Irish or Norman-Irish heiresses, or newcomers, favorites of John or of Henry III., or of their Ministers, enriched at the expense of the native population. Thomas, third son of Maurice Fitzgerald, claimed partly through his uncle Fitzstephen, and partly through his marriage with the daughter of another early adventurer, Sir William Morrie, those vast estates on which his descendants were afterwards known as Earls of Desmond, the White Knight, the Knight of Glynn, and the

Knight of Kerry. Robert de Carow and Patrick de Courcy claimed as heirs general to de Cogan. The de Mariscoes, de Barris, and le Poers were not extinct; and finally Edward I., soon after his accession, granted the whole land of Thomond to Thomas de Clare, son of the Earl of Gloucester, and son-in-law of Maurice, third Baron of Offaly. A contest very similar to that which was waged in Connaught between the O'Conors and de Burghs was consequently going on in Munster at the same time, between the old inhabitants and the new claimants, of all the three classes just indicated.

The principality of Desmond, containing angles of Waterford and Tipperary, with all Cork and Kerry, seemed at the beginning of the thirteenth century in greatest danger of conquest. The O'Callaghans, Lords of Cinel-Aedha, in the south of Cork, were driven into the mountains of Duhallow, where they rallied and held their ground for four centuries; the O'Sullivans, originally settled along the Suir, about Clonmel, were forced towards the mountain seacoast of Cork and Kerry, where they acquired new vigor in the less fertile soil of Beare and Bantry. The native families of the Desies, from their proximity to the port of Waterford, were harassed and overrun, and the ports of Dungarvan, Youghal and Cork, being also taken and garrisoned by the founder of the earldom of Desmond, easy entrance and egress by sea could always be obtained for his allies, auxiliaries and supplies. It was when these dangers were darkening and menacing on every side that the family of McCarthy, under a succession of able and vigorous chiefs, proved themselves worthy of the headship of the Eugenian race. Cormac McCarthy, who had expelled the first garrison from Waterford, ere he fell in a parley before Cork, had defeated the first enterprises of Fitzstephen and de Cogan; he left a worthy son in Donald na Curra, who, uniting his own co-relations, and acting in conjunction with O'Brien and O'Conor, retarded by his many exploits the progress of the invasion in Munster. He recovered Cork, and razed King John's castle at Knockgraffon on the Suir. He left two surviving sons, of whom the eldest, Donald *Gott*, or the Stammerer, took the title of *More*, or Great, and his posterity remained princes of Desmond, until that title merged in the earldom of Glencare

(A. D. 1565); the other, Cormac, after taking his brother prisoner compelled him to acknowledge him as lord of the four baronies of Carbury. From this Cormac the family of McCarthy Reagh descended, and to them the O'Driscolls, O'Donovans, O'Mahonys, and other Eugenian houses became tributary. The chief residence of McCarthy Reagh was long fixed at Dunmanway; his castles were also at Baltimore, Castlehaven, Lough-Fyne, and in Inis-Sherkin and Clear Island. The power of McCarthy More extended at its greatest reach from Tralee in Kerry to Lismore in Waterford. In the year 1229, Dermid McCarthy had peaceable possession of Cork, and founded the Franciscan Monastery there. Such was his power, that, according to Hamner and his authorities, the Geraldines "dare not for twelve years put plough into the ground in Desmond." At last, another generation rose, and fierce family feuds broke out between the branches of the family. The Lord of Carbury now was Fineen, or Florence, the most celebrated man of his name, and one whose power naturally encroached upon the possession of the elder house. John, son of Thomas Fitzgerald of Desmond, seized the occasion to make good the enormous pretension of his family. In the expedition which he undertook for this purpose, in the year 1260, he was joined by the Justiciary, William Dene, by Walter de Burgo, Earl of Ulster, by Walter de Riddlesford, Baron of Bray, by Donnel Roe, a chief of the hostile house of McCarthy. The Lord of Carbury united under his standard the chief Eugenian families, not only of the Coast, but even of McCarthy More's principality, and the battle was fought with great ferocity at Callan-glen, near Kenmare, in Kerry. There the Anglo-Normans received the most complete defeat they had yet experienced on Irish ground. John Fitz-Thomas, his son Maurice, eight barons, fifteen knights, and "countless numbers of common soldiers were slain." The Monastery of Tralee received the dead body of its founder and his son, while Florence McCarthy, following up his blow, captured and broke down in swift succession all the English castles in his neighborhood, including those of Macroom, Dunnamark, Dunloe, and Killorglin. In besieging one of these castles, called Ringrone, the victorious chief, in the full tide of conquest, was cut off, and his brother, called the *Athcleireach* (or suspended priest), succeeded to his possessions. The death of the victor arrested the panic of the defeat, but Munster saw another generation before her invaders had shaken off the depression of the battle of Callan-glen.

Before the English interest had received this severe blow in the south, a series of events had transpired in Leinster going to show that its aspiring barons had been seized with the madness which precedes destruction. William, Earl Marshal and Protector of England during the minority of Henry III., had married Isabella, the daughter of Strongbow and granddaughter of Dermid, through whom he assumed the title of Lord of Leinster. He procured the office of Earl Marshal of Ireland—originally conferred on the first de Lacy—for his own nephew, and thus converted the de Lacys into mortal enemies. His son and successor Richard, having made himself obnoxious, soon after his accession to that title, to the young King, or to Hubert de Burgh, was outlawed, and letters were despatched to the Justiciary, Fitzgerald, to de Burgo, de Lacy, and other Anglo-Irish lords, if he landed in Ireland, to seize his person, alive or dead, and send it to England. Strong in his estates and alliances, the young Earl came; while his enemies employed the wily Geoffrey de Mountmorres to entrap him into a conference, in order to his destruction. The meeting was appointed for the first day of April, 1234, and while the outlawed Earl was conversing with those who had invited him, an affray began among their servants by design, he himself was mortally wounded and carried to one of Fitzgerald's castles, where he died. He was succeeded in his Irish honors by three of his brothers, who all died without heirs male. Anselme, the last Earl Marshal of his family, dying in 1245, left five co-heiresses, Maud, Joan, Isabel, Sybil, and Eva, between whom the Irish estates—or such portions of them in actual possession—were divided. They married respectively the Earls of Norfolk, Suffolk, Gloucester, Ferrers, and Braos, or Bruce, Lord of Brecknock, in whose families, for another century or more, the secondary titles were Catherlogh, Kildare, Wexford, Kilkenny, and Leix,—those fine districts being supposed, most absurdly, to have come into the Marshal family, from the daughter of Strongbow. The false knights and dishonored nobles concerned in the murder of Richard Marshal were disappointed of the prey which had been promised them—the partition of his estates. And such was the horror which the deed excited in England, that it hastened the fall of Hubert de Burgh, though Maurice Fitzgerald, of Offally —ancestor of the Kildare family—having cleared himself of all complicity in it by oath—was continued as Justiciary for ten years longer. In the year 1245, for his tardiness in joining the King's army in Wales, he was succeeded by the false-hearted Geoffrey de Mountmorres, who held the office till 1247. During the next twenty-five years, about half as many Justices were placed and displaced, according to the whim of the successive favorites at the English Court. In 1252, Prince Edward, afterwards Edward I., was appointed with the title of Lord Lieutenant, but never came over. Nor is there in the series of rulers we have numbered, with, perhaps, two exceptions, any who have rendered their names memorable by great exploits, or lasting legislation. So little inherent power had the incumbents of the highest office—unless when they employed their own proper forces in their sovereign's name—that we read without surprise, how the bold mountaineers of Wicklow at the opening of the century (A.D. 1209) slaughtered the Bristolians of Dublin, engaged at their archery in Cullenswood, and at the close of it, how "one of the Kavanaghs, of the blood of McMurrogh, living at Leinster," "displayed his standards within sight of the city." Yet this is commonly spoken of as a country overrun by a few score Norman Knights, in a couple of campaigns!

The maintenance of the conquest was in these years less the work of the King's Justices than of the great houses. Of these, two principally profitted, by the untimely felling of that great tree which overshadowed all others in Leinster, the Marshals. The descendants of the eldest son of Maurice Fitzgerald clung to their Leinster possessions, while their equally vigorous cousins pushed their fortunes in Desmond. Maurice, grandson of Maurice, and second Baron of Offally, from the year 1229 to the year 1246, was three times Lord Justice. "He was a valiant Knight, a very pleasant man, and inferior to none in the kingdom," by Matthew Paris's account. He introduced the Franciscan and Dominican orders into Ireland, built many castles, churches, and abbeys at Youghal, at Sligo, at Armagh, at Maynooth, and in other places. In the year 1257, he was wounded in single combat by O'Donnell, Lord of Tyrconnell, near Sligo, and died soon after in the Franciscan habit in Youghal. He left his successor so powerful, that in the year 1264, there being a feud between the Geraldines and de Burghs, he seized the Lord Justice and the whole de Burgh party at a conference at Castledermot, and carried them to his own castles of Lea and Dunamase as prisoners. In 1272, on the accidental death of the Lord Justice Audley by a fall from his horse, "the council" elected this the third Baron of Offally in his stead.

The family of Butler were of slower growth, but of equal tenacity with the Geraldines. They first seem to have attached themselves to the Marshals, for whom they were indebted for their first holding in Kilkenny. At the Conference of Castledermot Theobald Butler, the fourth in descent from the founder of the house, was numbered among the adherents of de Burgh, but a few years later we find him the ally of the Geraldines in the invasion of Thomond. In the year 1247, the title of Lord of Carrick had been conferred on him, which in 1315 was converted into Earl of Carrick, and this again into that of Ormond. The Butlers of this house, when they had attained their growth of power, became the hereditary rivals of the Kildare Geraldines, whose earldom dates from 1316, as that of Ormond does from 1328, and Desmond from 1329.

The name of Maurice, the third Baron of Offally, and uncle of John, the first Earl of Kildare, draws our attention naturally to the last enterprize of his life—the attempt to establish his son-in-law, Thomas de Clare, in possession of Thomond. The de Clares, Earls of Gloucester, pretended a grant from Henry II. of the whole of Thomond, as their title to invade that principality; but their real grant was bestowed by Edward I., in the year 1275. The state of the renowned patrimony of Brian had long seemed to invite such an aggression. Murtogh, son of Donnell More, who succeeded his father in 1194, had early signalized himself by capturing the castles of Birr, Kinnetty, Ballyroane and Lothra, in Leix, and razing them to the ground.

But these castles were reconstructed in 1213, when the feuds between the rival O'Briens—Murtogh and Donogh Cairbre—had paralyzed the defence force of Thomond. It was, doubtless, in the true divide-and-conquer spirit, that Henry the Third's advisers confirmed to Donogh the lordship of Thomond in 1220, leaving to his elder brother the comparatively barren title of King of Munster. Both brothers, by alternately working on their hopes and fears, were thus for many years kept in a state of dependence on the foreigner. One gleam of patriotic virtue illumines the annals of the house of O'Brien, during the first forty years of the century—when, in the year 1225, Donogh Cairbre assisted Felim O'Conor to resist the Anglo-Norman army, then pouring over Connaught, in the quarrel of de Burgh. Conor, the son of Donogh, who succeeded his father in the year 1242, animated by the example of his cotemporaries, made successful war against the invaders of his Province, more especially in the year 1257, and the next year; attended with O'Conor the meeting at Beleek, on the Erne, where Brian O'Neil was acknowledged, by both the Munster and the Connaught Prince, as *Ard-Righ*. The untimely end of this attempt at national union will be hereafter related; meantime, we proceed to mention that, in 1260, the Lord of Thomond defeated the Geraldines and their Welsh auxiliaries, at Kilbarran, in Clare. He was succeeded the following season by his son, Brian Roe, in whose time Thomas de Clare again put to the test of battle his pretensions to the lordship of Thomond.

It was in the year 1277, that supported by his father-in-law, the Kildare Fitzgerald, de Clare marched into Munster, and sought an interview with the O'Brien. The relation of gossip, accounted sacred among the Irish, existed between them, but Brien Roe, having placed himself credulously in the hands of his invaders, was cruelly drawn to pieces between two horses. All Thomond rose in arms, under Donogh, son of Brian, to revenge this infamous murder. Near Ennis the Normans met a terrible defeat, from which de Clare and Fitzgerald fled for safety into the neighboring Church of Quin. But Donogh O'Brien burned the Church over their heads, and forced them to surrender at discretion. Strange to say they were held to ransom, on conditions, we may suppose, sufficiently hard. Other days of blood were yet to decide the claims of the family of de Clare. In 1287, Turlogh, then the O'Brien, defeated an invasion similar to the last, in which Thomas de Clare was slain, together with Patrick Fitzmaurice of Kerry, Richard Taafe, Richard Deriter, Nicholas Teeling, and other knights, and Gerald, the fourth Baron of Offally, brother-in-law to de Clare, was mortally wounded. After another interval, Gilbert de Clare, son of Thomas, renewed the contest, which he bequeathed to his brother Richard. This Richard, whose name figures more than his brother in the events of his time, made a last effort, in the year 1318, to make good the claims of his family. On the 5th of May, in that year, he fell in battle against McCarthy and O'Brien, and there fell with him Sir Thomas de Naas, Sir Henry Capell, Sir James and Sir John Caunton, with four other knights and a proportion of men-at-arms. From thenceforth that proud offshoot of the house of Gloucester, which, at its first settling in Munster, flourished as bravely as the Geraldines themselves, became extinct in the land.

Such were the varying fortunes of the two races in Leinster and Munster, and such the men who rose and fell. We must now turn to the contest as maintained at the same period in Meath and Ulster.

CHAPTER X.

EVENTS OF THE THIRTEENTH CENTURY—THE NORMANS IN MEATH AND ULSTER.

WE may estimate the power of the de Lacy family in the second generation, from the fact that their expulsion required a royal army and navy, commanded by the King in person, to come from England. Although pardoned by John, the brothers took care never to place themselves in that cowardly tyrant's power, and they observed the same precaution on the accession of his son, until well assured that he did not share the antipathy of his father. After their restoration the Lacys had no rivals among the Norman Irish except the Marshal family, and though both houses in half a century became extinct, not so those they had planted, or patronized, or who claimed from them collaterally. In Meath the Tuites, Cusacks, Flemings, Daltons, Petits, Husseys, Nangles, Tyrrells, Nugents, Verdons, and Gennevilles, struck deep into the soil. The co-heiresses, Margaret and Matilda de Lacy, married Lord Theobald de Verdon and Sir Geoffrey de Genneville, between whom the estate of their father was divided; both these ladies dying without male issue, the lordship was, in 1286, claimed by Richard de Burgo, Earl of Ulster, whose mother was their cousin-germain. But we are anticipating time.

No portion of the island, if we except, perhaps, Wexford and the shores of Strangford Lough, was so thoroughly castellated as the ancient Meath from the sea to the Shannon. Trim, Kells, and Durrow were the strongest holds; there were keeps or castles at Ardbraccan, Slane, Rathwyre, Navan, Skreen, Santry, Clontarf, and Castleknock—for even these places, almost within sight of Dublin, were included in de Lacy's original grant. None of these fortresses could have been more than a few miles distant from the next, and once within their thick-ribbed walls, the Norman, Saxon, Cambrian, or Danish serf or tenant might laugh at the Milesian arrows and battle-axes without. With these fortresses, and their own half-Irish origin and policy, the de Lacys, father and son, held Meath for two generations in general subjection. But the banishment of the brothers in 1210, and the death of Walter of Meath, presented the family of O'Melaghlin and the whole of the Methian tribes with opportunities of insurrection not to be neglected. We read, therefore, under the years 1211, 12 and 13, that Art O'Melaghlin and Cormac, his son, took the castles of Killclane, Ardinurcher, Athboy, and Smerhie, killing knights and wardens, and enriching themselves with booty; that the whole English of Ireland turned out *en masse* to the rescue of their brethren in Meath; that the castles of Birr, Durrow, and Kinnetty were strengthened against Art, and a new one erected at Clonmacnoise. After ten years of exile, the banished de Lacys returned, and by alliance with O'Neil, no less than their own prowess, recovered all their former influence. Cormac, son of Art, left a son and successor also named Art, who, we read at the year 1264, gave the English of Meath a great defeat upon the Brosna, where he that was not slain was drowned. Following the blow, he burned their villages and broke the castles of the stranger throughout Devlin, Calry, and Brawny, and replaced in power over them the McCoghlans, Magawleys, and O'Breens, from whom he took hostages, according to ancient custom. Two years afterwards he repulsed Walter de Burgh at Shannon harbor, driving his men into the river, where many of them perished. At his death (A. D. 1283) he is eulogized for having destroyed seven-and-twenty English castles in his lifetime. From these exploits he was called Art *na Caislean,* a remarkable distinction when we remember that the Irish were, up to this time, wholly unskilled in besieging such strongholds as the Norman engineers knew so well how to construct. His only rival in Meath in such meritorious works of destruction was Conor, son of Donnell, and O'Melaghlin of East-Meath, or *Bregia,* whose death is recorded at the year 1277, " as one of the three men in Ireland" whom the midland English most feared.

From the ancient mensal the transition is easy to the north. The border-land of Breffni, whose chief was the first of the native nobles that perished by Norman perfidy, was at the beginning of the century swayed by Ulgarg O'Rourke. Of Ulgarg we know little, save that in the year 1231 he "died on his way to the river Jordan"—a not uncommon pilgrimage with the Irish of those days. Nial, son of Congal, succeeded, and about the middle of the century we find Breffni divided into two lordships, from the mountain of Slieve-an-eiran eastward, or Cavan, being given to ART, son of Cathal, and from the mountain westward, or Leitrim, to Donnell, son of Conor, son of Tiernan, de Lacy's victim. This subdivision conduced neither to the strengthening of its defenders nor to the satisfaction of O'Conor, under whose auspices it was made. Family feuds and household treasons were its natural results for two or three generations; in the midst of these broils two neighboring families rose into greater importance, the O'Reillys in Cavan and the Maguires in Fermanagb. Still, strong in their lake and mountain region, the tribes of Breffni were comparatively unmolested by foreign enemies, while the stress of the northern battle fell upon the men of Tyrconnell and Tyrone, of Oriel and of the coast country, from Carlingford to the Causeway.

The borders of Tyrconnell and Tyrone, like every other tribeland, were frequently enlarged or contracted, according to the vigor or weakness of their chiefs or neighbors. In the age of which we now speak, Tyrconnell extended from the Erne to the Foyle, and Tyrone from the Foyle to Lough Neagh, with the exception of the extreme north of Derry and Antrim, which belonged to the O'Kanes. It was not till the fourteenth century that the O'Neils spread their power east of Lough Neagh, over those baronies of Antrim long known as north and south *Clan-Hugh-Buidhe*, (Clandeboy.) North Antrim was still known as Dalriada, and South Antrim and Down, as Ulidia. Oriel, which has been usually spoken of in this history as Louth, included angles of Monaghan and Armagh, and was anciently the most extensive lordship in Ulster. The chieftain families of Tyrconnell were the O'Donnells; of Tyrone, the O'Neils and McLaughlins; of Dalriada, O'Kanes, O'Haras and O'Shields; of Ulidia, the Magennis of Iveagh and the Donlevys of Down; of Oriel, the McMahons and O'Hanlons. Among these populous tribes the invaders dealt some of their fiercest blows, both by land and sea, in the thirteenth century. But the north was fortunate in its chiefs; they may fairly contest the laurel with the O'Conors, O'Briens and McCarthys of the west and south.

In the first third of the century, Hugh O'Neil, who succeeded to the lordship of Tyrone in 1198, and died in 1230, was cotemporary with Donnell More O'Donnell, who, succeeding to the lordship of Tyrconnell in 1208, died in 1241, after an equally long and almost equally distinguished career. Melaghlin O'Donnell succeeded Donnell More from '41 to '47, Godfrey from '48 to '57, and Donnell Oge from 1257 to 1281, when he was slain in battle. Hugh O'Neil was succeeded in Tyrone by Donnell McLaughlin, of the rival branch of the same stock, who in 1241 was subdued by O'Donnell, and the ascendancy of the family of O'Neil established in the person of Brian, afterwards chosen

King of Ireland, and slain at Down. Hugh Boy, or the Swarthy, was elected O'Neil on Brian's death, and ruled till the year 1283, when he was slain in battle, as was his next successor, Brian, in the year 1295. These names and dates are worthy to be borne in mind, because on these two great houses mainly devolved the brunt of battle in their own province.

These northern chiefs had two frontiers to guard or to assail: the north-eastern, extending from the glens of Antrim to the hills of Mourne, and the southern stretching from sea to sea, from Newry to Sligo. This country was very assailable by sea; to those whose castles commanded its harbors and rivers, the fleets of Bristol, Chester, Man, and Dublin could always carry supplies and reinforcements. By the interior line one road threaded the Mourne mountains, and deflected towards Armagh, while another, winding through west Breffni, led from Sligo into Donegal by the cataract of Assaroe,—the present Ballyshannon. Along these ancient lines of communication, by fords, in mountain passes, and near the landing places for ships, the struggle for the possession of that end of the Island went on, at intervals, whenever large bodies of men could be spared from garrisons and from districts already occupied.

In the year 1210, we find that there was an English Castle at Cael-uisge, now Castle-Caldwell, on Lough Erne, and that it was broke down and its defenders slain by Hugh O'Neil and Donald More O'Donnell acting together. After this event we have no trace of a foreign force in the interior of Ulster for several years. Hugh O'Neil, who died in 1230, is praised by the Bards for "never having given hostages, pledges, or tributes to English or Irish," which seems a compliment well founded. During several years following that date the war was chiefly centered in Connaught, and the fighting men of the north who took part in it were acting as allies to the O'Conors. Donald More O'Donnell had married a daughter of Cathal Crovdearg, so that ties of blood, as well as neighboring interests, united these two great families. In the year 1247, an army under Maurice Fitzgerald, then Lord Justice, crossed the Erne in two divisions, one above and the other at Ballyshannon. Melaghlin O'Donnell was defending the passage of the river when he was taken unexpectedly in the rear by those who had crossed higher up, and thus was defeated and slain. Fitzgerald then ravaged Tyrconnell, set up a rival chief O'Canavan, and rebuilt the Castle at Cael-uisge, near Beleek. Ten years afterwards Godfrey O'Donnell, the successor of Melaghlin, avenged the defeat at Ballyshannon, in the sanguinary battle of Credran, near Sligo, where engaging Fitzgerald in single combat, he gave him his death-stroke. From wounds received at Credran, Godfrey himself, after lingering twelve months in great suffering, died. But his bodily afflictions did not prevent him discharging all the duties of a great Captain; he razed a second time the English Castle on Lough Erne, and stoutly protected his own borders against the pretensions of O'Neil, being carried on his bier in the front of the battle of Lough Swilly in 1258.

It was while Tyrconnell was under the rule of this heroic soldier that the unfortunate feud arose between the O'Neils and O'Donnells. Both families, sprung from a common ancestor, of equal antiquity and equal pride, neither would yield a first place to the other. "Pay me my tribute," was O'Neil's demand; "I owe you no tribute, and if I did ——" was O'Donnell's reply. The O'Neil at this time—Brian—aspiring to restore the Irish sovereignty in his own person, was compelled to begin the work of exercising authority over his next neighbor. More than one border battle was the consequence, not only with Godfrey, but with Donnell Oge, his successor. In the year 1258, Brian was formally recognized by O'Conor and O'Brien as chief of the kingdom, in the conference of Cael-uisge, and two years later, at the battle of Down, gallantly laid down his life, in defence of the kingdom he claimed to govern. In this most important battle no O'Donnell is found fighting with King Brian, though immediately afterwards we find Donnell Oge of Tyrconnell endeavoring to subjugate Tyrone, and active afterwards in the aid of his cousins, the grandsons of Cathal Crovdearg, in Connaught.

The Norman commander in this battle was Stephen de Longespay, then Lord Justice, Earl of Salisbury in England, and Count de Rosman in France. His marriage with the widow of Hugh de Lacy and daughter of de Riddlesford connected him closely with Irish affairs, and in the battle of Down he seems to have had all the Anglo-Irish chivalry, "in gold and iron," at his back. With King Brian O'Neil fell, on that crimson day, the chiefs of the O'Hanlons, O'Kanes, McLaughlins, O'Gormlys, McCanns, and other families who followed his banner. The men of Connaught suffered hardly less than those of Ulster. McDermott, Lord of Moylurgh, Cathal O'Conor, O'Gara, McDonogh, O'Mulrony, O'Quinn, and other chiefs were among the slain. In Hugh *Bwee* O'Neil the only hope of the house of Tyrone seemed now to rest; and his energy and courage were all taxed to the uttermost to retain the place of his family in the Province, beating back rapacious neighbors on the one hand, and guarding against foreign enemies on the other. For twelve years, Hugh *Bwee* defended his lordship against all aggressors. In 1283, he fell at the hands of the insurgent chiefs of Oriel and Breffni, and a fierce contest for the succession arose between his son Brian and Donald, son of King Brian, who fell at Down. A contest of twelve years saw Donald successful over his rival (A.D. 1295), and his rule extended from that period until 1325, when he died at Leary's lake, in the present diocese of Clogher.

It was this latter Donnell or Donald O'Neil, who, towards the end of his reign, addressed to Pope John XXII. (elected to the pontificate in 1316) that powerful indictment against the Anglo-Normans, which has ever since remained one of the cardinal texts of our history. It was evidently written after the unsuccessful attempt, in which Donald was himself a main actor, to establish Edward Bruce on the throne of Ireland. That period we have not yet reached, but the merciless character of the warfare waged against the natives of the country could hardly have been aggravated by Bruce's defeat. "They oblige us by open force," says the Ulster Prince, "to give up to them our houses and our lands, and to seek shelter like wild beasts upon the mountains, in woods, marshes and caves. Even there we are not secure against their fury; they even envy us those dreary and terrible abodes; they are incessant and unremitting in their pursuit after us, endeavoring to chase us from among them; they lay claim to every place in which they can discover us with unwarranted audacity and injustice; they allege that the whole kingdom belongs to them of right, and that an Irishman has no longer a right to remain in his own country."

After specifying in detail the proofs of these and other general charges, the eloquent Prince concludes by uttering the memorable vow that the Irish "will not cease to fight against and among their invaders until the day when they themselves, for want of power, shall have ceased to do us harm, and that a Supreme Judge shall have taken just vengeance on their crimes, which we firmly hope will sooner or later come to pass."

CHAPTER XI.

RETROSPECT OF THE NORMAN PERIOD IN IRELAND—A GLANCE AT THE MILITARY TACTICS OF THE TIMES—NO CONQUEST OF THE COUNTRY IN THE THIRTEENTH CENTURY.

THOUGH the victorious and protracted career of Richard de Burgh, the "Red Earl" of Ulster, might, without overstraining, be included in the Norman period, yet as introductory to the memorable advent and election of King Edward Bruce, we must leave it for the succeeding book. Having brought down the narrative, as regards all the Provinces, to the end of the first century, from the invasion, we must now cast a backward glance on the events of that hundred years before passing into the presence of other times and new combinations.

"There were," says *Giraldus Cambrensis*, "three sundry sorts of servitors which served in the realm of Ireland, Normans, Englishmen, and the Cambrians, which were the first conquerors of the land: the first were in most credit and estimation, the second next, but the last were not accounted or regarded of." "The Normans," adds that author, "were very fine in their apparel, and delicate in their diets; they could not feed but upon dainties, neither could their meat digest without wine at each meal; yet would they not serve in the marches or any remote place against the enemy, neither would they lie in garrison to keep any remote castle or fort, but would be still about their lord's side to serve and guard his person; they would be where they might be full and have plenty, they could talk and brag, swear and stare, and, standing in their own reputation, disdain all others." This is rather the language of a partizan than of an historian; of one who felt and spoke for those, his own kinsmen many of them, who, he complains, although the first to enter on the conquest, were yet held in contempt and disdain, "and only new-comers called to council."

The Normans were certainly the captains in every campaign from Robert Fitzstephen to Stephen de Longespay. They made the war and they maintained it. In the rank and file, and even among the knighthood, men of pure Welsh, English, and Flemish and Danish blood, may be singled out, but each host was marshalled by Norman skill, and every defeat was borne with Norman fortitude. It may seem strange, then, that these greatest masters of the art of war, as waged in the middle ages, invincible in England, France, Italy, and the East, should after a hundred years be no nearer to the conquest of Ireland than they were at the end of the tenth year.

The main causes of the fluctuations of the war were, no doubt, the divided military command, and the frequent change of their civil authorities. They had never marched, or colonized before without their Duke, or King at their head, and in their midst. One supreme chief was necessary to keep to any common purpose the minds of so many proud, intractable nobles. The feuds of the de Lacys with the Marshalls, of the Geraldines with the de Burghs, broke out periodically during the thirteenth century, and were naturally seized upon by the Irish as opportunities for attacking either or both. The secondary nobles and all the adventurers understood their danger and its cause, when they petitioned Henry II. and Henry III. so often and so urgently as they did, that a member of the royal family might reside permanently in Ireland, to exercise the supreme authority, military and civil.

The civil administration of the colonists passing into different hands every three or four years, suffered from the absence of permanent authority. The law of the marches was, of necessity, the law of the strong hand, and no other. But *Cambrensis*, whose personal prejudices are not involved in this fact, describes the walled towns as filled with litigation in his time. "There was," he says, "such *lawing* and vexation, that the veteran was more troubled in *lawing* within the town than he was in peril at large with the enemy." This being the case, we must take with great caution the bold assertions so often made of the zeal with which the natives petitioned the Henrys and Edwards that the law of England might be extended to them. Certain Celts whose lands lay within or upon the marches, others who compounded with their Norman invaders, a chief or prince, hard-pressed by domestic enemies, may have wished to be in a position to quote Norman law against Norman spoilers, but the popular petitions which went to England, beseeching the extension of its laws to Ireland, went only from the townsmen of Dublin, and the new settlers in Leinster or Meath, harassed and impoverished by the arbitrary jurisdiction of manorial courts, from which they had no appeal. The great mass of the Irish remained as warmly attached to their Brehon code down to the seventeenth century as they were before the invasion of Norman or Dane. It may sound barbarous to our ears that, according to that code, murder should be compounded by an *eric*, or fine; that putting out the eyes should be the usual punishment of treason; that maiming should be judicially inflicted for sundry offences; and that the land of a whole clan should be equally shared between the free members of that clan. We are not yet in a position to form an intelligent opinion upon the primitive jurisprudence of our ancestors, but the system itself could not have been very viscious which nourished in the governed such a thirst for justice, that, according to one of their earliest English law reformers, they were anxious for its execution, even against themselves.

The distinction made in the courts of the adventurers against natives of the soil, even when long domiciled within their borders, was of itself a sufficient cause of war between the races. In the eloquent letter of the O Neil to Pope John XXII.—written about the year 1318—we read, that no man of Irish origin could sue in an English court; that no Irishman, within the marches, could make a legal will; that his property was appropriated by his English neighbors; and that the murder of an

Irishman was not even a felony punishable by fine. This latter charge would appear incredible, if we had not the record of more than one case where the homicide justified his act by the plea that his victim was a mere native, and where the plea was held good and sufficient.

A very vivid picture of Hiberno-Norman town-life in those days is presented to us in an old poem, on the "Entrenchment of the Town of Ross," in the year 1265. We have there the various trades and crafts—mariners, coat-makers, fullers, cloth-dyers and sellers, butchers, cordwainers, tanners, hucksters, smiths, masons, carpenters, arranged by guilds, and marching to the sound of flute and tabor, under banners bearing a fish and platter, a painted ship, and other "rare devices." On the walls, when finished, cross-bows hung, with store of arrows ready to shoot; when the city horn sounded twice burgess and batchelor vied with each other in warlike haste. In time of peace the stranger was always welcome in the streets; he was free to buy and sell without toll or tax, and to admire the fair dames who walked the quiet ramparts, clad in mantles of green, or russet, or scarlet. Such is the poetic picture of the town of Ross in the thirteenth century; the poem itself is written in Norman-French, though evidently intended for popular use, and the author is called "Friar Michael of Kildare." It is pretty evident from this instance, which is not singular, that a century after the first invasion, the French language was still the speech of part, if not the majority, of these Hiberno-Norman townsmen.

So walls, and laws, and language arose, a triple barrier between the races. That common religion which might be expected to form a strong bond between them had itself to adopt a twofold organization. Distinctions of nationality were carried into the Sanctuary and into the Cloister. The historian *Giraldus*, in preaching at Dublin against the alleged vices of the native Clergy, sounded the first note of a long and bitter controversy. He was promptly answered from the same pulpit on the next occasion by Albin O'Mulloy, the patriot Abbot of Baltinglass. In one of the early Courts or Parliaments of the Adventurers, they decreed that no Monastery in those districts of which they had possession, should admit any but natives of England, as novices,—a rule, which, according to O'Neil's letter, was faithfully acted upon by English Dominicans, Franciscans, Benedictines, and regular canons. Some of the great Cistercian houses on the marches, in which the native religious predominated, adopted a retaliatory rule, for which they were severely censured by the general Chapter of their Order. But the length to which this feud was carried may be imagined by the sweeping charge O'Neil brings against "Brother Symon, a relative of the Bishop of Coventry," and other religious of his nation, who openly maintained, he says, that the killing of a mere Irishmen was no murder.

When this was the feeling on one side, or was believed to be the feeling, we cannot wonder that the war should have been renewed as regularly as the seasons. No sooner was the husbandman in the field, than the knight was upon the road. Some peculiarities of the wars of those days gleam out at intervals through the methodic indifference to detail of the old annals, and reveal to us curious conditions of society. In the Irish country, where castle-building was but slowly introduced, we see, for example, that the usual storage for provisions, in time of war, was in churches and churchyards. Thus de Burgh, in his expedition to Mayo, in 1236, "left neither rick nor basket of corn in the large churchyard of Mayo, or in the yard of the Church of Saint Michael the Archangel, and carried away eighty baskets out of the churches themselves." When we read, therefore, as we frequently do, of both Irish and Normans plundering churches in the land of their enemies, we are not to suppose the plunder of the sanctuary. Popularly this seizing the supplies of an enemy on consecrated ground was considered next to sacrilege; and well it was for the fugitives in the sanctuary in those iron times that it should be so considered. Yet not the less is it necessary for us to distinguish a high-handed military measure from actual sacrilege, for which there can be no apology, and hardly any earthly atonement.

In their first campaigns the Irish had one great advantage over the Normans in their familiarity with the country. This helped them to their first victories. But when the invaders were able to set up rival houses against each other and to secure the co-operation of natives, the advantage was soon equalized. Great importance was attached to the intelligence and good faith of the *guides*, who accompanied every army, and were personally consulted by the leaders in determining their march. A country so thickly studded with the ancient forest, and so netted with rivers (then of much greater volume than since they have been stripped of their guardian woods), afforded constant occasion for the display of minute local knowledge. To miss a pass or to find a ford might determine a campaign, almost as much as the skill of the chief, or the courage of the battalion.

The Irish depended for their knowledge of the English towns and castles on their daring *spies*, who continually risked their necks in acquiring for their clansmen such needful information. This perilous duty, when undertaken by a native for the benefit of his country, was justly accounted highly honorable. Proud poets, educated in all the mysteries of their art, and even men of chieftain rank, did not hesitate to assume disguises and act the patriot spy. One of the most celebrated spies of this century was Donough Fitzpatrick, son of the Lord of Ossory, who was slain by the English in 1250. He was said to be "one of the three men" most feared by the English in his day. "He was in the habit of going about to reconnoitre their market towns," say the Annalists, "in various disguises." An old quatrain gives us a list of some of the parts he played when in the towns of his enemies—

> "He is a carpenter, he is a turner,
> My nursling is a bookman,
> He is selling wine and hides
> Where he sees a gathering."

An able captain, as well as an intrepid spy, he met his fate in acting out his favorite part, "which," adds our justice-loving Four Masters, "was a retaliation due to the English, for, up to that time, he had killed, burned, and destroyed many of them."

Of the equipments and tactics of the belligerents we get from our Annals but scanty details. The Norman battalion, according to the usage of that people, led by the marshal of the field, charged, after the archers had delivered their fire. But these wars had bred a new mounted force, called hobiller-archers, who were found so effective that they were adopted into all the armies of Europe. Although the bow was never a favorite weapon with the Irish, particular tribes seem to have been noted for its use. We hear in the campaigns of this century of the archers of Breffni, and we may probably interpret as referring to the same weapon, Felim O'Conor's order to his men, in his combat with the sons of Roderick at Drumraitte (1237), "not to shoot but to come to a close fight." It is possible, however, that this order may have reference to the old Irish weapon, the javelin or dart. The pike, the battle-axe, the sword, and skein, or dagger, both parties had in common, though their construction was different. The favorite tactique, on both sides, seems to have been the old military expedient of outflanking an enemy, and attacking him simultaneously in front and rear. Thus, at the year 1225, in one of the combats of the O'Conors, when the son of Cathal *Crovdearg* endeavored to surround Turlogh O'Conor, the latter ordered his recruits to the van, and Donn Oge Magheraty, with some Tyronian and other soldiers to cover the rear, "by which means they escaped without the loss of a man." The flank movement by which the Lord Justice Fitzgerald carried the passage of the Erne (A. D. 1247) against O'Donnell, according to the Annalists, was suggested to Fitzgerald by Cormac, the grandson of Roderick O'Conor. By that period in their intercourse the Normans and Irish had fought so often together that their stock of tactical knowledge must have been, from experience, very much common property. In the eyes of the Irish chiefs and chroniclers, the foreign soldiers who served with them were but hired mercenaries. They were sometimes repaid by the plunder of the country attacked, but usually they received fixed wages for the length of time they entered. "Hostages for the payment of wages" are frequently referred to, as given by native nobles to these foreign auxiliaries. The chief expedient for subsisting an army was driving before them herds and flocks; free quarters for men and horses were supplied by the tenants of allied chiefs within their territory, and for the rest, the simple outfit was probably not very unlike that of the Scottish borderers described by Froissart, who cooked the cattle they captured in their skins, carrying a broad plate of metal and a little bag of oatmeal trussed up behind the saddle.

One inveterate habit clung to the ancient race, even until long after the times of which we now speak—their unconquerable prejudice against defensive armor. Gilbride McNamee, the laureat to King Brian O'Neil, gives due prominence to this fact in his poem on the death of his patron in the battle of Down (A. D. 1260). Thus sings the northern bard—

> "The foreigners from London,
>   The hosts from Port-Largy*
> Came in a bright green body,
>   In gold and iron armor.
>
> "Unequal they engage in the battle,
>   The foreigners and the Gael of Tara,
> *Fine linen shirts on the race of Conn*,
>   And the strangers *one mass of iron*."

With what courage they fought, these scorners of armor, their victories of Ennis, of Callanglen, and of Credran, as well as their defeats at the Erne and at Down, amply testify. The first hundred years of war for native land, with their new foes, had passed over, and three-fourths of the *Saer Clanna* were still as free as they had ever been. It was not reserved even for the Norman race—the conquest of Innisfail!

CHAPTER XII.

STATE OF SOCIETY AND LEARNING IN IRELAND DURING THE NORMAN PERIOD.

WE have already spoken of the character of the war waged by and against the Normans on Irish soil, and as war was then almost every man's business, we may be supposed to have described all that is known of the time in describing its wars.

* Port-Largy, Waterford.

What we have to add of the other pursuits of the various orders of men, into which society was divided, is neither very full nor very satisfactory.

The rise, fall and migrations of some of the clans, have been already alluded to. In no age did more depend on the personal character of the chief than then. When the death of the heroic Godfrey left the free clansmen of Tyrconnell without a lord to lead them to battle, or rule them in peace, the Annalists represent them to us as meeting in great perplexity, and engaged "in making speeches" as to what was to be done, when suddenly, to their great relief, Donnell Oge, son of Donnell More, who had been fostered in Alba (Scotland), was seen approaching them. Not more welcome was Tuathal, the well-beloved, the restorer of the Milesian monarchy, after the revolt of the *Tuatha*. He was immediately elected chief, and the emissaries of O'Niel, who had been waiting for an answer to his demand of tribute, were brought before him. He answered their proposition by a proverb expressed in the Gaelic of Alba, which says that "every man should possess his own country," and Tyrconnell armed to make good this maxim.

The Bardic order still retained much of their ancient power, and all their ancient pride. Of their most famous names in this period we may mention Murray O'Daly of Lissadil, in Sligo, Donogh O'Daly of Finvarra, sometimes called Abbot of Boyle, and Gilbride McNamee, laureate to King Brian O'Neil. McNamee, in lamenting the death of Brian, describes himself as defenceless, and a prey to every spoiler, now that his royal protector is no more. He gave him, he tells us, for a poem on one occasion, besides gold and raiment, a gift of twenty cows. On another, when he presented him a poem, he gave in return twenty horned cows, and a gift still more lasting, "the blessing of the King of Erin." Other chiefs, who fell in the same battle, and to one of whom, named Auliffe O'Gormley, he had often gone "on a visit of pleasure," are lamented with equal warmth by the bard. The poetic Abbot of Boyle is himself lamented in the Annals as the Ovid of Ireland, as "a poet who never had and never will have an equal." But the episode which best illustrates, at once the address and the audacity of the bardic order, is the story of Murray O'Daly of Lissadil, and Donnell More O'Donnell, Lord of Tyrconnell.

In the year 1213, O'Donnell despatched Finn O'Brollaghan, his *Aes graidh* or Steward, to collect his tribute in Connaught, and Finn, putting up at the house of O'Daly, near Drumcliff, and being a plebeian who knew no better, began to wrangle with the poet. The irritable master of song, seizing a sharp axe, slew the steward on the spot, and then to avoid O'Donnell's vengeance fled into Clanrickarde. Here he announced himself by a poem addressed to de Burgh, imploring his protection, setting forth the claims of the Bardic order on all high-descended heroes, and contending that his fault was but venial, in killing a clown, who insulted him. O'Donnell pursued the fugitive to Athenry, and de Burgh sent him away secretly into Thomond. Into Thomond, the Lord of Tyrconnell marched, but O'Brien sent off the Bard to Limerick. The enraged Ulsterman soon appeared at the gates of Limerick, when O'Daly was smuggled out of the town, and "passed from hand to hand," until he reached Dublin. The following spring O'Donnell appeared in force before Dublin, and demanded the fugitive, who, as a last resort, had been sent for safety into Scotland. From the place of his exile he addressed three deprecatory poems to the offended Lord of Tyrconnell, who finally allowed him to return to Lissadill in peace, and even restored him to his friendship.

The introduction of the new religious orders—Dominicans, Franciscans, and the order for the redemption of Captives into Ireland, in the first quarter of this century gradually extinguished the old Columban and Brigintine houses. In Leinster they made way most rapidly; but Ulster clung with its ancient tenacity to the Columban rule. The Hierarchy of the northern half-kingdom still exercised a protectorate over Iona itself, for we read, at the year 1203, how Kellagh having erected a monastery in the middle of Iona, in despite of the religious, that the Bishops of Derry and Raphoe, with the Abbots of Armagh and Derry and numbers of the Clergy of the North of Ireland, passed over to Iona, pulled down the unauthorized monastery, and assisted at the election of a new Abbot. This is almost the last important act of the Columban order in Ireland. By the close of the century, the Dominicans had some thirty houses, and the Franciscans as many more, whether in the walled towns or the open country. These monasteries became the refuge of scholars, during the stormy period we have passed, and in other days full as troubled, which were to come. Moreover, as the Irish student, like all others in that age, desired to travel from school to school, these orders admitted him to the ranks of widespread European brotherhoods, from whom he might always claim hospitality. Nor need we reject as anything incredible the high renown for scholarship and ability obtained in those times by such men as Thomas Palmeran of Naas, in the University of Paris; by Peter and Thomas Hibernicus in the University of Naples, in the age of Aquinas; by Malachy of Ireland, a Franciscan, Chaplain to King Edward II. of England and Professor at Oxford; by the Danish Dominican, Gotofrid of Waterford; and above all, by John Scotus of Down, the subtle doctor, the luminary of the Franciscan schools, of Paris and Cologne. The native schools of Ireland had lost their early ascendancy, and are no longer traceable in our annals; but Irish scholarship when arrested in its full development at home, transferred its efforts to foreign Universities, and there maintained the ancient honor of the country among the studious " nations" of Christendom. Among the " nations" involved in the college riots at Oxford, in the year 1274, we find mention of the Irish, from which fact it is evident there must have been a considerable number of natives of that country, then frequenting the University.

The most distinguished native ecclesiastics of this century were Matthew O'Heney, Archbishop of Cashel, originally a Cistercian monk, who died in retirement at Holy Cross in 1207; Albin O'Mulloy, the opponent of *Giraldus*, who died Bishop of Ferns in 1222; and Clarus McMailin, Erenach of Trinity Island, Lough Key—if an *Erenach* may be called an ecclesiastic. It was O'Heney made the Norman who said the Irish Church had no martyrs, the celebrated answer, that now men had come into the country who knew so well how to make martyrs, that reproach would soon be taken away. He is said to have written a life of Saint Cuthbert of Lindisfarne, and we know that he had legantine powers at the opening of the century. The *Erenach* of Lough Key, who flourished in its second half, plays an important part in all the western feuds and campaigns; his guarantee often preserved peace and protected the vanquished. Among the church-builders of his age, he stands conspicuous. The ordinary churches were indeed easily built, seldom exceeding 60 or 70 feet in length, and one half that width, and the material still most in use was, for the church proper, timber. The towers, cashels, or surrounding walls, and the cells of the religious, as well as the great monasteries and collegiate and cathedral churches, were of stone, and many of them remain monuments of the skill and munificence of their founders.

Of the consequences of the abolition of slavery by the Council of Armagh, at the close of the twelfth century, we have no tangible evidence. It is probable that the slave trade, rather than domestic servitude, was abolished by that decree. The cultivators of the soil were still divided into two orders—Biataghs and Brooees. "The former," says O'Donovan, "who were comparatively few in number, would appear to have held their lands free of rent, but were obliged to entertain travellers, and the chief's soldiers when on their march in his direction; and the latter (the Brooees) would appear to have been subject to a stipulated rent and service." From "the Book of Lecan," a compilation of the fourteenth century, we learn that the Brooee was required to keep an hundred laborers, and an hundred of each kind of domestic animals. Of the rights or wages of the laborers, we believe, there is no mention made.

BOOK V.
THE ERA OF KING EDWARD BRUCE.

CHAPTER I.

THE RISE OF "THE RED EARL"—RELATIONS OF IRELAND AND SCOTLAND.

During the half century which comprised the reigns of Edward I. and II. in England (1272 to A.D. 1327), Scotland saw the last of her first race of Kings, and the elevation of the family of Bruce, under whose brilliant star Ireland was, for a season, drawn into the mid-current of Scottish politics. Before relating the incidents of that revolution of short duration but long enduring consequences, we must note the rise to greatness of the one great Norman name, which in that era mainly represented the English interest and influence in Ireland.

Richard de Burgh, called from his ruddy complexion "the Red Earl," of Ulster, nobly bred in the court of Henry III. of England, had attained man's age about the period when the de Lacies, the Geraldines, de Clares, and other great Anglo-Irish families, either through the fortune of war or failure of issue, were deprived of most of their natural leaders. Uniting in his own person the blood of the O'Conors, de Lacies, and de Burghs, his authority was great from the beginning in Meath and Connaught. In his inroads on Westmeath he seems to have been abetted by the junior branches of the de Lacies, who were with his host in the year 1286, when he besieged Theobald de Verdon in Athlone, and advanced his banner as far eastward as the strong town of Trim, upon the Boyne. Laying claim to the possessions of the Lord of Meath, which touched the Kildare Geraldines at so many points, he inevitably came into contact with that powerful family. In 1288, in alliance with Manus O'Conor, they compelled him to retreat from Roscommon into Clanrickarde, in Mayo. De Verdon, his competitor for Westmeath, naturally entered into alliance with the Kildare Geraldine, and in the year 1294, after many lesser conflicts, they took the Red Earl and his brother William prisoners, and carried them in fetters to the Castle of Lea, in Offally. This happened on the 6th day of December; a Parliament, assembled at Kilkenny on the 12th of March following, ordered their release; and a peace was made between these powerful houses. De Burgh gave his two sons as hostages to Fitzgerald, and the latter surrendered the Castle of Sligo to de Burgh. From the period of this peace the power of the last named nobleman outgrew anything that had been known since the Invasion. In the year 1291, he banished the O'Donnell out of his territory, and set up another of his own choosing; he deposed one O'Neil and raised up another; he so straitened O'Conor in his patrimony of Roscommon, that that Prince also entered his camp at Meelick, and gave him hostages. He was thus the first and only man of his race who had ever had in his hand the hostages both of Ulster and Connaught. When the King of England sent writs into Ireland, he usually addressed the Red Earl, before the Lord Justice or Lord Deputy—a compliment which, in that ceremonious age, could not be otherwise than flattering to the pride of de Burgh. Such was the order of summons, in which, in the year 1296, he was required by Edward I. to attend him into Scotland, which was then experiencing some of the worst consequences of a disputed succession. As Ireland's interest in this struggle becomes in the sequel second only to that of Scotland, we must make brief mention of its origin and progress.

By the accidental death of Alexander III., in 1286, the McAlpine, or Scoto-Irish dynasty, was suddenly terminated. Alexander's only surviving child, Margaret, called from her mother's country, "the Maid of Norway," soon followed her father; and no less than eight competitors, all claiming collateral descent from the former Kings, appeared at the head of as many factions to contest the succession. This number was, however, soon reduced to two men—John Baliol and Robert Bruce—the former the grandson of the eldest, the latter the son of the second daughter of King David I. After many bickerings these powerful rivals were induced to refer their claims to the decision of Edward I. of England, who, in a Great Court held at Berwick in the year 1292, decided in favor of Baliol, not in the character of an indifferent arbitrator, but as lord paramount of Scotland. As such, Baliol there and then rendered him feudal homage, and became, in the language of the age, "his man." This sub-sovereignty could not but be galling to the proud and warlike nobles of Scotland, and accordingly, finding Edward embroiled about his French possessions, three years after the decision, they caused Baliol to enter into an alliance, offensive and defensive, with Philip IV. of France, against his English suzerain. The nearer danger compelled Edward to march with 40,000 men, which he had raised for the war in France, towards the Scottish border, whither he summoned the Earl of Ulster, the Geraldines, Butlers, de Verdons, de Genvilles, Birminghams, Poers, Purcells, de Cogans, de Barrys, de Lacys, d'Exeters and other minor nobles to come to him in his camp early in March, 1296. The Norman-Irish obeyed the call, but the pride of de Burgh would not permit him to embark in the train of the Lord Justice Wogan, who had been also summoned; he sailed with his own forces in a separate fleet, having conferred the honor of knighthood on thirty of his younger followers before embarking at Dublin. Whether these forces arrived in time to take part in the bloody siege of Berwick, and the panic-route at Dunbar, does not appear; they were in time, however, to see the strongest places in Scotland yielded up, and John Baliol a prisoner on his way to the Tower of London. They were sumptuously entertained by the conqueror in the Castle of Roxburgh, and returned to their western homes deeply impressed with the power of England, and the puissance of her warrior-king.

But the independence of Scotland was not to be trodden out in a single campaign. During Edward's absence in France, William Wallace and other guerilla chiefs arose, to whom were soon united certain patriot nobles and bishops. The English deputy de Warrane fought two unsuccessful campaigns against these leaders, until his royal master, having concluded peace with France, summoned his Parliament to meet him at York, and his Norman-Irish lieges to join him in his northern camp, with all their forces on the 1st of March, 1299. In June the English King found himself at Roxburgh, at the head of 8,000 horse, and 80,000 foot, "chiefly Irish and Welsh." With this immense force he routed Wallace at Falkirk on the 22d of July, and reduced him to his original rank of a guerilla chief, wandering with his bands of partizans from one fastness to another. The Scottish cause gained in Pope Boniface VII. a powerful advocate soon after, and the unsubdued districts continued to obey a Regency composed of the Bishop of St. Andrews, Robert Bruce, and John Comyn. These regents exercised their authority in the name of Baliol, carried on negotiations with France and Rome, convoked a Parliament, and, among other military operations, captured Stirling Castle. In the documentary remains of this great controversy, it is curious to find Edward claiming the entire island of Britain in virtue of the legend of Brute the Trojan, and the Scots rejecting it with scorn, and displaying their true descent and origin from Scota, the fabled first mother of the Milesian Irish. There is ample evidence that the claims of kindred were at this period keenly felt by the Gael of Ireland, for the people of Scotland, and men of our race are mentioned among the companions of Wallace and the allies of Bruce. But the Norman-Irish were naturally drawn to the English banner, and when, in 1303, it was again displayed north of the Tweed, the usual noble names are found among its followers. In 1307 Scotland lost her most formidable foe, by the death of Edward, and at the same time began to recognize her appointed deliverer in the person of Robert Bruce. But we must return to "the Red Earl," the central figure in our own annals during this half century.

The new King, Edward II., compelled by his English barons to banish his minion, Gaveston, Earl of Cornwall, had created him his lieutenant of Ireland, endowed him with a grant of the royalties of the whole island, to the prejudice of the Earl and other noblemen. The sojourn of this brilliant parasite in Ireland lasted but a year—from June, 1308, till the June following. He displayed both vigor and munificence, and acquired friends. But the Red Earl, sharing to the full the antipathy of the great barons of England, kept apart from his court, maintained a rival state at Trim, as Commander-in-Chief, conferring knighthood, levying men, and imposing taxes at his own discretion. A challenge of battle is said to have passed between him and the Lieutenant, when the latter was recalled into England by the King, where he was three years later put to death by the barons, into whose hands he had fallen. Sir John Wogan and Sir Edmund Butler succeeded him in the Irish administration; but the real power long remained with Richard de Burgh. He was appointed plenipotentiary to treat with Robert Bruce, on behalf of the King of England, "upon which occasion the Scottish deputies waited on him in Ireland." In the year 1302 Bruce had married his daughter, the Lady Ellen, while of his other daughters one was Countess of Desmond, and another became Countess of Kildare in 1312. A thousand marks—the same sum at which the town and castle of Sligo were then valued—was allowed by the Earl for the marriage portion of his last-mentioned daughter. His power and reputation, about the period of her marriage, were at the full. He had long held the title of Commander of the *Irish* forces, "in Ireland, Scotland, Wales, and Gascony;" he had successfully resisted Gaveston in the meridian of his court favor; the father-in-law of a King, and of Earls of almost royal power, lord paramount of half the island—such a subject England had not seen on Irish ground since the Invasion. This prodigious power he retained, not less by his energy than his munificence. He erected castles at Carlingford, at Sligo, on the Upper Shannon, and on Lough Foyle. He was a generous patron of the Carmelite Order, for whom he built the Convent of Loughrea. He was famed as a princely entertainer, and before retiring from public affairs, characteristically closed his career with a magnificent banquet at Kilkenny, where the whole Parliament were his guests. Having reached an age bordering upon fourscore he retired to the Monastery of Athassel, and there expired within sight of his family vault, after half a century of such sway as was rarely enjoyed in that age, even by Kings. But before that peaceful close he was destined to confront a storm the like of which had not blown over Ireland during the long period since he first began to perform his part in the affairs of that kingdom.

CHAPTER II.

THE NORTHERN IRISH ENTER INTO ALLIANCE WITH KING ROBERT BRUCE—ARRIVAL AND FIRST CAMPAIGN OF EDWARD BRUCE.

No facts of the ages over which we have already passed are better authenticated than the identity of origin and feeling which existed between the Celts of Erin and of Albyn. Nor was this sympathy of race diminished by their common dangers from a common enemy. On the eve of the Norman invasion we saw how heartily the Irish were with Somerled and the men of Moray in resisting the feudal polity of the successors of Malcolm *Caen-More*. As the Plantagenet Princes in person led their forces against Scotland, the interest of the Irish, especially those of the North, increased, year by year, in the struggles of the Scots. Irish adherents followed the fortunes of Wallace to the close; and when Robert Bruce, after being crowned and seated in the chair of the McAlpin line, on the summit of the hill of Scone, had to flee into exile, he naturally sought refuge where he knew he would find friends. Accompanied by three of his brothers, several adherents, and even by some of the females of his family, he steered, in the autumn of 1306, for the little island of Rathlin—seven miles long by a mile wide—one point of which is within three miles of the Antrim beach. In its most populous modern day Rathlin contained not above 1,000 souls, and little wonder if its still smaller population five centuries ago fled in terror at the approach of Bruce. They were, however, soon disarmed of their fears, and agreed to supply the fugitive King daily with provisions for 300 persons, the whole number who accompanied or followed him into exile. His faithful adherents soon erected for him a castle, commanding one of the few landing places on the island, the ruins of which are still shown to strangers as "Bruce's Castle." Here he passed in perfect safety the winter of 1306, while his emissaries were recruiting in Ulster, or passing to and fro, in the intervals of storm, among the western islands. Without waiting for the spring to come round again, they issued from their retreat in different directions; one body of 700 Irish sailed under Thomas and Alexander, the King's brothers, for the Clyde, while Robert and Edward took the more direct passage towards the coast of Argyle, and, after many adventures, found themselves strong enough to attack the foreign forces in Perth and Ayrshire. The opportune death of Edward of England the same summer, and the civil strife bred by his successor's inordinate favor towards Gaveston, enabled the Bruces gradually to root out the internal garrisons of their enemies; but the party that had sailed, under the younger brothers, from Rathlin, were attacked and captured in Loch Ryan by McDowell, and the survivors of the engagement, with Thomas and Alexander Bruce, were carried prisoners to Carlisle and there put to death.

The seven years' war of Scottish independence was drawn to a close by the decisive campaign of 1314. The second Edward prepared an overwhelming force for this expedition, summoning, as usual, the Norman-Irish Earls, and inviting in different language his "beloved" cousins, the native Irish Chiefs, not only such as had entered into English alliances at any time, but also notorious allies of Bruce, like O'Neil, O'Donnell, and O'Kane. These writs were generally unheeded; we have no record of either Norman-Irish or native-Irish Chief having responded to Edward's summons, nor could nobles so summoned have been present without some record remaining of the fact. On the contrary all the wishes of the old Irish went with the Scots, and the Normans were more than suspected of leaning the same way. Twenty-one clans, Highlanders and Islemen, and many Ulstermen, fought on the side of Bruce, on the field of Bannockburn; the grant of "Kincardine-O'Neil," made by the victor-King to his Irish followers, remains a striking evidence of their fidelity to his person, and their sacrifices in his cause. The result of that glorious day was, by the testimony of all historians, English as well as Scottish, received with enthusiasm on the Irish side of the channel.

Whether any understanding had been come to between the northern Irish and Bruce, during his sojourn in Rathlin, or whether the victory of Bannochburn suggested the design, Edward Bruce, the gallant companion of all his brother's fortunes and misfortunes, was now invited to place himself at the head of the men of Ulster, in a war for Irish independence. He was a soldier of not inferior fame to his brother for courage and fortitude, though he had never exhibited the higher qualities of general and statesman which crowned the glory of King Robert. Yet as he had never held a separate command of consequence, his rashness and obstinacy, though well known to his intimates, were lost sight of, at a distance, by those who gazed with admiration on the brilliant achievements, in which he had certainly borne the second part. The chief mover in the negotiation by which this gallant soldier was brought to embark his fortunes in an Irish war, was Donald, Prince of Ulster. This Prince, whose name is so familiar from his celebrated remonstrance addressed to Pope John XXII., was son of King Brian of the battle of Down, who, half a century before, at the Conference of Caeluisge, was formally chosen Ard-Righ, by the nobles of three Provinces. He had succeeded to the principality—not without a protracted struggle with the Red Earl—some twenty years before the date of the battle of Bannochburn. Endued with an intensely national spirit, he seems to have fully adopted the views of Nicholas McMaelisa, the Primate of Armagh, his early cotemporary. This Prelate—one of the most resolute opponents of the Norman conquest—had constantly refused to instal any foreigner in a northern diocese. When the Chapter of Ardagh delayed their election, he nominated a suitable person to the Holy See; when the See of Meath was distracted between two national parties he installed his nominee; when the Countess of Ulster caused Edward I. to issue his writ for the installation of John, Bishop of Connor, he refused his acquiescence. He left nearly every See in his Province, at the time of his decease (the year

1303), under the administration of a native ecclesiastic; a dozen years before he had established a formal "association" among the Prelates at large, by which they bound themselves to resist the interference of the Kings of England in the nomination of Bishops, and to be subject only to the sanction of the See of Rome. In the Provinces of Cashel and Tuam, in the fourteenth century, we do not often find a foreign born Bishop; even in Leinster double elections and double delegations to Rome, show how deeply the views of the patriotic Nicholas McMaelisa had seized upon the clergy of the next age. It was Donald O'Neil's darling project to establish a unity of action against the common enemy among the chiefs, similar to that which the Primate had brought about among the Bishops. His own pretensions to the sovereignty were greater than that of any Prince of his age; his house had given more monarchs to the island than any other; his father had been acknowledged by the requisite majority; his courage, patriotism, and talents, were admittedly equal to the task. But he felt the utter impossibility of conciliating that fatal family pride, fed into extravagance by Bards and Senachies, which we have so often pointed out as the worst consequence of the Celtic system. He saw chiefs, proud of their lineage and their name, submit to serve a foreign Earl of Ulster, who refused homage to the native Prince of Ulster; he saw the seedlings of a vice of which we have seen the fruit—that his countrymen would submit to a stranger rather than to one of themselves, and he reasoned, not unnaturally, that, by the hand of some friendly stranger, they might be united and liberated. The attempt of Edward Bruce was a failure, and was followed by many disasters; but a more patriotic design, or one with fairer omens of success, could not have entered the mind or heart of a native Prince, after the event of the battle at Bannockburn. Edward of England, having intelligence of the negotiations on foot between the Irish and Scots, after his great defeat, summoned over to Windsor during the winter, de Burgh, Fitzgerald, de Verdun, and Edmund Butler, the Lord Deputy. After conferring with them, and confirming Butler in his office, they were despatched back in all haste to defend their country. Nor was there time to lose. Edward Bruce, with his usual impetuosity,

without waiting for his full armament, had sailed from Ayr with
6,000 men in 300 galleys, accompanied by Thomas Randolph,
Earl of Moray, Sir John Stuart, Sir Philip Moubray, Sir Fergus
of Androssan, and other distinguished knights. He landed on
the 25th day of May, 1315, in the Glendun river, near Glenarm,
and was promptly joined by Donald O'Neil, and twelve other
chiefs. Their first advance was from the coast towards that
angle of Lough Neagh, near which stands the town of Antrim.
Here, at Rathmore, in the plain of Moylinny, they were attacked by the Mandevilles and Savages of the Ards of Down,
whom they defeated. From Antrim they continued their route
evidently towards Dublin, taking Dundalk and Ardee, after a
sharp resistance. At Ardee they were but 35 miles north of
Dublin, easy of conquest, if they had been provided with siege
trains—which it seemed they were not.

While Bruce and O'Neil were coming up from the north,
Hugh O'Donnell, lord of Tyrconnell, as if to provide occupation for the Earl of Ulster, attacked and sacked the castle
and town of Sligo, and wasted the adjacent country. The Earl,
on hearing of the landing of the Scots, had mustered his forces
at Athlone, and compelled the unwilling attendance of Felim
O'Conor, with his clansmen. From Athlone he directed his
march towards Drogheda, where he arrived with "20 cohorts,"
about the same time that the Lord Deputy Butler came up with
"30 cohorts." Bruce unprepared to meet so vast a force—
taken together some 25,000 or 30,000 men—retreated slowly
towards his point of debarkation. De Burgh, who, as Commander-in-Chief, took precedence in the field of the Lord Deputy,
ordered the latter to protect Meath and Leinster, while he pursued the enemy. Bruce, having despatched the Earl of Moray to
his brother, was now anxious to hold some northern position where
they could most easily join him. He led de Burgh therefore
into the north of Antrim, thence across the Bann at Coleraine,
breaking down the bridge at that point. Here the armies
encamped for some days, separated by the river, the outposts occasionally indulging in "a shooting of arrows." By
negotiation, Bruce and O'Neil succeeded in detaching O'Conor
from de Burgh. Under the plea—which really had sufficient

foundation—of suppressing an insurrection headed by one of his rivals, O'Conor returned to his own country. No sooner had he left than Bruce assumed the offensive, and it was now the Red Earl's turn to fall back. They retreated towards the castle of Conyre (probably Connor, near Ballymena, in Antrim), where an engagement was fought, in which de Burgh was defeated, his brother William, Sir John Mandeville, and several other knights being taken prisoners. The Earl continued his retreat through Meath towards his own possession; Bruce followed, capturing in succession Granard, Fenagh, and Kells, celebrating his Christmas at Loughsweedy, in Westmeath, in the milst of the most considerable chiefs of Ulster, Meath, and Connaught. It was probably at this stage of his progress that he received the adhesion of the junior branches of the Lacies—the chief Norman family that openly joined his standard.

This termination of his first campaign on Irish soil might be considered highly favorable to Bruce. More than half the clans had risen, and others were certain to follow their example; the clergy were almost wholly with him; and his heroic brother had promised to lead an army to his aid in the ensuing spring.

CHAPTER III.

BRUCE'S SECOND CAMPAIGN, AND CORONATION AT DUNDALK—
THE RISING IN CONNAUGHT—BATTLE OF ATHENRY—ROBERT
BRUCE IN IRELAND.

From Loughsweedy, Bruce broke up his quarters, and marched into Kildare, encamping successively at Naas, Kildare, and Rathangan. Advancing in a southerly direction, he found an immense, but disorderly Anglo-Irish host drawn out, at the moat of Ardscull, near Athy, to dispute his march. They were commanded by the Lord Justice Butler, the Baron of Offally, the Lord Arnold Poer, and other magnates; but so divided were these proud Peers, in authority and in feeling, that, after a severe skirmish with Bruce's vanguard, in which some knights were killed on both sides, they retreated before the Hiberno-Scottish army, which continued its march unmolested, and took possession of Castledermot.

Animated by these successes, won in their midst, the clans of Leinster began in succession to raise their heads. The tribes of Wicklow, once possessors of the fertile plains to the east and west, rallied in the mountain glens to which they had been driven, and commenced that long guerilla war, which centuries only were to extinguish. The McMurroghs along the ridge of Leinster, and all their kindred upon the Barrow and the Slaney, mustered under a chief, against whom the Lord Justice was compelled to march in person, later in the campaign of 1316. The Lord of Dunamase was equally sanguine, but 800 men of the name of O'Moore, slain in one disastrous encounter, crippled for the time the military strength of that great house. Having thus kindled the war, in the very heart of Leinster, Bruce retraced his march, through Meath and Louth, and held at Dundalk that great assembly in which he was solemnly elected King of Ireland. Donald O'Neil, by letters patent, as son of Brian "of the battle of Down," the last acknowledged native king, formally resigned his right, in favor of Bruce, a proceeding which he defends in his celebrated letter to Pope John XXII., where he speaks of the new Sovereign as the illustrious Earl of Carrick, Edward de Bruce, a nobleman descended from the same ancestors with themselves, whom they had called to their aid, and freely chosen, as their king and lord. The ceremony of inauguration seems to have been performed, in the Gaelic fashion, on the hill of Knocknemelan, within a mile of Dundalk, while the solemn consecration took place in one of the churches of the town. Surrounded by all the external marks of royalty, Bruce established his court in the castle of Northburgh, (one of de Conrcy's or de Verdon's fortresses,) adjoining Dundalk, where he took cognizance of all pleas that were brought before him. At that moment his prospects compared favorably with those of his illustrious brother a few years earlier. The Anglo-Irish were bitterly divided against each other; while, according to their joint declaration of loyalty, signed before de Hothun, King Edward's special agent, "all the Irish of Ireland, several great lords, and many English people," had given in their adhesion to Bruce. In Ulster, except Carrickfergus, no place of strength remained in the hands of any subject of Edward of England. The arrival of supplies from Scotland enabled Bruce to resume that siege in the autumn of 1316, and the castle, after a heroic defence by Sir Thomas de Mandeville, was surrendered in midwinter. Here, in the month of February, 1317, the new King of Ireland had the gratification of welcoming his brother of Scotland, at the head of a powerful auxiliary force, and here, according to Barbour's *Chronicle*, they feasted for three days, in mirth and jollity, before entering on the third campaign of this war.

We have before mentioned that one of the first successes obtained by Bruce was through the withdrawal of Felim O'Conor from the Red Earl's alliance. The Prince thus won over to what may be fairly called the national cause, had just then attained his majority, and his martial accomplishments reflected honor on his fosterer, McDermott of Moylurg, while they filled with confidence the hearts of his own clansmen. After his secession from de Burgh at Coleraine, he had spent a whole year in suppressing the formidable rival, who had risen to dispute his title. Several combats ensued between their respective adherents, but at length Roderick, the pretender, was defeated and slain, and Felim turned all his energies to co-operate with Bruce, by driving the foreigner out of his own province. Having secured the assistance of all the chief tribes of the west, and established the ancient supremacy of his house over Breffni, he first attacked the town of Ballylahen, in Mayo, the seat of the family of de Exeter, slew Slevin de Exeter, the lord de Cogan, and other knights and barons, and plundered the town. At the beginning of August in the same year, in pursuance of his plan, Felim mustered the most numerous force which Connaught had sent forth, since the days of Cathal More. Under his leadership marched the Prince of Meath, the lords of Breffni, Leyny, Annally, Teffia, Hy-Many, and Hy-Fiachra, with their men. The point of attack was the town of Athenry, the chief fortified stronghold of the de Burghs and Berminghams in that region. Its importance dated from the reign of

King John; it had been enriched with convents and strengthened by towers; it was besides the burial place of the two great Norman families just mentioned, and their descendants felt that before the walls of Athenry their possessions were to be confirmed to them by their own valor, or lost forever. A decisive battle was fought on St. Laurence's day—the 10th of August—in which the steel-clad Norman battalion once more triumphed over the linen-shirted clansmen of the west. The field was contested with heroic obstinacy; no man gave way; none thought of asking or giving quarter. The standard bearer, the personal guard, and the Brehon of O'Conor fell around him. The lords of Hy-Many, Teffia, and Lesny, the heir of the house of Moylurg, with many other chiefs, and, according to the usual computation, 8,000 men were slain. Felim O'Conor himself, in the twenty-third year of his age, and the very morning of his fame, fell with the rest, and his kindred, the Sil-Murray, were left for a season an easy prey to William de Burgh and John de Bermingham, the joint commanders in the battle. The spirit of exaggeration common in most accounts of killed and wounded, has described this day as fatal to the name and race of O'Conor, who are represented as cut off to a man in the conflict; the direct line which Felim represented was indeed left without an immediate adult representative; but the offshoots of that great house had spread too far and flourished too vigorously to be shorn away, even by so terrible a blow as that dealt at Athenry. The very next year we find chiefs of the name making some figure in the wars of their own province, but it is observable that what may be called the national party in Connaught for some time after Athenry, looked to McDermott of Moylurg as their most powerful leader.

The moral effect of the victory of Athenry was hardly to be compensated for by the capture of Carrickfergus the next winter. It inspired the Anglo-Irish with new courage. De Bermingham was created commander-in-chief. The citizens of Dublin burned their suburbs to strengthen their means of defence. Suspecting the zeal of the Red Earl, so nearly connected with the Bruces by marriage, their Mayor proceeded to Saint Mary's abbey where he lodged, arrested and confined him to the castle. To that building the Bermingham tower was added about this time, and the strength of the whole must have been great when the skilful leaders who had carried Stirling and Berwick abandoned the siege of Dublin as hopeless. In Easter week, 1317, Roger Mortimer, afterwards Earl of March, nearly allied to the English King on the one hand, and maternally descended from the Marshalls and McMurroghs on the other, arrived at Youghal, as Lord Justice, released the Earl of Ulster on reaching Dublin, and prepared to dispute the progress of the Bruces towards the South.

The royal brothers had determined, according to their national Bard, to take their way with all their host, from one end of Ireland to the other. Their destination was Munster, which populous province had not yet ratified the recent election. Ulster and Meath were with them; Connaught, by the battle of Athenry, was rendered incapable of any immediate effort, and therefore Edward Bruce, in true Gaelic fashion, decided to proceed on his royal visitation, and so secure the hostages of the southern half-kingdom. At the head of 20,000 men, in two divisions, the brothers marched from Carrickfergus; meeting, with the exception of a severe skirmish in a wood near Slane, with no other molestation till they approached the very walls of Dublin. Finding the place stronger than they expected, or unwilling to waste time at that season of the year, the Hiberno-Scottish army, after occupying Castleknock, turned up the valley of the Liffey, and encamped for four days by the pleasant waterfall of Leixlip. From Leixlip to Naas, they traversed the estates of one of their active foes, the new made Earl of Kildare, and from Naas they directed their march to Callan in Ossory, taking special pleasure, according to Anglo-Irish Annals, in harrying the lands of another enemy, the Lord Butler, afterwards Earl of Ormond. From Callan their route lay to Cashel and Limerick, at each of which they encamped two or three days without seeing the face of an enemy. But if they encountered no enemies in Munster neither did they make many friends by their expedition. It seems that on further acquaintance rivalries and enmities sprung up between the two nations who composed the army; that Edward Bruce, while styling himself King of Ireland, acted more like a vigorous conqueror exhausting his enemies, than a prudent Prince careful for his friends and adherents. His army is accused, in terms of greater vehemence than are usually employed in our cautious chronicles, of plundering churches and monasteries, and even violating the tombs of the dead in search of buried treasure. The failure of the harvest, added to the effect of a threefold war, had so diminished the stock of food that numbers perished of famine, and this dark, indelible remembrance was, by an arbitrary notion of cause and effect, inseparably associated in the popular mind, both English and Irish, with the Scottish invasion. One fact is clear, that the election of Dundalk was not popular in Munster, and that the chiefs of Thomond and Desmond were uncommitted, if not hostile towards Bruce's sovereignty. McCarthy and O'Brien seized the occasion, indeed, while he was campaigning in the North, to root out the last representative of the family of de Clare, as we have already related, when tracing the fortunes of the Normans in Munster. But of the twelve reguli, or Princes in Bruce's train, none are mentioned as having come from the Southern provinces.

This visitation of Munster occupied the months of February and March. In April, the Lord Justice Mortimer summoned a Parliament at Kilkenny, and there, also, the whole Anglo-Irish forces, to the number of 30,000 men, were assembled. The Bruces on their return northward might easily have been intercepted, or the genius which triumphed at Bannockburn might have been as conspicuously signalized on Irish ground. But the military authorities were waiting orders from the Parliament, and the Parliament were at issue with the new Justice, and so the opportunity was lost. Early in May, the Hiberno-Scottish army re-entered Ulster, by nearly the same route as they had taken going southwards, and King Robert soon after returned into Scotland, promising faithfully to rejoin his brother, as soon as he disposed of his own pressing affairs. The King of England in the meantime, in consternation at the news from Ireland, applied to the Pope, then at Avignon, to exercise his influence with the Clergy and Chiefs of Ireland, for the preservation of the English interest in that country. It was in answer to the Papal rescripts so procured that Donald O'Neil despatched his celebrated Remonstrance, which the Pontiff enclosed to Edward II., with an urgent recommendation that the wrongs therein recited, might be atoned for, and avoided in the future.

CHAPTER IV.

BATTLE OF FAUGHARD AND DEATH OF KING EDWARD BRUCE—CONSEQUENCES OF HIS INVASION—EXTINCTION OF THE EARLDOM OF ULSTER—IRISH OPINION OF EDWARD BRUCE.

It is too commonly the fashion, as well with historians as with others, to glorify the successful and censure severely the unfortunate. No such feeling actuates us in speaking of the character of Edward Bruce, King of Ireland. That he was as gallant a knight as any in that age of gallantry, we know; that he could confront the gloomiest aspect of adversity with cheerfulness, we also know. But the united testimony, both of history and tradition, in his own country, so tenacious of its anecdotical treasures, describes him as rash, headstrong, and intractable, beyond all the captains of his time. And in strict conformity with this character is the closing scene of his Irish career.

The harvest had again failed in 1317, and enforced a melancholy sort of truce between all the belligerents. The scarcity was not confined to Ireland, but had severely afflicted England and Scotland, compelling their rulers to bestow a momentary attention on the then abject class, the tillers of the soil. But the summer of 1318 brightened above more prosperous fields, from which no sooner had each party snatched or purchased his share of the produce, than the war-note again resounded through all the four Provinces. On the part of the Anglo-Irish, John de Bermingham was confirmed as Commander-in-Chief, and departed from Dublin with, according to the chronicles of the Pale, but 2,000 chosen troops, while the Scottish biographer of the Bruces gives him "20,000 trapped horse." The latter may certainly be considered an exaggerated account, and the former must be equally incorrect. Judged by the other

armaments of that period, from the fact that the Normans of
Meath, under Sir Miles de Verdon and Sir Richard Tuit, were
in his ranks, and that he then held the rank of Commander-in-
Chief of all the English forces in Ireland, it is incredible that de
Bermingham should have crossed the Boyne with less that eight
or ten thousand men. Whatever the number may have been
Bruce resolved to risk the issue of battle contrary to the advice
of all his officers, and without awaiting the reinforcements hourly
expected from Scotland, and which shortly after the engagement did arrive. The native chiefs of Ulster, whose counsel
was also to avoid a pitched battle, seeing their opinions so
lightly valued, are said to have withdrawn from Dundalk.
There remained with the iron-headed King the Lords Mowbray,
de Soulis, and Stewart, with the three brothers of the latter;
MacRory, lord of the Isles, and McDonald, chief of his clan.
The neighborhood of Dundalk, the scene of his triumphs and
coronation, was to be the scene of this last act of Bruce's chivalrous and stormy career.

On the 14th of October, 1318, at the hill of Faughard, within
a couple of miles of Dundalk, the advance guard of the hostile
armies came into the presence of each other, and made ready
for battle. Roland de Jorse, the foreign Archbishop of Armagh
—who had not been able to take possession of his see, though
appointed to it seven years before—accompanied the Anglo-
Irish, and moving through their ranks, gave his benediction to
their banners. But the impetuosity of Bruce gave little time
for preparation. At the head of the vanguard, without waiting
for the whole of his company to come up, he charged the enemy
with impetuosity. The action became general, and the skill
of de Bermingham as a leader was again demonstrated. An incident common to the warfare of that age was, however, the
immediate cause of the victory. Master John de Maupas, a
burgher of Dundalk, believing that the death of the Scottish
leader would be the signal for the retreat of his followers, disguised as a jester or fool, sought him throughout the field. One
of the royal esquires named Gilbert Harper wearing the sur-
coat of his master, was mistaken for him, and slain; but the true
leader was at length found by de Maupas, and struck down

with the blow of a leaden plummet or slung-shot. After the battle when the field was searched for his body, it was found under that of de Maupas, who had bravely yielded up life for life. The Hiberno-Scottish forces dispersed in dismay, and when King Robert of Scotland landed a day or two afterwards, he was met by the fugitive men of Carrick, under their leader Thompson, who informed him of his brother's fate. He returned at once into his own country, carrying off the few Scottish survivors. The head of the impetuous Edward was sent to London; but the body was interred in the churchyard of Faughard, where, within living memory, a tall pillar stone was pointed out by every peasant of the neighborhood as marking the grave of "King Bruce."

The fortunes of the principal actors, native and Norman, in the invasion of Edward Bruce, may be briefly recounted before closing this book of our history. John de Bermingham, created for his former victory Baron of Athenry, had now the Earldom of Louth conferred on him with a royal pension. He promptly followed up his blow at Faughard by expelling Donald O'Neil, the mainspring of the invasion, from Tyrone; but Donald, after a short sojourn among the mountains of Fermanagh, returned during the winter and resumed his lordship, though he never wholly recovered from the losses he had sustained. The new Earl of Louth continued to hold the rank of Commander-in-Chief in Ireland, to which he added in 1322 that of Lord Justice. He was slain in 1329, with some 200 of his personal adherents, in an affair with the natives of his new earldom at a place called Ballybeagan. He left by a daughter of the Earl of Ulster three daughters; the title was perpetuated in the family of his brothers.

In 1319, the Earls of Kildare and Louth, and the Lord Arnold le Poer, were appointed a commission to inquire into all treasons committed in Ireland during Bruce's invasion. Among other outlawries they decreed those of the three de Lacies, the chiefs of their name, in Meath and Ulster. That illustrious family, however, survived even this last confiscation, and their descendants, several centuries later, were large proprietors in the midland counties.

Three years after the battle of Faughard died Roland de Jorse, Archbishop of Armagh, it was said, of vexations arising out of Bruce's war, and other difficulties which beset him in taking possession of his see. Adam, Bishop of Ferns, was deprived of his revenues for taking part with Bruce, and the Friars Minor of the Franciscan order, were severely censured in a Papal rescript for their zeal on the same side.

The great families of Fitzgerald and Butler obtained their earldoms of Kildare, Desmond and Ormond, out of this dangerous crisis, but the premier earldom of Ulster disappeared from our history soon afterwards. Richard, the Red Earl, having died in the Monastery of Athassil, in 1326, was succeeded by his son, William, who, seven years later, in consequence of a family feud, instigated by one of his own female relatives, Gilla de Burgh, wife of Walter de Mandeville, was murdered at the Fords, near Carrickfergus, in the 21st year of his age. His wife, Maud, daughter of Henry Plantagenet, Earl of Lancaster, fled into England with her infant, afterwards married to Lionel, Duke of Clarence, son of King Edward III., who thus became personally interested in the system which he initiated by the odious Statute of Kilkenny. But the misfortunes of the Red Earl's posterity did not end with the murder of his immediate successor. Edmond his surviving son, five years subsequently, was seized by his cousin Edmond, the son of William, and drowned in Lough Mask, with a stone about his neck. The posterity of William de Burgh then assumed the name of McWilliam, and renounced the laws, language and allegiance of England. Profitting by their dissensions, Turlogh O'Conor, towards the middle of the century, asserted supremacy over them, thus practising against the descendants the same policy which the first de Burghs had successfully employed among the sons of Roderick.

We must mention here a final consequence of Edward Bruce's invasion seldom referred to,—namely, the character of the treaty between Scotland and England, concluded and signed at Edinburgh, on St. Patrick's Day, 1328. By this treaty, after arranging an intermarriage between the royal families, it was stipulated in the event of a rebellion against Scotland, in Skye, Man, or the Islands, or against England, in Ireland, that the several

Kings would not abet or assist each other's rebel subjects. Remembering this article we know not what to make of the entry in our own Annals, which states that Robert Bruce landed at Carrickfergus, in the same year 1328, "and sent word to the Justiciary and Council, that he came to make peace between Ireland and Scotland, and that he would meet them at Green Castle; but that the latter failing to meet him, he returned to Scotland." This, however, we know: high hopes were entertained and immense sacrifices were made, for Edward Bruce, but were made in vain. His proverbial rashness in battle with his total disregard of the opinion of the country into which he came, alienated from him those who were at first disposed to receive him with enthusiasm. It may be an instructive lesson to such as look to foreign leaders and foreign forces for the means of national deliverance to read the terms in which the native Annalists record the defeat and death of Edward Bruce: "No achievement had been performed in Ireland, for a long time," say the Four Masters, "from which greater benefit had accrued to the country than from this." "There was not a better deed done in Ireland since the banishment of the Formorians," says the Annalist of Clonmacnoise! So detested may a foreign liberating chief become, who outrages the feelings and usages of the people he pretends, or really means to emancipate!

BOOK VI.

THE NATIVE, THE NATURALIZED, AND "THE ENGLISH INTEREST."

CHAPTER I.

CIVIL WAR IN ENGLAND—ITS EFFECTS ON THE ANGLO-IRISH—THE KNIGHTS OF SAINT JOHN—GENERAL DESIRE OF THE ANGLO-IRISH TO NATURALIZE THEMSELVES AMONG THE NATIVE POPULATION—A POLICY OF NON-INTERCOURSE BETWEEN THE RACES RESOLVED ON, IN ENGLAND.

THE closing years of the reign of Edward II. of England were endangered by the same partiality for favorites, which had disturbed its beginning. The de Spensers, father and son, played at this period the part which Gaveston had performed twenty years earlier. The Barons, who undertook to rid their country of this pampered family, had, however, at their head Queen Isabella, sister of the King of France, who had separated from her husband under a pretended fear of violence at his hands, but in reality to enjoy more freely her criminal intercourse with her favorite, Mortimer. With the aid of French and Flemish mercenaries, they compelled the unhappy Edward to fly from London to Bristol, whence he was pursued, captured, and after being confined for several months in different fortresses, was secretly murdered in the autumn of 1327, by thrusting a red hot iron into his bowels. His son, Edward, a lad of fifteen years of age, afterwards the celebrated Edward III., was proclaimed King, though the substantial power remained for some years longer with Queen Isabella, and her paramour, now elevated to the rank of Earl of March. In the year 1330, however, their guilty prosperity was brought to a sudden close; Mortimer was seized by surprise, tried by his peers, and executed at Tyburn; Isabella was imprisoned for life, and the young King, at the age of eighteen, began in reality that reign, which, through half a century's continuance, proved so glorious and advantageous for England.

It will be apparent that during the last few years of the second, and under the minority of the third Edward, the Anglo-Irish Barons would be left to pursue undisturbed their own particular interests and enmities. The renewal of war with Scotland, on the death of King Robert Bruce, and the subsequent protracted wars with France, which occupied, with some intervals of truce, nearly thirty years of the third Edward's reign, left ample time for the growth of abuses of every description among the descendants of those who had invaded Ireland, under the pretext of its reformation, both in morals and government. The contribution of an auxiliary force to aid him in his foreign wars was all the warlike King expected from his lords of Ireland, and at so cheap a price they were well pleased to hold their possessions under his guarantee. At Halidon hill the Anglo-Irish, led by Sir John Darcy, distinguished themselves against the Scots in 1333; and at the siege of Calais, under the Earls of Kildare and Desmond, they acquired additional reputation in 1347. From this time forward it became a settled maxim of English policy to draft native troops out of Ireland for foreign service, and to send English soldiers into it in times of emergency.

In the very year when the tragedy of Edward the Second's deposition and death was enacted in England, a drama of a lighter kind was performed among his new made earls in Ireland. The Lord Arnold le Poer gave mortal offence to Maurice, first Earl of Desmond, by calling him "a Rhymer," a term synonymous with poetaster. To make good his reputation as a Bard, the Earl summoned his allies, the Butlers and Birminghams, while le Poer obtained the aid of his maternal relatives, the de Burghs, and several desperate conflicts took place between them. The Earl of Kildare, then deputy, summoned both parties to meet him at Kilkenny, but le Poer and William de Burgh fled into England, while the victors, instead of obeying the deputy's summons, enjoyed themselves in ravaging his estate. The following year (A. D. 1328), le Poer and de Burgh returned from England, and were reconciled with Desmond and Ormond by the mediation of the new deputy, Roger Outlaw, Prior of the Knights of the Hospital at Kilmainham. In honor of this reconciliation de Burgh gave a banquet at the castle, and Maurice of Desmond reciprocated by another the next day, in St. Patrick's Church, though it was then, as the Anglo-Irish Annalist remarks, the penitential season of lent. A work of peace and reconciliation, calculated to spare the effusion of Christian blood, may have been thought some justification for this irreverent use of a consecrated edifice.

The mention of the Lord Deputy, Sir Roger Outlaw, the second Prior of his order though not the last, who wielded the highest political power over the English settlements, naturally leads to the mention of the establishment in Ireland, of the illustrious orders of the Temple and the Hospital. The first foundation of the elder order is attributed to Strongbow, who erected for them a castle at Kilmainham, on the high ground to the south of the Liffey, about a mile distant from the Danish wall of old Dublin. Here, the Templars flourished, for nearly a century and a half, until the process for their suppression was instituted under Edward II., in 1308. Thirty members of the order were imprisoned and examined in Dublin, before three Dominican inquisitors—Father Richard Balbyn, Minister of the Order of St. Dominick in Ireland, Fathers Philip de Slane and Hugh de St. Leger. The decision arrived at was the same as in France and England; the order was condemned and suppressed; and their Priory of Kilmainham, with sixteen benefices in the diocese of Dublin, and several others, in Ferns, Meath, and Dromore, passed to the succeeding order, in 1311. The state maintained by the Priors of Kilmainham in their capacious residence often rivalled that of the Lords Justices. But though their rents were ample, they did not collect them without service. Their house might justly be regarded as an advanced fortress on the south side of the city, constantly open to attacks from the mountain tribes of

Wicklow. Although their vows were for the Holy Land, they were ever ready to march, at the call of the English Deputies, and their banner, blazoned with the *Agnus Dei*, waved over the bloodiest border frays of the XIVth century. The Priors of Kilmainham sat as Barons in the Parliaments of "the Pale," and the office was considered the first in ecclesiastical rank among the regular orders.

During the second quarter of this century, an extraordinary change became apparent in the manners and customs of the descendants of the Normans, Flemings, and Cambrians, whose ancestors an hundred years earlier were strangers in the land. Instead of intermarrying exclusively among themselves, the prevailing fashion became to seek for Irish wives, and to bestow their daughters on Irish husbands. Instead of clinging to the language of Normandy or England, they began to cultivate the native speech of the country. Instead of despising Irish law, every nobleman was now anxious to have his Brehon, his Bard, and his Senachie. The children of the Barons were given to be fostered by Milesian mothers, and trained in the early exercises so minutely prescribed by Milesian education. Kildare, Ormond, and Desmond, adopted the old military usages of exacting "coyne and livery"—horse meat and man's meat—from their feudal tenants. The tie of Gossipred, one of the most fondly cherished by the native population, was multiplied between the two races, and under the wise encouragement of a domestic dynasty might have become a powerful bond of social union. In Connaught and Munster where the proportion of native to naturalized was largest, the change was completed almost in a generation, and could never afterwards be wholly undone. In Ulster the English element in the population towards the end of this century was almost extinct, but in Meath and Leinster, and that portion of Munster immediately bordering on Meath and Leinster, the process of amalgamation required more time than the policy of the Kings of England allowed it to obtain.

The first step taken to counteract their tendency to *Hibernicize* themselves, was to bestow additional honors on the great families. The barony of Offally was enlarged into the earldom of Kildare; the lordship of Carrick into the earldom of Ormond;

the title of Desmond was conferred on Maurice Fitz-Thomas Fitzgerald, and that of Louth on the Baron de Bermingham. Nor were they empty honors; they were accompanied with something better. The "royal liberties" were formally conceded, in no less than nine great districts, to their several lords. Those of Carlow, Wexford, Kilkenny, Kildare, and Leix, had been inherited by the heirs of the Earl Marshal's five daughters; four other counties Palatine were now added—Ulster, Meath, Ormond, and Desmond. "The absolute lords of those palatinates," says Sir John Davis, "made barons and knights, exercised high justice within all their territories; erected courts for civil and criminal causes, and for their own revenues, in the same form in which the king's courts were established at Dublin; they constituted their own judges, seneschals, sheriffs, coroners, and escheators. So that the king's writs did not run in their counties, which took up more than two parts of the English colony; but ran only in the church-lands lying within the same, which were therefore called THE CROSSE, wherein the Sheriff was nominated by the King. By "high-justice" is meant the power of life and death, which was hardly consistent with even a semblance of subjection. No wonder such absolute lords should be found little disposed to obey the summons of deputies, like Sir Ralph Ufford and Sir John Morris, men of merely knightly rank, whose equals they had the power to create, by the touch of their swords.

For a season their new honors quickened the dormant loyalty of the recipients. Desmond, at the head of 10,000 men, joined the lord deputy, Sir John Darcy, to suppress the insurgent tribes of South Leinster; the Earls of Ulster and Ormond united their forces for an expedition into Westmeath against the brave McGeoghegans and their allies; but even these services—so complicated were public and private motives in the breasts of the actors—did not allay the growing suspicion of what were commonly called " the old English," in the minds of the English King and his council. Their resolution seems to have been fixed to entrust no native of Ireland with the highest office in his own country; in accordance with which decision Sir Anthony Lucy was appointed, (1331;) Sir John Darcy, (1832-34;

again in 1341;) and Sir Ralph Ufford, (1343-1346.) During the incumbency of these English knights, whether acting as justiciaries or as deputies, the first systematic attempts were made to prevent, both by the exercise of patronage and by penal legislation, the fusion of races, which was so universal a tendency of that age. And although these attempts were discontinued on the recommencement of war with France in 1345, the conviction of their utility had seized too strongly on the tenacious will of Edward III. to be wholly abandoned. The peace of Bretigni in 1360 gave him leisure to turn again his thoughts in that direction. The following year he sent over his third son, Lionel, Duke of Clarence and Earl of Ulster, (in right of his wife,) who boldly announced his object to be the total separation, into hostile camps, of the two populations.

This first attempt to enforce non-intercourse between the natives and the naturalized deserves more particular mention. It appears to have begun in the time of Sir Anthony Lucy, when the King's Council sent over certain "Articles of Reform," in which it was threatened that if the native nobility were not more attentive in discharging their duties to the King, his Majesty would resume into his own hands all the grants made to them by his royal ancestors or himself, as well as enforce payment of debts due to the Crown which had been formerly remitted. From some motive, these articles were allowed, after being made public, to remain a dead letter, until the administration of Darcy, Edward's confidential agent in many important transactions. English and Irish. They were proclaimed with additional emphasis by this deputy, who convoked a Parliament or Council, at Dublin, to enforce them as law. The same year, 1342, a new ordinance came from England, prohibiting the public employment of men born or married, or possessing estates in Ireland, and declaring that all offices of state should be filled in that country by "fit Englishmen, having lands, tenements, and benefices in England." To this sweeping proscription the Anglo-Irish, as well townsmen as nobles, resolved to offer every resistance, and by the convocation of the Earls of Desmond, Ormond, and Kildare, they agreed to meet, for that purpose, at Kilkenny. Accordingly, what is called Darcy's Parliament, met at Dublin in October, while Desmond's rival assembly gathered at Kilkenny in November. The proceedings of the former, if it agreed to any, are unrecorded, but the latter despatched to the King, by the hands of the Prior of Kilmainham, a Remonstrance couched in Norman-French, the court language, in which they reviewed the state of the country; deplored the recovery of so large a portion of the former conquest by the old Irish; accused, in round terms, the successive English officials sent into the land, with a desire suddenly to enrich themselves at the expense both of sovereign and subject; pleaded boldly their own loyal services, not only in Ireland, but in the French and Scottish wars; and finally, claimed the protection of the Great Charter, that they might not be ousted of their estates, without being called in judgment. Edward, sorely in need of men and subsidies for another expedition to France, returned them a conciliatory answer, summoning them to join him in arms, with their followers, at an early day; and although a vigorous effort was made by Sir Ralph Ufford to enforce the articles of 1331, and the ordinance of 1341, by the capture of the Earls of Desmond and Kildare, and by military execution on some of their followers, the policy of non-intercourse was tacitly abandoned for some years after the Remonstrance of Kilkenny. In 1353, under the lord deputy, Rokeby, an attempt was made to revive it, but it was quickly abandoned, and two years later, Maurice, Earl of Desmond, the leader of the opposition, was appointed to the office of Lord Justice for life! Unfortunately that high-spirited nobleman died the year of his appointment before its effects could begin to be felt. The only legal concession which marked his period was a royal writ constituting the "Parliament" of the Pale the court of last resort for appeals from the decisions of the King's courts in that province. A recurrence to the former favorite policy signalized the year 1357, when a new set of ordinances were received from London, denouncing the penalties of treason against all who intermarried, or had relations of fosterage with the Irish; and proclaiming war upon all kerns and idle men found within the English districts. Still severer measures, in the same direction, were soon afterwards decided upon by the English King and his council.

Before relating the farther history of this penal code as applied to race, we must recall the reader's attention to the important date of the Kilkenny Remonstrance, 1342. From that year may be distinctly traced the growth of two parties, among the subjects of the English Kings in Ireland. At one time they are distinguished as "the old English" and "the new English," at another, as "English by birth" and "English by blood." The new English, fresh from the Imperial island, seem to have usually conducted themselves with a haughty sense of superiority; the old English, more than half *Hibernicized*, confronted these strangers with all the self-complacency of natives of the soil, on which they stood. In their frequent visits to the Imperial capital, the old English were made sensibly to feel that their country was not there; and as often as they went, they returned with renewed ardor to the land of their possessions and their birth. Time, also, had thrown its reverent glory round the names of the first invaders, and to be descended from the companions of Earl Richard, or the captains who accompanied King John, was a source of family pride, second only to that which the native princes cherished, in tracing up their lineage to Milesius of Spain. There were many reasons, good, bad, and indifferent for the descendants of the Norman adventurers adopting Celtic names, laws, and customs, but not the least potent, perhaps, was the fostering of family pride and family dependence, which, judged from our present stand-points, were two of the worst possible preparations for our national success in modern times.

CHAPTER II.

LIONEL, DUKE OF CLARENCE, LORD LIEUTENANT—THE PENAL CODE OF RACE—"THE STATUTE OF KILKENNY," AND SOME OF ITS CONSEQUENCES.

WHILE the grand experiment for the separation of the population of Ireland into two hostile camps was being matured in England, the Earls of Kildare and Ormond were, for four or five years, alternately entrusted with the supreme power. Fresh ordinances, in the spirit of those despatched to Darcy, in 1342, continued annually to arrive. One commanded all lieges of the English King, having grants upon the marches of the Irish enemy, to reside upon and defend them, under pain of revocation. By another entrusted to the Earl of Ormond for promulgation, "no mere Irishman" was to be made a Mayor or bailiff, or other officer of any town within the English districts; nor was any mere Irishman "thereafter, under any pretence of kindred, or from any other cause, to be received into holy orders, or advanced to any ecclesiastical benefice." A modification of this last edict was made the succeeding year, when a royal writ explained that exception was intended to be made of such Irish clerks as had given individual proofs of their loyalty.

Soon after the peace of Bretigni had been solemnly ratified at Calais, in 1360, by the Kings of France and England, and the latter had returned to London, it was reported that one of the Princes would be sent over to exercise the supreme power at Dublin. As no member of the royal family had visited Ireland since the reign of John—though Edward I., when Prince, had been appointed his father's lieutenant—this announcement naturally excited unusual expectations. The Prince chosen was the King's third son, Lionel, Duke of Clarence; and every preparation was made to give *eclat* and effect to his administration. This Prince had married, a few years before, Elizabeth de Burgh, who brought him the titles of Earl of Ulster and Lord of Connaught, with the claims which they covered. By a proclamation, issued in England, all who held possessions in Ireland were commanded to appear before the King, either by proxy or in person, to take measures for resisting the continued encroachments of the Irish enemy. Among the absentees compelled to contribute to the expedition accompanying the Prince, are mentioned Maria, Countess of Norfolk, Agnes, Countess of Pembroke, Margery de Roos, Anna le Despenser, and other noble ladies, who, by a strange recurrence, represented in this age the five co-heiresses of the first Earl Marshal, granddaughters of Eva McMurrogh. What exact force was equipped from all these contributions is not mentioned; but the Prince arrived in Ireland with no more than 1,500 men, under the command of Ralph, Earl of Strafford, James, Earl of Ormond, Sir William Windsor, Sir John Carew, and other knights. He landed at Dublin on the 15th of September, 1361, and remained in office for three years. On landing he issued a proclamation, prohibiting natives of the country, of all origins, from approaching his camp or court, and having made this hopeful beginning he marched with his troops into Munster, where he was defeated by O'Brien, and compelled to retreat. Yet by the flattery of courtiers he was saluted as the conqueror of Clare, and took from the supposed fact, his title of *Clarence*. But no adulation could blind him to the real weakness of his position; he keenly felt the injurious consequences of his proclamation, revoked it, and endeavored to remove the impression he had made, by conferring knighthood on the Prestons, Talbots, Cusacks, De la Hydes, and members of other families, not immediately connected with the Palatine Earls. He removed the Exchequer from Dublin to Carlow, and expended 500 pounds—a large sum for that age—in fortifying the town. The barrier of Leinster was established at Carlow, from which it was removed, by an act of the English Parliament ten years afterwards; the town and castle were retaken in 1397, by the celebrated Art McMorrogh, and long remained in the hands of his posterity.

In 1364, Duke Lionel went to England, leaving de Windsor as his deputy, but in 1365, and again in 1367, he twice returned to his government. This latter year is memorable as the date of the second great stride towards the establishment of a Penal

Code of race, by the enactment of the "Statute of Kilkenny." This memorable Statute was drawn with elaborate care, being intended to serve as the corner stone of all future legislation, and its provisions are deserving of enumeration. The Act sets out with this preamble: "Whereas, at the conquest of the land of Ireland, and for a long time after, the English of the said land used the English language, mode of riding, and apparel, and were governed and ruled, both they and their subjects, called Betaghese, (villeins,) according to English law, &c., &c.,—but now many English of the said land, forsaking the English language, manners, mode of riding, laws, and usages, live, and govern themselves according to the manners, fashion, and language of the Irish enemies, and also have made divers marriages and alliances between themselves and the Irish enemies aforesaid—it is therefore enacted, among other provisions, that all intermarriages, fosterings, gossipred, and buying or selling with the 'enemie, shall be accounted treason—that English names, fashions, and manners shall be resumed under penalty of the confiscation of the delinquent's lands—that March-law and Brehon-law are illegal, and that there shall be no law but English law—that the Irish shall not pasture their cattle on English lands—that the English shall not entertain Irish rhymers, minstrels, or newsmen; and, moreover, that no 'mere Irishmen,' shall be admitted to any ecclesiastical benefice or religious house, situated within the English districts."

All the names of those who attended at this Parliament of Kilkenny are not accessible to us; but that the Earls of Kildare, Ormond and Desmond, were of the number need hardly surprise us, alarmed as they all were by the late successes of the native princes, and overawed by the recent prodigious victories of Edward III. at Cressy and Poictiers. What does at first seem incomprehensible is that the Archbishop not only of Dublin, but of Cashel and Tuam—in the heart of the Irish country—and the Bishops of Leighlin, Ossory, Lismore, Cloyne and Killala, should be parties to this statute. But on closer inspection our surprise, at their presence, disappears. Most of these prelates were at that day nominees of the English King, and many of them were English by birth. Some of them never had possession of their Sees, but dwelt within the nearest strong town, as pensioners on the bounty of the Crown, while the dioceses were administered by native rivals, or tolerated vicars. Le Reve, Bishop of Lismore, was Chancellor to the Duke in 1367; Young, Bishop of Leighlin, was Vice-Treasurer, the Bishop of Ossory, John of Tatendale, was an English Augustinian, whose appointment was disputed by Milo Sweetman, the native Bishop elect; the Bishop of Cloyne, John de Swasham, was a Carmelite of Lyn, in the county of Norfolk, afterwards Bishop of Bangor, in Wales, where he distinguished himself in the controversy against Wyckliff; the Bishop of Killala we only know by the name of Robert—at that time very unusual among the Irish. The two native names are those of the Archbishops of Cashel and Tuam, Thomas O'Carrol and John O'Grady. The former was probably, and the latter certainly, a nominee of the Crown. We know that Dr. O'Grady died an exile from his see—if he ever was permitted to enter it—in the city of Limerick, four years after the sitting of the Parliament of Kilkenny. Shortly after the enactment of this law, by which he is best remembered, the Duke of Clarence returned to England, leaving to Gerald, fourth Earl of Desmond, the task of carrying it into effect. In the remaining years of this reign the office of Lord Lieutenant was held by Sir William de Windsor, during the intervals of whose absence in England the Prior of Kilmainham, or the Earl of Kildare or of Ormond, discharged the duties with the title of Lord Deputy or Lord Justice.

It is now time that we should turn to the native annals of the country to show how the Irish princes had carried on the contest during the eventful half century which the reign of Edward III. occupies in the history of England.

In the generation which elapsed from the death of the Earl of Ulster, or rather from the first avowal of the policy of proscription in 1342—the native tribes had on all sides and continuously gained on the descendants of their invaders. In Connaught, the McWilliams, McWattins, and McFeoriss retained part of their estates only by becoming as Irish as the Irish. The lordships of Leyny and Corran, in Sligo and Mayo, were recovered by the heirs of their former chiefs, while the powerful family of O'Conor's Sligo converted that strong town into a formidable centre of operations. Rindown, Athlone, Roscommon, and Bunratty, all frontier posts fortified by the Normans, were in 1342, as we learn from the Remonstrance of Kilkenny, in the hands of the elder race.

The war, in all the Provinces, was in many respects a war of posts. Towards the north Carrickfergus continued the outwork till captured by Niel O'Neil, when Downpatrick and Dundalk became the northern barriers. The latter town, which seems to have been strengthened after Bruce's defeat, was repeatedly attacked by Niel O'Neil, and at last entered into conditions, by which it procured his protection. At Downpatrick also, in the year 1375, he gained a signal victory over the English of the town and their allies, under Sir James Talbot of Malahide, and Burke of Camline, in which both these commanders were slain. This O'Neil, called from his many successes Neil *More*, or the Great, dying in 1397, left the borders of Ulster more effectually cleared of foreign garrisons than they had been for a century and a half before. He enriched the churches of Armagh and Derry, and built a habitation for students resorting to the primatial city, on the site of the ancient palace of Emania, which had been deserted before the coming of St. Patrick.

The northern and western chiefs seem in this age to have made some improvements in military equipments and tactics. *Cooey-na-gall*, a celebrated captain of the O'Kanes, is represented on his tomb at Dungiven as clad in complete armor—though that may be the fancy of the sculptor. Scottish gallowglasses —heavy-armed infantry, trained in Bruce's campaigns, were permanently enlisted in their service. Of their leaders the most distinguished were McNeil *Cam*, or the Crooked, and McRory, in the service of O'Conor, and McDonnell, McSorley, and McSweeney, in the service of O'Neil, O'Donnell, and O'Conor Sligo. The leaders of these warlike bands are called the Constables of Tyr-Owen, of North Connaught, or of Connaught, and are distinguished in all the warlike encounters in the north and west.

The midland country—the counties now of Longford, Westmeath, Meath, Dublin, Kildare, King's and Queen's, were almost constantly in arms, during the latter half of this century. Th lords of Annally, Moy-Cashel, Carbry, Offally, Ely, and Leix, rivalled each other in enterprize and endurance. In 1329, McGeoghegan of Westmeath defeated and slew Lord Thomas Butler, with the loss of 120 men at Mullingar; but the next year suffered an equal loss from the combined forces of the Earls of Ormond and Ulster; his neighbor, O'Farrell, contended with even better fortune, especially towards the close of Edward's reign (1372), when in one successful foray he not only swept their garrisons out of Annally, but rendered important assistance to the insurgent tribes of Meath. In Leinster, the house of O'Moore, under Lysaght their Chief, by a well concerted conspiracy, seized in one night (in 1327) no less than eight castles, and razed the fort of Dunamase, which they despaired of defending. In 1346, under Conal O'Moore, they destroyed the foreign strongholds of Ley and Kilmehedie; and though Conal was slain by the English, and Rory, one of their creatures, placed in his stead, the tribe put Rory to death as a traitor in 1354, and for two centuries thereafter upheld their independence. Simultaneously, the O'Conors of Offally, and the O'Carrolls of Ely, adjoining and kindred tribes, so straightened the Earl of Kildare on the one hand, and the Earl of Ormond on the other, that a cess of 40 pence on every carucate (140 acres) of tilled land, and of 40 pence on chattels of the value of six pounds, was imposed on all the English settlements, for the defence of Kildare, Carlow, and the marches generally. Out of the amount collected in Carlow, a portion was paid to the Earl of Kildare, "for preventing the O'Moores from burning the town of Killahan." The same nobleman was commanded, by an order in Council, to strengthen his Castles of Rathmore, Kilkea, and Ballymore, under pain of forfeiture. These events occurred in 1356, '7, and '8.

In the south the same struggle for supremacy proceeded with much the same results. The Earl of Desmond, fresh from his Justiceship in Dublin, and the penal legislation of Kilkenny, was, in 1370, defeated and slain near Adare, by Brian O'Brien, Prince of Thomond, with several knights of his name, and "an indescribable number of others." Limerick was next assailed, and capitulated to O'Brien, who created Sheedy

McNamara, Warden of the City. The English burghers, however, after the retirement of O'Brien, rose, murdered the new Warden, and opened the gates to Sir William de Windsor, the Lord Lieutenant, who had hastened to their relief. Two years later the whole Anglo-Irish force, under the fourth Earl of Kildare, was summoned to Limerick, in order to defend it against O'Brien. So desperate now became the contest, that William de Windsor only consented to return a second time as Lord Lieutenant in 1374, on condition that he was to act strictly on the defensive, and to receive annually the sum of £11,213 6s. 8d.—a sum exceeding the whole revenue which the English King derived from Ireland at that period; which, according to Sir John Davies, fell short of £11,000. Although such was the critical state of the English interest, this lieutenant obtained from the fears of successive Parliaments annual subsidies of £2,000 and £3,000. The deputies from Louth having voted against his demand, were thrown into prison; but a direct petition from the Anglo-Irish to the King brought an order to de Windsor not to enforce the collection of these grants, and to remit in favor of the petitioners the scutage "on all those lands of which the Irish enemy had deprived them."

In the last year of Edward III. (1376), he summoned the magnates and the burghers of towns to send representatives to London to consult with him on the state of the English settlements in Ireland. But those so addressed having assembled together, drew up a protest, setting forth that the great Council of Ireland had never been accustomed to meet out of that kingdom, though, saving the rights of their heirs and successors, they expressed their willingness to do so, for the King's convenience, on that occasion. Richard Deno and William Stapolyn were first sent over to England to exhibit the evils of the Irish administration; the proposed general assembly of representatives seems to have dropped. The King ordered the two delegates just mentioned to be paid ten pounds out of the Exchequer for their expenses.

The series of events, however, which most clearly exhibits the decay of the English interest, transpired within the limits of Leinster, almost within sight of Dublin. Of the actors in these events the most distinguished for energy, ability, and good fortune was Art McMurrogh, whose exploits are entitled to a separate and detailed account.

CHAPTER III.

ART M'MURROGH, LORD OF LEINSTER—FIRST EXPEDITION OF RICHARD II., OF ENGLAND, TO IRELAND.

WHETHER Donald Kavanagh McMurrogh, son of Dermid, was born out of wedlock, as the Lady Eva was made to depose, in order to create a claim of inheritance for herself as sole heiress, this, at least, is certain, that his descendants continued to be looked upon by the kindred clans of Leinster as the natural lords of that principality. Towards the close of the XIIIth century, in the third or fourth generation, after the death of their immediate ancestor, the Kavanaghs of Leighlin and Ballyloughlin begin to act prominently in the affairs of their Province, and their chief is styled both by Irish and English "the McMurrogh." In the era of King Edward Bruce, they were sufficiently formidable to call for an expedition of the Lord Justice into their patrimony, by which they are said to have been defeated. In the next age, in 1335, Maurice, "the McMurrogh," was granted by the Anglo-Irish Parliament or Council, the sum of 80 marks annually, for keeping open certain roads and preserving the peace within his jurisdiction. In 1358, Art, the successor of Maurice, and Donald Revagh were proclaimed "rebels" in a Parliament held at Castledermot, by the Lord Deputy Sancto Amando, the said Art being further branded with deep ingratitude to Edward III., who had acknowledged him as "the Mac-Murch." To carry on a war against him the whole English interest was assessed with a special tax. Louth contributed £20; Meath and Waterford, 2s. on every carucate (140 acres) of tilled land; Kilkenny the same sum, with the addition of 6d. in the pound on chattels. This Art captured the strong castles of **Kilbelle, Galbarstown, Rathville,** and although his career was not one of invariable success, he bequeathed to his son, also called Art, in 1375, an inheritance extending over a large portion—perhaps one-half—of the territory ruled by his ancestors before the invasion.

Art McMurrogh, or Art Kavanagh, as he is more commonly called, was born in the year 1357, and from the age of sixteen and upwards was distinguished by his hospitality, knowledge, and feats of arms. Like the great Brian, he was a younger son, but the fortune of war removed one by one those who would otherwise have preceded him in the captaincy of his clan and connections. About the year 1375—while he was still under age—he was elected successor to his father, according to the Annalists, who record his death in 1417, "after being forty-two years in the government of Leinster." Fortunately he attained command at a period favorable to his genius and enterprize. His own and the adjoining tribes were aroused by tidings of success from other Provinces, and the partial victories of their immediate predecessors, to entertain bolder schemes, and they only waited for a chief of distinguished ability to concentrate their efforts. This chief they found, where they naturally looked for him, among the old ruling family of the Province. Nor were the English settlers ignorant of his promise. In the Parliament held at Castledermot in 1377, they granted to him the customary annual tribute paid to his house, the nature of which calls for a word of explanation. This tribute was granted, "as the late King had done to his ancestors;" it was again voted in a Parliament held in 1380, and continued to be paid so late as the opening of the seventeenth century (A. D. 1603). Not only was a fixed sum paid out of the Exchequer for this purpose—inducing the native chiefs to grant a right of way through their territories—but a direct tax was levied on the inhabitants of English origin for the same privilege. This tax, called "black mail," or "black rent," was sometimes differently regarded by those who paid and those who received it. The former looked on it as a stipend, the latter as a tribute; but that it implied a formal acknowledgment of the local jurisdiction of the chief cannot be doubted. Two centuries after the time of which we speak, Baron Finglas, in his suggestions to King Henry VIII.

for extending his power in Ireland, recommends that "no black rent be paid to any Irishman *for the four shires*"—of the Pale—"and any black rent they had afore this time be paid to them for ever." At that late period "the McMurrogh" had still his 80 marks annually from the Exchequer, and £40 from the English settled in Wexford; O'Carroll of Ely had £40 from the English in Kilkenny, and O'Conor of Offally £20 from those of Kildare, and £300 from Meath. It was to meet these and other annuities to more distant chiefs, that William of Windsor, in 1369, covenanted for a larger revenue than the whole of the Anglo-Irish districts then yielded, and which led him besides to stipulate that he was to undertake no new expeditions, but to act entirely on the defensive. We find a little later, that the necessity of sustaining the Dublin authorities at an annual loss was one of the main motives which induced Richard II. of England to transport two royal armies across the channel, in 1394 and 1399.

Art McMurrogh, the younger, not only extended the bounds of his own inheritance and imposed tribute on the English settlers in adjoining districts, during the first years of his rule, but having married a noble lady of the "Pale," Elizabeth, heiress to the barony of Norragh, in Kildare, which included Naas and its neighborhood, he claimed her inheritance in full, though forfeited under "the statute of Kilkenny," according to English notions. So necessary did it seem to the Deputy and Council of the day to conciliate their formidable neighbor, that they addressed a special representation to King Richard, setting forth the facts of the case, and adding that McMurrogh threatened, until this lady's estates were restored and the arrears of tribute due to him fully discharged, he should never cease from war, "but would join with the Earl of Desmond against the Earl of Ormond, and afterwards return with a great force out of Munster to ravage the country." This allusion most probably refers to James, second Earl of Ormond, who from being the maternal grandson of Edward I. was called the noble Earl, and was considered in his day the peculiar representative of the English interest. In the last years of Edward III., and the first of his successor, he was constable of the Castle of Dublin, with a fee of £18 5s. per annum. In 1381—the probable date of the address just quoted—he had a commission to treat with certain rebels, in order to reform them and promote peace. Three years later he died and was buried in the Cathedral of St. Canice, Kilkenny, the place of sepulture of his family.

When, in the year 1389, Richard II. having attained his majority demanded to reign alone, the condition of the English interest was most critical. During the twelve years of his minority the Anglo-Irish policy of the Council of Regency had shifted and changed, according to the predominance of particular influences. The Lord Lieutenancy was conferred on the King's relatives, Edmund Mortimer, Earl of March (1379), and continued to his son, Roger Mortimer, a minor (1381); in 1383, it was transferred to Philip de Courtenay, the King's cousin. The following year, de Courtenay having been arrested and fined for mal-administration, Robert de Vere, Earl of Oxford, the special favorite of Richard, was created Marquis of Dublin and Duke of Ireland, with a grant of all the powers and authority exercised at any period in Ireland by that King or his predecessors. This extraordinary grant was solemnly confirmed by the English Parliament, who, perhaps willing to get rid of the favorite at any cost, allotted the sum of 30,000 marks due from the King of France, with a guard of 500 men at arms and 1,000 archers for de Vere's expedition. But that favored nobleman never entered into possession of the principality assigned him; he experienced the fate of the Gavestons and de Spencers of a former reign; fleeing, for his life, from the Barons he died in exile in the Netherlands. The only real rulers of the Anglo-Irish in the years of the King's minority, or previous to his first expedition in 1394, (if we except Sir John Stanley's short terms of office in 1385 and 1389,) were the Earls of Ormond, second and third, Colton, Dean of Saint Patrick's, Petit, Bishop of Meath, and White, Prior of Kilmainham. For thirty years after the death of Edward III., no Geraldine was entrusted with the highest office, and no Anglo-Irish layman of any other family but the Butlers. In 1393, Thomas of Woodstock, Duke of Gloucester, uncle to Richard, was appointed Lord Lieutenant, and was on the point of embarking when a royal order reached him announcing the determination of the King to take command of the forces in person.

The immediate motives for Richard's expedition are variously stated by different authors. That usually assigned by the English—a desire to divert his mind from brooding over the loss of his wife, "the good Queen Anne," seems wholly insufficient. He had announced his intention a year before her death; he had called together, before the Queen fell ill, the Parliament at Westminster, which readily voted him "a tenth" of the revenues of all their estates for the expedition. Anne's sickness was sudden, and her death took place in the last week of July. Richard's preparations at that date were far advanced towards completion, and Sir Thomas Scroope had been already some months u Dublin to prepare for his reception. The reason assigned by Anglo-Irish writers is more plausible: he had been a candidate for the Imperial Crown of Germany, and was tauntingly told by his competitors to conquer Ireland before he entered the lists for the highest political honor of that age. This rebuke, and the ill-success of his arms against France and Scotland, probably made him desirous to achieve in a new field some share of that military glory which was always so highly prized by his family.

Some events which immediately preceded Richard's expedition may help us to understand the relative positions of the natives and the naturalized to the English interest in the districts through which he was to march. By this time the banner of Art McMurrogh floated over all the castles and raths, on the slope of the Ridge of Leinster, or the steps of the Blackstair hills; while the forests along the Barrow and the Upper Slaney, as well as in the plain of Carlow and in the south-western angle of Wicklow (now the barony of Shillelagh), served still better his purposes of defensive warfare. So entirely was the range of country thus vaguely defined under native sway that John Griffin, the English Bishop of Leighlin, and Chancellor of the Exchequer, obtained a grant in 1389 of the town of Gulroestown, in the county of Dublin, "near the marches of O'Toole, seeing he could not live within his own see for the rebels." In 1390, Peter Creagh, Bishop of Limerick, on his way to attend an Anglo-Irish Parliament, was taken prisoner in that region, and in consequence the usual fine was remitted in his favor. In 1392, James, the third Earl of Ormond, gave McMurrogh a severe check at Tiscoffin, near Shankill, where 600 of his clansmen were left dead among the hills.

This defeat, however, was thrown into the shade by the capture of New Ross, on the very eve of Richard's arrival at Waterford. In a previous chapter we have described the fortifications erected round this important seaport towards the end of the XIIIth century. Since that period its progress had been steadily onward. In the reign of Edward III. the controversy which had long subsisted between the merchants of Ross and those of Waterford, concerning the trade monopolies claimed by the latter, had been decided in favor of Ross. At this period it could muster in its own defence 363 cross-bowmen, 1,200 long-bowmen, 1,200 pikemen, and 104 horsemen—a force which would seem to place it second to Dublin in point of military strength. The capture of so important a place by McMurrogh was a cheering omen to his followers. He razed the walls and towers, and carried off gold, silver and hostages.

On the 2d of October, 1394, the royal fleet of Richard arrived from Milford Haven, at Waterford. To those who saw Ireland for the first time, the rock of Dundonolf, famed for Raymond's camp, the abbey of Dunbrody looking calmly down on the confluence of the three rivers, and the half-Danish, half-Norman port before them, must have presented scenes full of interest. To the townsmen the fleet was something wonderful. The endless succession of ships of all sizes and models, which had wafted over 30,000 archers and 4,000 men at arms; the royal galley leading on the fluttering penons of so many great nobles, was a novel sight to that generation. Attendant on the King were his uncle, the Duke of Gloucester, the young Earl of March, heir apparent, Thomas Mowbray, Earl of Nottingham, the Earl of Rutland, the Lord Thomas Percy, afterwards Earl of Westmoreland, and father of Hotspur, and Sir Thomas Moreley, heir to the last Lord Marshal of the "Pale." Several dignitaries of the English Church, as well Bishops as Abbots, were also with the fleet. Immediately after landing a *Te Deum* was sung in the Cathedral, where Earl Richard had wedded the Princess Eva, where Henry II. and John had offered up similar thanksgivings.

Richard remained a week at Waterford; gave splendid *fetes*, and received some lords of the neighboring country, Le Poers, Graces and Butlers. He made gifts to churches, and ratified the charter given by John to the abbey of Holy Cross in Munster. He issued a summons to Gerald, Earl of Desmond, to appear before him by the feast of the Purification, "in whatever part of Ireland he should then be," to answer to the charge of having usurped the manor, revenues, and honor of Dungarvan. Although it was then near the middle of October, he took the resolution of marching to Dublin, through the country of McMurrogh, and knowing the memory of Edward the Confessor to be popular in Leinster, he furled the royal banner, and hoisted that of the saintly Saxon king, which bore " a cross patence, or, on a field gules, with four doves argent on the shield." His own proper banner bore lioncels and fleur-de-lis. His route was by Thomastown to Kilkenny, a city which had risen into importance with the Butlers. Nearly half a century before, this family had brought artizans from Flanders, who established the manufacture of woollens, for which the town was ever after famous. Its military importance was early felt and long maintained. At this city Richard was joined by Sir William de Wellesley, who claimed to be hereditary standard-bearer for Ireland, and by other Anglo-Irish nobles. From thence he despatched his Earl Marshal into "Catherlough" to treat with McMurrogh. On the plain of Ballygorry, near Carlow, Art, with his uncle, Malachy, O'Moore, O'Nolan, O'Byrne, MacDavid and other chiefs, met the Earl Marshal. The terms proposed were almost equivalent to extermination. They were, in effect, that the Leinster chieftains, under fines of enormous amount, payable into the Apostolic chamber, should before the first Sunday of Lent surrender to the English King " the full possession of all their lands, tenements, castles, woods and forts, which by them and all other of the Kenseologhes, their companions, men, or adherents, late were occupied within the province of Leinster." And the condition of this surrender was to be, that they should have unmolested possession of any and all lands they could conquer from the King's other Irish enemies elsewhere in the kingdom. To these hard conditions some of the minor chiefs, overawed by the immense force brought against them, would, it seems, have submitted, but Art sternly refused to treat, declaring that if he made terms at all, it should be with the King and not with the Earl Marshal; and that instead of yielding his own lands, his wife's patrimony in Kildare should be restored. This broke up the conference, and Mowbray returned discomfitted to Kilkenny.

King Richard, full of indignation, put himself at the head of his army and advanced against the Leinster clans. But his march was slow and painful: the season and the forest fought against him; he was unable to collect by the way sufficient fodder for the horses or provisions for the men. McMurrogh swept off everything of the nature of food—took advantage of his knowledge of the country to burst upon the enemy by night, to entrap them into ambuscades, to separate the cavalry from the foot, and by many other stratagems to thin their ranks and harass the stragglers. At length Richard despairing of dislodging him from his fastnesses in Idrone, or fighting a way out of them, sent to him another deputation of "the English and Irish of Leinster," inviting him to Dublin to a personal interview. This proposal was accepted, and the English king continued his way to Dublin, probably along the sea coast by Bray and the white strand, over Killiney and Dunleary. Soon after his arrival at Dublin, care was taken to repair the highway which ran by the sea, towards Wicklow and Wexford.

CHAPTER IV.

SUBSEQUENT PROCEEDINGS OF RICHARD II.—LIEUTENANCY AND DEATH OF THE EARL OF MARCH—SECOND EXPEDITION OF RICHARD AGAINST ART M'MURROGH—CHANGE OF DYNASTY IN ENGLAND.

At Dublin, Richard prepared to celebrate the festival of Christmas, with all the splendor of which he was so fond. He had received letters from his council in England warmly congratulating him on the results of his "noble voyage" and his successes against "his rebel Make Murgh." Several lords and chiefs were hospitably entertained by him during the holidays—but the greater magnates did not yet present themselves—unless we suppose them to have continued his guests at Dublin, from Christmas till Easter, which is hardly credible.

The supplies which he had provided were soon devoured by so vast a following. His army, however, were paid their wages weekly, and were well satisfied. But whatever the King or his flatterers might pretend, the real object of all the mighty preparations made was still in the distance, and fresh supplies were needed for the projected campaign of 1395. To raise the requisite funds, he determined to send to England his uncle, the Duke of Gloucester. Gloucester carried a letter to the regent, the Duke of York, countersigned "Lincolne," and dated from Dublin, "Feb. 1, 1395." The council, consisting of the Earls of Derby, Arundel, de Ware, Salisbury, Northumberland, and others, was convened, and they "readily voted a tenth off the clergy, and a fifteenth off the laity, for the King's supply." This they sent with a document, signed by them all, exhorting him to a vigorous prosecution of the war, and the demolition of all forts belonging to "MacMourgh [or] le grand O'Nel." They also addressed him another letter, complimentary of his valor and discretion in all things.

While awaiting supplies from England, Richard made a progress as far northward as Drogheda, where he took up his abode in the Dominican Convent of St. Mary Magdalen. On the eve of St. Patrick's Day, O'Neil, O'Donnell, O Reilly, O'Hanlon, and MacMahon, visited and exchanged professions of friendship with him. It is said they made "submission" to him as their sovereign lord, but until the Indentures, which have been spoken of, but never published, are exhibited, it will be impossible to determine what, in their minds and in his, were the exact relations subsisting between the native Irish princes and the King of England at that time. O'Neil, and other lords of Ulster, accompanied him back to Dublin, where they found O'Brien, O'Conor, and McMurrogh, lately arrived. They were all lodged in a fair mansion, according to the notion of Master Castide, Froissart's informant, and were under the care of the Earl of Ormond and Castide himself, both of whom spoke familiarly the Irish language.

The glimpse we get through Norman spectacles of the manners and customs of these chieftains is eminently instructive, both as regards the observers and the observed. They would have, it seems, very much to the disedification of the English esquire, "their minstrels and principal servants sit at the same table and eat from the same dish." The interpreters employed all their eloquence in vain to dissuade them from this lewd habit, which they perversely called " a praiseworthy custom," till at last, to get rid of importunities, they consented to have it ordered otherwise, during their stay, as King Richard's guests.

On the 24th of March the Cathedral of Christ's Church beheld the four kings devoutly keeping the vigil preparatory to knighthood. They had been induced to accept that honor from Richard's hand. They had apologized at first, saying they were all knighted at the age of seven. But the ceremony, as performed in the rest of Christendom, was represented to them as a great and religious custom, which made the simplest knight the equal of his sovereign, which added new lustre to the crowned head, and fresh honor to the victorious sword. On the Feast of the Annunciation they went through the imposing ceremony, according to the custom obtaining among their entertainers.

While the native Princes of the four Provinces were thu

lodged together in one house, it was inevitable that plans of cooperation for the future should be discussed between them. Soon after the Earl of Ormond, who knew their language, appeared before Richard as the accuser of McMurrogh, who was, on his statement, committed to close confinement in the Castle. He was, however, soon after set at liberty, though O'Moore, O'Byrne, and John O'Mullain were retained in custody, probably as hostages, for the fulfilment of the terms of his release. By this time the expected supplies had arrived from England, and the festival of Easter was happily passed. Before breaking up from his winter quarters Richard celebrated with great pomp the festival of his namesake, St. Richard, Bishop of Chichester, and then summoned a parliament to meet him at Kilkenny on the 12th of the month. The acts of this parliament have not seen the light; an obscurity which they share in common with all the documents of this Prince's progress in Ireland. The same remark was made three centuries ago by the English chronicler, Grafton, who adds with much simplicity, that as Richard's voyage into Ireland "was nothing profitable nor honorable to him, therefore the writers think it scant worth the noting."

Early in May a deputation, at the head of which was the celebrated William of Wyckham, arrived from England invoking the personal presence of the King to quiet the disturbances caused by the progress of Lollardism. With this invitation he decided at once to comply, but first he appointed the youthful Earl of March his lieutenant in Ireland, and confirmed the ordinance of Edward III., empowering the chief governor in council to convene parliament by writ, which writ should be of equal obligation with the King's writ in England. He ordained that a fine of not less than fifty marks and not more than one hundred should be exacted of every representative of a town or shire, who, being elected as such, neglected or refused to attend. He reformed the royal courts, and appointed Walter de Hankerford and William Sturmey, two Englishmen, "well learned in the law" as judges, whose annual salaries were to be forty pounds each. Having made these arrangements, he took an affectionate leave of his heir and cousin, and sailed for England, whither he was accompanied by most of the great nobles who had passed over with him to the Irish wars. Little dreamt they of the fate which impended over many of their heads. Three short years and Gloucester would die by the assassin's hand, Arundel by the executioner's axe, and Mowbray, Earl Marshal, the ambassador at Ballygorry, would pine to death in Italian banishment. Even a greater change than any of these—a change of dynasty—was soon to come over England.

The young Earl of March, now left in the supreme direction of affairs, so far as we know, had no better title to govern than that he was heir to the English throne, unless it may have been considered an additional recommendation that he was sixth in descent from the Lady Eva McMurrogh. To his English title, he added that of Earl of Ulster and Lord of Connaught, derived from his mother, the daughter of Lionel, Duke of Clarence, and those of Lord of Trim and Clare, from other relations. The councillors with whom he was surrounded included the wisest statesmen and most experienced soldiers of "the Pale." Among them were Almaric, Baron Grace, who, contrary to the statute of Kilkenny, had married an O'Meagher of Ikerrin, and whose family had intermarried with the McMurroghs; the third Earl of Ormond, an indomitable soldier, who had acted as Lord Deputy, in former years of this reign; Cranley, Archbishop of Dublin, and Roche, the Cistertian Abbot of St. Mary's, lately created Lord Treasurer of Ireland; Stephen Bray, Chief Justice; and Gerald, fifth Earl of Kildare. Among his advisers of English birth were Roger Grey, his successor; the new Judges Hankerford and Sturmey, and others of less pacific reputation. With the dignitaries of the Church, and the innumerable priors and abbots, in and about Dublin, the court of the Heir Presumptive must have been a crowded and imposing one for those times, and had its external prospects been peaceful, much ease and pleasure might have been enjoyed within its walls.

In the three years of this administration, the struggle between the natives, the naturalized, and the English interest knew no cessation in Leinster. Some form of submission had been wrung from McMurrogh before his release from Dublin Castle, in the spring of 1395, but this engagement extorted under duress, from a guest towards whom every rite of hospitality had been violated, he did not feel bound by after his enlargement. In the same year an attempt was made to entrap him at a banquet given in one of the castles of the frontier, but warned by his bard, he made good his escape "by the strength of his arm, and by bravery." After this double violation of what among his countrymen, even of the fiercest tribes, was always held sacred, the privileged character of a guest, he never again placed himself at the mercy of prince or peer, but prosecuted the war with unfaltering determination. In 1396, his neighbor, the chief of Imayle, carried off from an engagement near Dublin, six score heads of the foreigners; and the next year—an exploit hardly second in its kind to the taking of Ross—the strong castle and town of Carlow were captured by McMurrogh himself. In the campaign of 1398, on the 20th of July, was fought the eventful battle of Kenlis, or Kells, on the banks of the stream called "the King's river," in the barony of Kells, and county of Kilkenny. Here fell the Heir Presumptive to the English crown, whose premature removal was one of the causes which contributed to the revolution in England, a year or two later. The tidings of this event filled "the Pale" with consternation, and thoroughly aroused the vindictive temper of Richard. He at once despatched to Dublin his half-brother, Thomas Holland, Earl of Kent, recently created Duke of Surrey. To this duke he made a gift of Carlow castle and town, to be held (if taken) by knights' service. He then, as much, perhaps, to give occupation to the minds of his people, as to prosecute his old project of subduing Ireland, began to make preparations for his second expedition thither. Death again delayed him. John of Ghent, Duke of Lancaster, his uncle, and one of the most famous soldiers of the time, suddenly sickened, and died. As Henry, his son, was in banishment, the King, under pretence of appropriating his vast wealth to the service of the nation, seized it into his own hands, and, despite the warnings of his wisest councillors as to the disturbed state of the kingdom, again took up his march for Milford Haven.

A French knight, named Creton, had obtained leave with a brother-in-arms to accompany this expedition, and has left us a very vivid account of its progress. Quitting Paris they reached

London just as King Richard was about "to cross the sea on account of the injuries and grievances that his mortal enemies had committed against him in Ireland, where they had put to death many of his faithful friends." Wherefore they were further told, "he would take no rest until he had avenged himself upon MacMore, who called himself most excellent King and Lord of great Ireland; where he had but little territory of any kind."

They at once set out for Milford, where, "waiting for the north wind," they remained "ten whole days." Here they found King Richard with a great army, and a corresponding fleet. The clergy were taxed to supply horses, wagons, and money—the nobles, shires and towns, their knights, men-at-arms, and archers—the seaports, from Whitehaven to Penzance, were obliged, by an order in council, dated February 7th, to send vessels rated at twenty-five tons and upwards to Milford, by the octave of Easter. King's letters were issued whenever the usual ordinances failed, and even the press-gang was resorted to, to raise the required number of mariners. Minstrels of all kinds crowded to the camp, enlivening it by their strains, and enriching themselves the while. The wind coming fair, the vessels "took in their lading of bread, wine, cows and calves, salt meat and plenty of water," and the King taking leave of his ladies, they set sail.

In two days they saw "the tower of Waterford." The condition to which the people of this English stronghold had been reduced by the war was pitiable in the extreme. Some were in rags, others girt with ropes, and their dwellings seemed to the voyagers but huts and holes. They rushed into the tide up to their waists, for the speedy unloading of the ships, especially attending to those that bore the supplies of the army. Little did the proud cavaliers and well-fed yeomen, who then looked on, imagine, as they pitied the poor wretches of Waterford, that before many weeks were over, they would themselves be reduced to the like necessity—even to rushing into the sea to contend for a morsel of food.

Six days after his arrival, which was on the 1st of June, King Richard marched from Waterford "in close order to Kilkenny."

He had now the advantage of long days and warm nights which in his first expedition he had not. His forces were rather less than in 1394; some say twenty, some twenty-four thousand in all. The Earl of Rutland, with a reinforcement in one hundred ships, was to have followed him, but this unfaithful courtier did not greatly hasten his preparations to overtake his master. With the King were the Lord Steward of England, Sir Thomas Percy; the Duke of Exeter; De Spencer, Earl of Gloucester; the Lord Henry of Lancaster, afterwards King Henry V.; the son of the late Duke of Gloucester; the son of the Countess of Salisbury; the Bishop of Exeter and London; the Abbot of Westminster, and a gallant Welsh gentleman, afterwards known to fame as Owen Glendower. He dropped the subterfuge of bearing Edward the Confessor's banner, and advanced his own standard, which bore leopards and flower de luces. In this order, "riding boldly," they reached Kilkenny, where Richard remained a fortnight awaiting news of the Earl of Rutland from Waterford. No news, however, came. But while he waited, he received intelligence from Kildare which gratified his thirst for vengeance. Jenico d'Artois, a Gascon knight of great discretion and valor who had come over the preceding year with the Duke of Surrey, marching towards Kilkenny, had encountered some bands of the Irish in Kildare, (bound on a like errand to their prince,) whom he fought and put to flight, leaving two hundred of them dead upon the field. This Jenico, relishing Irish warfare more than most foreign soldiers of his age, continued long after to serve in Ireland—married one of his daughters to Preston, Baron of Naas, and another to the first Lord Portlester.

On the 23d of June, "the very vigil of St. John," a saint to whom the King was very much devoted, Richard, resolving to delay no longer, left Kilkenny, and marched directly towards Catherlough. He sent a message in advance to McMurrogh, "who would neither submit nor obey him in any way; but affirmed that he was the rightful King of Ireland, and that he would never cease from war and the defence of his country until his death; and said that the wish to deprive him of it by conquest was unlawful."

Art McMurrogh, now some years beyond middle age, had

with him in arms "three thousand hardy men," "who did not appear," says our French knight, "to be much afraid of the English." The cattle and corn, the women and the helpless, he had removed into the interior of the fastnesses, while he himself awaited, in Idrone, the approach of the enemy.

This district which lies north and south between the rivers Slaney and Barrow is of a diversified and broken soil, watered with several small streams, and patched with tracts of morass and marsh. It was then half covered with wood, except in the neighborhood of Old Leighlin, and a few other places where villages had grown up around the castles, raths and monasteries of earlier days. On reaching the border of the forest, King Richard ordered all the habitations in sight to be set on fire; and then "two thousand five hundred of the well affected people," or, as others say, prisoners, "began to hew a highway into the woods."

When the first space was cleared, Richard, ever fond of pageantry, ordered his standard to be planted on the new ground, and pennons and banners arrayed on every side. Then he sent for the sons of the Dukes of Gloucester and Lancaster, his cousins, and the son of the Countess of Salisbury and other bachelors-in-arms, and there knighted them with all due solemnity. To young Lancaster, he said, "My fair cousin, henceforth, be preux and valiant, for you have some valiant blood to conquer." The youth to whom he made this address was little more than a boy, but tall of his age, and very vigorous. He had been a hard student at Oxford, and was now as unbridled as a colt new loosed into a meadow. He was fond of music, and afterwards became illustrious as the Fifth Henry of English history. Who could have foreseen when first he put on his spurs by the wood's side, in Catherlough, that he would one day inherit the throne of England and make good the pretensions of all his predecessors to the throne of France?

Richard's advance was slow and wearisome in the forests of Idrone. His route was towards the eastern coast. McMurrogh retreated before him, harassing him dreadfully, carrying off everything fit for food for man or beast, surprising and slaying his foragers, and filling his camp nightly with alarm and blood. The English archers got occasional shots at his men, "so that they did not all escape;" and they in turn often attacked the rear-guard, " and threw their darts with such force that they pierced haubergeon and plates through and through." The Leinster King would risk no open battle so long as he could thus cut off the enemy in detail. Many brave knights fell, many men-at-arms and archers; and a deep disrelish for the service began to manifest itself in the English camp.

A party of Wexford settlers, however, brought one day to his camp Malachy McMurrogh, uncle to Art, a timid, treaty-making man. According to the custom of that century—observed by the defenders of Stirling and the burgesses of Calais—he submitted with a *wythe* about his neck, rendering up a naked sword. His retinue, bareheaded and barefoot, followed him into the presence of Richard, who received them graciously. "Friends," said he to them, "as to the evils and the wrongs that you have committed against me, I pardon you on condition that each of you will swear to be faithful to me for the time to come." Of this circumstance he made the most, as our guide goes on to tell in these words: "Then every one readily complied with his demand; and took the oath. "When this was done he sent word to MacMore, who called himself Lord and King of Ireland, (*that country*,) where he has many a wood but little cultivated land, that if he would come straightways to him with a rope about *his* neck, as his uncle had done, he would admit him to mercy, and elsewhere give him castles and lands in abundance." The answer of King Art is thus reported: "MacMore told the King's people he would do no such thing for all the treasures of the sea or on this side, (the sea,) but would continue to fight and harass him."

For eleven days longer Richard continued his route in the direction of Dublin, McMurrogh and his allies falling back towards the hills and glens of Wicklow. The English could find nothing by the way but "a few green oats" for the horses, which being exposed night and day and so badly fed, perished in great numbers. The general discontent now made itself audible even to the ears of the King. For many days five or six men had but a "single loaf." Even gentlemen, knights and squires, fasted in succession; and our chivalrous guide, for his part, " would have been heartily glad to have been penniless at Poitiers or Paris." Daily deaths made the camp a scene of continued mourning, and all the minstrels that had come across the sea to amuse their victor countrymen, like the poet who went with Edward II. to Bannochburn to celebrate the conquest of the Scots, found their gay imaginings turned to a sorrowful reverse.

At last, however, they came in sight of the sea-coast, where vessels laden with provisions, sent from Dublin, were awaiting them. So eager were the famished men for food, that " they rushed into the sea as eagerly as they would into their s'raw." All their money was poured into the hands of the merchants; some of them even fought in the water about a morsel of food, while in their thirst they drank all the wine they could lay hands on. Our guide saw full a thousand men drunk that day on "the wine of Ossey and Spain." The scene of this extraordinary incident is conjectured to have been at or near Arklow, where the beach is sandy and flat, such as it is not at any point of Wicklow north of that place.

The morning after the arrival of these stores, King Richard again set forward for Dublin, determining to penetrate Wicklow by the valleys that lead from the Meeting of the Waters to Bray. He had not proceeded far on his march, when a Franciscan friar reached his camp as Ambassador from the Leinster King. This unnamed messenger, whose cowl history cannot raise, expressed the willingness of his lord to treat with the King, through some accredited agent—" some lord who might be relied upon"—" so that *their* anger (Richard's and his own), that had long been cruel, might now be extinguished." The announcement spread " great joy" in the English camp. A halt was ordered, and a council called. After a consultation, it was resolved that De Spencer, Earl of Gloucester, should be empowered to confer with Art. This nobleman, now but 26 years of age, had served in the campaign of 1394. He was one of the most powerful peers of England, and had married Constance, daughter of the Duke of York, Richard's cousin. From his possessions in Wales, he probably knew something of the Gaelic customs and speech. He was captain of the rear-guard on this expedition, and now, with 200 lances, and 1,000 archers, all of whom were chosen men, he set out for the conference. The French knight also went with him, as he himself relates in these words:

"Between two woods, at some distance from the sea, I beheld MacMore and a body of the Irish, more than I can number, descend the mountain. He had a horse, without housing or saddle, which was so fine and good, that it had cost him, they said, four hundred cows; for there is little money in the country, wherefore their usual traffic is only with cattle. In coming down, it galloped so hard, that, in my opinion, I never saw hare, deer, sheep, or any other animal, I declare to you for a certainty, run with such speed as it did. In his right hand he bore a great long dart, which he cast with much skill. * * * * His people drew up in front of the wood. These two (Gloucester and the King), like an out-post, met near a little brook. There MacMore stopped. He was a fine large man—wondrously active. To look at him, he seemed very stern and savage, and an able man. He and the Earl spake of their doings, recounting the evil and injury that MacMore had done towards the King at sundry times; and how they all foreswore their fidelity when wrongfully, without judgment or law, they most mischievously put to death the courteous Earl of March. Then they exchanged much discourse, but did not come to agreement; they took short leave, and hastily parted. Each took his way apart, and the Earl returned towards King Richard."

This interview seems to have taken place in the lower vale of Ovoca, locally called Glen-Art, both from the description of the scenery, and the stage of his march at which Richard halted. The two woods, the hills on either hand, the summer-shrunken river, which, to one accustomed to the Seine and the Thames, naturally looked no bigger than a brook, form a picture, the original of which can only be found in that locality. The name itself, a name not to be found among the immediate chiefs of Wicklow, would seem to confirm this hypothesis.

The Earl on his return declared, "he could find nothing in him, (Art,) save only that he would ask for *pardon*, truly, upon condition of having *peace without reserve*, free from any molestation or imprisonment; otherwise, he will never come to agreement as long as he lives; and, (he said,) 'nothing venture, nothing have.' This speech," says the French knight, "was not agreeable to the King; it appeared to me that his face grew pale with anger; he swore in great wrath by St. Edward, that, no, never, would he depart from Ireland, till, alive or dead, he had him in his power."

The King, notwithstanding, was most anxious to reach Dublin: He at once broke up his camp, and marched on through Wicklow, "for all the shoutings of the enemie." What other losses he met in those deep valleys our guide deigns not to tell, but only that they arrived at last in Dublin "more than 30,000" strong, which includes, of course, the forces of the Anglo-Irish lords that joined them on the way. There "the whole of their ills were soon forgotten, and their sorrow removed." The provost and sheriffs feasted them sumptuously, and they were all well-housed and clad. After the dangers they had undergone, these attentions were doubly grateful to them. But for long years the memory of this doleful march lived in the recollection of the English on both sides the Irish sea, and but once more for above a century did a hostile army venture into the fastnesses of Idrone and Hy-Kinsellah.

When Richard arrived in Dublin, still galled by the memory of his disasters, he divided his force into three divisions, and sent them out in quest of McMurrogh, promising to whosoever should bring him to Dublin, alive or dead, "100 marks, in pure gold." "Every one took care to remember these words," says Creton, "for it was a good hearing." And Richard, moreover, declared that if they did not capture him, when the autumn came, and the trees were leafless and dry, he would burn "all the woods, great and small," or find out that troublous rebel. The same day he sent out his three troops, the Earl of Rutland, his laggard cousin, arrived at Dublin with 100 barges. His unaccountable delay he submissively apologized for, and was readily pardoned. "Joy and delight" now reigned in Dublin. The crown jewels shone at daily banquets, tournaments, and mysteries. Every day some new pastime was invented, and thus six weeks passed, and August drew to an end. Richard's happiness would have been complete had any of his soldiers brought in McMurrogh's head: but far other news was on the way to him. Though there was such merriment in Dublin, a long-continued storm swept the channel. When good weather returned, a barge arrived from Chester, bearing Sir William Bagot, who brought intelligence that Henry of Lancaster, the banished Duke, had landed at Ravenspur, and raised a formidable insurrection amongst the people, winning over the Archbishop of Canterbury, the Duke of York, and other great nobles. Richard was struck with dismay. He at once sent the Earl of Salisbury into Wales to announce his return, and then, taking the evil counsel of Rutland, marched himself to Waterford, with most part of his force, and collected the remainder on the way. Eighteen days after the news arrived he embarked for England, leaving Sir John Stanley as Lord Lieutenant in Ireland. Before quitting Dublin, he confined the sons of the Dukes of Lancaster, and Gloucester, in the strong fortress of Trim, from which they were liberated to share the triumph of the successful usurper, Henry IV.

It is beyond our province to follow the after-fate of the monarch, whose Irish campaigns we have endeavored to restore to their relative importance. His deposition and cruel death, in the prison of Pontefract, are familiar to readers of English history. The unsuccessful insurrections suppressed during his rival's reign, and the glory won by the son of that rival, as Henry V., seemed to have established the house of Lancaster firmly on the throne; but the long minority of Henry VI.—who inherited the royal dignity at nine months old—and the factions among the other members of that family opened opportunities, too tempting to be resisted, to the rival dynasty of York. During the first sixty years of the century on which we are next to enter, we shall find the English interest in Ireland controlled by the house of Lancaster; in the succeeding twenty-five years the partizans of the house of York are in the ascendant; until at length, after the victory of Bosworth field (A.D. 1485), the wars of the roses are terminated by the coronation of the Earl of Richmond as Henry VIIth, and his politic marriage with the Princess Elizabeth—the representative of the Yorkist dynasty. It will be seen how these rival houses had their respective factions among the Anglo-

Irish; how these factions retarded two centuries the establishment of English power in Ireland; how the native lords and chiefs took advantage of the disunion among the foreigners to circumscribe more and more the narrow limits of the Pale; and lastly, how the absence of national unity alone preserved the power so reduced from utter extinction. In considering all these far extending consequences of the deposition of Richard II., and the substitution of Henry of Lancaster in his stead, we must give due weight to his unsuccessful Irish wars as proximate causes of that revolution. The death of the Heir Presumptive in the battle of Kel's; the exactions and ill-success of Richard in his wars; the seizure of John of Ghent's estates and treasures; the absence of the sovereign at the critical moment: all these are causes which operated powerfully to that end. And of these all that relate to Irish affairs were mainly brought about by the heroic constancy in the face of enormous odds, the unwearied energy, and high military skill exhibited by one man—Art McMurrogh.

CHAPTER V.

PARTIES WITHIN "THE PALE"—BATTLES OF KILMAINHAM AND KILLUCAN—SIR JOHN TALBOT'S LORD LIEUTENANCY.

ONE leading fact, which we have to follow in all its consequences through the whole of the XVth century, is the division of the English and of the Anglo-Irish interest into two parties, Lancasterians and Yorkists. This division of the foreign power will be found to have produced a corresponding sense of security in the minds of the native population, and thus deprived them of that next best thing to a united national action, the combining effects of a common external danger.

The new party lines were not drawn immediately upon the English revolution of 1399, but a very few years sufficed to infuse among settlers of English birth or descent the partizan passions which distracted the minds of men in their original country. The third Earl of Ormond, although he had received so many favors from the late King and his grandfather, yet by a common descent of five generations from Edward I., stood in relation of cousinship to the Usurper. On the arrival of the young Duke of Lancaster as Lord Lieutenant, in 1402, Ormond became one of his first courtiers, and dying soon after, he chose the Duke guardian to his heir, afterwards the fourth Earl. This heir, while yet a minor (1407), was elected or apppointed deputy to his guardian, the Lord Lieutenant; during almost the whole of the short reign of Henry Vth (1413-1421) he resided at the English Court, or accompanied the King in his French campaigns, thus laying the foundations of that influence which, six several times during the reign of Henry VI., procured his appointment to office as Lord Deputy, Lord Justice, or Lord Lieutenant. At length, in the mid-year of the century, his successor was created Earl of Wiltshire, and entrusted with the important duties of one of the Commissioners for the Fleet, and Lord Treasurer of England; favors and employments which sufficiently account for how the Ormond family became the leaders of the Lancaster party among the Anglo-Irish.

The bestowal of the first place on another house tended to estrange the Geraldines, who, with some reason, regarded themselves as better entitled to such honors. During the first official term of the Duke of Lancaster, no great feeling was exhibited, and on his departure in 1405, the 5th Earl of Kildare was, for a year, entrusted with the office of Deputy. On the return of the Duke, in August, 1408, the Earl rode out to meet him, but was suddenly arrested with three other members of his family, and imprisoned in the Castle. His house in Dublin was plundered by the servants of the Lord Lieutenant, and the sum of 300 marks was exacted for his ransom. Such injustice and indignity, as well as the subsequent arrest of the sixth Earl, in 1418, "for having communicated with the Prior of Kilmainham" —still more than their rivalry with the Ormonds, drove the Kildare family into the ranks of the adherents of the Dukes of York. We shall see in the sequel the important reacting influence of these Anglo-Irish combinations upon the fortunes of the white rose and the red.

To signalize his accession and remove the reproach of inaction which had been so often urged against his predecessor, Henry IV. was no sooner seated on the throne than he summoned the military tenants of the Crown to meet him in arms upon the Tyne, for the invasion of Scotland. It seems probable that he summoned those of Ireland with the rest, as we find in that year (1400) that an Anglo-Irish fleet, proceeding northwards from Dublin, encountered a Scottish fleet in Strangford Lough, where a fierce engagement was fought, both sides claiming the victory. Three years later the Dubliners landed at Saint Ninians, and behaved valiantly, as their train bands did the same summer against the mountain tribes of Wicklow. Notwithstanding the personal sojourn of the unfortunate Richard, and his lavish expenditure among them, these warlike burghers cordially supported the new dynasty. Some privileges of trade were judiciously extended to them, and, in 1407, Henry granted to the Mayors of the city the privilege of having a gilded sword carried before them, in the same manner as the Mayors of London.

At the period when these politic favors were bestowed on the citizens of Dublin, Henry was contending with a formidable insurrection in Wales, under the leadership of Owen Glendower, who had learned in the fastnesses of Idrone, serving under King Richard, how brave men, though not formed to war in the best schools, can defend their country against invasion. In the struggle which he maintained so gallantly during this and the next reign, though the fleet of Dublin at first assisted his enemies, he was materially aided afterwards by the constant occupation furnished them by the clans of Leinster. The early years of the Lancasterian dynasty were marked by a series of almost invariable defeats in the Leinster counties. Art. McMurrogh, whose activity defied the chilling effects of age, poured his cohorts through Sculloge gap, on the garrisons of Wexford, taking in rapid possession in one campaign (1406) the castles of Camolin, Ferns, and Enniscorthy. Returning northward he retook Castledermot, and inflicted chastisement on the warlike

Abbot of Conal, near Naas, who shortly before attacked some Irish forces on the Curragh of Kildare, slaying two hundred men. Castledermot was retaken by the Lord Deputy Scrope the next year, with the aid of the Earls of Ormond and Desmond, and the Prior of Kilmainham, at the head of his Knights. These allies were fresh from a Parliament in Dublin, where the Statute of Kilkenny had been, according to custom, solemnly re-enacted as the only hope of the English interest, and they natura'ly drew the sword in maintenance of their palladium. Within six miles of Callan, in "McMurrogh's country," they encountered that chieftain and his clansmen. In the early part of the day the Irish are stated to have had the advantage, but some Methian captains coming up in the afternoon turned the tide in favor of the English. According to the chronicles of the Pale, they won a second victory before nightfall at the town of Callan, over O'Carroll of Ely, who was marching to the aid of McMurrogh. But so confused and unsatisfactory are the accounts of this twofold engagement on the same day, in which the Deputy in person, and such important persons as the Earls of Desmond, of Ormond, and the Prior of Kilmainham commanded, that we cannot reconcile it with probability. The Irish Annals simply record the fact that a battle was gained at Callan over the Irish of Munster, in which O'Carroll was slain. Other native authorities add that 800 of his followers fell with O'Carroll, but no mention whatever is made of the battle with McMurrogh. The English accounts gravely add, that the evening sun stood still, while the Lord Deputy rode six miles, from the place of the first engagement to that of the second. This was the last campaign of Sir Stephen Scrope; he died soon after by the pestilence which swept over the island, sparing neither rich nor poor.

The Duke of Lancaster resumed the Lieutenancy, arrested the Earl of Kildare as before related, convoked a Parliament at Dublin, and with all the forces he could muster, determined on an expedition southwards. But McMurrogh and the mountaineers of Wicklow now felt themselves strong enough to take the initiative. They crossed the plain which lies to the north of Dublin, and encamped at Kilmainham, where Roderick when he besieged the city, and Brien before the battle of Clontarf, had pitched their tents of old. The English and Anglo-Irish forces, under the eye of their Prince, marched out to dislodge them, in four divisions. The first was led by the Duke in person; the second by the veteran knight, Jenicho d'Artois, the third by Sir Edward Perrers, an English knight, and the fourth by Sir Thomas Butler, Prior of the Order of Saint John, afterwards created by Henry Vth, for his distinguished service, Earl of Kilmain. With McMurrogh were O'Byrne, O'Nolan and other chiefs, besides his sons, nephews, and relatives. The numbers on each side could hardly fall short of ten thousand men, and the action may be fairly considered one of the most decisive of those times. The Duke was carried back wounded into Dublin; the slopes of Inchicore and the valley of the Liffey were strewn with the dying and the dead; the river at that point obtained from the Leinster Irish the name of *Athcroe*, or the ford of slaughter; the widowed city was filled with lamentation and dismay. In a petition addressed to King Henry by the Council, apparently during his son's confinement from the effects of his wound, they thus describe the Lord Lieutenant's condition: "His soldiers have deserted him; the people of his household are on the point of leaving him; and though they were willing to remain, our lord is not able to keep them together; our said lord, your son, is so destitute of money, that he hath not a penny in the world, nor a penny can he get credit for."

One consequence of this battle of Kilmainham was, that while Art McMurrogh lived, no further attacks were made upon his kindred or country. He died at Ross, on the first day of January, 1417, in the 60th year of his age. His Brehon O'Doran having also died suddenly on the same day, it was supposed they were both poisoned by a drink prepared for them by a woman of the town. "He was," say our impartial *Four Masters*, who seldom speak so warmly of any Leinster Prince, "a man distinguished for his hospitality, knowledge, and feats of arms; a man full of prosperity and royalty; a founder of churches and monasteries by his bounty and contributions," and one who had defended his Province from the age of sixteen to sixty.

On his recovery from the effects of his wound, the Duke of Lancaster returned finally to England, appointing Prior Butler his Deputy, who filled that office for five consecutive years. Butler was an illegitimate son of the late Earl of Ormond, and naturally a Lancasterian: among the Irish he was called Thomas *Baccagh*, on account of his lameness. He at once abandoned South Leinster as a field of operations, and directed all his efforts to maintain the Pale in Kildare, Meath, and Louth. His chief antagonist in this line of action was Murrough or Maurice O'Conor, of Offally. This powerful chief had lost two or three sons, but had gained as many battles over former deputies. He was invariably aided by his connexions and neighbors, the MacGeoghegans of Westmeath. Conjointly they captured the castles and plundered the towns of their enemies, holding their prisoners to ransom or carrying off their flocks. In 1411 O'Conor held to ransom the English sheriff of Meath, and somewhat later defeated Prior Butler in a pitched battle. His greatest victory was the battle of Killucan, fought on the 10th day of May, 1414. In this engagement MacGeoghegan was as usual his comrade. All the power of the English Pale was arrayed against them. Sir Thomas Mereward, Baron of Screen, "and a great many officers and common soldiers were slain," and among the prisoners were Christopher Fleming, son of the Baron of Slane, for whom a ransom of 1,400 marks was paid, and the ubiquitous Sir Jenicho d'Artois, who, with some others, paid "twelve hundred marks, beside a reward and fine for intercession." A Parliament which sat at Dublin for thirteen weeks, in 1413, and a foray into Wicklow, complete the notable acts of Thomas *Baccagh's* viceroyalty. Soon after the accession of Henry Vth (1413), he was summoned to accompany that warlike monarch into France, and for a short interval the government was exercised by Sir John Stanley, who died shortly after his arrival, and by the Archbishop of Dublin, as Commissioner. On the eve of St. Martin's Day, 1414, Sir John Talbot, afterwards so celebrated as first Earl of Shrewsbury, landed at Dalkey, with the title of Lord Lieutenant.

The appointment of this celebrated Captain, on the brink of a war with France, was an admission of the desperate strait to which the English interest had been reduced. And if the end could ever justify the means, Henry Vth from his point of view might have defended on that ground the appointment of this inexorable soldier. Adopting the system of Sir Thomas Butler, Talbot paid little or no attention to South Leinster, but aimed in the first place to preserve to his sovereign, Louth and Meath. His most southern point of operation, in his first Lieutenancy, was Leix, but his continuous efforts were directed against the O'Conors of Offally and the O'Hanlons and McMahons of Oriel. For three succeeding years he made circuits through these tribes, generally by the same route, west and north, plundering chiefs and churches, sparing " neither saint nor sanctuary." On his return to Dublin after these forays, he exacted with a high hand whatever he wanted for his household. When he returned to England, 1419, he carried along with him, according to the chronicles of the Pale—" the curses of many, because he, being run much in debt for victuals, and divers other things, would pay little or nothing at all." Among the natives he left a still worse reputation. The plunder of a bard was regarded by them as worse, if possible, than the spoliation of a sanctuary. One of Talbot's immediate predecessors was reputed to have died of the malediction of a bard of Westmeath, whose property he had appropriated; but as if to show his contempt of such superstition, Talbot suffered no son of song to escape him. Their satires fell powerless on his path. Not only did he enrich himself, by means lawful and unlawful, but he created interest, which a few years afterwards was able to checkmate the Desmonds and Ormonds. The see of Dublin falling vacant during his administration, he procured the appointment of his brother Richard as Archbishop, and left him, at his departure, in temporary possession of the office of Lord Deputy. Branches of his family were planted at Malahide, Belgarde, and Talbotstown, in Wicklow, the representatives of which survive till this day.

One of this Lieutenant's most acceptable offices to the State was the result of stratagem rather than of arms. The celebrated Art McMurrogh was succeeded, in 1417, by his son, Donogh, who seems to have inherited his valor, without his prudence.

In 1419, in common with the O'Conor of Offally, his father's friend, he was entrapped into the custody of Talbot. O'Conor, the night of his capture, escaped with his companions, and kept up the war until his death: McMurrogh was carried to London and confined in the Tower. Here he languished for nine weary years. At length, in 1428, Talbot, having "got license to make the best of him," held him to ransom. The people of his own province re'eaed him, "which was joyful news to the Irish."

But neither the aggrandizement of new nor the depression of old families affected any cardinal change in the direction of events. We have traced for half a century, and are still farther to follow out, the natural consequences of the odious *Statute of Kilkenny*. Although every successive Parliament of the Pale recited and re-enacted that statute, every year saw it dispensed in particular cases, both as to trading, intermarriage, and fostering with the natives. Yet the virus of national proscription outlived all the experience of its futility. In 1417, an English petition was presented to the English Parliament, praying that the law, excluding Irish ecclesiastics from Irish benefices, should be strictly enforced; and the same year they prohibited the influx of fugitives from Ireland, while the Pale Parliament passed a corresponding act against allowing any one to emigrate without special license. At a Parliament held at Dublin in 1421, O'Hedian, Archbishop of Cashel, was impeached by Gese, Bishop of Waterford, the main charges being that he loved none of the English nation; that he presented no Englishman to a living; and that he designed to make himself King of Munster. This zealous assembly also adopted a petition of grievances to the King, praying that as the Irish, who had done homage to King Richard, "had long since taken arms against the government notwithstanding their recognizances payable in the Apostolic chamber, his Highness the King would lay their conduct before the Pope, and prevail on the Holy Father to publish *a crusade against them*, to follow up the intention of his predecessor's grant to Henry II!"

In the temporal order, as we have seen, the policy of hatred brought its own punishment. "The Pale," which may be said to date from the passing of *the Statute of Kilkenny* (1367), was already abridged more than one-half. The Parliament of Kilkenny had defined it as embracing "Louth, Meath, Dublin, Kildare, Catherlough, Klikenny, Wexford, Waterford, and Tipperary," each governed by Seneschals or Sheriffs. In 1422 Dunlavan and Ballymore are mentioned as the chief keys of Dublin and Kildare—and in the succeeding reign Callan in Oriel is set down as the chief key of that part. Dikes to keep out the enemy were made from Tallaght to Tassagard, at Rathconnell in Meath, and at other places in Meath and Kildare. These narrower limits it long retained, and the usual phrase in all future legislation by which the assemblies of the Anglo-Irish define their jurisdiction is "the four shires." So completely was this enclosure isolated from the rest of the country that, in the reign at which we have now arrived, both the Earls of Desmond and Ormond were exempted from attending certain sittings of Parliament, and the Privy Council, on the ground that they could not do so without marching through the enemy's country at great risk and inconvenience. It is true occasional successes attended the military enterprizes of the Anglo-Irish even in these days of their lowest fortunes. But they had chosen to adopt a narrow, bigoted, unsocial policy; a policy of exclusive dealing and perpetual estrangement from their neighbors dwelling on the same soil, and they had their reward. Their borders were narrowed upon them; they were penned up in one corner of the kingdom, out of which they could not venture a league without license and protection, from the free clansmen they insincerely affected to despise.

CHAPTER VI.

ACTS OF THE NATIVE PRINCES—SUBDIVISION OF TRIBES AND TERRITORIES—ANGLO-IRISH TOWNS UNDER NATIVE PROTECTION—ATTEMPT OF THADDEUS O'BRIEN, PRINCE OF THOMOND, TO RESTORE THE MONARCHY—RELATIONS OF THE RACES IN THE FIFTEENTH CENTURY.

THE history of " the Pale" being recounted down to the period of its complete isolation, we have now to pass beyond its entrenched and castellated limits, in order to follow the course of events in other parts of the kingdom.

While the highest courage was everywhere exhibited by chiefs and clansmen, no attempt was made to bring about another National Confederacy, after the fall of Edward Bruce. One result of that striking *denouement* of a stormy career—in addition to those before mentioned—was to give new life to the jealousy which had never wholly subsided, between the two primitive divisions of the Island. Bruce welcomed, sustained, and lamented by the Northern Irish, was distrusted, avoided, and execrated by those of the South. There may have been exceptions, but this was the rule. The Bards and Newsmen of subsequent times, according to their Provincial bias, charged the failure of Bruce upon the Eugenian race, or justified his fate by aspersing his memory and his adherents of the race of Conn. This feeling of irritation, always most deep-seated when driven in by a consciousness of mismanagement or of self-reproach, goes a great way to account for the fact, that more than one generation was to pass away, before any closer union could be brought about between the Northern and Southern Milesian Irish.

We cannot, therefore, in the period embraced in our present book, treat the Provinces otherwise than as estranged communities, departing farther and farther from the ancient traditions of one central legislative council and one supreme elective chief. Special, short-lived alliances between lords of different Provinces are indeed frequent; but they were brought about mostly by ties of relationship or gossipred, and dissolved with the disappearance of the immediate danger. The very idea of national unity, once so cherished by all the children of *Miledh Espaigne*, seems to have been as wholly lost as any of those secrets of ancient handiwork, over which modern ingenuity puzzles itself in vain. In the times to which we have descended, it was every principality and every lordship for itself. As was said of old in Rome, "Antony had his party, Octavius had his party, but the Commonwealth had none."

Not alone was the greater unity wholly forgotten, but no sooner were the descendants of the Anglo-Normans driven into their eastern enclosure, or thoroughly amalgamated in language, laws and costume with themselves, than the ties of particular clans began to loose their binding force, and the tendency to subdivide showed itself on every opportunity. We have already, in the book of the "War of Succession," described the subdivisions of Breffni and of Meath as measures of policy, taken by the O'Conor Kings, to weaken their too powerful suffragans. But that step, which might have strengthened the hands of a native dynasty, almost inevitably weakened the tribes themselves in combatting the attacks of a highly organized foreign power. Of this the O'Conors themselves became afterwards the most striking example. For half a century following the Red Earl's death, they had gained steadily on the foreigners settled in Connaught. The terrible defeat of Athenry was more than atoned for by both other victories. At length the descendants of the vanquished on that day ruled as proudly as ever did their ancestors in their native Province. The posterity of the victors were merely tolerated on its soil, or anxiously building up new houses in Meath and Louth. But in an evil hour, on the death of their last King (1384), the O'Conors agreed to settle the conflicting claims of rival candidates for the succession by dividing the common inheritance. From this date downwards we have an O'Conor Don and an O'Conor Roe in the Annals of that Province, each rallying a separate band of partizans; and according to the accidents of age, minority, alliance, or personal reputation, infringing, harassing, or domineering over the other. Powerful lords they long continued, but as Provincial Princes we meet them no more.

This fatal example—of which there had been a faint foreshadowing in the division of the McCarthys in the preceding century—in the course of a generation or two, was copied by almost every great connexion, north and south. The descendants of yellow Hugh O'Neil in Clandeboy claimed exemption from the supremacy of the elder family in Tyrone; the O'Farells, acknowledged two lords of Annally; the McDonoghs, two lords of Tirerril; there was McDermott of the Wood claiming independence of McDermott of the Rock; OBrien of Ara asserted equality with O'Brien of Thomond; the nephews of Art McMurrogh contested the superiority of his sons; and thus slowly but surely the most powerful clans were hastening the day of their own dissolution.

A consequence of these subdivisions was the necessity which arose for new and opposite alliances, among those who had formerly looked on themselves as members of one family, with common dangers and common enemies. The pivot of policy now rested on neighborhood rather than on pedigree; a change in its first stages apparently unnatural and deplorable, but in the long run not without its compensating advantages. As an instance of these new necessities, we may adduce the protection and succor steadily extended by the O'Neils of Clandeboy, to the McQuillans, Bissets, of the Antrim coast, and the McDonnells of the Glens, against the frequent attacks of the O'Neils of Tyrone. The latter laid claim to all Ulster, and long refused to acknowledge these foreigners, though men of kindred race and speech. Had it not been that the interest of Clandeboy pointed the other way, it is very doubtful if either the Welsh or Scottish settlers by the bays of Antrim could have made a successful stand against the overruling power of the house of Dungannon. The same policy, adopted by native chiefs under similar circumstances, protected the minor groups of settlers of foreign origin in the most remote districts—like the Barretts and other Welsh people of Tyrawley—long after the Deputies of the Kings of

England had ceased to consider them as fellow-subjects, or to be concerned for their existence.

In like manner the detached towns, built by foreigners, of Welsh, Flemish, Saxon or Scottish origin, were now taken "under the protection" of the neighboring chief, or Prince, and paid to him or to his bailiff an annual tax for such protection. In this manner Wexford purchased protection of McMurrogh, Limerick from O'Brien, and Dundalk from O'Neil. But the yoke was not always borne with patience, nor did the bare relation of tax-gatherer and tax-payer generate any very cordial feeling between the parties. Emboldened by the arrival of a powerful Deputy, or a considerable accession to the Colony, or taking advantage of contested elections for the chieftaincy among their protectors, these sturdy communities sometimes sought by force to get rid of their native masters. Yet in no case at this period were such town risings ultimately successful. The appearance of a menacing force, and the threat of the torch, soon brought the refractory burgesses to terms. On such an occasion (1444) Dundalk paid Owen O'Neil the sum of 60 marks and two tuns of wine to avert his indignation. On another, the townsmen of Limerick agreed about the same period to pay annually forever to O'Brien the sum of 60 marks. Notwithstanding the precarious tenure of their existence they all continued jealously to guard their exclusive privileges. In the oath of office taken by the Mayor of Dublin (1388) he is sworn to guard the city's franchises, so that no Irish rebel shall intrude upon the limits. Nicholas O'Grady, Abbot of a Monastery in Clare, is mentioned in 1485 as "the twelfth Irishman that ever possessed the freedom of the city of Limerick" up to that time. A special by-law, at a still later period, was necessary to admit Colonel William O'Shaughnessy, of one of the first families in that county, to the freedom of the Corporation of the town of Galway. Exclusiveness on the one side, and arbitrary taxation on the other, were ill means of ensuring the prosperity of these new trading communities; Freedom and Peace have ever been as essential to commerce as the winds and waves are to navigation.

The dissolution and reorganization of the greater clans necessarily included the removal of old, and the formation of new boundaries, and these changes frequently .ed to border battles between the contestants. The most striking illustration of the struggles of this description, which occurs in our Annals in the fifteenth century, is that which was waged for three generations between a branch of the O'Conors established at Sligo, calling themselves "lords of Lower Connaught," and the O'Donnells of Donegal. The country about Sligo had anciently been subject to the Donegal chiefs, but the new masters of Sligo, after the era of Edward Bruce, not only refused any longer to pay tribute, but endeavored by the strong hand to extend their sway to the banks of the Drowse and the Erne. The pride not less than the power of the O'Donnells was interested in resisting this innovation, for in the midst of the debateable land rose the famous mountain of Ben Gulban (now Benbulben), which bore the name of the first father of their tribe. The contest was, therefore, bequeathed from father to son, but the family of Sligo, under the lead of their vigorous chiefs, and with the advantage of actual possession, prevailed in establishing the exemption of their territory from the ancient tribute. The Drowse, which carries the surplus waters of the beautiful Lough Melvin into the bay of Donegal, finally became the boundary between Lower Connaught and Tyrconnell.

We have already alluded to the loss of the arts of political combination among the Irish in the Middle Ages. This loss was occasionally felt by the superior minds both in church and state. It was felt by Donald More O'Brien and those who went with him into the house of Conor Moinmoy O'Conor, in 1188; it was felt by the nobles who, at Cael-uisge, elected Brian O'Neil in 1258; it was felt by the twelve reguli, who, in 1315, invited Edward Bruce, "a man of kindred blood," to rule over them; it was imputed as a crime to Art McMurrogh in 1397, that he designed to claim the general sovereignty; and now in this century, Thaddeus O'Brien, Prince of Thomond, with the aid of the Irish of the southern half-kingdom, began (to use the phrase of the last Antiquary of Lecan) "working his way to Tara." This Prince united all the tribes of Munster in his favor, and needing, according to ancient usage, the suffrages of two other Provinces to ensure his election, he crossed the Shannon in the summer of 1466 at the head of the largest army which had followed any of his ancestors since the days of King Brian. He renewed his protection to the town of Limerick, entered into an alliance with the Earl of Desmond—which alliance seems to have cost Desmond his head—received in his camp the hostages of Ormond and Ossory, and gave gifts to the lords of Leinster. Simultaneously, O'Conor of Offally had achieved a great success over the Palesmen, taking prisoner the Earl of Desmond, the Prior of Trim, the Lords Barnwall, Plunkett, Nugent, and other Methian magnates—a circumstance which also seems to have some connection with the fate of Desmond and Plunkett, who were the next year tried for treason and executed at Drogheda, by order of the Earl of Worcester, then deputy. The usual Anglo-Irish tales, as to the causes of Desmond's losing the favor of Edward IV., seem very like after-inventions. It is much more natural to attribute that sudden change to some connection with the attempt of O'Brien the previous year—since this only makes intelligible the accusation against him of "*alliance*, fosterage, and alterage with the King's Irish enemies."

From Leinster O'Brien recrossed the Shannon, and overran the country of the Clan-William Burke. But the ancient jealousy of Leath-Conn would not permit its proud chiefs to render hostage or homage to a Munster Prince, of no higher rank than themselves. Disappointed in his hopes of that union which could alone restore the monarchy in the person of a native ruler, the descendant of Brian returned to Kinkora, where he shortly afterwards fell ill of fever and died. "It was commonly reported," says the Antiquary of Lecan, "that the multitudes envious eyes and hearts shortened his days."

The naturalized Norman noble spoke the language of the Gael, and retained his Brehons and Bards like his Milesian compeer. For generations the daughters of the elder race had been the mothers of his house; and the milk of Irish foster-mothers had nourished the infancy of its heirs. The Geraldines, the McWilliams, even the Butlers, among their tenants and soldiers, were now as Irish as the Irish. Whether allies or enemies, rivals or as relatives, they stood as near to their neighbors of

Celtic origin as they did to the descendants of those who first landed at Bannow and at Waterford. The "Statute of Kilkenny" had proclaimed the eternal separation of the races, but up to this period it had failed, and the men of both origins were left free to develope whatever characteristics were most natural to them. What we mean by being left free is, that there was no general or long-sustained combination of one race for the suppression of the other from the period of Richard the Second's last reverses (A. D. 1399) till the period of the Reformation. Native Irish life, therefore, throughout the whole of the XVth, and during the first half of the XVIth century, was as free to shape and direct itself, to ends of its own choosing, as it had been at almost any former period in our history. Private wars and hereditary blood-feuds, next after the loss of national unity, were the worst vices of the nation. Deeds of violence and acts of retaliation were as common as the succession of day and night. Every free clansman carried his battle-axe to church and chase, to festival and fairgreen. The strong arm was prompt to obey the fiery impulse, and it must be admitted in solemn sadness, that almost every page of our records at this period is stained with human blood. But though crimes of violence are common, crimes of treachery are rare. The memory of a McMahon, who betrayed and slew his guest, is execrated by the same stoical scribes, who set down, without a single expression of horror, the open murder of chief after chief. Taking off by poison, so common among their cotemporaries, seems to have been altogether unknown, and the cruelties of the State Prisons of the Middle Ages undreamt of by our fierce, impetuous, but not implacable ancestors. The facts which go to affix the imputation of cruelty on those ages are, the frequent entries which we find of deposed chiefs, or conspicuous criminals, having their eyes put out, or being maimed in their members. By these barbarous punishments they lost caste, if not life; but that indeed must have been a wretched remnant of existence which remained to the blinded lover, or the maimed warrior, or the crippled tiller of the soil. Of the social and religious relations existing between the races, we shall have occasion to speak more fully before closing the present Book.

CHAPTER VII.

CONTINUED DIVISION AND DECLINE OF "THE ENGLISH INTEREST"—RICHARD, DUKE OF YORK, LORD LIEUTENANT—CIVIL WAR AGAIN IN ENGLAND—EXECUTION OF THE EARL OF DESMOND—ASCENDANCY OF THE KILDARE GERALDINES.

WE have already described the limits to which "the Pale" was circumscribed at the beginning of the XIVth century. The fortunes of that inconsiderable settlement during the following century hardly rise to the level of historical importance, nor would the recital of them be at all readable but for the ultimate consequences which ensued from the preservation of those last remains of foreign power in the island. On that account, however, we have to consult the barren annals of "the Pale" through the intermediate period, that we may make clear the accidents by which it was preserved from destruction, and enabled to play a part in after-times, undreamt of and inconceivable, to those who tolerated its existence in the ages of which we speak.

On the northern coasts of Ireland the co-operation of the friendly Scots with the native Irish had long been a source of anxiety to the Palesmen. In the year 1404, Dougan, Bishop of Derry, and Sir Jenicho d'Artois, were appointed Commissioners by Henry IV., to conclude a permanent peace with McDonald, Lord of the Isles, but notwithstanding that form was then gone through, during the reigns of all the Lancasterian Kings, evidence of the Hiberno-Scotch alliance being still in existence, constantly recurs. In the year 1430 an address or petition of the Dublin Council to the King sets forth "that the enemies and rebels, *aided by the Scots*, had conquered or rendered tributary almost every part of the country, *except the county of Dublin*." The presence of Henry Vth in Ireland had been urgently solicited by his lieges in that kingdom, but without effect. The hero of Agincourt having set his heart upon the conquest of France, left Ireland to his lieutenants and their deputies. Nor could his attention be aroused to the English interest in that country, even by the formal declaration of the Speaker of the English Parliament, that "the greater part of the lordship of Ireland" had been "conquered" by the natives.

The comparatively new family of Talbot, sustained by the influence of the great Earl of Shrewsbury, now Seneschal of France, had risen to the highest pitch of influence. When on the accession of Henry VIth, Edward Mortimer, Earl of March, was appointed Lord Lieutenant, and Dantsey, Bishop of Meath, his deputy, Talbot, Archbishop of Dublin, and Lord Chancellor, refused to acknowledge Dantsey's pretensions because his commission was given under the private seal of Lord Mortimer. Having effected his object in this instance, the Archbishop directed his subsequent attacks against the House of Ormond, the chief favorites of the King, or rather of the Council, in that reign. In 1441, at a Dublin Parliament, messengers were appointed to convey certain articles to the King, the purport of which was to prevent the Earl of Ormond from being made lord lieutenant, alleging against him many misdemeanors in his former administration, and praying that some "mighty lord of England" might be named to that office to execute the laws more effectually "than any Irishman ever did or ever will do."

This attempt to destroy the influence of Ormond led to an alliance between that Earl and Sir James, afterwards seventh Earl of Desmond. Sir James was son of Gerald, fourth Earl (distinguished as "the Rhymer," or Magician), by the lady Eleanor Butler, daughter of the second Earl of Ormond. He stood, therefore, in the relation of cousin to the cotemporary head of the Butler family. When his nephew Thomas openly violated the Statute of Kilkenny, by marrying the beautiful Catherine McCormac, the ambitious and intriguing Sir James, anxious to enforce that statute, found a ready seconder in Ormond. Earl Thomas, forced to quit the country, died an exile at Rouen, in France, and Sir James, after many intrigues and negotiations, obtained the title and estates. For once the necessities of Desmond and Ormond united these houses, but the money of the English Archbishop of Dublin, backed by the influence of his illustrious brother, proved equal to them both. In the first twenty-five years of the reign of Henry VIth, (1422–1447,) Ormond was five times lieutenant or deputy, and Talbot five times Deputy, Lord Justice, or Lord Commissioner. Their factious controversy culminated with "the articles" adopted in 1441, which altogether failed of the intended effect; Ormond was reappointed two years afterwards to his old office; nor was it till 1446, when the Earl of Shrewsbury was a third time sent over, that the Talbots had any substantial advantage over their rivals. The recall of the Earl for service in France, and the death of the Archbishop two years later, though it deprived the party they had formed of a resident leader, did not lead to its dissolution. Bound together by common interests and dangers, their action may be traced in opposition to the Geraldines, through the remaining years of Henry VIth, and perhaps so late as the earlier years of Henry VIIth (1485–1500).

In the struggle of dynasties from which England suffered so severely during the XVth century, the drama of ambition shifted its scenes from London and York to Calais and Dublin. The appointment of Richard, Duke of York, as Lord Lieutenant, in 1449, presented him an opportunity of creating a Yorkist party among the nobles and people of "the Pale." This able and ambitious Prince possessed in his hereditary estate resources equal to great enterprizes. He was in the first place the representative of the third son of Edward III.; on the death of his cousin the Earl of March, in 1424, he became heir to that property and title. He was Duke of York, Earl of March, and Earl of Rutland, in England; Earl of Ulster and Earl of Cork, Lord of Connaught, Clare, Meath, and Trim, in Ireland. He had been twice Regent of France, during the minority of Henry, where he upheld the cause of the Plantagenet King with signal ability. By the peace concluded at Tours, between England, France, and Burgundy, in 1444, he was enabled to return to England, where the King had lately come of age, and begun to exhibit the weak though amiable disposition which

led to his ruin. The events of the succeeding two or three
years were calculated to expose Henry to the odium of his
subjects and the machinations of his enemies. Town after
town and province after province were lost in France; the
Regent Somerset returned to experience the full force of this
unpopularity; the royal favorite Suffolk was banished, pursued,
and murdered at sea; the King's uncles, Cardinal Beaufort and
the Duke of Gloucester, were removed by death—so that every
sign and circumstance of the time whispered encouragement to
the ambitious Duke. When, therefore, the Irish lieutenancy
was offered, in order to separate him from his partizans, he at
first refused it; subsequently, however, he accepted, on conditions dictated by himself, calculated to leave him wholly his
own master. These conditions, reduced to writing in the form
of an Indenture between the King and the Duke, extended his
lieutenancy to a period of ten years; allowed him, besides the
entire revenue of Ireland, an annual subsidy from England;
full power to let the King's land, to levy and maintain soldiers,
to place or displace all officers, to appoint a Deputy, and to
return to England at his pleasure. On these terms the ex-
Regent of France undertook the government of the English
settlement in Ireland.

Arrived at Dublin, *the* Duke (as in his day he was always called)
employed himself rather to strengthen his party than to extend
the limits of his government. Soon after his arrival a son was
born to him, and baptized with great pomp in the Castle. James,
fifth Earl of Ormond, and Thomas, eighth Earl of Desmond, were
invited to stand as sponsors. In the line of policy indicated by this
choice, he steadily persevered during his whole connection with
Ireland—which lasted till his death, in 1460. Alternately he
named a Butler and a Geraldine as his deputy, and although he
failed ultimately to win the Earl of Ormond from the traditional
party of his family, he secured the attachment of several of his
kinsmen. Stirring events in England, the year after his appointment, made it necessary for him to return immediately. The
unpopularity of the administration which had banished him had
rapidly augmented. The French King had recovered the whole
of Normandy, for four centuries annexed to the English Crown.

Nothing but Calais remained of all the Continental possessions which the Plantagenets had inherited, and which Henry Vth had done so much to strengthen and extend. Domestic abuses aggravated the discontent arising from foreign defeats. The Bishop of Chichester, one of the ministers, was set upon and slain by a mob at Portsmouth. Twenty thousand men of Kent, under the command of Jack Cade, an Anglo-Irishman, who had given himself out as a son of the last Earl of March, who died in the Irish government twenty-five years before, marched upon London. They defeated a royal force at Sevenoaks, and the city opened its gate at the summons of Cade. The Kentish men took possession of Southwark, while their Irish leader for three days, entering the city every morning, compelled the mayor and the judges to sit in the Guildhall, tried and sentenced Lord Say to death, who, with his son-in-law, Cromer, Sheriff of Kent, was accordingly executed. Every evening, as he had promised the citizens, he retired with his guards across the river, preserving the strictest order among them. But the royalists were not idle, and when, on the fourth morning, Cade attempted as usual to enter London proper, he found the bridge of Southwark barricaded and defended by a strong force under the Lord Scales. After six hours' hard fighting his raw levies were repulsed, and many of them accepted a free pardon tendered to them in the moment of defeat. Cade retired with the remainder on Deptford and Rochester, but gradually abandoned by them, he was surprised, half famished in a garden at Heyfield, and put to death. His captor claimed and received the large reward of a thousand marks offered for his head. This was in the second week of July; on the 1st of September, news was brought to London that the Duke of York had suddenly landed from Ireland. His partizans eagerly gathered round him at his castle of Fotheringay, but for five years longer, by the repeated concessions of the gentle-minded Henry, and the interposition of powerful mediators, the actual war of the roses was postponed.

It is beyond our province to follow the details of that ferocious struggle, which was waged almost incessantly from 1455 till 1471—from the first battle of St. Albans till the final battle at Tewksbury. We are interested in it mainly as it connects the fortunes of the Anglo-Irish Earls with one or other of the dynasties; and their fortunes again, with the benefit or disadvantage of their allies and relatives among our native Princes. Of the transactions in England, it may be sufficient to say that the Duke of York, after his victory at St. Albans in '55, was declared Lord Protector of the realm during Henry's imbecility; that the next year the King recovered and the Protector's office was abolished; that in '57 both parties stood at bay; in '58 an insincere peace was patched up between them; in '59 they appealed to arms, the Yorkists gained a victory at Bloreheath, but being defeated at Ludiford, Duke Richard, with one of his sons, fled for safety into Ireland.

It was the month of November when the fugitive Duke arrived to resume the Lord Lieutenancy which he had formerly exercised. Legally, his commission, for those who recognized the authority of King Henry, had expired four months before— as it bore date from July 5th, 1449; but it is evident the majority of the Anglo-Irish received him as a Prince of their own election rather than as an ordinary Viceroy. He held, soon after his arrival, a Parliament at Dublin, which met by adjournment at Drogheda the following spring. The English Parliament having declared him, his duchess, sons, and principal adherents traitors, and writs to that effect having been sent over, the Irish Parliament passed a declaratory Act (1460) making the service of all such writs treason against *their* authority—"it having been ever customary in their land to receive and entertain strangers with due respect and hospitality." Under this law, an emissary of the Earl of Ormond, upon whom English writs against the fugitives were found, was executed as a traitor. This independent Parliament confirmed the Duke in his office; made it high treason to imagine his death, and—taking advantage of the favorable conjuncture of affairs—they further declared that the inhabitants of Ireland could only be bound by laws made in Ireland; that no writs were of force unless issued under the great seal of Ireland; that the realm had of ancient right its own Lord Constable and Earl Marshal, by whom alone trials for treason alleged to have been committed in Ireland could be conducted. In the same busy spring, the Earl of Warwick (so celebrated as "the Kingmaker" of English history) sailed from Calais, of which he was Constable, with the Channel-fleet, of which he was also in command, and doubling the Land's end of England, arrived at Dublin to concert measures for another rising in England. He found the Duke at Dublin, "surrounded by his Earls and homagers," and measures were soon concerted between them.

An appeal to the English nation was prepared at this Conference, charging upon Henry's advisers that they had written to the French King to besiege Calais, and to the Irish Princes to expel the English settlers. The loyalty of the fugitive lords, and their readiness to prove their innocence before their sovereign, were stoutly asserted. Emissaries were despatched in every direction; troops were raised; Warwick soon after landed in Kent—always strongly pro-Yorkist—defeated the royalists at Northampton in July, and the Duke reaching London in October a compromise was agreed to, after much discussion, in which Henry was to have the crown for life, while the Duke was acknowledged as his successor, and created president of his council.

We have frequently remarked in our history the recurrence of conflicts between the north and south of the island. The same thing is distinctly traceable through the annals of England down to a quite recent period. Whether difference of race, or of admixture of race, may not lie at the foundation of such long-living enmities, we will not here attempt to discuss; such, however, is the fact. Queen Margaret had fled northward after the defeat of Northampton towards the Scottish border, from which she now returned at the head of 20,000 men. The Duke advanced rapidly to meet her, and engaging with a far inferior force at Wakefield, was slain in the field, or beheaded after the battle. All now seemed lost to the Yorkist party, when young Edward, son of Duke Richard, advancing from the marches of Wales at the head of an army equal in numbers to the royalists, won in the month of February, 1461, the battles of Mortimers-cross and Barnet, and was crowned at Westminster in March, by the title of Edward IV. The sanguinary battle of Towton, soon after his coronation, where 38,000 dead were reckoned by the heralds, confirmed his title and established his throne. Even the subsequent hostility of Warwick—though it compelled him once to surrender himself a prisoner, and once to fly the country—did not finally transfer the sceptre to his rival. Warwick was slain in the battle of Tewkesbury (1471), the Lancasterian Prince Edward was put to death on the field, and his unhappy father was murdered in prison. Two years later, Henry, Earl of Richmond, grandson of Catherine, Queen of Henry V. and Owen Ap Tudor, the only remaining leader capable of rallying the beaten party, was driven into exile in France, from which he returned fourteen years afterwards to contest the crown with Richard III.

In these English wars, the only Irish nobleman who sustained the Lancasterian cause was James V., Earl of Ormond. He had been created by Henry, Earl of Wiltshire, during his father's lifetime, in the same year in which his father stood sponsor in Dublin for the son of the Duke. He succeeded to the Irish title and estates in 1451; held a foremost rank in almost all the engagements from the battle of Saint Albans to that of Towton, in which he was taken prisoner and executed by order of Edward IV. His blood was declared attainted and his estates forfeited; but a few years later both the title and property were restored to Sir John Butler, the sixth Earl. On the eve of the open rupture between the Roses, another name intimately associated with Ireland disappeared from the roll of the English nobility. The veteran Talbot, Earl of Shrewsbury, in the eightieth year of his age, accepted the command of the English forces in France, retook the city of Bordeaux, but fell in attack on the French camp at Chatillon, in the subsequent campaign—1453. His son, Lord Lisle, was slain at the same time defending his father's body. Among other consequences which ensued, the Talbot interest in Ireland suffered from the loss of so powerful a patron at the English court. We have only to add that at Wakefield, and in most of the other engagements, there was a strong Anglo-Irish contingent in the Yorkist ranks, and a smaller one—chiefly tenants of Ormond—on the opposite side. Many writers complain that the House of York drained "the Pale" of its defenders, and thus still further diminished the resources of the English interest in Ireland.

In the last forty years of the fifteenth century, the history of "the Pale" is the biography of the family of the Geraldines. We must make some brief mention of the remarkable men to whom we refer.

THOMAS, VIIIth Earl of Desmond, for his services to the House of York, was appointed Lord Deputy in the first years of Edward IV. He had naturally made himself obnoxious to the Ormond interest, but still more so to the Talbots, whose leader in civil contests was Sherwood, Bishop of Meath—for some years, in despite of the Geraldines, Lord Chancellor. Between him and Desmond there existed the bitterest animosity. In 1464, nine of the Deputy's men were slain in a broil in Fingall, by tenants or servants of the Bishop. The next year each party repaired to London to vindicate himself and criminate his antagonist. The Bishop seems to have triumphed, for in 1466, John Tiptoft, Earl of Worcester, called in England for his barbarity to Lancasterian prisoners "the Butcher," superseded Desmond. The movement of Thaddeus O Brien, already related, the same year, gave Tiptoft grounds for accusing Desmond, Kildare, Sir Edward Plunkett, and others, of treason. On this charge he summoned them before him at Drogheda in the following February. Kildare wisely fled to England, where he pleaded his innocence successfully with the King. But Desmond and Plunkett, over-confident of their own influence, repaired to Drogheda, were tried, condemned, and beheaded. Their execution took place on the 15th day of February, 1467. It is instructive to add that Tiptoft, a few years later, underwent the fate in England, without exciting a particle of the sympathy felt for Desmond.

THOMAS, VIIth Earl of Kildare, succeeded on his safe return from England to more than the power of his late relative. The office of Chancellor, after a sharp struggle, was taken from Bishop Sherwood, and confirmed to him for life by an act of the twelfth, Edward III. He had been named Lord Justice after Tiptoft's recall, in 1467, and four years later exchanged the title for that of Lord Deputy to the young Duke of Clarence—the nominal Lieutenant. In 1475, on some change of Court-favor, the supreme power was taken from him, and conferred on the old enemy of his House, the Bishop of Meath. Kildare died two years later, having signalized his latter days by founding an Anglo-Irish order of chivalry, called "the Brothers of St. George." This order was to consist of 13 persons of the highest rank, within the Pale, 120 mounted archers, and 40 horsemen attended by 40 pages. The officers were to assemble annually in Dublin, on St. George's Day, to elect their Captain from their own number. After having existed twenty years the Brotherhood was suppressed by the jealousy of Henry VIIth, in 1494.

GERALD, VIIIth Earl of Kildare (called in the Irish Annals Geroit More, or "the Great"), succeeded his father in 1477. He had the gratification of ousting Sherwood from the government the following year, and having it transferred to himself. For nearly forty years he continued the central figure among the Anglo-Irish, and as his family were closely connected by marriage with the McCarthys, O'Carrolls of Ely, the O'Conors of Offally, O'Neils and O'Donnells, he exercised immense influence over the affairs of all the Provinces. In his time, moreover, the English interest, under the auspices of an undisturbed dynasty, and a cautious, politic Prince (Henry VII.), began by slow and almost imperceptible degrees to recover the unity and compactness it had lost ever since the Red Earl's death.

CHAPTER VIII.

THE AGE AND RULE OF GERALD, EIGHTH EARL OF KILDARE—THE TIDE BEGINS TO TURN FOR THE ENGLISH INTEREST—THE YORKIST PRETENDERS, SIMNEL AND WARBECK—POYNING'S PARLIAMENT—BATTLES OF KNOCKDOE AND MONABRAHER.

PERHAPS no preface could better introduce to the reader the singular events which marked the times of Gerald, VIIIth Earl of Kildare, than a brief account of one of his principal partizans —Sir James Keating, Prior of the Knights of St. John. The family of Keating, of Norman-Irish origin, were most numerous in the XVth century in Kildare, from which they afterwards spread into Tipperary and Limerick. Sir James Keating, "a mere Irishman," became Prior of Kilmainham about the year 1461, at which time Sir Robert Dowdal, deputy to the Lord Treasurer, complained in Parliament, that being on a pilgrimage to one of the shrines of the Pale, he was assaulted near Cloniff, by the Prior, with a drawn sword, and thereby put in danger of his life. It was accordingly decreed that Keating should pay to the King a hundred pounds fine, and to Sir Robert a hundred marks; but, from certain technical errors in the proceedings, he successfully evaded both these penalties. When in the year 1478 the Lord Grey of Codner was sent over to supersede Kildare, he took the decided step of refusing to surrender to that nobleman the Castle of Dublin, of which he was Constable. Being threatened with an assault, he broke down the bridge and prepared his defence, while his friend, the Earl of Kildare, called a Parliament at Naas, in opposition to Lord Grey's Assembly at Dublin. In 1480, after two years of rival parties and viceroys, Lord Grey was feign to resign his office, and Kildare was regularly appointed Deputy to Richard, Duke of Gloucester, afterwards Richard III. Two years later, Keating was deprived of his rank by Peter d'Aubusson, Grand Master of Rhodes, who appointed Sir Marmaduke Lumley, an English knight, in his stead. Sir Marmaduke landed soon after at Clontarf, where he was taken prisoner by Keating, and kept in close confinement until he had surrendered all the instruments of his election and confirmation. He was then enlarged, and appointed to the commandery of Kilseran, near Castlebellingham, in Louth. In the year 1488, Keating was one of those who took an active part in favor of the pretender Lambert Simnel, and although his pardon had been sternly refused by Henry VII., he retained possession of the Hospital until 1491, when he was ejected by force, "and ended his turbulent life," as we are told, "in the most abject poverty and disgrace." All whom he had appointed to office were removed; an Act of Parliament was passed, prohibiting the reception of any "mere Irishman" into the Order for the future, and enacting that whoever was recognized as Prior by the Grand Master should be of English birth, and one having such a connection with the Order there as might strengthen the force and interest of the Kings of England in Ireland.

The fact most indicative of the spirit of the times is, that a man of Prior Keating's disposition could, for thirty years, have played such a daring part as we have described in the city of Dublin. During the greater part of that period, he held the office of Constable of the Castle and Prior of Kilmainham, in defiance of English Deputies and English Kings; than which no farther evidence may be adduced to show how completely the English interest was extinguished, even within the walls of Dublin, during the reign of the last of the Plantagenet Princes, and the first years of Henry VIIth.

In 1485, Henry, Earl of Richmond, grandson of Queen Catherine and Owen ap Tudor, returned from his fourteen years' exile in France, and, by the victory of Bosworth, took possession of the throne. The Earl of Kildare, undisputed Deputy during the last years of Edward IV., had been continued by Richard, and was not removed by Henry VII. Though a staunch Yorkist, he showed no outward opposition to the change of dynasty, for which he found a graceful apology soon afterwards. Being at Mass, in Christ's Church Cathedral, on the 2d of February, 1486, he received intelligence of Henry's marriage with Elizabeth of York, which he at once communicated to the Archbishop of Dublin, and ordered an additional Mass for the King and Queen. Yet, from the hour of that union of the houses of York and Lancaster, it needed no extraordinary wisdom to foresee that the exemption of the Anglo-Irish nobles from the supremacy of their nominal King must come to an end, and the freedom of the old Irish from any formidable external danger must also close. The union of the Roses, so full of the promise of peace for England, was to form the date of a new era in her relations with Ireland. The tide of English power was at that hour at its lowest ebb; it had left far in the interior the landmarks of its first irresistible rush; it might be said, without exaggeration, that Gaelic children now gathered shells and pebbles where that tide once rolled, charged with all its thunders; it was now about to turn; the first murmuring menace of new encroachments began to be heard under Henry VIIth; as we listen they grow louder on the ear; the waves advance with a steady, deliberate march, unlike the first impetuous onslaught of the Normans; they advance and do not recede, till they recover all the ground they had abandoned. The era which we dated from the Red Earl's death, in 1333, has exhausted its resources of aggression and assimilation; a new era opens with the reign of Henry VII.—or, more distinctly still, with that of his successor, Henry VIII. We must close our account with the old era, before entering upon the new.

The contest between the Earl of Kildare and Lord Grey for the government (1478-1480) marks the lowest ebb of the English power. We have already related how Prior Keating shut the Castle gates on the English deputy, and threatened to fire on his guard if he attempted to force them. Lord Portlester also, the Chancellor, and father-in-law to Kildare, joined that Earl in his Parliament at Naas with the great seal. Lord Grey, in his Dublin Assembly, declared the great seal cancelled, and ordered a new one to be struck, but after a two years' contest he was obliged to succumb to the greater influence of the Geraldines. Kildare was regularly acknowledged Lord Deputy, under the King's privy seal. It was ordained that thereafter there should be but one Parliament convoked during the year; that but one subsidy should be demanded, annually, the sum "not to exceed a thousand marks." Certain Acts of both Parliaments—Grey's and Kildare's—were by compromise confirmed. Of these were two which do not seem to collate very well with each other; one prohibiting the inhabitants of the Pale from holding any intercourse whatsoever with the mere Irish; the other extending to Con O'Neil, Prince of Tyrone, and brother-in-law of Kildare, the rights of a naturalized subject within the Pale. The former was probably Lord Grey's; the latter was Lord Kildare's legislation.

Although Henry VII. had neither disturbed the Earl in his governments, nor his brother, Lord Thomas, as Chancellor, it was not to be expected that he could place entire confidence in the leading Yorkist family among the Anglo-Irish. The restoration of the Ormond estates, in favor of Thomas, VIIth Earl, was both politic and just, and could hardly be objectionable to Kildare, who had just married one of his daughters to Pierce Butler, nephew and heir to Thomas. The want of confidence between the new King and his Deputy was first exhibited in 1486, when the Earl being summoned to attend on his Majesty, called a Parliament at Trim, which voted him an address, representing that in the affairs about to be discussed, his presence was absolutely necessary. Henry affected to accept the excuse as valid, but every arrival of Court news contained some fresh indication of his deep-seated mistrust of the Lord Deputy, who, however, he dared not yet dismiss.

The only surviving Yorkists who could put forward pretensions to the throne were the Earl of Lincoln, Richard's declared heir, and the young Earl of Warwick, son of that Duke of Clarence who was born in Dublin Castle in 1449. Lincoln, with Lord Lovell and others of his friends, was in exile at the court of the dowager Duchess of Burgundy, sister to Edward IV.; and the son of Clarence—a lad of fifteen years of age—was a prisoner in the Tower. In the year 1486, a report spread of the escape of this Prince, and soon afterwards Richard Symon, a Priest of Oxford, landed in Dublin with a youth of the same age, of prepossessing appearance and address, who could relate with the minutest detail the incidents of his previous imprisonment. He was at once recognized as the son of Clarence by the Earl of Kildare and his party, and preparations were made for his coronation by the title of Edward VI. Henry, alarmed, produced from the Tower the genuine Warwick, whom he publicly paraded through London, in order to prove that the pretender in Dublin was an impostor. The Duchess of Burgundy, however, fitted out a fleet, containing 2,000 veteran troops under the command of Martin Swart, who, sailing up the channel, reached Dublin without interruption. With this fleet came the Earl of Lincoln, Lord Lovell, and the other English refugees, who all recognized the *protégé* of Father Symon as the true Prince. Octavius, the Italian Archbishop of Armagh, then residing at Dublin, the Bishop of Clogher, the Butlers, and the Baron of Howth, were incredulous or hostile. The great majority of the Anglo-Irish lords, spiritual and temporal, favored his cause, and he was accordingly crowned in Christ Church Cathedral, with a diadem taken from an image of our Lady, on the 24th of May, 1487; the Deputy, Chancellor, and Treasurer were present; the sermon was preached by Pain, Bishop of Meath. A Parliament was next convoked in his name, in which the Butlers and citizens of Waterford were proscribed as traitors. A herald from the latter city, who had spoken over boldly, was hanged by the Dubliners as a proof of their loyalty. The Council ordered a force to be equipped for the service of his new Majesty in England, and Lord Thomas Fitzgerald resigned the Chancellorship to take the command. This expedition—the last which invaded England from the side of Ireland—sailed from Dublin about the first of June, and landing on the Lancashire shore, at the pile of Foudray, marched to Ulverstone, where they were joined by Sir Thomas Broughton and other devoted Yorkists. From Ulverstone the whole force, about 8,000 strong, marched into Yorkshire, and from Yorkshire southwards into Nottingham. Henry, who had been engaged in making a progress through the southern counties, hastened to meet them, and both armies met at Stoke-upon Trent, near Newark, on the 16th day of June, 1487. The battle was contested with the utmost obstinacy, but the English prevailed. The Earl of Lincoln, the Lords Thomas and Maurice Fitzgerald, Plunket, son of Lord Killeen, Martin Swart, and Sir Thomas Broughton were slain; Lord Lovell escaped, but was never heard of afterwards; the pretended Edward VIth was captured, and spared by Henry only to be made a scullion in his kitchen. Father Symon was cast into prison, where he died, after having confessed that his *protégé* was Lambert Simnel, the son of a joiner at Oxford.

Nothing shows the strength of the Kildare party, and the weakness of the English interest, more than that the deputy and his partizans were still continued in office. They despatched a joint letter to the King, deprecating his anger, which he was prudent enough to conceal. He sent over, the following spring, Sir Richard Edgecombe, Comptroller of his household, accompanied by a guard of 500 men. Sir Richard first touched at

Kinsale, where he received the homage of the Lords Barry and de Courcy; he then sailed to Waterford, where he delivered to the Mayor royal letters confirming the city in its privileges, and authorizing its merchants to seize and distress those of Dublin, unless they made their submission. After leaving Waterford, he landed at Malahide, passing by Dublin, to which he proceeded by land, accompanied with his guard. The Earl of Kildare was absent on a pilgrimage, from which he did not return for several days. His first interviews with Edgecombe were cold and formal, but finally on the 21st of July, after eight or ten days' disputation, the Earl and the other lords of his party did homage to King Henry, in the great chamber of his townhouse in Thomas Court, and thence proceeding to the chapel, took the oath of allegiance on the consecrated host. With this submission Henry was fain to be content; Kildare, Portlester and Plunkett were continued in office. The only one to whom the King's pardon was persistently refused was Sir James Keating, Prior of Kilmainham.

In the subsequent attempts of Perkin Warbeck (1492–1499), in the character of Richard, Duke of York, one of the Princes murdered in the Tower by Richard III., the Anglo-Irish took a less active part. Warbeck landed at Cork from Lisbon, and despatched letters to the Earls of Kildare and Desmond, to which they returned civil but evasive replies. At Cork he received an invitation from the King of France to visit that country, where he remained till the conclusion of peace between France and England. He then retired to Burgundy, where he was cordially received by the Duchess; after an unsuccessful descent on the coast of Kent he took refuge in Scotland, where he married a lady closely allied to the crown. In 1497 he again tried his fortune in the South of Ireland, was joined by Maurice, Xth Earl of Desmond, the Lord Barry and the citizens of Cork. Having laid siege to Waterford he was compelled to retire with loss, and Desmond having made his peace with Henry, Warbeck was forced again to fly into Scotland. In 1497 and '8, he made new attempts to excite insurrection in his favor in the north of England and in Cornwall. He was finally taken and put to death on the 16th of November, 1499.

With him suffered his first and most faithful adherent, John Waters, who had been Mayor of Cork at his first landing from Lisbon in 1492, and who is ignorantly or designedly called by Henry's partizan "O'Water." History has not yet positively established the fraudulency of this pretender. A late eminently cautious writer, with all the evidence which modern research has accumulated, speaks of him as "one of the most myterious persons in English history:" and in mystery we must leave him.

We have somewhat anticipated events, in other quarters, in order to dispose of both the Yorkist pretenders at the same time. The situation of the Earls of Kildare in this and the next reign, though full of grandeur, was also full of peril. Within the Pale they had one part to play, without the Pale another. Within the Pale they held one language, without it another. At Dublin they were English Earls, beyond the Boyne or the Barrow, they were Irish chiefs. They had to tread their cautious, and not always consistent way, through the endless complications which must arise between two nations occupying the same soil, with conflicting allegiance, language, laws, customs, and interests. While we frequently feel indignant at the tone they take towards the "Irish enemy" in their despatches to London—the pretended enemies being at that very time their confidants and allies—on farther reflection we feel disposed .o make some allowance on the score of circumstance and necessity, for a duplicity which, in the end, brought about, as duplicity in public affairs ever does, its own punishment.

In Ulster as well as in Leinster, the ascendency of the Earl of Kildare over the native population was widespread and long sustained. Con O'Neil, Lord of Tyrone, from 1483 to 1491, and Turlogh, Con and Art, his sons and successors (from 1498 to 1548), maintained the most intimate relations with this Earl and his successors. To the former he was brother-in-law, and to the latter, of course, uncle; to all he seems to have been strongly attached. Hugh Roe O'Donnell, Lord of Tyrconnell (1450–1505), and his son and successor, Hugh Dhu O'Donnell, (1505–1530), were also closely connected with Kildare both by friendship and intermarriage. In 1491, O'Neil and O'Donnell mutually submitted their disputes to his decision, at his Castle of Maynooth, and though he found it impossible to reconcile them at the moment, we find both of these houses cordially united with him afterwards. In 1498, he took Dungannon and Omagh, "with great guns," from the insurgents against the authority of his grandson, Turlogh O'Neil, and restored them to Turlogh; the next year he visited O'Donnell, and brought his son Henry to be fostered among the kindly Irish of Tyrconnell. In the year 1500 he also placed the Castle of Kinnaird in the custody of Turlogh O'Neil. In Leinster, the Geraldine interest was still more entirely bound up with that of the native population. His son, Sir Oliver of Killeigh, married an O'Conor of Offally; the daughter of another son, Sir James of Leixlip, (sometimes called the Knight of the Valley), became the wife of the chief of Imayle. The Earl of Ormonde, and Ulick Burke of Clanrickarde, were also sons-in-law of the VIIIth Earl, but in both these cases the old family feuds survived in despite of the new family alliances.

In the fourth year after his accession, Henry VII., proceeding by slow degrees to undermine Kildare's enormous power, summoned the chief Anglo-Irish nobles to his Court at Greenwich, where he reproached them with their support of Simnel, who, to their extreme confusion, he caused to wait on them as butler, at dinner. A year or two afterwards, he removed Lord Portlester from the Treasurship, which he conferred on Sir James Butler, the bastard of Ormond. Plunkett the Chief Justice was promoted to the Chancellorship, and Kildare himself was removed to make way for Fitzsymons, Archbishop of Dublin. This, however, was but a government *ad interim*, for in the year 1494, a wholly English administration was appointed. Sir Edward Poynings, with a picked force of 1,000 men, was appointed Lord Deputy; the Bishop of Bangor was appointed Chancellor, Sir Hugh Conway, an Englishman, was to be Treasurer; and these officials were accompanied by an entirely new bench of judges, all English, whom they were instructed to instal immediately on their arrival. Kildare had resisted the first changes with vigor, and a bloody feud had taken place between his retainers and those of Sir James of Ormond, on the green of

Oxmantown—now Smithfield, in Dublin. On the arrival of Poynings, however, he submitted with the best possible grace, and accompanied that deputy to Drogheda, where he had summoned a Parliament to meet him. From Drogheda, they made an incursion into O'Hanlon's country (Orior in Armagh). On returning from Drogheda, Poynings, on a real or pretended discovery of a secret understanding between O'Hanlon and Kildare, arrested the latter, in Dublin, and at once placed him on board a barque "kept waiting for that purpose," and despatched him to England. On reaching London, he was imprisoned in the Tower, for two years, during which time his party in Ireland were left headless and dispirited.

The government of Sir Edward Poynings, which lasted from 1494 till Kildare's restoration, in August, 1496, is most memorable for the character of its legislation. He assembled a Parliament at Drogheda, in November, 1495, at which were passed the statutes so celebrated in our Parliamentary history as the "10th Henry VII." These statutes were the first enacted in Ireland in which the English language was employed. They confirmed the Provisions of the Statute of Kilkenny, except that prohibiting the use of the Irish language, which had now become so deeply rooted even within the Pale as to make its immediate abolition impracticable. The hospitable law passed in the time of Richard, Duke of York, against the arrest of refugees by virtue of writs issued in England, was repealed. The English acts, against provisors to Rome—ecclesiastics who applied for or accepted preferment directly from Rome—were adopted. It was also enacted that all offices should be held at the King's pleasure; that the Lords of Parliament should appear in their robes as the Lords did in England; that no one should presume to make peace or war except with license of the Governor; that no great guns should be kept in the fortresses except by similar license; and that men of English *birth* only should be appointed constables of the Castles of Dublin, Trim, Leixlip, Athlone, Wicklow, Greencastle, Carlingford, and Carrickfergus. But the most important measure of all was one which provided that thereafter no legislation whatever should be proceeded with in Ireland, unless the bills to be proposed were first submitted to the King and Council in England, and were returned, certified under the great seal of the realm. This is what is usually and specially called in our Parliamentary history "Poyning's Act," and next to the Statute of Kilkenny, it may be considered the most important enactment ever passed, at any Parliament, of the English settlers.

The liberation of the Earl of Kildare from the Tower, and his restoration as Deputy, seems to have been hastened by the movements of Perkin Warbeck, and by the visit of Hugh Roe O'Donnell to James IV., King of Scotland. O'Donnell had arrived at Ayr in the month of August, 1495, a few weeks after Warbeck had reached that court. He was received with great splendor and cordiality by the accomplished Prince, then lately come of age, and filled with projects natural to his youth and temperament. With O'Donnell, according to the Four Masters, he formed a league, by which they bound themselves "mutually to assist each other in all their exigencies."* The knowledge of this alliance, and of Warbeck's favor at the Scottish Court, no doubt decided Henry to avail himself, if possible, of the assistance of his most powerful Irish subject. There was, moreover, another influence at work. The first countess had died soon after her husband's arrest, and he now married, in England, Elizabeth St. John, cousin to the King. Fortified in his allegiance and court favor by this alliance, he returned in triumph to Dublin, where he was welcomed with enthusiasm.

In his subsequent conduct as Lord Deputy, an office which he continued to hold till his death in 1513, this powerful nobleman seems to have steadily upheld the English interest, which was now in harmony with his own. Having driven off Warbeck in his last visit to Ireland (1497), he received extensive estates in England, as a reward for his zeal, and after the victory of Knockdoe (1505), he was installed by proxy at Windsor as Knight of the Garter. This long-continued reign—for such in truth it may be called—left him without a rival in his latter years. He marched to whatever end of the island he would, pulling down and setting up chiefs and castles; his garrisons were to be found from Belfast to Cork, and along the valley of the Shannon, from Athleague to Limerick.

The last event of national importance connected with the name of Geroit More arose out of the battle of KNOCK-DOE, ("battle-axe hill"), fought within seven or eight miles of Galway town, on the 19th of August, 1504. Few of the cardinal facts in our history have been more entirely misapprehended and misrepresented than this. It is usually described as a pitched battle between English and Irish—the turning point in the war of races—and the second foundation of English power. The simple circumstances are these: Ulick III., Lord of Clanrickarde, had married and misused the lady Eustacia Fitzgerald, who seems to have fled to her father, leaving her children behind. This led to an embittered family dispute, which was expanded into a public quarrel by the complaint of William O'Kelly, whose Castles of Garbally, Monivea, and Gallagh, Burke had seized and demolished. In reinstating O Kelly, Kildare found the opportunity which he sought to punish his son-in-law, and both parties prepared for a trial of strength. It so happened that Clanrickarde's alliances at that day were chiefly with O'Brien and the southern Irish, while Kildare's were with those of Ulster. From these causes, what was at first a family quarrel, and at most a local feud, swelled into the dimensions of a national contest between North and South—Leath-Moghda and Leath-Conn. Under these terms, the native Annalists accurately describe the belligerents on either side. With Kildare were the Lords of Tyrconnell, Sligo, Moylurg, Breffni, Oriel and Orior; O'Farrell, Bishop of Ardagh, the Tanist of Tyrowen, the heir of Iveagh, O'Kelly of Hy-Many, McWilliam of Mayo, the Barons of Slane, Delvin, Howth, Dunsany, Gormanstown, Trimblestown, and John Blake, Mayor of Dublin, with the city militia. With Clanrickarde were Turlogh O'Brien, son of the Lord of Thomond, McNamara of Clare, O'Carroll of Ely, O'Brien of Ara, and O'Kennedy of Ormond. The battle was obstinate and bloody. Artillery and musketry, first introduced from Germany some twenty years before (1487), were freely used, and the ploughshare of the peasant has often turned up bullets, large and small, upon the hillside where the battle was fought. The most credible account sets down the number of the slain at 2,000 men—the most exaggerated at

9,000. The victory was with Kildare, who after encamping on the field for twenty-four hours, by the advice of O'Donnell, marched next day to Galway where he found the children of Clanrickarde, whom he restored to their injured mother. Athenry opened its gates to receive the conquerors, and after celebrating their victory in the stronghold of the vanquished, the Ulster Chiefs returned to the North and Kildare to Dublin.

Less known is the battle of Monabraher, which may be considered the offset of Knockdoe. It was fought in 1510—the first year of Henry VIII., who had just confirmed Lord Kildare in the government. The younger O'Donnell joined him in Munster, and after taking the Castles of Kanturk, Pallas, and Castlemaine, they marched to Limerick where the Earl of Desmond, the McCarthys of both branches, and "the Irish of Meath and Leinster," in alliance with Kildare, joined them with their forces. The old allies, Turlogh O'Brien, Clanrickarde, and the McNamaras attacked them at the bridge of Portrush, near Castleconnell, and drove them through Monabraher ("the friar's bog"), with the loss of the Barons Barnwall and Kent, and many of their forces; the survivors were feign to take refuge within the walls of Limerick.

Three years later, Earl Gerald set out to besiege Leap Castle, in O'Moore's country; but it happened that as he was watering his horse in the little river Greese, at Kilkea, he was shot by one of the O'Moores; he was immediately carried to Athy, where shortly afterwards he expired. If we except the first Hugh de Lacy and the Red Earl of Ulster, the Normans in Ireland had not produced a more illustrious man than Gerald, VIIIth Earl of Kildare. He was, says Stainhurst, "of tall stature and goodly presence; very liberal and merciful; of strict piety; mild in his government; passionate, but easily appeased And our justice-loving *Four Masters* have described him as "a knight in valor, and princely and religious in his words and judgments."

CHAPTER IX.

STATE OF IRISH AND ANGLO-IRISH SOCIETY DURING THE FOURTEENTH AND FIFTEENTH CENTURIES.

The main peculiarities of social life among the Irish and Anglo-Irish during the XIVth and XVth centuries are still visible to us. Of the drudges of the earth, as in all other histories, we see or hear little or nothing, but of those orders of men of whom the historic muse takes count, such as bards, rulers, builders, and religious, there is much information to be found scattered up and down our annals, which, if properly put together and clearly interpreted, may afford us a tolerably clear view of the men and their times.

The love of learning, always strong in this race of men and women, revived in full force with their exemption from the immediate pressure of foreign invasion. The person of Bard and Brehon was still held inviolable; to the malediction of the Bard of Usnagh was attributed the sudden death of the Deputy, Sir John Stanley; to their murder of the Brehon McEgan is traced all the misfortunes which befel the sons of Irial O Farrell. To receive the poet graciously, to seat him in the place of honor at the feast, to listen to him with reverence, and to reward him munificently, were considered duties incumbent on the princes of the land. And these duties, to do them justice, they never neglected. One of the O'Neils is specially praised for having given more gifts to poets, and having "a larger collection of poems" than any other man of his age. In the struggle between O'Donnell and O'Conor for the northern corner of Sligo, we find mention made of books accidentally burned in "the house of the manuscripts," in Lough Gill. Among the spoils carried off by O'Donnell, on another occasion, were two famous books—one of which, the Leahar Gear (Short Book), he afterwards paid back, as part of the ransom for the release of his friend, O'Doherty.

The Bards and Ollams, though more dependant on their Princes than we have seen them in their early palmy days, had yet ample hereditary estates in every principality and lordship. If natural posterity failed, the incumbent was free to adopt some capable person as his heir. It was in this way the family of O'Clery, originally of Tyrawley, came to settle in Tyrconnell, towards the end of the XIVth century. At that time O Sgingin, chief Ollam to O'Donnell, offered his daughter in marriage to Cormac O'Clery, a young professor of both laws, in the monastery near Ballyshannon, on condition that the first male child born of the marriage should be brought up to his own profession. This was readily agreed to, and from this auspicious marriage descended the famous family, which produced three of the Four Masters of Donegal.

The virtue of hospitality was, of all others, that which the old Irish of every degree in rank and wealth most cheerfully practised. In many cases it degenerated into extravagance and prodigality. But in general it is presented to us in so winning a garb that our objections on the score of prudence vanish before it. When we read of the freeness of heart of Henry Avery O Neil, who granted all manner of things "that came into his hands," to all manner of men, we pause and doubt whether such a virtue in such excess may not lean towards vice. But when we hear of a powerful lord, like William O'Kelly of Galway, entertaining throughout the Christmas holydays all the poets musicians, and poor persons who choose to flock to him, or of the pious and splendid Margaret O'Carroll, receiving twice a year in Offally all the Bards of Albyn and Erin, we cannot but envy the professors of the gentle art their good fortune in having lived in such times, and shared in such assemblies. As hospitality was the first of social virtues, so inhospita'ity was the worst of vices; the unpopularity of a churl descended to his posterity through successive generations.

The high estimation in which women were held among the tribes is evident from the particularity with which the historians record their obits and marriages. The maiden name of the wife was never wholly lost in that of her husband, and if her family were of equal standing with his before marriage, she generally retained her full share of authority afterwards. The Margaret O'Carroll already mentioned, a descendant and progenitress of illustrious women, rode privately to Trim, as we are told, with some English prisoners, taken by her husband, O'Conor of Offally, and exchanged them for others of equal worth lying in that fortress; and "this she did," it is added, "without the knowledge of" her husband. This lady was famed not only for her exceeding hospitality and her extreme piety, but for other more unexpected works. Her name is remembered in connection with the erection of bridges and the making of highways, as well as the building of churches, and the presentation of missals and mass-books. And the grace she thus acquired long brought blessings upon her posterity, among whom there never were wanting able men and heroic women while they kept their place in the land. An equally celebrated but less amiable woman was Margaret Fitzgerald, daughter of the VIIIth Earl of Kildare, and wife of Pierce, VIIIth Earl of Ormonde. "She was," says the Dublin Annalist, "a lady of such port that all the estates of the realm couched to her, so politique that nothing was thought substantially debated without her advice." Her decision of character is preserved in numerous traditions in and around Kilkenny, where she lies buried. Of her is told the story that when exhorted on her death-bed to make restitution of some ill-got lands, and being told the penalty that awaited her if she died impenitent, she answered, "it was better one old woman should burn for eternity than that the Butlers should be curtailed of their estates."

The fame of virtuous deeds, of generosity, of peace-making, of fidelity, was in that state of society as easily attainable by women as by men. The Unas, Finolas, Sabias, Lasarinas, were as certain of immortality as the Hughs, Cathals, Donalds and Conors, their sons, brothers, or lovers. Perhaps it would be impossible to find any history of those or of later ages in which women are treated upon a more perfect equality with men, where their virtues and talents entitled them to such consideration.

The piety of the age, though it had lost something of the simplicity and fervor of elder times, was still conspicuous and edifying. Within the island, the pilgrimage of Saint Patrick's purgatory, the shrine of our Lady of Trim, the virtues of the holy cross of Raphoe, the miracles wrought by the *Baculum Christi*, and other relics of Christ Church, Dublin, were implicitly believed and piously frequented. The long and dangerous journeys to Rome and Jerusalem were frequently taken, but the favorite foreign vow was to Compostella, in Spain. Chiefs, Ladies, and Bards, are almost annually mentioned as having sailed or returned from the city of St. James; generally these pilgrims left in companies, and returned in the same way. The great Jubilee of 1450, so enthusiastically attended from every corner of Christendom, drew vast multitudes from our island to Rome. By those who returned tidings were first brought to Ireland of the capture of Constantinople by the Turks. On receipt of this intelligence, which sent a thrill through the heart of Europe, Tregury, Archbishop of Dublin, proclaimed a fast of three days, and on each day walked in sackcloth, with his clergy, through the streets of the city, to the Cathedral. By many in that age the event was connected with the mystic utterances of the Apocalypse, and the often-apprehended consummation of all Time.

Although the Irish were then, as they still are, firm believers in supernatural influence working visibly among men, they do not appear to have ever been slaves to the terrible delusion of witchcraft. Among the Anglo-Irish we find the first instance of that mania which appears in our history, and we believe the only one, if we except the Presbyterian witches of Carrickfergus, in the early part of the XVIIIth century. The scene of the ancient delusion was Kilkenny, where Bishop Ledred accused the Lady Alice Kettel, and William her son, of practising black magic, in the year 1327. Sir Roger Outlaw, Prior of Kilmainham, and stepson to Lady Alice, undertook to protect her; but the fearful charge was extended to him also, and he was compelled to enter on his defence. The tribunal appointed to try the charge—one of the main grounds on which the Templars had been suppressed twenty-five years before—was composed of the Dean of St. Patrick's, the Prior of Christ Church, the Abbots of St. Mary's and St. Thomas's, Dublin Mr. Elias Lawless, and Mr. Peter Willeby, lawyers. Outlaw was acquitted, and Ledred forced to fly for safety to England, of which he was a native. It is pleasant to remember that, although Irish credulity sometimes took shapes absurd and grotesque enough, it never was perverted into diabolical channels, or directed to the barbarities of witch-finding.

About the beginning of the XVth century we meet with the first mention of the use of Usquebagh, or *Aqua Vitæ*, in our Annals Under the date of 1405 we read that McRannal, or Reynolds, chief of Muntireolais, died of a surfeit of it, about Christmas. A quaint Elizabethan writer thus descants on the properties of that liquor, as he found them, by personal experience: " For the rawness" (of the air) they (the Irish) have an excellent remedy by their *Aqua Vitæ*, vulgarly called *Usquebagh*, which binds up the belly and drieth up moisture more than our *Aqua Vitæ*, yet inflameth not so much."

And as the opening of the century may be considered notable for the first mention of *Usquebagh*, so its close is memorable for the first employment of firearms. In the year 1489, according to Anglo-Irish Annals, "six hand guns or musquets were sent to the Earl of Kildare out of Germany," which his guard bore while on sentry at Thomas Court—his Dublin residence. But two years earlier (1487) we have positive mention of the employment of guns at the siege of Castlecar, in Leitrim, by Hugh Roe O'Donnell. Great guns were freely used ten years later in the taking of Dungannon and Omagh, and contributed not a little to the victory of Knockdoe—in 1505. About the same time we begin to hear of their employment by sea in rather a curious connection. A certain French Knight, returning from the pilgrimage of Lough Derg, visiting O'Donnell at Donegal heard of the anxiety of his entertainer to take a certain Castle which stood by the sea, in Sligo. This Knight promised to send him, on his return to France, "a vessel carrying great guns," which he accordingly did, and the Castle was in consequence taken. Nevertheless the old Irish, according to their habit, took but slowly to this wonderful invention, though destined to revolutionize the art to which they were naturally predisposed—the art of war.

The dwellings of the chiefs, and of the wealthy among the

proprietors, near the marches, were chiefly situated amid pallisaded islands, or on promontories naturally moated by lakes. The houses, in those circumstances, were mostly of framework, though the Milesian nobles, in less exposed districts, had castles of stone, after the Norman fashion. The Castle "bawn" was usually enclosed by one or more strong walls, the inner sides of which were lined with barns, stables, and the houses of the retainers. Not unfrequently the thatched roofs of these out-buildings taking fire, compelled the castle to surrender, The Castle "green," whether within or without the walls, was the usual scene of rural sports and athletic games, of which, at all periods, our ancestors were so fond. Of the interior economy of the Milesian rath, or dun, we know less than of the Norman tower, where, before the huge kitchen chimney, the heavy-laden spit was turned by hand, while the dining-hall was adorned with the glitter of the dresser, or by tapestry hangings;—the floors of hall and chambers being strewn with rushes and odorous herbs. We have spoken of the zeal of the Milesian Chiefs in accumulating MSS. and in rewarding Bards and Scribes. We are enabled to form some idea of the mental resources of an Anglo-Irish nobleman of the XVth century, from the catalogue of the library remaining in Maynooth Castle, in the reign of Henry VIIIth. Of Latin books, there were the works of several of the schoolmen, the dialogues of St. Gregory, Virgil, Juvenal, and Terence; the Holy Bible; Boethius' Consolations of Philosophy, and Saint Thomas's Summa; of French works, Froissart, Mandeville, two French Bibles, a French Livy and Cæsar, with the most popular romances; in English, there were the Polychronicon, Cambrensis, Lyttleton's Tenures, Sir Thomas More's book on Pilgrimages, and several romances. Moreover there were copies of the Psalter of Cashel, a book of Irish chronicles, lives of St. Beraghan, St. Ficch and St. Finian, with various religious tracts, and romantic tales. This was, perhaps, the most extensive private collection to be found within the pale; we have every reason to infer, that, at least in Irish and Latin works, the Castles of the older race—lovers of learning and entertainers of learned men—were not worse furnished than Maynooth.

CHAPTER X.

STATE OF RELIGION AND LEARNING DURING THE FOURTEENTH AND FIFTEENTH CENTURIES.

ALTHOUGH the English and Irish professed the same religion during these ages, yet in the appointment of Bishops, the administration of ecclesiastical property, and in all their views of the relation of the Church to the State, the two nations differed almost as widely as in their laws, language, and customs. The Plantagenet princes and their Parliaments had always exhibited a jealousy of the See of Rome, and statute upon statute was passed, from the reign of Henry II. to that of Richard II., in order to diminish the power of the Supreme Pontiffs in nominating to English benefices. In the second Richard's reign, so eventful for the English interest in Ireland, it had been enacted that any of the clergy procuring appointments directly from Rome, or exercising powers so conferred, should incur the penalty of a præmunire—that is, the forfeiture of their lands and chattels, beside being liable to imprisonment during the King's pleasure. This statute was held to apply equally to Ireland, being confirmed by some of those petty conventions of "the Pale," which the Dublin Governors of the XIVth century dignified with the name of Parliaments.

The ancient Irish method of promotion to a vacant see, or abbacy, though modelled on the electoral principle which penetrated all Celtic usages, was undoubtedly open to the charge of favoring nepotism, down to the time of Saint Malachy, the restorer of the Irish Church. After that period, the Prelates elect were ever careful to obtain the sanction of the Holy See, before consecration. Such habitual submission to Rome was seldom found, except in cases of disputed election, to interfere with the choice of the clergy, and the custom grew more and more into favor, as the English method of nomination by the crown was attempted to be enforced, not only throughout "the Pale," but, by means of English agents at Rome and Avignon, in the appointment to sees, within the provinces of Armagh, Cashel, and Tuam. The ancient usage of farming the church lands, under the charge of a lay steward, or *Erenach*, elected by the clan, and the division of all the revenues into four parts—for the Bishop, the Vicar and his priests, for the poor, and for repairs of the sacred edifice, was equally opposed to the pretensions of Princes, who looked on their Bishops as Barons, and Church temporalities, like all other fiefs, as held originally of the crown. Even if there had not been those differences of origin, interest, and government which necessarily brought the two populations into collision, these distinct systems of ecclesiastical polity could not well have existed on the same soil without frequently clashing, one with the other.

In our notice of the association promoted among the clergy, at the end of the XIIIth century, by the patriotic McMaelisa, ("follower of Jesus"), and in our own comments on the memorable letter of Prince Donald O'Neil to Pope John XXII., written in the year 1317 or '18, we have seen how wide and deep was the gulf then existing between the English and Irish churchmen. In the year 1324, an attempt to heal this unchristian breach was made by Philip of Slane, the Dominican who presided at the trial of the Knights Templars, who afterwards became Bishop of Cork, and rose into high favor with the Queen-Mother, Isabella. As her Ambassador, or in the name of King Edward III., still a minor, he is reported to have submitted to Pope John certain propositions for the promotion of peace in the Irish Church, some of which were certainly well calculated to promote that end. He suggested that the smaller Bishoprics, yielding under sixty pounds per annum, should be united to more eminent sees, and that Irish Abbots and Priors should admit English lay brothers to their houses, and English Superiors Irish brothers, in like manner. The third proposition, however, savors more of the politician than of the peacemaker; it was to bring under the bann of excommunication, with all its rigorous consequences in that age, those "disturbers of the peace" who invaded the authority of the English King in Ireland. As a consequence of this mission, a Concordat for Ireland seems to have been concluded at Avignon, embracing the two first points, but omitting the third, which was, no doubt, with the English Court, the main object of. Friar Philip's embassy.

During the XIVth century, and down to the election of Martin Vth (A. D. 1417), the Popes sat mainly at Avignon, in France. In the last forty years of that melancholy period, other Prelates sitting at Rome, or elsewhere in Italy, claimed the Apostolic primacy. It was in the midst of these troubles and trials of the Church that the powerful Kings of England, who were also sovereigns of a great part of France, contrived to extort from the embarrassed pontiffs concessions which, however gratifying to royal pride, were abhorrent to the more Catholic spirit of the Irish people. A constant struggle was maintained during the entire period of the captivity of the Popes in France between Roman and English influence in Ireland. There were often two sets of Bishops elected in such border sees as Meath and Louth, which were districts under a divided influence. The Bishops of Limerick, Cork, and Waterford, liable to have their revenues cut off, and their personal liberty endangered by sea, were almost invariably nominees of the English Court; those of the Province of Dublin were necessarily so; but the prelates of Ulster, of Connaught, and of Munster—the southern seaports excepted—were almost invariably native ecclesiastics, elected in the old mode, by the assembled clergy, and receiving letters of confirmation direct from Avignon or Italy.

A few incidents in the history of the Church of Cashel will better illustrate the character of the contest between the native episcopacy and the foreign power. Towards the end of the XIIIth century, Archbishop McCarwill maintained with great courage the independence of his jurisdiction against Henry III. and Edward I. Having inducted certain Bishops into their sees without waiting for the royal letters, he sustained a long litigation in the Anglo-Irish courts, and was much harassed in his goods and person. Seizing from a usurer £400, he successfully resisted the feudal claim of Edward I., as lord paramount, to pay over the money to the royal exchequer Edward having undertaken to erect a prison—or fortress in disguise—in his episcopal city, the bold Prelate publicly excommunicated the Lord Justice who undertook the work, the escheator who supplied the funds, and all those engaged in its construction, nor did he desist from his opposition until the obnoxious building was demolished. Ralph O'Kelly, who filled the same see from 1345 to 1361, exhibited an equally dauntless spirit. An Anglo-Irish Parliament having levied a subsidy on all property, lay and ecclesiastical, within their jurisdiction, to carry on the war of races before described, he not only opposed its collection within the Province of Cashel, but publicly excommunicated Epworth, Clerk of the Council, who had undertaken that task. For this offence an information was exhibited against him, laying the King's damages at a thousand pounds; but he pleaded the liberties of the Church, and successfully traversed the indictment. Richard O'Hedian, Archbishop from 1406 to 1440, was a Prelate of similar spirit to his predecessors. At a Parliament held in Dublin in 1421, it was formally alleged, among other enormities, that he made very much of the Irish and loved none of the English; that he presented no Englishman to a benefice and advised other Prelates to do likewise, and that he made himself King of Munster—alluding, probably, to some revival at this time of the old title of Prince-Bishop, which had anciently belonged to the Prelates of Cashel. O'Hedian retained his authority, however, till his death, after which the see remained twelve years vacant, the temporalities being farmed by the Earl of Ormond.

From this conflict of interests, frequently resulting in disputed possession and intrusive jurisdiction, religion must have suffered much, at least in its discipline and decorum. The English Archbishops of Dublin would not yield in public processions to the Irish Archbishops of Armagh, nor permit the crozier of St. Patrick to be borne publicly through their city; the English Bishop of Waterford was the public accuser of the Irish Archbishop of Cashel, last mentioned, before a lay tribunal—the knights and burgesses of "the Pale." The annual expeditions sent out from Dublin, to harass the nearest native clans, were seldom without a Bishop or Abbot, or Prior of the Temple or Hospital, in their midst. Scandals must have ensued; hatreds must have sprung up; prejudices, fatal to charity and unity, must have been engendered, both on the one side and the other. The spirit of party, carried into the Church, can be cherished in the presence of the Altar and Cross only by doing violence to the teachings of the Cross and the sanctity of the Altar.

While such was the troubled state of the Church, as exemplified in its twofold hierarchy, the religious orders continued to spread, with amazing energy, among both races. The orders of Saint Francis and Saint Dominick, those twin giants of the XIIIth century, already rivalled the mighty brotherhood which Saint Bernard had consecrated, and Saint Malachy had introduced into the Irish Church. It is observable that the Dominicans, at least at first, were most favored by the English and the Anglo-Irish; while the Franciscans were more popular with the native population. Exceptions may be found on both sides; but as a general rule this distinction can be traced in the strongholds of either order, and in the names of their most conspicuous members, down to that dark and trying hour when the tempest of "the Reformation" involved both in a common danger, and demonstrated their equal heroism. As elsewhere in Christendom, the sudden aggrandizement of these mendicant institutes excited jealousy and hostility among certain of the secular clergy and Bishops. This feeling was even stronger in England, during the reigns of Edward III. and Richard II., when, according to the popular superstition, the Devil appeared at various places "in the form of a grey friar." The great champion of the secular clergy, in the controversy which ensued, was Richard, son of Ralph, a native of Dundalk, the Erasmus of his age. Having graduated at Oxford, where the Irish were then classed as one of "the four nations" of students, Fitz-Ralph achieved distinction after distinction, till he rose to the rank of Chancellor of the University, in 1333. Fourteen years afterwards he was consecrated, by provision of

Pope Clement VIth, Archbishop of Armagh, and is by some writers styled "Cardinal of Armagh." Inducted into the chief see of his native Province and country, he soon commenced those sermons and writings against the mendicant orders which rendered him so conspicuous in the Church history of the XIVth century. Summoned to Avignon, in 1350, to be examined on his doctrine, he maintained before the Consistory the following propositions: 1st, that our Lord Jesus Christ, as a man, was very poor, not that He loved poverty for itself; 2d, that our Lord had never begged; 3d, that He never taught men to beg; 4th, that, on the contrary, He taught men not to beg; 5th, that man cannot, with prudence and holiness, confine himself by vow to a life of constant mendicity; 6th, that minor brothers are not obliged by their rule to beg; 7th, that the bull of Alexander IV., which condemns the Book of Masters, does not invalidate any of the aforesaid conclusions; 8th, that by those who, wishing to confess, exclude certain churches, their parish one should be preferred to the oratories of monks; and 9th, that, for auricular confession, the diocesan bishop should be chosen in preference to friars.

In a "defence of Parish Priests," and many other tracts, in several sermons, preached at London, Litchfield, Drogheda, Dundalk, and Armagh, he maintained the thesis until the year 1357, when the Superior of the Franciscans at Armagh, seconded by the influence of his own and the Dominican order, caused him to be summoned a second time before the Pope. Fitz-Ralph promptly obeyed the summons, but before the cause could be finally decided he died at Avignon in 1361. His body was removed from thence to Dundalk in 1370 by Stephen de Valle, Bishop of Meath. Miracles were said to have been wrought at his tomb; a process of inquiry into their validity was instituted by order of Boniface IX., but abandoned without any result being arrived at. The bitter controversy between the mendicant and other orders was revived towards the end of the century by Henry, a Cistertian monk of Baltinglass, who maintained opinions still more extreme than those of Fitz-Ralph; but he was compelled publicly and solemnly to retract them before Commissioners appointed for that purpose in the year 1882.

The range of mental culture in Europe during the XIVth century included only the scholastic philosophy and theology with the physics, taught in the scnools of the Spanish Arabs. The XVth century saw the revival of Greek literature in Italy, and the general restoration of classical learning. The former century is especially barren of original *belles lettres* writings; but the next succeeding ages produced Italian poetry, French chronicles, Spanish ballads, and all that wonderful efflorescence of popular literature, which, in our far advanced cultivation, we still so much envy and admire. In the last days of Scholasticism, Irish intelligence asserted its ancient equality with the best minds of Europe; but in the new era of national literature, unless there are buried treasures yet to be dug out of their Gaelic tombs, the country fell altogether behind England, and even Scotland, not to speak of Italy or France. Archbishop Fitz-Ralph, John Scotus of Down, William of Drogheda, Professor of both laws at Oxford, are respectable representatives among the last and greatest group of the Schoolmen. Another illustrious name remains to be added to the roll of Irish Scholastics, that of Maurice O'Fihely, Archbishop of Tuam. He was a thorough Scotist in philosophy, which he taught at Padua, in discourses long afterwards printed at Venice. His Commentaries on *Scotus*, his Dictionary of the Sacred Scriptures, and other numerous writings go far to justify the compliments of his cotemporaries, though the fond appellation of the "flower of the earth" given him by some of of them sounds extravagant and absurd. Soon after arriving from Rome to take possession of his see he died at Tuam in 1513, in the fiftieth year of his age—an early age to have won so colossal a reputation.

Beyond some meagre annals, compiled in monastic houses and a few rhymed panegyrics, the muses of history and of poetry seem to have abandoned the island to the theologians, jurists, and men of science. The Bardic order was still one of the recognized estates, and found patrons worthy of their harps in the lady Margaret O'Carroll, of Offally, William O'Kelley, of Galway, and Henry Avery O'Neil. Full collections of the original Irish poetry of the Middle Ages are yet to be made public, but it is scarcely possible that if any composition of eminent merit existed, we should not have had editions and translations of it before now.

BOOK VII.

UNION OF THE CROWNS OF ENGLAND AND IRELAND.

CHAPTER I.

IRISH POLICY OF HENRY THE EIGHTH DURING THE LIFETIME OF CARDINAL WOLSEY.

Henry the Eighth of England succeeded his father on the throne, early in the year 1509. He was in the eighteenth year of his age, when he thus found himself master of a well-filled treasury and an united kingdom. Fortune, as if to complete his felicity, had furnished him from the outset of his reign with a minister of unrivalled talent for public business. This was Thomas Wolsey, successively royal Chaplain, Almoner, Archbishop of York, Papal Legate, Lord Chancellor, and Lord Cardinal. From the fifth to the twentieth year of King Henry, he was, in effect, sovereign in the state, and it is wonderful to find how much time he contrived to borrow from the momentous foreign affairs of that eventful age for the obscurer intrigues of Irish politics.

Wolsey kept before his mind, more prominently than any previous English statesman, the design of making his royal master as absolute in Ireland as any King in Christendom. He determined to abolish every pretence to sovereignty but that of the King of England, and to this end he resolved to circumscribe the power of the Anglo-Irish Barons, and to win over by "dulce ways" and "politic drifts," as he expressed it, the

Milesian-Irish Chiefs. This policy, continued by all the Tudor sovereigns till the latter years of Elizabeth, so far as it distinguished between the Barons and Chiefs, always favored the latter. The Kildares and Desmonds were hunted to the death, in the same age, and by the same authority, which carefully fostered every symptom of adhesion or attachment on the part of the O'Neils and O'Briens. Neither were these last loved or trusted for their own sakes, but the natural enemy fares better in all histories than the unnatural rebel.

We must enumerate some of the more remarkable instances of Wolsey's twofold policy of concession and intimidation. In the third and fourth years of Henry, Hugh O'Donnell, lord of Tyrconnell, passing through England, on a pilgrimage to Rome, was entertained with great honor at Windsor and Greenwich for four months each time. He returned to Ulster deeply impressed with the magnificence of the young monarch and the resources of his kingdom. During the remainder of his life he cherished a strong predilection for England; he dissuaded James IV. of Scotland from leading a liberating expedition to Ireland in 1513—previous to the ill-fated campaign which ended on Flodden field, and he steadily resisted the influx of the Islesmen into Down and Antrim. In 1521 we find him described by the Lord Lieutenant, Surrey, as being of all the Irish chiefs the best disposed "to fall into English order." He maintained a direct correspondence with Henry until his death, 1537, when the policy he had so materially assisted had progressed beyond the possibility of defeat. Simultaneously with O'Donnell's adhesion, the same views found favor with the powerful chief of Tyrone. The O'Neils were now divided into two great septs, those of Tyrone, whose seat was at Dungannon, and those of Clandeboy, whose strongholds studded the eastern shores of Lough Neagh. In the year 1480, Con O'Neil, lord of Tyrone, married his cousin-germain, Lady Alice Fitzgerald, daughter of the Earl of Kildare. This alliance tended to establish an intimacy between Maynooth and Dungannon, which subserved many of the ends of Wolsey's policy. Turlogh, Art, and Con, sons of Lady Alice, and successively chiefs of Tyrone, adhered to the fortunes of the Kildare family, who were, however unwillingly, controlled by the superior power of Henry. The Clandeboy O'Neils, on the contrary, regarded this alliance as nothing short of apostacy, and pursued the exactly opposite course, repudiating English and cultivating Scottish alliances. Open ruptures and frequent collisions took place between the estranged and exasperated kinsmen; in the sequel we will find how the last surviving son of Lady Alice became in his old age the first Earl of Tyrone, while the House of Clandeboy took up the title of "the O'Neil." The example of the elder branch of this ancient royal race, and of the hardly less illustrious family of Tyrconnell, exercised a potent influence on the other chieftains of Ulster.

An elaborate report on "the State of Ireland," with "a plan for its Reformation"—submitted to Henry in the year 1515—gives us a tolerably clear view of the political and military condition of the several provinces. The only portions of the country in any sense subject to English law, were half the counties of Louth, Meath, Dublin, Kildare, and Wexford. The residents within these districts paid "black rent" to the nearest native chiefs. Sheriffs were not permitted to execute writs, beyond the bounds thus described, and even within thirty miles of Dublin, March-law and Brehon-law were in full force. Ten native magnates are enumerated in Leinster as "chief captains" of their "nations"—not one of whom regarded the English King as his Sovereign. Twenty chiefs in Munster, fifteen in Connaught, and three in Westmeath, maintained their ancient state, administered their own laws, and recognized no superiority, except in one another, as policy or custom compelled them. Thirty chief English captains, of whom eighteen resided in Munster, seven in Connaught, and the remainder in Meath, Down, and Antrim, are set down as "rebels" and followers of "the Irish order." Of these, the principal in the midland counties were the Dillons and Tyrrells, in the West the Burkes and Berminghams, in the South the Powers, Barrys, Roches—the Earl of Desmond and his relatives. The enormous growth of these Munster Geraldines, and their not less insatiable greed, produced many strange complications in the politics of the South. Not content with the moiety of Kerry, Cork and Waterford, they had planted their landless cadets along the Suir and the Shannon, in Ormond and Thomond. They narrowed the dominions of the O'Briens on the one hand and the McCarthys on the other. Concluding peace or war with their neighbors, as suited their own convenience, they sometimes condescended to accept further feudal privileges from the Kings of England. To Maurice, Xth Earl, Henry VIIth had granted "all the customs, cockets, poundage, prize wines of Limerick, Cork, Kinsale, Baltimore and Youghall, with other privileges and advantages." Yet Earl James, in the next reign, did not hesitate to treat with Francis of France and the Emperor of Germany, as an independent Prince, long before the pretence of resisting the Reformation could be alleged in his justification. What we have here to observe is, that this predominance of the Munster Geraldines drove first one and then another branch of the McCarthys, and O'Briens, into the meshes of Wolsey's policy. Cormac Oge, lord of Muskerry, and his cousin, the lord of Carbery, defeated the XIth Earl (James), at Moore Abbey, in 1521, with a loss of 1,500 foot and 5 or 600 horsemen. To strengthen himself against the powerful adversary so deeply wounded, Cormac sought the protection of the lord lieutenant, the Earl of Surrey, and of Pierce Roe, the VIIIth Earl of Ormond, who had common wrongs to avenge. In this way McCarthy became identified with the English interest, which he steadily adhered to till his death ——— in 1536. Driven by the same necessity to adopt the same expedient, Murrough O'Brien, lord of Thomond, a few years later visited Henry at London, where he resigned his principality, received back his lands, under a royal patent conveying them to him as "Earl of Thomond, and Baron of Inchiquin." Henry was but too happy to have raised up such a counterpoise to the power of Desmond, at his own door, while O'Brien was equally anxious to secure foreign aid against such intolerable encroachments. The policy worked effectually; it brought the succeeding Earl of Desmond to London, an humble suitor for the King's mercy, and favor, which were after some demur granted.

The event, however, which most directly tended to the establishment of an English royalty in Ireland, was the depression of the family of Kildare in the beginning of this reign, and its all but extinction a few years later. Gerald the IXth Earl of that title, succeeded his father in the office of lord deputy in the first years of Henry. He had been a ward at the court of the preceding King, and by both his first and second marriages was closely connected with the royal family. Yet he stood in the way of the settled plans of Wolsey, before whom the highest heads in the realm trembled. His father, as if to secure him against the hereditary enmity of the Butlers, had married his daughter Margaret to Pierce Roe, Earl of Ossory, afterwards VIIIth Earl of Ormond—the restorer of that house. This lady, however, entered heartily into the antipathies of her husband's family, and being of masculine spirit, with an uncommon genius for public affairs, helped more than any Butler had ever done to humble the overshadowing house of which she was born. The weight of Wolsey's influence was constantly exercised in favor of Ormond, who had the skill to recommend himself quite as effectually to Secretary Cromwell, after the Cardinal's disgrace and death. But the struggles of the house of Kildare were bold and desperate.

CHAPTER II.

THE INSURRECTION OF SILKEN THOMAS—THE GERALDINE LEAGUE—ADMINISTRATION OF LORD LEONARD GRAY.

THE IXth and last *Catholic* Earl of Kildare, in the ninth year of Henry VIIIth, had been summoned to London to answer two charges preferred against him by his political enemies: "1st, that he had enriched himself and his followers out of the crown lands and revenues. 2d, that he had formed alliances and corresponded with divers Irish enemies of the State." Pending these charges the Earl of Surrey, the joint-victor with his father at Flodden field, was despatched to Dublin in his stead, with the title of Lord Lieutenant.

Kildare, by the advice of Wolsey, was retained in a sort of honorable attendance on the person of the King for nearly four years. During this interval he accompanied Henry to "the field of the cloth of Gold," so celebrated in French and English chronicles. On his return to Dublin, in 1523, he found his enemy the Earl of Ormond in his old office, but had the pleasure of supplanting him one year afterwards. In 1525, on the discovery of Desmond's correspondence with Francis of France, he was ordered to march into Munster and arrest that nobleman. But, though he obeyed the royal order, Desmond successfully evaded him, not, as was alleged, without his friendly connivance. The next year this evasion was made the ground of a fresh impeachment by the implacable Earl of Ormond; he was again summoned to London, and committed to the Tower. In 1530 he was liberated, and sent over, with Sir William Skeffington, whose authority to some extent he shared. The English Knight had the title of Deputy, but Kildare was, in effect, Captain General, as the Red Earl had formerly been. Skeffington was instructed to obey him in the field, while it was expected that the Earl, in return, would sustain his colleague in the Council. A year had not passed before they were declared enemies, and Skeffington was recalled to England, where he added another to the number of Kildare's enemies. After a short term of undisputed power, the latter found himself, in 1533, for the third time, an inmate of the Tower. It is clear that the impetuous Earl, after his second escape, had not conducted himself as prudently as one so well forewarned ought to have done. He played more openly than ever the twofold part of Irish Chief among the Irish, and English Baron within the Pale. His daughters were married to the native lords of Offally and Ely, and he frequently took part as arbitrator in the affairs of those clans. The anti-Geraldine faction were not slow to torture these facts to suit themselves. They had been strengthened at Dublin by three English officials, Archbishop Allan, his relative John Allan, afterwards Master of the Rolls, and Robert Cowley, the Chief Solicitor,

Lord Ormond's confidential agent. The reiterated representations of these personages induced the suspicious and irascible King to order the Earl's attendance at London, authorizing him at the same time to appoint a substitute, for whose conduct he would be answerable. Kildare nominated his son, Lord Thomas, though not yet of man's age; after giving him many sage advices, he sailed for England no more to return.

The English interest at that moment had apparently reached the lowest point. The O'Briens had bridged the Shannon, and enforced their ancient claims over Limerick. So defenceless, at certain periods, was Dublin itself that Edmond Oge O'Byrne surprised the Castle by night, liberated the prisoners, and carried off the stores. This daring achievement, unprecedented even in the records of the fearless mountaineers of Wicklow, was thrown in to aggravate the alleged offences of Kildare. He was accused moreover of having employed the King's great guns and other munitions of war to strengthen his own Castles of Maynooth and Ley—a charge more direct and explicit than had been alleged against him at any former period.

While the Earl lay in London Tower, an expedient very common afterwards in our history—the forging of letters and despatches—was resorted to by his enemies in Dublin, to drive the young Lord Thomas into some rash act which might prove fatal to his father and himself. Accordingly the packets brought from Chester, in the spring of 1534, repeated reports, one confirming the other, of the execution of the Earl in the Tower. Nor was there anything very improbable in such an occurrence. The cruel character of Henry had, in these same spring months, been fully developed in the execution of the reputed prophetess, Elizabeth Barton, and all her abettors. The most eminent layman in England, Sir Thomas More, and the most illustrious ecclesiastic, Bishop Fisher, had at the same time been found guilty of misprison of treason for having known of the pretended prophecies of Elizabeth without communicating their knowledge to the King. That an Anglo-Irish Earl, even of the first rank, could hope to fare better at the hands of the tyrant, than his aged tutor and his trusted Chancellor, was not to be expected. When, therefore, Lord Thomas Fitzgerald flung down the sword of State on the Council table, in the hall of St. Mary's Abbey, on the 11th day of June, 1534, and formally renounced his allegiance to King Henry as the murderer of his father, although he betrayed an impetuous and impolitic temper, there was much in the events of the times to justify his belief in the rumors of his father's execution.

This renunciation of allegiance was a declaration of open war. The chapter thus opened in the memoirs of the Leinster Geraldines closed at Tyburn on the 3d of February, 1537. Within these three years, the policy of annexation was hastened by several events—but by none more than this unconcerted, unprepared, reckless revolt. The advice of the imprisoned Earl to his son had been "to play the gentlest part," but youth and rash counsels overcame the suggestions of age and experience. One great excess stained the cause of "Silken Thomas," while it was but six weeks old. Towards the end of July, Archbishop Allan, his father's deadly enemy, left his retreat in the Castle, and put to sea by night, hoping to escape into England. The vessel, whether by design or accident, ran ashore at Clontarf, and the neighborhood being overrun by the insurgents, the Archbishop concealed himself at Artane. Here he was discovered, dragged from his bed, and murdered, if not in the actual presence, under the same roof with Lord Thomas. King Henry's Bishops hurled against the assassins the greater excommunication, with all its penalties; a terrific malediction, which was, perhaps, more than counterbalanced by the Papal Bull issued against Henry and Anne Boleyn on the last day of August—the knowledge of which must have reached Ireland before the end of the year. This Bull cited Henry to appear within ninety days in person, or by attorney, at Rome, to answer for his offences against the Apostolic See; failing which, he was declared excommunicated, his subjects were absolved from their allegiance, and commanded to take up arms against their former sovereign. The ninety days expired with the month of November, 1534.

Lord Thomas, as he acted without consultation with others, so he was followed, but by few persons of influence. His

brothers-in-law, the chiefs of Ely and Offally, O'Moore of
Leix, two of his five uncles, his relatives the Delahides, mustered their adherents, and rallied to his standard. He held
the castles of Carlow, Maynooth, Athy, and other strongholds
in Kildare. He besieged Dublin, and came to a composition
with the citizens, by which they agreed to allow him free
ingress to assail the Castle, into which his enemies had withdrawn. He despatched agents to the Emperor, Charles Vth,
and the Pope, but before those agents could well have returned
—March, 1535—Maynooth had been assaulted and taken by
Sir William Skeffington—and the bands collected by the young
lord had melted away. Lord Leonard Gray, his maternal
uncle, assumed the command for the King of England, instead
of Skeffington, disabled by sickness, and the abortive insurrection was extinguished in one campaign. Towards the end
of August, 1535, the unfortunate Lord Thomas surrendered on
the guarantee of Lord Leonard and Lord Butler; in the following year his five uncles—three of whom had never joined
in the rising—were treacherously seized at a banquet given to
them by Gray, and were all, with their nephew, executed at Tyburn, on the 3d of February, 1537. The imprisoned Earl having
died in the Tower on the 12th of December, 1534, the sole survivor of this historic house was now a child of twelve years of
age, whose life was sought with an avidity equal to Herod's, but
who was protected with a fidelity which defeated every attempt
to capture him. Alternately the guest of his aunts married to
the chiefs of Offally and Donegal, the sympathy everywhere
felt for him led to a confederacy between the Northern and
Southern Chiefs, which had long been wanting. A loose league
was formed, including the O'Neils of both branches, O'Donnell,
O'Brien, the Earl of Desmond, and the chiefs of Moylurg and
Breffni. The lad, the object of so much natural and chivalrous
affection, was harbored for a time in Munster, thence transported through Connaught into Donegal, and finally, after four
years, in which he engaged more of the minds of statesmen
than any other individual under the rank of royalty, was
safely landed in France. We shall meet him again in another
reign, under more fortunate auspices.

Lord Leonard Gray continued in office as Deputy for nearly five years (1535-40). This interval was marked by several successes against detached clans and the parties to the Geraldine league, whom he was careful to attack only in succession. In his second campaign, O'Brien's bridge was carried and demolished, one O'Brien was set up against another, and one O'Conor against another; the next year the Castle of Dungannon was taken from O'Neil, and Dundrum from Magennis. In 1539, he defeated O'Neil and O'Donnell at Belahoe, on the borders of Farney, in Monaghan, with a loss of 400 men and the spoils they had taken from the English of Navan and Ardee. The Mayors of Dublin and Drogheda were knighted on the field for the valor they had shown at the head of their train-bands. The same year, he made a successful incursion into the territory of the Earl of Desmond, receiving the homage of many of the inferior lords, and exonerating them from the exactions of those haughty Palatines. Recalled to England in 1540, he, too, in turn, fell a victim to the sanguinary spirit of King Henry, and perished on the scaffold.

CHAPTER III.

SIR ANTHONY ST. LEGER, LORD DEPUTY—NEGOTIATIONS OF THE IRISH CHIEFS WITH JAMES THE FIFTH OF SCOTLAND—FIRST ATTEMPTS TO INTRODUCE THE PROTESTANT REFORMATION—OPPOSITION OF THE CLERGY—PARLIAMENT OF 1541—THE PROCTORS OF THE CLERGY EXCLUDED—STATE OF THE COUNTRY—THE CROWNS UNITED—HENRY THE EIGHTH PROCLAIMED AT LONDON AND DUBLIN.

Upon the disgrace of Lord Leonard Gray in 1540, Sir Anthony St. Leger was appointed Deputy. He had previously been employed as chief of the commission issued in 1537, to survey land subject to the King, to inquire into, confirm, or cancel titles, and abolish abuses which might have crept in among the Englishry, whether upon the marches or within the Pale. In this employment he had at his disposal a guard of

840 men, while the Deputy and Council were ordered to obey his mandates as if given by the King in person. The commissioners were further empowered to reform the Courts of Law; to enter as King's Counsel into both Houses of Parliament, there to urge the adoption of measures, upholding English laws and customs, establishing the King's supremacy, in spirituals as in temporals, to provide for the defence of the marches, and the better collection of the revenues. In the three years which he spent at the head of this commission, St. Leger, an eminently able and politic person, made himself intimately acquainted with Irish affairs; as a natural consequence of which knowledge he was entrusted, upon the first vacancy, with their supreme directions. In this situation he had to contend, not only with the complications long existing in the system itself, but with the formidable disturbing influence, exercised by the Court of Scotland, chiefly upon and by means of, the Ulster Princes.

Up to this period, the old political intimacy of Scotland and Ireland had known no diminution. The Scots in Antrim could reckon, soon after Henry's accession to the throne, 2,000 fighting men. In 1513, in order to co-operate with the warlike movement of O'Donnell, the Scottish fleet, under the Earl of Arran, in his famous flagship, "the great Michael," captured Carrickfergus, putting its Anglo-Irish garrison to the sword. In the same Scottish reign (that of James IV.), one of the O'Donnells had a munificent grant of lands in Kirkcudbright, as other adventurers from Ulster had from the same monarch, in Galloway and Kincardine. In 1523, while hostilities raged between Scotland and England, the Irish Chiefs entered into treaty with Francis the First of France, who bound himself to land in Ireland 15,000 men, to expel the English from "the Pale," and to carry his arms across the channel in the quarrel of Richard de la Pole, father of the famous Cardinal, and at this time a formidable pretender to the English throne. The imbecile conduct of the Scottish Regent, the Duke of Albany, destroyed this enterprize, which, however, was but the forerunner, if it was not the model, of several similar combinations. When the Earl of Bothwell took refuge at the

English Court, in 1531, he suggested to Henry VIII., among other motives for renewing the war with James Vth, that the latter was in league "with the Emperor, the Danish King, and O'Donnell." The following year, a Scottish force of 4,000 men, under John, son of Alexander McDonald, Lord of the Isles, served, by permission of their King, under the banner of the Chieftain of Tyrconnell. An uninterrupted correspondence between the Ulster Chiefs, and the Scottish Court may be traced through this reign, forming a curious chapter of Irish diplomacy. In 1535, we have a letter from O'Neil to James Vth, from which it appears that O'Neil's Secretary was then residing at the Scottish Court; and as the crisis of the contest for the Crown drew near, we find the messages and overtures from Ulster multiplying in number and earnestness. In that critical period, James Vth was between twenty and thirty years old, and his powerful minister, Cardinal Beaton, was acting by him the part that Wolsey had played by Henry at a like age. The Cardinal, favoring the French and Irish alliances, had drawn a line of Scottish policy, in relation to both those countries, precisely parallel to Wolsey's. During the Geraldine insurrection, Henry was obliged to remonstrate with James on favors shown to his rebels of Ireland. This charge James' ministers, in their correspondence of the year 1535, strenuously denied, while admitting that some insignificant Islesmen, over whom he could exercise no control, might have gone privily thither. In the spring of 1540, Bryan Layton, one of the English agents at the Scottish Court, communicated to Secretary Cromwell that James had fitted out a fleet of 15 ships, manned by 2,000 men, and armed with all the ordnance that he could muster; that his destination was Ireland, the Crown of which had been offered to him, the previous Lent, by "eight gentlemen," who brought him written tenders of submission "from all the great men of Ireland," with their seals attached; and, furthermore, that the King had declared to Lord Maxwell his determination to win such a prize as "never King of Scotland had before," or to loose his life in the attempt. It is remarkable that in this same spring of 1540-- while such was understood to be the destination of the Scottish fleet—a congress of the Chiefs of all Ireland was appointed to be held at the Abbey of Fore, in Westmeath. To prevent this meeting taking place, the whole force of the Pale, with the judges, clergy, townsmen and husbandmen, marched out under the direction of the Lords of the Council (St. Leger not having yet arrived to replace Lord Gray), but finding no such assembly as they had been led to expect, they made a predatory incursion into Roscommon, and dispersed some armed bands belonging to O'Conor. The commander in this expedition was the Marshal Sir William Brereton, for the moment one of the Lords Justices. He was followed to the field by the last Prior of Kilmainham, Sir John Rawson, the Master of the Rolls, the Archbishop of Dublin, the Bishop of Meath, Mr. Justice Luttrell, and the Barons of the Exchequer—a strange medley of civil and military dignitaries.

The prevention or postponement of the Congress at Fore must have exercised a decided influence on the expedition of James Vth. His great armada having put to sea, after coasting among the out-Islands, and putting into a northern English port from stress of weather, returned home without achievement of any kind. Diplomatic intercourse was shortly renewed between him and Henry, but, in the following year, to the extreme displeasure of his royal kinsman, he assumed the much-prized title of "Defender of the Faith." Another rupture took place, when the Irish card was played over again with the customary effect. In a letter of July, 1541, introducing to the Irish Chiefs the Jesuit Fathers, Salmeron, Broet, and Capata, who passed through Scotland on their way to Ireland, James styles himself "Lord of Ireland"—another insult and defiance to Henry, whose newly-acquired kingly style was then but a few weeks old. By way of retaliation Henry ordered the Archbishop of York to search the registers of that see for evidence of *his* claim to the Crown of Scotland, and industriously cultivated the disaffected party amongst the Scottish nobility. At length these bickerings broke out into open war, and the short, but fatal campaign of 1542, removed another rival for the English King. The double defeat of Fala and of Solway Moss, the treason of his nobles, and the failure of his hopes, broke the heart of the high-spirited James Vth. He died in December, 1542, in the 33d year of his age, a few hours after learning the birth of his daughter, so celebrated as Mary, Queen of Scots. In his last moments he pronounced the doom of the Stuart dynasty—"it came with a lass," he exclaimed, "and it will go with a lass." And thus it happened that the image of Ireland which unfolds the first scene of the War of the Roses; which is inseparable from the story of the two Bruces; and which occupies so much of the first and last years of the Tudor dynasty, stands mournfully by the death-bed of the last Stuart King who reigned in Scotland— the only Prince of his race that had ever written under his name the title of "*Dominus Hibernice.*"

The premature death of James was hardly more regretted by his immediate subjects than by his Irish allies. All external events now conspired to show the hopelessness of resistance to the power of King Henry. From Scotland, destined to half a century of anarchy, no help could be expected. Wales, another ancient ally of the Irish, had been incorporated with England, in 1536, and was fast becoming reconciled to the rule of a Prince, sprung from a Welsh ancestry. Francis of France and Charles Vth, rivals for the leadership of the Continent, were too busy with their own projects to enter into any Irish alliance. The Geraldines had suffered terrible defeats; the family of Kildare was without an adult representative; the O'Neils and O'Donnells had lost ground at Bellahoe, and were dismayed by the unlooked-for death of the King of Scotland. The arguments, therefore, by which many of the chiefs might have justified themselves to their clans in 1541, '2 and '3, for submitting to the inevitable laws of necessity in rendering homage to Henry VIIIth, were neither few nor weak. Abroad there was no hope of an alliance sufficient to counterbalance the immense resources of England; at home life-wasting private wars, the conflict of laws, of languages, and of titles to property, had become unbearable. That fatal family pride, which would not permit an O'Brien to obey an O'Neil, nor an O'Conor to follow either, rendered the establishment of a native monarchy—even if there had been no other obstacle—

wholly impracticable. Among the clergy alone did the growing supremacy of Henry meet with any effective opposition.

At its first presentation in Ireland, and during the whole of Henry's lifetime, the "Reformation" wore the guise of schism, as distinguished from heresy. To deny the supremacy of the Pope and admit the supremacy of the King were almost its sole tests of doctrine. All the ancient teaching in relation to the Seven Sacraments, the Holy Sacrifice of the Mass, the Real Presence, Purgatory, and Prayers for the Dead, were scrupulously retained. Subsequently, the necessity of auricular confession, the invocation of Saints, and the celibacy of the clergy came to be questioned, but they were not dogmatically assailed during this reign. The common people, where English was understood, were slow in taking alarm at these masked innovations; in the Irish-speaking districts—three-fourths of the whole country—they were only heard of as rumors from afar, but the clergy, secular and regular, were not long left in doubt as to where such steps must necessarily lead.

From 1534, the year of his divorce, until 1541, the year of his election, Henry attempted, by fits and starts, to assert his supremacy in Ireland. He appointed George Browne, a strenuous advocate of the divorce, some time Provincial of the order of St. Augustine in England, Archbishop of Dublin, vacant by the murder of Archbishop Allan. On the 12th of March, 1535, Browne was consecrated by Cranmer, whose opinions, as well as those of Secretary Cromwell, he echoed through life. He may be considered the first agent employed to introduce the Reformation into Ireland, and his zeal in that work seems to have been unwearied. He was destined, however, to find many opponents, and but few converts. Not only the Primate of Armagh, George Cromer, and almost all the episcopal order, resolutely resisted his measures, but the clergy and laity of Dublin refused to accept his new forms of prayer, or to listen to his strange teaching. He inveighs in his correspondence with Cromwell against Bassenet, Dean of St. Patrick's, Castele, Prior of Christ's Church, and generally against all the clergy. Of the twenty-eight secular priests in Dublin but three could be induced to act with him; the regular orders he found equally intractable—more especially the Observantins, whose name he endeavored to change to Conventuals. "The spirituality," as he calls them, refused to take the oaths of abjuration and supremacy; refused to strike the name of the Bishop of Rome from their primers and mass-books, and seduced the rest into like contumacy. Finding persuasion of little avail, he sometimes resorted to harsher measures.

Dr. Sall, a grey friar of Waterford, was brought to Dublin and imprisoned for preaching the new doctrines in the Spring of 1538; Thaddeus Byrne, another friar, was put in the pillory, and was reported to have committed suicide in the Castle, on the 14th of July of the same year; Sir Humfrey, parson of Saint Owens, and the suffragan Bishop of Meath, were "clapped in ward," for publicly praying for the Pope's weal and the King's conversion; another Bishop and friar were arrested and carried to Trim, for similar offences, but were liberated without trial, by Lord Deputy Gray; a friar of Waterford, in 1539, by order of the St. Leger Commission, was executed in the habit of his order, on a charge of "felony," and so left hanging "as a mirror for all his brethren." Yet, with all this severity, and all the temptations held out by the wealth of confiscated monasteries, none would abide the preaching of the new religion, except the "Lord Butler, the Master of the Rolls (Allan), Mr. Treasurer (Brabazon), and one or two more of small reputation."

The first test to which the firmness of the clergy had been put was in the Parliament convoked at Dublin by Lord Deputy Gray in May, 1537. Anciently in such assemblies two proctors of each diocese, within the Pale, had been accustomed to sit and vote in the Upper House as representing their order, but the proposed tests of supremacy and abjuration were so boldly resisted by the proctors and spiritual peers on this occasion that the Lord Deputy was compelled to prorogue the Parliament without attaining its assent to those measures. During the recess a question was raised by the Crown lawyers as to the competency of the proctors to vote, while admitting their right to be present as councillors and assistants; this question, on an appeal to England, was declared in the negative, whereupon that learned body were excluded from all share in the future Irish legislation of this reign. Hence, whoever else are answerable for the election of 1541 the proctors of the clergy are not.

Having thus reduced the clerical opposition in the Upper House, the work of monastic spoliation, covertly commenced two years before under the pretence of reforming abuses, was more confidently resumed. In 1536, an act had been passed vesting the property of all religious houses in the Crown; at which time the value of their moveables was estimated at £100,000 and their yearly value at £32,000. In 1537, eight abbeys were suppressed during the King's pleasure; in 1538, a commission issued for the suppression of monasteries; and in 1539, twenty-four great Houses, whose Abbots and Priors had been lords of Parliament, were declared "surrendered" to the King, and their late superiors were granted pensions for life. How these "surrenders" were procured we may judge from the case of Manus, Abbot of St. Mary's, Thurles, who was carried prisoner to Dublin and suffered a long confinement for refusing to yield up his trust according to the desired formula. The work of confiscation was in these first years confined to the walled towns in English hands, the district of the Pale, and such points of the Irish country as could be conveniently reached. The great order of the Cistercians, established for more than four centuries at Mellifont, at Monastereven, at Bective, at Jerpoint, at Tintern, and at Dunbrody, were the first expelled from their cloisters and gardens. The Canons regular of St. Augustine at Trim, at Conal, at Athassel and at Kells, were next assailed by the degenerate Augustinian, who presided over the commission. The orders of St. Victor, of Aroacia, of St. John of Jerusalem, were extinguished wherever the arm of the Reformation could reach. The mendicant orders, spread into every district of the island, were not so easily erased from the soil; very many of the Dominican and Franciscan houses standing and flourishing far into the succeeding century.

If the influence of the clergy counterbalanced the policy of the chiefs, the condition of the mass of the population—more

especially of the inhabitants of the pale and the marches—
was such as to make them cherish the expectation that any
governmental change whatever should be for the better. It
was, under these circumstances, a far-reaching policy, which
combined the causes and the remedy for social wrongs,
with invectives against the old, and arguments in favor of the
new religion. In order to understand what elements of discontent there were to be wrought to such conclusions, it is
enough to give the merest glance at the social state of the
lower classes under English authority. The St. Leger Commission represents the mixed population of the marches, and
the Englishry of "the Pale" as burthened by accumulated
exactions. Their lords quartered upon them at pleasure
their horses, servants, and guests. They were charged with
coin and livery—that is, horse-meat and man's-meat—when
their lords travelled from place to place—with summer-oats,
with providing for their cosherings, or feasts, at Christmas and
Easter, with " black men and black money," for border defence,
and with workmen and axemen from every ploughland, to
work in the ditches, or to hew passages for the soldiery through
the woods. Every aggravation of feudal wrong was inflicted
on this harassed population. When a le Poer or a Butler
married a daughter he exacted a sheep from every flock, and
a cow from every village. When one of his sons went to England a special tribute was levied on every village and ploughland to bear the young gentleman's travelling expenses.
When the heads of any of the great houses hunted, their dogs
were to be supplied by the tenants " with bread and milk, or
butter." In the towns tailors, masons, and carpenters, were
taxed for coin and livery; "mustrons" were employed in
building halls, castles, stables, and barns, at the expense of the
tenantry, for the sole use of the lord. The only effective law
was an undigested jumble of the Brehon, the Civil, and the
Common law; with the arbitrary ordinances of the marches,
known as "the Statutes of Kilcash"—so called from a border
stronghold near the foot of Slievenamon—a species of wild justice, resembling too often that administered by Robin Hood, or
Bob Roy.

Many circumstances concurring to promote plans so long cherished by Henry, St. Leger summoned a Parliament for the morrow after Trinity Sunday, being the 13th of the month of June, 1541. The attendance on the day named was not so full as was expected, so the opening was deferred till the following Thursday—being the feast of Corpus Christi. On that festival the Mass of the Holy Ghost was solemnly celebrated in St. Patrick's Cathedral, in which "two thousand persons" had assembled. The Lords of Parliament rode in cavalcade to the Church doors, headed by the Deputy. There were seen side by side in this procession the Earls of Desmond and Ormond, the Lords Barry, Roche and Berningham; thirteen Barons of "the Pale," and a long train of Knights; Donogh O'Brien, Tanist of Thomond, the O'Reilly, O'Moore and McWilliam; Charles, son of Art Kavanagh, lord of Leinster, and Fitzpatrick, lord of Ossory. Never before had so many Milesian chiefs and Norman barons been seen together, except on the field of battle; never before had Dublin beheld marshalled in her streets what could by any stretch of imagination be considered a national representation. For this singularity, not less than for the business it transacted, the Parliament of 1541 will be held in lasting remembrance.

In the sanctuary of St. Patrick's, two Archbishops and twelve Bishops assisted at the solemn Mass, and the whole ceremony was highly imposing. "The like thereof," wrote St. Leger to Henry, "has not been seen here these many years." On the next day, Friday, the Commons elected Sir Thomas Cusack speaker, who, in "a right solemn proposition," opened at the bar of the Lords' House the main business of the session—the establishment of King Henry's supremacy. To this address Lord Chancellor Allen—"well and prudentlie answered;"—and the Commons withdrew to their own chamber. The substance of both speeches was "briefly and prudentlie" declared in the Irish language to the Gaelic Lords, by the Earl of Ormond, "greatly to their contentation." Then St. Leger proposed that Henry and his heirs should have the title of King, and caused the "bill devised for the same to be read." This bill having been put to the Lords' House, both in Irish and English, passed its three readings at the same sitting. In the Commons it was adopted with equal unanimity the next day, when the Lord Deputy most joyfully gave his consent. Thus on Saturday, June 19th, 1541, the royalty of Ireland was first formally transferred to an English dynasty. On that day the triumphant St. Leger was enabled to write his royal master his congratulations on having added to his dignities "another imperial crown." On Sunday bonfires were made in honor of the event, guns fired, and wine on stoop was set in the streets. All prisoners, except those for capital offences, were liberated; *Te Deum* was sung in St. Patrick's, and King Henry issued his proclamation, on receipt of the intelligence, for a general pardon throughout *all* his dominions. The new title was confirmed with great formality by the English Parliament in their session of 1542. Proclamation was formally made of it in London, on the 1st of July of that year, when it was moreover declared that after that date all persons being lawfully convicted of opposing the new dignity should "be adjudged high traitors"—"and suffer the pains of death."

Thus was consummated the first political union of Ireland with England. The strangely-constituted Assembly, which had given its sanction to the arrangement, in the language of the Celt, the Norman, and the Saxon, continued in session till the end of July, when they were prorogued till November. They enacted several statutes, in completion of the great change they had decreed; and while some prepared for a journey to the court of their new sovereign, others returned to their homes, to account as best they could for the part they had played at Dublin.

CHAPTER IV.

ADHESION OF O'NEIL, O'DONNELL AND O'BRIEN—A NEW ANGLO-IRISH PEERAGE—NEW RELATIONS OF LORD AND TENANT—BISHOPS APPOINTED BY THE CROWN—RETROSPECT.

The Act of Election could hardly be considered as the Act of the Irish nation, so long as several of the most distinguished chiefs withheld their concurrence. With these, therefore, Saint Leger entered into separate treaties, by separate instruments, agreed upon, at various dates, during the years 1542 and 1543. Manus O'Donnell, lord of Tyrconnell, gave in his adhesion in August, 1541, Con O'Neil, lord of Tyrowen, Murrogh O'Brien, lord of Thomond, Art O'Moore, lord of Leix, and Ulick Burke, lord of Clanrickarde, 1542 and 1543; but during the reign of Henry, no chief of the McCarthys, the O'Conors of Roscommon or of Offally, entered into any such engagement. The election, therefore, was far from unanimous, and Henry VIIIth would perhaps be classed by our ancient Senachies among the "Kings with opposition," who figure so often in our Annals during the Middle Ages.

Assuming, however, the title conferred upon him with no little complacency, Henry proceeded to exercise the first privilege of a sovereign, the creation of honors. Murrogh O'Brien, chief of his name, became Earl of Thomond, and Donough, his nephew, Baron of Ibrackan; Ulick McWilliam Burke became Earl of Clanrickarde and Baron of Dunkellin; Hugh O'Donnell was made Earl of Tyrconnell, Fitzpatrick became Baron of Ossory, and Kavanagh, Baron of Ballyan; Con O'Neil was made Earl of Tyrone, having asked, and been refused, the higher title of Earl of Ulster. The order of Knighthood was conferred on several of the principal attendants, and to each of the new peers the King granted a house in or near Dublin, for their accommodation, when attending the sittings of Parliament.

The imposing ceremonial of the transformation of these Celtic chiefs into English Earls has been very minutely described by an eye-witness. One batch were made at Greenwich Palace, after High Mass on Sunday, the 1st of July, 1543. The Queen's closet "was richly hanged with cloth of arras and well strawed with rushes," for their robing room. The King received them under a canopy of state, surrounded by his Privy Council, the peers, spiritual and temporal, the Earl of Glencairn, Sir George Douglas, and the other Scottish Commissioners. The Earls of Derby and Ormond led in the new Earl of Thomond, Viscount Lisle, carrying before them the sword. The Chamberlain handed his letters patent to the Secretary who read them down to the words *Cincturam gladii*, when the King girt the kneeling Earl, baldrick-wise, with the sword, all the company standing. A similar ceremony was gone through with the others, the King throwing a gold chain having a cross hanging to it round each of their necks. Then, preceded by the trumpeters blowing, and the officers at arms, they entered the dining-hall, where, after the second course, their titles were proclaimed aloud in Norman-French by Garter, King at Arms. Nor did Henry, who prided himself on his munificence, omit even more substantial tokens of his favor to the new Peers. Besides the town houses near Dublin, before mentioned, he granted to O'Brien all the abbeys and benefices of Thomond, bishoprics excepted; to McWilliam Burke, all the parsonages and vicarages of Clanrickarde, with one-third of the first-fruits, the Abbey of *Via Nova*, and £30 a year compensation for the loss of the customs of Galway; to Donogh O'Brien, the Abbey of Ellenegrane, the moiety of the Abbey of Clare, and an annuity of £20 a year. To the new lord of Ossory he granted the monasteries of Aghadoe and Aghmacarte, with the right of holding court lete and market, every Thursday, at his town of Aghadoe. For these and other favors the recipients had been instructed to petition the King, and drafts of such petitions had been drawn up in anticipation of their arrival in England by some official hand. The petitions are quoted by most of our late historians as their own proper act, but it is quite clear, though willing enough to present them and to accept such gifts, they had never dictated them.

In the creation of this Peerage Henry proclaimed, in the most practical manner possible, his determination to assimilate the laws and institutions of Ireland to those of England. And the new made Earls, forgetting their ancient relations to their clans—forgetting, as O'Brien had answered St. Leger's first overtures three years before, "that though he was captain of his nation he was still but one man," by suing out royal patents for their lands, certainly consented to carry out the King's plans. The Brehon law was doomed from the date of the creation of the new Peers at Greenwich, for such a change entailed among its first consequences a complete abrogation of the Gaelic relations of clansman and chief.

By the Brehon law every member of a free clan was as truly a proprietor of the tribe-land as the chief himself. He could sell his share, or the interest in it, to any other member of the tribe—the origin, perhaps, of what is now called tenant-right; he could not, however, sell to a stranger without the consent of the tribe and the chief. The stranger coming in under such an arrangement, held by a special tenure, yet if he remained during the time of three lords he became thereby naturalized. If the unnaturalized tenant withdrew of his own will from the land he was obliged to leave all his improvements behind; but if he was ejected he was entitled to get their full value. Those who were immediate tenants of the chief, or of the church, were debarred this privilege of tenant-right, and if unable to keep their holdings were obliged to surrender them unreservedly to the church or the chief. All the tribesmen, according to the extent of their possessions, were bound to maintain the chief's household, and to sustain him, with men and means, in his offensive and defensive wars. Such were, in brief, the land laws in force over three-fourths of the country in the XVIth century; laws which partook largely of the spirit of an ancient patriarchal justice, but which, in ages of movement, exchange, and enterprise would have been found the reverse of favorable to individual freedom and national strength. There were not wanting, we may be assured, many minds to whom this truth was apparent so early as the age of Henry VIIIth. And it may not be unreasonable to suppose that one of the advantages which the chief found in exchanging his partriarchal position for a feudal Earldom would be the greater degree of independence on the will of the tribe, which the new system conferred on him. With the mass of the clansmen, however, for the very same reason the change was certain to be unpopular, if not odious. But a still more serious change—a change of religion—was evidently contemplated by those Earls who accepted the property of the confiscated religious houses. The receiver of such estates could hardly pretend to belong to the ancient religion of the country.

It is impossible to understand Irish history from the reign of Henry VIII. till the fall of James II.—nearly two hundred years—without constantly keeping in mind the dilemma of the chiefs and lords between the requirements of the English Court on one hand and of the native clans on the other. Expected to obey and to administer conflicting laws, to personate two characters, to speak two languages, to uphold the old, yet to patronize the new order of things, distrusted at Court if they inclined to the people, detested by the people if they leaned towards the Court—a more difficult situation can hardly be conceived. Their perilous circumstances brought forth a new species of Irish character in the Chieftain-Earls of the Tudor and Stuart times. Not less given to war than their forefathers, they were now compelled to study the politician's part, even more than the soldier's. Brought personally in contact with powerful Sovereigns, or pitted at home against the Sydneys, Mountjoys, Chichesters, and Straffords, the lessons of Bacon and Machiavelli found apt scholars in the halls of Dunmanway and Dungannon. The multitude, in the meanwhile, saw only the broad fact that the Chief had bowed his neck to the hated Saxon yoke, and had promised, or would be by and by compelled, to introduce foreign garrisons, foreign judges, and foreign laws, amongst the sons of the Gael. Very early they perceived this; on the adhesion of O'Donnell to the Act of Election, a part of his clansmen, under the lead of his own son, rose up against his authority. A rival McWilliam, was at once chosen to the new Earl of Clanrickarde, in the West. Con O'Neil, the first of his race who had accepted an English title, was imprisoned by his son, John the Proud, and died of grief during his confinement. O'Brien found, on his return from Greenwich, half his territory in revolt; and this was the general experience of all Henry's electors. Yet such was the power of the new Sovereign that, we are told in our Annals, at the year 1547—the year of Henry's death—" no one dared give food or protection" to those few patriotic chiefs who still held obstinately out against the election of 1541.

The creation of a new peerage coincided in point of time with the first unconditional nomination of new Bishops by the Crown. The Plantagenet Kings, in common with all feudal Princes, had always claimed the right of investing Bishops with their temporalities and legal dignities; while, at the same time, they recognized in the See of Rome the seat and centre of Apostolic authority. But Henry, excommunicated and incorrigible, had procured from the Parliament of "the Pale," three years before the Act of Election, the formal recognition of his spiritual supremacy, under which he proceeded, as often as he had an opportunity, to promote candidates for the episcopacy to vacant sees. Between 1537 and 1547, thirteen or fourteen such vacancies having occurred, he nominated to the succession whenever the diocese was actually within his power. In this way the Sees of Dublin, Kildare, Ferns, Ardagh, Emly, Tuam and Killaloe were filled up; while the vacancies which occurred about the same period in Armagh, Clogher, Clonmacnoise, Clonfert, Kilmore, and Down and Connor were supplied from Rome. Many of the latter were allowed to take possession of their temporalities—so far as they were within English power—by taking an oath of allegiance, specially drawn for them. Others, when prevented from so doing by the penalties of *præmunire*, delegated their authority to Vicars General, who contrived to elude the provisions of the statute. On the other hand, several of the King's Bishops, excluded by popular hostility from the nominal sees, never resided upon them; some of them spent their lives in Dublin, and others were entertained as suffragans by Bishops in England.

In March, 1543, Primate Cromer, who had so resolutely led the early opposition to Archbishop Browne, died, whereupon Pope Paul III. appointed Robert Waucop, a Scotsman (by some writers called *Venantius*), to the See of Armagh. This remarkable man, though afflicted with blindness from his youth upwards, was a doctor of the Sorbonne, and one of the most distinguished Prelates of his age. He introduced the first Jesuit Fathers into Ireland, and to him is attributed the establishment of that intimate intercourse between the Ulster Princes and the See of Rome, which characterized the latter half of the century. He assisted at the Council of Trent from 1545 to 1547, was subsequently employed as Legate in Germany, and died abroad during the reign of Edward VIth. Simultaneously with the appointment of Primate Waucop, Henry VIIIth had nominated to the same dignity George Dowdal, a native of Louth, formerly Prior of the crutched friars at Ardee, in that county. Though Dowdal accepted the nomination, he did so without acknowledging the King's supremacy in spirituals. On the contrary he remained attached to the Holy See, and held his claims in abeyance, during the lifetime of Waucop. On the death of the latter, he assumed his rank, but was obliged to fly into exile, during the reign of Edward. On the accession of Mary he was recalled from his place of banishment in Brabant, and his first official act on returning home was to proclaim a Jubilee for the public restoration of the Catholic worship.

The King's Bishops during the last years of Henry, and the brief reign of Edward, were, besides Browne of Dublin, Edward Staples, Bishop of Meath, Matthew Saunders and Robert Travers, successively Bishops of Leighlin, William Miagh and Thomas Lancaster, successively Bishops of Kildare, and John Bale, Bishop of Ossory—all Englishmen. The only native names, before the reign of Elizabeth, which we find associated in any sense with the "reformation," are John Coyn, or Quin, Bishop of Limerick, and Dominick Tirrey, Bishop of Cork and Cloyne. Dr. Quin was promoted to the See in 1522, and resigned his charge in the year 1551. He is called a "favorer" of the new doctrines, but it is not stated how far he went in their support. His successor, Dr. William Casoy, was one of the six Bishops deprived by Queen Mary on her accession to the throne. As Bishop Tirrey is not of the number—although he lived till the third year of Mary's reign—we may conclude that he became reconciled to the Holy See.

The native population became, before Henry's death, fully aroused to the nature of the new doctrines, to which at first they had paid so little attention. The Commission issued in 1539 to Archbishop Browne and others for the destruction of images and relics, and the prevention of pilgrimages, as well as the ordering of English prayers as a substitute for the Mass, brought home to all minds the sweeping character of the change. Our native Annals record the breaking out of the English schism from the year 1537, though its formal introduction into Ireland may, perhaps, be more accurately dated from the issuing of the Ecclesiastical Commission of 1539. In their eyes it was the offspring of "pride, vain-glory, avarice, and lust," and its first manifestations were well calculated to make it forever odious on Irish soil. "They destroyed the religious orders," exclaim the Four Masters! "They broke down the monasteries, and sold their roofs and bells, from Aran of the Saints to the Iccian Sea!" "They burned the images, shrines, and relics of the Saints; they destroyed the Statue of our Lady of Trim, and the Staff of Jesus, which had been in the hand of St. Patrick!" Such were the works of that Commission as seen by the eyes of Catholics, natives of the soil. The Commissioners themselves, however, gloried in their work, and pointed with complacency to their success. The "innumerable images" which adorned the churches were dashed to pieces; the ornaments of shrines and altars, when not secreted in time, were torn from their places, and beaten into shapeless masses of metal. This harvest yielded in the first year nearly £3,000, on an inventory, wherein we find 1,000 lbs. weight of wax, manufactured into candles and tapers, valued at £20. Such was the return made to the revenue; what share of the spoil was appropriated by the agents employed may never be known. It would be absurd, however, to expect a scrupulous regard to honesty in men engaged in the work of sacrilege! And this work, it must be added, was carried on in the face of the stipulation entered into with the **Parliament** of 1541, that "the Church of Ireland shall be free, and enjoy all its accustomed privileges."

The death of Henry in January, 1547, found the Reformation in Ireland at the stage just described. But though all attempts to diffuse a general recognition of his spiritual power had failed, his reign will ever be memorable as the epoch of the union of the English and Irish Crowns. Before closing the present Book of our History, in which we have endeavored to account for that great fact, and to trace the progress of the negotiations which led to its accomplishment, we must briefly review the relations existing between the Kings of England and the Irish nation, from Henry II. to Henry VIII.

If we are to receive a statement of considerable antiquity, a memorable compromise effected at the Council of Constance, between the ambassadors of France and England, as to who should take precedence, turned mainly on this very point. The French monarchy was then at its lowest, the English at its highest pitch, for Charles VI. was but a nominal sovereign of France, while the conqueror of Azincourt sat on the throne of England. Yet in the first assembly of the Prelates and Princes of Europe, we are told that the ambassadors of France raised a question of the right of the English envoys to be received as representing a nation, seeing that they had been conquered not only by the Romans, but by the Saxons. Their argument further was, that, "as the Saxons were tributaries to the German Empire, and never governed by native sovereigns, they [the English] should take place as a branch only of the German empire, and not as a free nation. For," argued the French, "it is evident from Albertus Magnus and Bartholomew Glanville, that the world is divided into three parts, Europe, Asia and Africa;—that Europe is divided into four empires, the Roman, Constantinopolitan, the Irish, and the Spanish." "The English advocates," we are told, "admitting the force of these allegations, claimed their precedency and rank from Henry's being monarch of Ireland, and it was accordingly granted."

If this often-told anecdote is of any historical value, it only shows the ignorance of the representatives of France in yielding their pretensions on so poor a quibble. Neither Henry Vth, nor any other English sovereign before him, had laid claim to the title of "Monarch of Ireland." The indolence or ignorance of modern writers has led them, it is true, to adopt the whole series of the Plantagenet Kings as sovereigns of Ireland—to set up in history a dynasty which never existed for us; to leave out of their accounts of a monarchical people all question of their crown; and to pass over the election of 1541 without adequate, or any inquiry.

It is certain that neither Henry II., nor Richard I., ever used in any written instrument, or graven sign, the style of king, or even lord of Ireland; though in the Parliament held at Oxford in the year 1185, Henry conferred on his youngest son, John *lack-land*, a title which he did not himself possess, and John is thenceforth known in English history as "Lord of Ireland." This honor was not, however, of the exclusive nature of sovereignty, else John could hardly have borne it during the lifetime of his father and brother. And although we read that Cardinal Octavian was sent into England by Pope Urban III., authorized to consecrate John, *King* of Ireland, no such consecration took place, nor was the lordship looked upon, at any period, as other than a creation of the royal power of England existing in Ireland, which could be recalled, transferred, or alienated, without detriment to the prerogative of the King.

Neither had this original view of the relations existing between England and Ireland undergone any change at the time of the Council of Constânce. Of this we have a curious illustration in the style employed by the Queen Dowager of Henry Vth, who, during the minority of her son, granted charters, as "Queen of England and France, and lady of Ireland." The use of different crowns in the coronations of all the Tudors subsequent to Henry VIIIth shows plainly how the recent origin of their secondary title was understood and acknowledged during the remainder of the XVIth century. Nothing of the kind was practised at the coronation of the Plantagenet Princes, nor were the arms of Ireland quartered with those of England previous to the period we have described—the memorable year, 1541.

BOOK VIII.

THE ERA OF THE REFORMATION.

CHAPTER I.

EVENTS OF THE REIGN OF EDWARD SIXTH.

On the last day of January, 1547, Edward, son of Henry, by Lady Jane Seymour, was crowned by the title of Edward VIth. He was then only nine years old, and was destined to wear the crown but for six years and a few months. No Irish Parliament was convened during his reign, but the Reformation was pushed on with great vigor, at first under the patronage of the Protector, his uncle, and subsequently of that uncle's rival, the Duke of Northumberland. Archbishop Cranmer suffered the zeal of neither of these statesmen to flag for want of stimulus, and the Lord Deputy Saint Leger, judging from the cause of his disgrace in the next reign, *approved himself a willing assistant in the work.

The Irish Privy Council, which exercised all the powers of government during this short reign, was composed exclusively of partizans of the Reformation. Besides Archbishop Browne and Staples, Bishop of Meath, its members were the Chancellor, Read, and the Treasurer, Brabazon, both English, with the Judges Aylmer, Luttrel, Bath, Cusack, and Howth—all proselytes, at least in form, to the new opinions. The Earl of Ormond, with sixteen of his household, having been poisoned at a banquet in Ely House, London, in October before Henry's death, the influence of that great house was wielded during the minority of his successor by Sir Francis Bryan, an English adventurer, who married the widowed countess. This lady being, moreover, daughter and heir general to James, Earl of Desmond, brought Bryan powerful connexions in the South, which he was not slow to turn to a politic account. His ambition aimed at nothing less than the supreme authority, military and civil; but when at length he attained the summit of his hopes, he only lived to enjoy them a few months.

To enable the Deputy and Council to carry out the work they had begun, an additional military force was felt to be necessary, and Sir Edward Bellingham was sent over, soon after Edward's accession, with a detachment of six hundred horse, four hundred foot, and the title of Captain General. This able officer, in conjunction with Sir Francis Bryan, who appears to have been everywhere, overran Offally, Leix, Ely and Westmeath, sending the chiefs of the two former districts as prisoners to London, and making advantageous terms with those of the latter. He was, however, supplanted in the third year of Edward by Bryan, who held successively the rank of Marshal of Ireland and Lord Deputy. To the latter office he was chosen on an emergency, by the Council, in December, 1549, but died at Clonmel, on an expedition against the O'Carrolls, in the following February. His successes and those of Bellingham hastened the reduction of Leix and Offally into shire ground in the following reign.

The total military force at the disposal of Edward's commanders was probably never less than 10,000 effective men. By the aid of their abundant artillery, they were enabled to take many strong places hitherto deemed impregnable to assault. The mounted men and infantry were, as yet, but partially armed with musquetons, or firelocks—for the spear and the bow still found advocates among military men. The spearmen or lances were chiefly recruited on the marches of Northumberland from the hardy race of border warriors; the mounted bowmen or hobillers were generally natives of Chester or North Wales. Between these newcomers and the native Anglo-Irish troops many contentions arose from time to time, but in the presence of the common foe these bickerings were completely forgotten. The townsmen of Waterford marched promptly at a call, under their standard of the three galleys, and those of Dublin as cheerfully turned out under their well-known banner, decorated with three flaming towers.

The *personnel* of the administration, in the six years of Edward, was continually undergoing change. Bellingham who succeeded St. Leger, was supplanted by Bryan, on whose death St. Leger was reappointed. After another year Sir James Croft was sent over to replace St. Leger, and continued to fill the office until the accession of Queen Mary. But whoever rose or fell to the first rank in civil affairs, the Privy Council remained exclusively Protestant, and the work of innovation was not suffered to languish. A manuscript account, attributed to Adam Loftus, Browne's successor, assigns the year 1549 as the date when "the Mass was put down," in Dublin, "and divine service was celebrated in English." Bishop Mant, the historian of the Established Church in Ireland, does not find any account of such an alteration, nor does the statement appear to him consistent with subsequent facts of this reign. We observe, also, that in 1550, Arthur Magennis, the Pope's Bishop of Dromore, was allowed by the government to enter on possession of his temporalities after taking an oath of allegiance, while King's Bishops were appointed in that and the next two years to the vacant sees of Kildare, Leighlin, Ossory, and Limerick. A vacancy having occurred in the See of Cashel, in 1551, it was unaccountably left vacant, as far as the Crown was concerned, during the remainder of this reign, while a similar vacancy in Armagh was filled, at least in name, by the appointment of Dr. Hugh Goodacre, chaplain to the Bishop of Winchester, and a favorite preacher with the Princess Elizabeth. This Prelate was consecrated, according to a new form, in Christ Church, Dublin, on 2d of February, 1523, together with his countryman, John Bale, Bishop of Ossory. The officiating Prelates were Browne, Staples, and Lancaster of Kildare—all English. The Irish Establishment, however, does not at all times rest its argument for the validity of its episcopal Order upon these consecrations. Most of their writers lay claim to the Apostolic succession, through Adam Loftus, consecrated in England, according to the ancient rite, by Hugh Curwen, an Archbishop in communion with the See of Rome, at the time of his elevation to the episcopacy.

In February, 1551, Sir Anthony St. Leger received the King's commands to cause the Scriptures translated into the English tongue, and the Liturgy and Prayers of the Church, also translated into English, to be read in all the churches of Ireland. To render these instructions effective the Deputy summoned a convocation of the Archbishops, Bishops, and Clergy, to meet in Dublin on the 1st of March, 1551. In this meeting—the first of two in which the defenders of the old and of the new religion met face to face—the Catholic party was led by the intrepid Dowdal, Archbishop of Armagh, and the Reformers by Archbishop Browne. The Deputy who, like most laymen of that age, had a strong theological turn, also, took an active part in the discussion. Finally delivering the royal order to Browne, the latter accepted it in a set form of words, without reservation; the Anglican Bishops of Meath, Kildare, and Leighlin, and Coyne, Bishop of Limerick, adhering to his act; Primate Dowdal, with the other Bishops, having previously retired from the Conference. On Easter day following, the English service was celebrated for the first time in Christ Church, Dublin, the Deputy, the Archbishop, and the Mayor of the city assisting. Browne preached from the text: "Open mine eyes that I may see the wonders of the law" —a sermon chiefly remarkable for its fierce invective against the new Order of Jesuits.

Primate Dowdal retired from the Castle Conference to Saint Mary's Abbey, on the north side of the Liffey, where he continued while these things were taking place in the city proper. The new Lord Deputy, Sir James Crofts, on his arrival in May, addressed himself to the Primate, to bring about, if possible, an accommodation between the Prelates. Fearing, as he said, an "order ere long to alter church matters, as well in offices as in ceremonies," the new Deputy urged another Conference, which was accordingly held at the Primate's lodgings, on the 16th of June. At this meeting Browne does not seem to have been present, the argument on the side of the Reformers being maintained by Staples. The points discussed were chiefly the essential character of the Holy Sacrifice of the Mass, and the invocation of Saints. The tone observed on both sides was full of high-bred courtesy. The letter of the Sacred Scriptures and the authority of Erasmus in Church History were chiefly relied upon by Staples; the common consent and usage of all Christendom, the primacy of Saint Peter, and the binding nature of the oath taken by Bishops at their consecration, were pointed out by the Primate. The disputants parted, with expressions of deep regret that they could come to no agreement; but the Primacy was soon afterwards transferred to Dublin, by order of the Privy Council, and Dowdal fled for refuge into Brabant. The Roman Catholic and the Anglican Episcopacy have never since met in oral controversy on Irish ground, though many of the second order of the clergy in both communions have, from time to time, been permitted by their superiors to engage in such discussions.

Whatever obstacles they encountered within the Church itself, the propagation of the new religion was not confined to moral means, nor was the spirit of opposition at all times restricted to mere argument. Bishop Bale having begun at Kilkenny to pull down the revered images of the Saints, and to overturn the Market Cross, was set upon by the mob, five of his servants, or guard, were slain, and himself narrowly escaped with his life by barricading himself in his palace. The garrisons in the neighborhood of the ancient seats of ecclesiastical power and munificence were authorized to plunder their sanctuaries and storehouses. The garrison of Down sacked the celebrated shrines and tomb of Patrick, Bridget, and Columbkill; the garrison of Carrickfergus ravaged Rathlin Island and attacked Derry, from which, however, they were repulsed with severe loss by John the Proud. But the most lamentable scene of spoliation, and that which excited the profoundest emotions of pity and anger in the public mind, was the violation of the churches of St. Kieran—the renowned Clonmacnoisé. This city of schools had cast its cross-crowned shade upon the gentle current of the Upper Shannon for a thousand years. Danish fury, civil storm, and Norman hostility had passed over it, leaving traces of their power in the midst of the evidences of its recuperation. The great Church to which pilgrims flocked from every tribe of Erin, on the 9th of September—St. Kieran's Day; the numerous chapels erected by the chiefs of all the neighboring clans; the halls, hospitals, book-houses, nunneries, cemeteries, granaries—all still stood, awaiting from Christian hands the last fatal blow. In the neighboring town of Athlone—seven or eight miles distant—the Treasurer, Brabazon, had lately erected a strong "Court" or Castle, from which, in the year 1552, the garrison sallied forth to attack "the place of the sons of the nobles,"— which is the meaning of the name. In executing this task they exhibited a fury surpassing that of Turgesius and his Danes. The pictured glass was torn from the window frames and the revered images from their niches; altars were overthrown; sacred vessels polluted. "They left not," say the Four Masters, "a book or a gem,' nor anything to show what Clonmacnoise had been, save the bare walls of the temples, the mighty shaft of the round tower, and the monuments in the cemeteries, with their inscriptions in Irish, in Hebrew, and in Latin. The Shannon re-echoed with their profane songs and laughter, as laden with chalices and crucifixes, brandishing croziers, and flaunting vestments in the air, their barges returned to the walls of Athlone.

In all the Gaelic speaking regions of Ireland, the new religion now began to be known by those fruits which it had so abundantly produced. Though the southern and midland districts had not yet recovered from the exhaustion consequent upon the suppression of the Geraldine league and the abortive insurrection of Silken Thomas, the northern tribes were still unbroken and undismayed. They had deputed George Paris, a kinsman of the Kildare Fitzgeralds, as their agent to the French King, in the latter days of Henry VIII., and had received two ambassadors on his behalf at Donegal and Dungannon. These ambassadors, the Baron de Forquevaux, and the Sieur de Montluc, who subsequently became Bishop of Valence, crossing over from the west of Scotland, entered into a league offensive and defensive with "the princes" of Tyrconnell and Tyrowen, by which the latter bound themselves to recognize on certain conditions, " whoever was King of France as King of Ireland likewise." This alliance, though prolonged into the reign of Edward, led to nothing definitive, and we shall see in the next reign how the hopes then turned towards France were naturally transferred to Spain.

The only native name which rises into historic importance at this period is that of Shane, or John O'Neil, "the Proud." He was the legitimate son of that Con O'Neil who had been girt with the Earl's baldric by the hands of Henry VIII. His father had procured at the same time for an illegitimate son, Ferodach, or Mathew, of Dundalk, the title of Baron of Dungannon, with the reversion of the Earldom. When, however, John the Proud came of age, he centered upon himself the hopes of his clansmen, deposed his father, subdued the Baron and assumed the title of O'Neil. In 1552 he defeated the efforts of Sir William Brabazon to fortify Belfast, and delivered Derry from its plunderers. From that time till his tragical death, in the ninth year of Queen Elizabeth, he stood unquestionably the first man of his race, both in lineage and action.

CHAPTER II.

EVENTS OF THE REIGN OF PHILIP AND MARY.

The death of Edward VI. and the accession of the lady Mary were known in Dublin by the middle of July, 1553, and soon spread all over the kingdom. On the 20th of that month, the form of proclamation was received from London, in which the new Queen was forbidden to be styled "head of the church," and this was quickly followed by another ordinance, authorizing all who would to publicly attend Mass, but not compelling thereto any who were unwilling. A curious legal difficulty existed in relation to Mary's title to the Crown of Ireland. By the Irish Statute, 28. Hen. VIII., the Irish crown was entailed by name on the Lady Elizabeth, and that act had not been repealed. It was, however, held to have been superseded by the English Statute, 35. Hen. VIII., which followed the election of 1541, and declared the Crown of Ireland "united and knit to the Imperial Crown of the Realm of England." Read in the light of the latter statute, the Irish sovereignty might be regarded a mere appurtenance of that of England, but Mary did not so consider it. At her coronation, a separate crown was used for Ireland, nor did she feel assured of the validity of her claim to wear it till she had obtained a formal dispensation to that effect from the Pope.

The intelligence of the new Queen's accession, and the public restoration of the old religion, diffused a general joy throughout Ireland. Festivals and pageants were held in the streets, and eloquent sermons poured from all the pulpits. Archbishop Dowdal was called from exile, and the Primacy was restored to Armagh. Sir Anthony St. Leger, his ancient antagonist, had now conformed to the Court fashion, and was sent over to direct the establishment of that religion which he had been so many years engaged in pulling down. In 1554, Browne, Staples, Lancaster, and Travers, were formally deprived of their sees; Bale and Casey of Limerick fled beyond seas, without awaiting judgment. Married clergymen were invariably silenced, and the children of Browne were declared by statute illegitimate.

What, however, gratified the public even more than these retributions was the liberation of the aged Chief of Offally from the Tower of London, at the earnest supplication of his heroic daughter, Margaret, who found her way to the Queen's presence to beg that boon; and the simultaneous restoration of the Earldom of Kildare, in the person of that Gerald, who had been so young a fugitive among the glens of Muskerry and Donegal, and had since undergone so many continental adventures. With O'Connor and young Gerald, the heir of the houses of Ormond and of Upper Ossory were also allowed to return to their homes to the great delight of the southern half of the kingdom. The subsequent marriage of Mary with Philip II.

of Spain gave an additional security to the Irish Catholics for the future freedom of their religion.

Great as was the change in this respect, it is not to be inferred that the national relations of Ireland and England were materially affected by such a change of sovereign. The maxims of conquest were not to be abandoned at the dictates of religion. The supreme power continued to be entrusted only to Englishmen; while the same Parliament (3d and 4th Philip and Mary) which abolished the title of head of the Church, and restored the Roman jurisdiction in matters spiritual, divided Leix and Offally, Glenmalier and Slewmargy, into shire ground, subject to English law, under the name of King's and Queen's County. The new forts of Maryborough and Philipstown, as well as the county names served to teach, the people of Leinster that the work of conquest could be as industriously prosecuted by Catholic as by Protestant rulers. Nor were these forts established and maintained without many a struggle. St. Leger, and his still abler successor, the Earl of Sussex, and the new Lord Treasurer, Sir Henry Sidney, were forced to lead many an expedition to the relief of those garrisons, and the dispersion of their assailants. It was not in Irish human nature to submit to the constant pressure of a foreign power without seizing every possible opportunity for its expulsion.

The new principle of primogeniture introduced at the commutation of chieftainries into earldoms was productive in this reign of much commotion and bloodshed. The seniors of the O'Briens resisted its establishment in Thomond, on the death of the first Earl; Calvagh O'Donnell took arms against his father, to defeat its introduction into Tyrconnell; John the Proud, as we have seen in the reign of Edward, had been one of its earliest opponents in Ulster. Being accused in the last year of Queen Mary of procuring the death of his illegitimate brother, the Baron of Dungannon, in order to remove him from his path, he was summoned to account for those circumstances before Sir Henry Sidney, then acting as Lord Justice. His plea has been preserved to us, and no doubt represents the prevailing opinion of the Gaelic-speaking population towards the new system. He answered, "that the surrender which his father had made to Henry VIII., and the restoration which Henry made to his father again were of no force; inasmuch as his father had no right to the lands which he surrendered to the King, except during his own life; that he (John) himself was the O'Neil by the law of Tanistry, and by popular election; and that he assumed no superiority over the chieftains of the North except what belonged to his ancestors." To these views he adhered to the last, accepting no English honors, though quite willing to live at peace with English sovereigns. When the title of Earl of Tyrone was revived, it was in favor of the son of the Baron, the celebrated Hugh O'Neil, the ally of Spain, and the most formidable antagonist of Queen Elizabeth.

In the Irish Parliament already referred to (3d and 4th Philip and Mary) an act was passed declaring it a felony to introduce armed Scotchmen into Ireland, or to intermarry with them without a license under the great seal. This statute was directed against those multitudes of Islesmen and Highlanders who annually crossed the narrow strait which separates Antrim from Argyle to harass the English garrisons alongshore, or to enlist as auxiliaries in Irish quarrels. In 1556, under one of their principal leaders, James, son of Conal, they laid siege to Carrickfergus and occupied Lord Sussex some six weeks in the glens of Antrim. Their leader finally entered into conditions, the nature of which may be inferred from the fact that he received the honor of knighthood on their acceptance. John O'Neil had usually in his service a number of these mercenary troops, from among whom he selected sixty body-guards, the same number supplied by his own clan. In his first attempt to subject Tyrconnell to his supremacy in 1557, his camp near Raphoe was surprised at night by Calvagh O'Donnell, and his native and foreign guards were put to the sword, while he himself barely escaped by swimming the Mourne and the Finn. O'Donnell had frequently employed a similar force, in his own defence; and we read of the Lord of Clanrickarde driving back a host of them engaged in the service of his rivals, from the banks of the Moy, in 1558.

Although the memory of Queen Mary has been hold up to

execration during three centuries as a bloody-minded and malignant persecutor of all who differed from her in religion, it is certain that in Ireland, where, if anywhere, the Protestant minority might have been extinguished by such severities as are imputed to her, no persecution for conscience' sake took place. Married Bishops were deprived, and married priests were silenced, but beyond this no coercion was employed. It has been said there was not time to bring the machinery to bear, but surely if there was time to do so in England, within the space of five years, there was time in Ireland also. The consoling truth—honorable to human nature and to Christian charity, is—that many families out of England, apprehending danger in their own country, sought and found a refuge from their fears in the western island. The families of Agar, Ellis, and Harvey, are descended from emigrants, who were accompanied from Cheshire by a clergyman of their own choice, whose ministrations they freely enjoyed during the remainder of this reign at Dublin. The story about Dr. Cole having been despatched to Ireland with a commission to punish heretics, and, losing it on the way, is unworthy of serious notice. If there had been any such determination formed there was ample time to put it into execution between 1553 and 1558.

CHAPTER III.

ACCESSION OF QUEEN ELIZABETH—PARLIAMENT OF 1560—THE ACT OF UNIFORMITY—CAREER AND DEATH OF JOHN O'NEIL "THE PROUD."

THE daughter of Anna Boleyn was promptly proclaimed Queen the same day on which Mary died—the 17th of November, 1558. Elizabeth was then in her 26th year, proud of her beauty, and confident in her abilities. Her great capacity had been cultivated by the best masters of the age, and the best of all ages, early adversity. Her vices were hereditary in her blood, but her genius for government so far surpassed any of her immediate predecessors as to throw her vices into the shade. During the forty-four years in which she wielded the English sceptre, many of the most stirring occurrences of our history took place; it could hardly have fallen out otherwise, under a sovereign of so much vigor, having the command of such immense resources.

On the news of Mary's death reaching Ireland the Lord Deputy Sussex returned to England, and Sir Henry Sidney, the Treasurer, was appointed his successor *ad interim*. As in England, so in Ireland, though for somewhat different reasons, the first months of the new reign were marked by a conciliating and temporizing policy. Elizabeth, who had not assumed the title of "Head of the Church," continued to hear Mass for several months after her accession. At her coronation she had a High Mass sung, accompanied, it is true, by a Calvinistic sermon. Before proceeding with the work of "reformation" inaugurated by her father, and arrested by her sister, she proceeded cautiously to establish herself, and her Irish deputy followed in the same careful line of conduct. Having first made a menacing demonstration against John the Proud, he entered into friendly correspondence with him, and finally ended the campaign by standing godfather to one of his children. This relation of gossip among the old Irish was no mere matter of ceremony, but involved obligations lasting as life, and sacred as the ties of kindred blood. By seeking such a sponsor O'Neil placed himself in Sidney's power, rather than Sidney in his, since the two men must have felt very differently bound by the connexion into which they had entered. As an evidence of the Imperial policy of the moment the incident is instructive.

Round the personal history of this splendid, but by no means stainless Ulster Prince, the events of the first nine years of Elizabeth's reign over Ireland naturally group themselves. Whether at her Majesty's council-board, or among the Scottish islands, or in hall or hut at home, the attention of all manner of men interested in Ireland was fixed upon the movements of John the Proud. In tracing his career we therefore naturally gather all, or nearly all, the threads of the national story, during the first ten years of Queen Mary's successor.

In the second year of Elizabeth, Lord Deputy Sussex, who returned fully possessed of her Majesty's views, summoned the Parliament to meet in Dublin on the 12th day of January, 1560. It is to be observed, however, that though the union of the crowns was now of twenty years' standing, the writs were not issued to the nation at large, but only to the ten counties of Dublin, Meath, Louth, Westmeath, Kildare, Carlow, Kilkenny, Wexford, Waterford and Tipperary, with their boroughs. The published instructions of Lord Sussex were "to make such statutes (concerning religion) as were made in England, *mutatis mutandis.*" As a preparation for the legislature, St. Patrick's Cathedral and Christ Church were purified by paint; the niches of the Saints were for the second time emptied of their images; texts of Scripture were blazoned upon the walls, and the Litany was chanted in English. After these preparatory demonstrations the Deputy opened the new Parliament, which sat for one short but busy month. The Acts of Mary's Parliament, re-establishing ecclesiastical relations with Rome, were the first thing repealed; then so much of the Act 33, Henry VIII., as related to the succession, was revived; all ecclesiastical jurisdiction was next declared vested in the Crown, and all "judges, justices, mayors and temporal officers were declared bound to take the oath of supremacy; the penalty attached to the refusal of the oath, by this statute, being "forfeiture of office and promotion during life." Proceeding rapidly in the same direction, it was declared that commissioners in ecclesiastical causes should adjudge nothing as heresy which was not expressly so condemned by the Canonical Scriptures, the received General Councils, or by Parliament. The penalty of *præmunire* was declared in force, and, to crown the work, the celebrated "Act of Uniformity" was passed. This was followed by other statutes for the restoration of first fruits and twentieths, and for the appointment of Bishops by the royal prerogative, or *conge d'elire*—elections by the chapter being declared mere "shadows of election, and derogatory to the prerogative." Such was in brief the legislation of that famous Parliament of ten counties—the often quoted statutes of the "2nd of Elizabeth." In the Act of Uniformity, the best known of all its statutes, there was this curious saving clause inserted: that whenever the "priest or common minister" could not speak English, he might still continue "to celebrate the service in the Latin tongue." Such other observances were to be had as were prescribed by the 2nd Edward VIth, until her Majesty should "publish further ceremonies or rites." We have no history of the debates of this Parliament of a month, but there is ample reason to believe that some of these statutes were resisted throughout by a majority of the Upper House, still chiefly composed of Catholic Peers; that the clause saving the Latin ritual was inserted as a compromise with this opposition; that some of the other Acts were passed by stealth in the absence of many members, and that the Lord Deputy gave his solemn pledge the statute of Uniformity should be enforced, if passed. So severe was the struggle, and so little satisfied was Sussex with his success, that he hastily dissolved the Houses and went over personally to England to represent the state of feeling he had encountered. Finally, it is remarkable that no other Parliament was called in Ireland till nine years afterwards—a convincing proof of how unmanageable that body, even constituted as it was, had shown itself to be in matters affecting religion.

The non-invitation of the Irish chiefs to this Parliament, contrary to the precedent set in Mary's reign and in 1541, the laws enacted, and the commotion they excited in the minds of the clergy, were circumstances which could not fail to attract the attention of John O'Neil. Even if insensible to what transpired at Dublin, the indefatigable Sussex—one of the ablest of Elizabeth's able Court—did not suffer him long to misunderstand his relations to the new Queen. He might be Sidney's gossip but he was not the less Elizabeth's enemy. He had been proclaimed "O'Neil" on the rath of Tullahoge, and had reigned at Dungannon, adjudging life and death. It was clear that two such jurisdictions as the Celtic and the Norman kingship could not stand long on the same soil, and the Ulster

Prince soon perceived that he must establish his authority, by arms, or perish with it. We must also read all Irish events of the time of Elizabeth by the light of foreign politics; during the long reign of that sovereign, England was never wholly free from fears of invasion, and many movements which now seem inexplicable will be readily understood when we recollect that they took place under the menaces of foreign powers.

The O'Neils had anciently exercised a high-handed superiority over all Ulster, and John the Proud was not the man to let his claim lie idle in any district of that wide-spread Province. But authority which has fallen into decay must be asserted only at a propitious time, and with the utmost tact; and here it was that Elizabeth's statesmen found their most effective means of attacking O'Neil. O'Donnell, who was his father-in-law, was studiously conciliated; his second wife, a lady of the Argyle family, received costly presents from the Queen; O'Reilly was created Earl of Breffny, and encouraged to resist the superiority to which the house of Dungannon laid claim. The natural consequences followed; John the Proud swept like a storm over the fertile hills of Cavan, and compelled the new-made Earl to deliver him tribute and hostages. O'Donnell, attended only by a few of his household, was seized in a religious house upon Lough Swilly, and subjected to every indignity which an insolent enemy could devise. His Countess, already alluded to, supposed to have been privy to this surprise of her husband, became the mistress of his captor and jailor, to whom she bore several children. What deepens the horror of this odious domestic tragedy is the fact that the wife of O'Neil, the daughter of O'Donnell, thus supplanted by her shameless stepmother, under her own roof, died soon afterwards of "horror, loathing, grief, and deep anguish," at the spectacle afforded by the private life of O'Neil, and the severities inflicted upon her wretched father. All the patriotic designs, and all the shining abilities of John the Proud, cannot abate a jot of our detestation of such a private life; though slandered in other respects as he was, by hostile pens, no evidence has been adduced to clear his memory of these indelible stains; nor after becoming acquainted with their existence can we follow his after career with that heartfelt sympathy with which the lives of purer patriots must always inspire us.

The pledge given by Sussex, that the penal legislation of 1560 should lie a dead letter, was not long observed. In May of the year following its enactment, a commission was appointed to enforce the 2nd Elizabeth, in Westmeath; and in 1562 a similar commission was appointed for Meath and Armagh. By these commissioners Dr. William Walsh, Catholic Bishop of Meath, was arraigned and imprisoned for preaching against the new liturgy; a Prelate who afterwards died an exile in Spain. The primatial see was for the moment vacant, Archbishop Dowdal having died at London three months before Queen Mary—on the Feast of the Assumption, 1558. Terence, Dean of Armagh, who acted as administrator, conveyed a Synod of the English-speaking clergy of the Province in July, 1559, at Drogheda, but as this dignitary followed in the steps of his faithful predecessors, his deanery was conferred upon Dr. Adam Loftus, Chaplain of the Lord Lieutenant; two years subsequently the dignity of Archbishop of Armagh was conferred upon the same person. Dr. Loftus, a native of Yorkshire, had found favor in the eyes of the Queen at a public exhibition at Cambridge University; he was but 28 years old, according to Sir James Ware, when consecrated Primate—but Dr. Mant thinks he must have attained at least the canonical age of 30. During the whole of this reign he continued to reside at Dublin, which see was early placed under his jurisdiction in lieu of the inaccessible Armagh. For forty years he continued one of the ruling spirits at Dublin, whether acting as Lord Chancellor, Lord Justice, Privy Councillor, or First Provost of Trinity College. He was a pluralist in Church and State, insatiable of money and honors; if he did not much assist in establishing his religion, he was eminently successful in enriching his family.

Having subdued every hostile neighbor and openly assumed the high prerogative of Prince of Ulster, John the Proud looked around him for allies in the greater struggle which he foresaw could not be long postponed. Calvagh O'Donnell was yielded up on receiving a munificent ransom, but his infamous wife remained with her paramour. A negotiation was set on foot with the chiefs of the Highland and Island Scots, large numbers of whom entered into O'Neil's service. Emissaries were despatched to the French Court, where they found a favorable reception, as Elizabeth was known to be in league with the King of Navarre and the Huguenot leaders against Francis II. The unexpected death of the King at the close of 1560; the return of his youthful widow, Queen Mary, to Scotland; the vigorous regency of Catherine de Medicis during the minority of her second son; the ill-success of Elizabeth's arms during the campaigns of 1561-2-3, followed by the humiliating peace of April, 1564—these events are all to be borne in memory when considering the extraordinary relations which were maintained during the same years by the proud Prince of Ulster, with the still prouder Queen of England. The apparently contradictory tactics pursued by the Lord Deputy Sussex, between his return to Dublin in the spring of 1561, and his final recall in 1564, when read by the light of events which transpired at Paris, London and Edinburgh, become easily intelligible. In the spring of the first mentioned year, it was thought possible to intimidate O'Neil, so Lord Sussex, with the Earl of Ormond as second in command, marched northwards, entered Armagh, and began to fortify the city, with a view to placing in it a powerful garrison. O'Neil, to remove the seat of hostilities, made an irruption into the plain of Meath, and menaced Dublin. The utmost consternation prevailed at his approach, and the Deputy, while continuing the fortification of Armagh, despatched the main body of his troops to press on the rear of the aggressor. By a rapid countermarch, O'Neil came up with this force, laden with spoils, in Louth, and after an obstinate engagement routed them with immense loss. On receipt of this intelligence, Sussex promptly abandoned Armagh, and returned to Dublin, while O'Neil erected his standard, as far South as Drogheda, within twenty miles of the capital. So critical at this moment was the aspect of affairs, that all the energies of the English interest were taxed to the utmost. In the autumn of the year, Sussex marched again from Dublin northward, having at his side the five powerful Earls of Kildare, Ormond, Desmond, Thomond, and Clanrickarde—whose mutual feuds had been healed or dissembled for the day. O'Neil prudently fell back before this powerful expedition, which found its way to the shores of Lough Foyle, without bringing him to an engagement and without any military advantage. As the shortest way of getting rid of such an enemy, the Lord Deputy, though one of the wisest and most justly celebrated of Elizabeth's Counsellors, did not hesitate to communicate to his royal mistress the project of hiring an assassin, named Nele Gray, to take off the Prince of Ulster, but the plot, though carefully elaborated, miscarried. Foreign news which probably reached him only on reaching the Foyle, led to a sudden change of tactics on the part of Sussex, and the young Lord Kildare—O'Neil's cousin germain, was employed to negotiate a peace with the enemy they had set out to demolish.

This Lord Kildare was Gerald, the XIth Earl, the same whom we have spoken of as a fugitive lad, in the last years of Henry VIIIth, and as restored to his estates and rank by Queen Mary. Although largely indebted to his Catholicity for the protection he had received while abroad from Francis Ist, Charles Vth, the Duke of Tuscany and the Roman See— especially the Cardinals Pole and Farnese—and still more indebted to the late Catholic Queen for the restoration of his family honors, this finished courtier, now in the very midsummer of life, one of the handsomest and most accomplished persons of his time, did not hesitate to conform himself, at least outwardly, to the religion of the State. Shortly before the campaign of which we have spoken, he had been suspected of treasonable designs, but had pleaded his cause successfully with the Queen in person. From Lough Foyle, accompanied by the Lord Slane, the Viscount Baltinglass, and a suitable guard, Lord Kildare set out for John O'Neil's camp, where a truce was concluded between the parties, Lord Sussex undertaking to withdraw his wardens from Armagh, and O'Neil engaging himself to live in peace with her Majesty, and to serve "when necessary against her enemies." The cousins also agreed personally to visit the English Court the following year, and accordingly in January ensuing they went to England, from which they returned home in the latter end of May.

The reception of John the Proud, at the Court of Elizabeth, was flattering in the extreme. The courtiers stared and smiled at his bareheaded body-guard, with their crocus-dyed vests, short jackets, and shaggy cloaks. But the broad-bladed battle-axe, and the sinewy arm which yielded it, inspired admiration for all the uncouth costume. The haughty indifference with which the Prince of Ulster treated every one about the Court, except the Queen, gave a keener edge to the satirical comments which were so freely indulged in at the expense of his style of dress. The wits proclaimed him "O'Neil the Great, cousin to Saint Patrick, friend to the Queen of England, and enemy to all the world besides!" O'Neil was well pleased with his reception by Elizabeth. When taxed upon his return with having made peace with her Majesty, he answered—"Yes, in her own bedchamber." There were, indeed, many points in common in both their characters.

Her Majesty, by letters patent dated at Windsor, on the 15th of January, 1563, recognized in John the Proud "the name and title of O'Neil, with the like authority, jurisdiction, and pre-eminence, as any of his ancestors." And O'Neil, by articles, dated at Benburb, the 18th of November of the same year, reciting the letters patent aforesaid, bound himself and his suffragans to behave as "the Queen's good and faithful subjects against all persons whatever." Thus, so far as an English alliance could guarantee it, was the supremacy of this daring chief guaranteed in Ulster from the Boyne to the North Sea.

In performing his part of the engagements thus entered into, O'Neil is placed in a less invidious light by English writers than formerly. They now describe him as scrupulously faithful to his word; as charitable to the poor, always carving and sending meat from his own table to the beggar at the gate before eating himself. Of the sincerity with which he carried out the expulsion of the Islesmen and Highlanders from Ulster, the result afforded the most conclusive evidence. It is true he had himself invited those bands into the Province to aid him against the very power with which he was now at peace, and, therefore, they might in their view allege duplicity and desertion against him. Yet enlisted as they usually were but for a single campaign, O'Neil expected them to depart as readily as they had come. But in this expectation he was disappointed. Their leaders, Angus, James, and Sorley McDonald, refused to recognize the new relations which had arisen, and O'Neil was, therefore, compelled to resort to force. He defeated the Scottish troops at Glenfesk, near Ballycastle, in 1564, in an action wherein Angus McDonald was slain, James died of his wounds, and Sorley was carried prisoner to Benburb. An English auxiliary force, under Colonel Randolph, sent round by sea, under pretence of co-operating against the Scots, took possession of Derry, and began to fortify it. But their leader was slain in a skirmish with a party of O'Neil's people who disliked the fortress, and whether by accident or otherwise their magazine exploded, killing a great part of the garrison and destroying their works. The remnant took to their shipping and returned to Dublin.

In the years 1565, 6 and 7, the internal dissensions of both Scotland and France, and the perturbations in the Netherlands giving full occupation to her foreign foes, Elizabeth had an interval of leisure to attend to this dangerous ally in Ulster. A second unsuccessful attempt on his life, by an assassin named Smith, was traced to the Lord Deputy, and a formal commission issued by the Queen to investigate the case. The result we know only by the event; Sussex was recalled, and Sir Henry Sidney substituted in his place! Death had lately made way in Tyrconnell and Fermanagh for new chiefs, and these leaders, more vigorous than their predecessors, were resolved to shake off the recently imposed and sternly exercised supremacy of Benburb. With these chiefs, Sidney, at the head of a veteran armament, cordially co-operated, and O'Neil's territory was now attacked simultaneously at three different points—in the year 1566. No considerable success was, however, obtained over him till the following year, when at the very opening of the campaign the brave O'Donnell arrested his march along the strand of the Lough Swilly, and the tide rising impetuously, as it does on that coast, on the rear of the men of Tyrone, struck them with terror, and completed their defeat. From 1,500 to 3,000 men perished by the sword or by the tide; John the Proud fled alone, along the river Swilly, and narrowly escaped by the fords of rivers and by solitary ways to his Castle on Lough Neagh. The Annalists of Donegal, who were old enough to have conversed with survivors of the battle, say that his mind became deranged by this sudden fall from the summit of prosperity to the depths of defeat. His next step would seem to establish the fact, for he at once despatched Sorley McDonald, the survivor of the battle of Glenfesk, to recruit a new auxiliary force for him amongst the Islesmen, whom he had so mortally offended. Then, abandoning his fortress upon the Blackwater, he set out with 50 guards, his secretary, and his mistress, the wife of the late O'Donnell, to meet these expected allies whom he had so fiercely driven off but two short years before. At Cushendun, on the Antrim coast, they met with all apparent cordiality, but an English agent, Captain Piers, or Pierce, seized an opportunity during the carouse which ensued to recall the bitter memories of Glenfesk. A dispute and a quarrel ensued; O'Neil fell covered with wounds, amid the exulting shouts of the avenging Islesmen. His gory head was presented to Captain Piers, who hastened with it to Dublin where he received a reward of a thousand marks for his success. High spiked upon the towers of the Castle, that proud head remained and rotted; the body, wrapped in a Kerns saffron shirt, was interred where he fell, a spot familiar to all the inhabitants of the Antrim glens as "the grave of Shane O'Neil." And so may be said to close the first decade of Elizabeth's reign over Ireland!

END OF VOL. I.

ERRATA.

In Contents, Book X., Chapter XII.—For "Grattan, Curran, and *his* friends," read *their* friends.

Page 8.—For *Eber* and *Gremhon*, read *Heber* and *Heremhon*.

Page 19.—For *Bilgee*, read *Belgic*.

Page 44.—For "*an-sufficient*," read "*all-sufficient*."

Page 97.—For *scanian*, read *Scanian*.

Page 145.—For *wear*, read *war*.